Whose Black Po

The past decade has witnessed the emergence of a new vanguard in African American political leaders. They came of age after Jim Crow segregation and the Civil Rights Movement, they were raised in integrated neighborhoods and educated in majority white institutions, and they are more likely to embrace deracialized campaign and governance strategies. Members of this new cohort, such as Cory Booker, Artur Davis, and Barack Obama, have often publicly clashed with their elders, either in campaigns or over points of policy. And because this generation did not experience codified racism, critics question whether these leaders will even serve the interests of African Americans once in office.

With these pressing concerns in mind, this volume uses multiple case studies to probe the implications of the emergence of these new leaders for the future of African American politics. Editor Andra Gillespie establishes a new theoretical framework based on the interaction of three factors: black leaders' crossover appeal, their political ambition, and connections to the black establishment. She sheds new light on the changing dynamics not only of Black politics but of the current American political scene.

Andra Gillespie is Assistant Professor of political science at Emory University, where she teaches courses in African American politics, political participation, and experimental methods.

Whose Black Politics?

Cases in Post-Racial Black Leadership

Edited by

Andra Gillespie

Routledge
Taylor & Francis Group

NEW YORK AND LONDON

First published 2010
by Routledge
270 Madison Avenue, New York, NY 10016

Simultaneously published in the UK
by Routledge
2 Park Square, Milton Park, Abingdon, Oxon OX14 4RN

Routledge is an imprint of the Taylor & Francis Group, an informa business

© 2010 Taylor & Francis

Typeset in Garamond by EvS Communication Networx, Inc.
Printed and bound in the United States of America on acid-free paper by Sheridan Books, Inc.

Library of Congress Cataloging in Publication Data
Gillespie, Andra.
Whose Black politics? : cases in post-racial Black leadership / Andra Gillespie.
p. cm.
Includes bibliographical references and index.
1. African American leadership—Case studies. 2. African Americans—Politics and
government—Case studies. 3. African American politicians—Case studies. 4. African
Americans—Race identity—Case studies. 5. Post-racialism—United States—Case studies.
6. United States—Race relations—Political aspects—Case studies. 7. African Americans—
History—1964– 8. United States—Politics and government—1989– I. Title.
E185.615.G535 2009
323.1196'073—dc22
2009025521

ISBN 10: 0-415-99215-X (hbk)
ISBN 10: 0-415-99216-8 (pbk)
ISBN 10: 0-203-89372-7 (ebk)

ISBN 13: 978-0-415-99215-2 (hbk)
ISBN 13: 978-0-415-99216-9 (pbk)
ISBN 13: 978-0-203-89372-2 (ebk)

To the trailblazers in our discipline: Ralph Bunche and
Jewel Limar Prestage

To the innovators in our specialty: Michael Dawson, Charles
Hamilton, Robert Smith, Ronald Walters, Michael Preston,
Paul Puryear, Lenneal Henderson, Georgia Persons,
and Huey Perry

And to our many mentors: Sharon Wright Austin, Cathy Cohen,
Donald Green, Michael Jones-Correa, Eric Mark Kramer,
Paula McClain, Joseph McCormick II, Cheryl Miller,
Dianne Pinderhughes, Randall Strahan, and Linda Faye Williams

Contents

List of Tables and Figures

Tables

Figures

Acknowledgments

The idea for this book germinated years ago at the 2006 annual meeting of the National Conference of Black Political Scientists. I have to thank Maya Rockeymoore for encouraging me to turn my conference paper into a book. And I am so grateful for having sat with Tyson King-Meadows and Sekou Franklin at the Awards Banquet that year. Otherwise, this book would have never happened.

Since that fateful conference, many of us—Sekou, Tyson, and I in particular—have had the privilege of refining our arguments at various conferences: the National Conference of Black Political Scientists, the Kirwan Institute Conference at Ohio State University, and the Annual Legislative Conference of the Congressional Black Caucus. We are eternally grateful to Joseph McCormick, Wendy Smooth, and Marjorie Innocent for extending us the invitations to present our work.

I am eternally grateful to the editorial staff at Routledge for their support of this project and their patience through this process. Michael Kerns has been exceptional, and he is ably assisted by Felisa Salvago-Keyes and Mary Altman. Thank you for everything you have done.

Clearly, this book would not have happened without the contributors who signed on board. You are all brilliant scholars, and it is my privilege to work with you.

I would also like to collectively thank the families of the contributors for their sacrifice. They gave up quality time to allow their authors to sit and research and write. I would be remiss not to acknowledge them.

Last but not least, I am grateful to God, for giving me the strength to make it through this process.

Introduction

Andra Gillespie

In 2008, *Time* magazine devoted its September 1 edition to coverage of the Democratic National Convention. Not surprisingly, Barack Obama's picture graced the cover. The most interesting part of the cover, though, was the half-cover listing all of the special articles in the issue. One title jumped out: "…The Obama Effect: New Black Leaders."

Barack Obama's meteoric rise to the presidency has drawn attention to a burgeoning public discourse about what the success of Black[1] politicians like him means for African-American politics. Certain tropes have emerged from this discussion: Barack Obama reflects a larger generational transition in African-American politics; new, racially moderate Black leaders are coming into their own politically; these moderate leaders are supplanting the older leaders who are associated with the protest phase of the Civil Rights and Black Power movements and are less likely to view themselves as race men and women than their predecessors (see Alleyne and Reed 2002; Starr 2002; Martin 2003; Samuel 2007; Ifill 2008; Bai 2008).

Much of the public discussion about this new cohort is extremely laudatory. For instance, after Barack Obama won the Iowa Caucus in 2008, the panelists of *The McLaughlin Group* used the event to discuss the future of Black politics. They agreed that Obama, Alabama Congressman Artur Davis, Massachusetts Governor Deval Patrick, former Tennessee Congressman Harold Ford Jr., and Washington, DC Mayor Adrian Fenty represented a sea change in Black politics. They noted that these politicians were different because of their moderate, less racialized political style and because of their Ivy League pedigrees. Some of the panel either hoped or acknowledged that these Black politicians would supplant the Jesse Jacksons and Al Sharptons who, in their minds, had defined Black politics for a generation (Schwartz 2008).

One would be remiss to not notice that a cohort of young Black elected officials has burst onto the national stage in the past few years. These politicians are largely Generation Xers, but they include a few, like Barack Obama, who were born at the tail end of the Baby Boom generation. A number of these young Black elected officials have garnered widespread attention for their historic victories or for challenging (and sometimes beating) established Black elected officials for power. Indeed, Barack Obama is chief among many young, Black elected officials who are poised to bring sweeping changes to both Black politics and national politics.

Because of Barack Obama's historic candidacy, many people have started paying attention to young Black politicians. It would be very easy for casual observers to assume that this cohort emerged only very recently and that all new Black politicians were like Barack Obama. My colleagues and I hope that we can dissuade readers from drawing such simplistic conclusions.

First and foremost, this cohort is extremely diverse, both stylistically and politically. Many are similar to Barack Obama in terms of background, telegenics, political style, policy preferences, and perceived ambitions for higher office. However, others are not so dissimilar from the elected officials who emerged from the Civil Rights and Black Power movements. While parts of the cohort eschew the "race man or woman" mantle, others fully embrace it.

Second, the path to power for politicians in this cohort is varied. Some of this cohort assumes office via traditional circumstances (i.e., they run for open seats or use their family's political connections). Others, particularly those without political connections, take huge risks to break into politics. They challenge strong incumbents at the height of their political power. Political scientists would argue that challenging strong incumbents is less than strategic (see Jacobsen and Kernell 1983), and political operatives would likely deem it quixotic and hubristic (Martin 2003). However, some young Black politicians have used such risks to create political opportunities for themselves where they did not previously exist.

Finally, the rise of this cohort reignites the discussion of the efficacy of racial moderation as a campaign and governance tactic. In the 1970s Charles Hamilton recommended that candidates aligned with the Civil Rights Movement adopt a race-neutral platform, called deracialization, in order to appeal to as many voters as possible. Critics saw the electoral efficacy of deracialization, but they contended that using such a strategy amounted to putting "golden handcuffs" on Black elected officials (Collins 1996, 89). They could get elected, but they would be unable to address explicitly racial issues as needed because that could upset the precarious electoral coalition that put them into office. Essentially, these critics charged that deracialized political candidates made a Faustian bargain with their non-Black constituents to not address racial issues in exchange for getting elected (McCormick and Jones 1993; Smith 1993). Now that some young Black politicians have been able to use deracialization to get elected to the highest offices in the country, will the critics' worst fears come true? Will non-Black constituents demand that they neglect addressing racial inequality in order to keep their jobs?

When we look at young Black politicians through these lenses, we realize that the rise of this new cohort raises new questions for the study of Black politics. As such, in this volume we hope to explore these questions in greater depth so that readers gain a complex, nuanced understanding of the issues surrounding the emergence of this cohort.

The rise of this cohort has tremendous implications for the study of African-

American politics. Will Black voters be satisfied now that Black politicians are descriptively represented in the country's highest political offices? Is this group of politicians poised to deliver on substantive goals as yet unattained in the African-American community? Will voters ultimately judge this cohort as being better able to deliver on the policy goals of interest to American Blacks such as the reduction of wealth, health, educational and income inequality, and the enforcement of existing civil rights legislation? Will Blacks embrace these leaders as representatives of their own community, or are they, as Matt Bai noted in his controversial *New York Times Magazine* article, "ambassadors **to** the Black community" (Bai 2008, author's emphasis)?

In the pages that follow, my colleagues and I will shed light on these and other issues. In the first chapter, I present a theoretical overview of this new cohort of young Black politicians. Readers will gain an understanding of the extant debates in Black politics that preceded the emergence of this cohort. I then propose a new model by which to assess and judge these emerging elected officials.

In part I of the volume, we look at the struggles some young Black politicians have had in getting elected to that first major office. Some of these officials appear to have the Midas touch today, but in reality, their paths to power have been difficult. In chapter 2, Emma Tolbert and I look at Congressman Artur Davis. It took him two tries to get elected to the House of Representatives. In this chapter, we compare the external political conditions in his first and second bids. We find that while his first attempt to run for office does not fit the classic model of a strategic election, his second attempt did resemble a conventionally strategic campaign. Davis was able to take advantage of redistricting changes in his district and a changed political dynamic in the wake of September 11 to best his once-victorious opponent.

Newark, New Jersey Mayor Cory Booker faced a similar situation to Artur Davis. In 2002, Booker lost a hard fought race to then four-term incumbent Sharpe James for Newark's mayoralty. In 2002, Newark voters, particularly Black voters, were skeptical of Booker, who was still a relative newcomer to the city. Before Booker could win his election, he had to burnish his local credentials. In chapter 3, I compare the 2002 and 2006 elections.

In part II, we turn our attentions to young Black politicians whose family connections made a transition to politics a little easier. In chapter 4, Randolph Burnside and Antonio Rodriguez look at the career of Congressman Jesse Jackson Jr., the son of the famed civil rights leader. Jackson's upbringing and socialization give him a different perspective on race politics than someone who was not necessarily raised in the heart of the Movement or in more integrated environs. Yet, Jackson's youth gives him a different perspective from politicians in his father's cohort. How does that legacy affect Jackson's legislative style? Burnside and Rodriguez analyze Jackson's sponsorship record and find that he tries to balance his support for racialized and racially transcendent policies.

Former Detroit Mayor Kwame Kilpatrick is perhaps the most infamous member of this cohort of young Black elected officials. In many ways, Kilpatrick was the epitome of the new, young Black politician. He came from a respected political family. He had been Michigan's youngest state House Majority Leader. When he was elected mayor in 2001, he was one of the youngest mayors in the country and considered a rising star in Democratic politics. Unfortunately, it all came crashing down under allegations of adultery and obstruction. In 2008, Kilpatrick resigned in shame and pleaded guilty to perjury. Athena King, Todd Shaw, and Lester Spence trace the rise and fall of Kilpatrick in chapter 5.

No volume of this sort would be complete without a discussion of Barack Obama. We devote part III to a discussion of the 44th President. While it is important to understand Obama's career since his election to the U.S. Senate in 2004, it is also important to look at his early career. By examining this phase of Obama's life, we find that Obama made risky campaign choices and was not always embraced by Black voters. Thus, the chapters in this volume seek to explain the evolution of Black and White support for Obama throughout his federal political career.

Lorrie Frasure begins our discussion of Barack Obama in chapter 6. She examines Obama's first attempts at federal office. In particular, Frasure looks at Obama's 2000 congressional primary defeat and his 2004 Senate primary victory. Why did Black voters soundly repudiate Obama in one election and then flock to his support four years later when he ran for statewide office?

Charlton McIlwain studies the 2008 Democratic primaries in chapter 7. For historical perspective, McIlwain examines White voter perceptions of Jesse Jackson in 1988. He finds that White voters did not view Jackson as a legitimate leader, and this hampered his ability to win the nomination. Early in the primary season, it was not clear that White voters viewed Obama as a strong leader. However, it was obvious that voters viewed Obama as a change agent. This contributed to his ability to secure the nomination and to his eventual victory.

We revisit the question of deracialization in part IV. In the 1990s scholars collaborated on two edited volumes devoted to deconstructing the strategy: Georgia Person's *Dilemmas of Black Politics* (1993a) and Huey Perry's 1996 *Race, Politics and Governance in the United States* (1996). The contributors to these volumes were particularly animated by the wave of historic Black electoral victories in 1989. That year, a number of Black candidates won high profile elections in majority White jurisdictions using deracialized campaign strategies. They include David Dinkins' election as New York City's first Black mayor and Douglas Wilder's election as Virginia and the nation's first Black governor since Reconstruction.

Making sense of deracialization was the main theme of both volumes. In the earlier volumes, contributors worked with the standard assumption that deracialization involved deemphasizing civil rights issues as much as possible in one's platform, avoiding racial appeals to Black voters, and cultivating a nonconfrontational persona that appeals to White voters (McCormick and Jones 1993, 76–77). Contributors to the Persons volume devoted time to discussing the consequences of adopting such a strategy. In their estimation, Black candidates who did not discuss race either were not standard bearers of Black politics, as in the case of former Connecticut Congressman Gary Franks (Persons 1993b); or, were susceptible to being the target of racially vitriolic campaign attacks or general anti-Black affect, as in the case of Harvey Gantt and Andrew Young (Z. Wilson 1993; Davis and Willingham 1993).

Contributors to the Perry volume did not challenge the fundamental definition of deracialization. Instead, they argued that many Black politicians of the day were in fact not deracialized. For instance, Mary Summers and Phillip Klinkner cited numerous examples of racially targeted campaigning and issue development to argue that John Daniels, New Haven, Connecticut's first Black mayor, was not actually a deracialized Black politician (Summers and Klinkner 1996). Lenneal Henderson asserted that former Baltimore Mayor Kurt Schmoke transcended race but was not deracialized (Henderson 1996).

The debate sparked by these two volumes suggests that we should reevaluate the standard definition of deracialization. We contend that the standard definition, while helpful, is far too black and white. In reality, candidates who are largely deracialized often do make racial appeals depending on the context.

With this in mind, the four chapters in this section add needed nuance to our understanding of deracialization as a campaign strategy and start to shed light on how deracialized candidates behave when they get elected. In chapter 8, Angela Lewis studies the election of Massachusetts Governor Deval Patrick. He ran a classic deracialized campaign. Like Harvey Gantt, his opponent used negative campaigning to try to prime racial fears during the campaign. Lewis explains why it did not work in this case.

In chapter 9, Rachel Yon turns her attention to a study of Washington, DC Mayor Adrian Fenty. In 2006, Fenty defeated City Council President and fellow African American Linda Cropp for the Democratic mayoral nomination. Fenty, a young, biracial, two-term councilman from a diverse ward, epitomized deracialized politics and is often compared to Artur Davis and Cory Booker. Both of those men had their racial bona fides challenged when they ran for their current political offices. Fenty, however, was not the target of such an attack. Yon conducts a historical analysis of race politics in Washington to explain why such an attack did not take place.

Chapter 10 focuses on the failed senatorial bid of former Tennessee Congressman Harold Ford Jr. In this chapter, Sekou Franklin explains Ford's campaign tactics using a theory called situational deracialization. Ford ran a largely deracialized campaign, but his campaign was not perfectly deracialized in the classic sense of the term. Instead, Ford targeted his message depending on his audience. He presented a deracialized image and platform to White audiences, while playing up his racial background for Black audiences.

While Black Republicans continue to make up a small fraction of the African-American electorate, it is still important to not exclude them from this analysis. Many would assume that Black Republicans would be the most likely to deemphasize race in their campaigns. However, Tyson King-Meadows shows otherwise. In chapter 11, he presents an analysis of former Maryland Lieutenant Governor (and future Republican National Committee Chairman) Michael Steele's 2006 Senate campaign. Instead of running a deracialized campaign, Steele racialized his campaign in an attempt to appeal to Black voters who may have been disaffected by the Democratic Party's failure to nominate a Black candidate in this and previous contests.

The final substantive section addresses the challenges of intersectionality. In part V, we look at the role played by candidates' multiple identities in affecting their public personas and ability to garner support. In chapter 12, Amber Perez and I study Congressman Keith Ellison, Minnesota's first Black and America's first Muslim congressman. Using content analysis, we determine how the public perceives him, both racially and religiously. Then, using his own words, we show how Ellison uses both of his perspectives to represent his district to the best of his ability.

Katrina Gamble explores the intersection of race and gender in chapter 13. Young Black men have been winning elective office at the big city executive and federal level since Cleo Fields won a congressional seat from Louisiana in 1992. However, no young woman achieved that feat until Yvette Clarke won a congressional seat from New York in 2006. Why was there a fourteen year gap? Are young, Black women more or less likely than their White peers or Black female elders to run for high office? The irony here is unmistakable. This generation of young Black politicians gets lauded for being progressive and for being antidiscriminatory; yet, for all this talk of being progressive, young Black women may not be fully empowered.

At the very end, I present a short conclusion. This conclusion ties all of the chapters together, and outlines the trends that are likely to emerge in this generation of Black elected leadership in the next one to two decades.

Note

1. The terms *Black* and *African American* will be used interchangeably in this book to describe people of African descent living in the United States.

References

Bai, Matt. 2008. Is Barack Obama the end of Black politics? *The New York Times Magazine*, August 6, http://www.nytimes.com/2008/08/10/magazine/10politicst.html?_r=1&scp=1&sq=is%20obama%20the%20end%20of%20black%20politics&st=cse (accessed September 2, 2008).

Collins, Sharon. 1996. *Black corporate executives*. Philadelphia: Temple University Press.

Davis, Marilyn, and Alex Willingham. 1993. Andrew Young and the Georgia state elections of 1990. In *Dilemmas of Black politics*, ed. Georgia Persons, 147–75. New York: HarperCollins.

Dawson, Michael C. 1994. *Behind the mule*. Princeton, NJ: Princeton University Press.

Henderson, Lenneal J. Jr. 1996. The governance of Kurt Schmoke as mayor of Baltimore. In *Race, governance, and politics in the United States*, ed. Huey L. Perry, 165–78. Gainesville: University of Florida Press.

Ifill, Gwen. 2008. Nothing unique about it. *Time*, September 1.

Jacobsen, Gary, and Samuel Kernell. 1983. *Strategy and choice in congressional elections*. 2nd ed. New Haven, CT: Yale University Press.

Martin, Roland. 2003. Ready or not… *Savoy*. March, 52–56.

McCormick, Joseph II, and Charles E. Jones. 1993. The conceptualization of deracialization: Thinking through the dilemma. In *Dilemmas of Black politics*, ed. Georgia Persons, 66–84. New York: HarperCollins.

Perry, Huey, ed. 1996. *Race, governance, and politics in the United States*. Gainesville: University of Florida Press.

Persons, Georgia, ed. 1993a. *Dilemmas of Black politics*. New York: HarperCollins.

———. 1993b. The election of Gary Franks and the ascendancy of the new Black conservatives. In *Dilemmas of Black politics*, ed. Georgia Persons, 194–208. New York: HarperCollins.

Samuel, Terence. 2007. Young, Black and post-civil rights. *The American Prospect*. September 4.

Schwartz, Sheldon, dir. 2008. *The McLaughlin group* [Syndicated television broadcast]. Washington, DC: Oliver Productions, January 4.

Smith, Robert C. 1993. Ideology as the enduring dilemma of Black politics. In *Dilemmas of Black politics*, ed. Georgia Persons, 211–25. New York: HarperCollins.

Starr, Alexandra. 2002. We shall overcome, too. *Business Week*. July 15. LexisNexis Academic Universe. http://www.web.lexis-nexis.com/universe (accessed January 20, 2003).

Summers, Mary, and Phillip Klinkner. 1996. The election and governance of John Daniels as mayor of New Haven. In *Race, governance, and politics in the United States*, ed. Huey L. Perry,127–50. Gainesville: University of Florida Press.

Time. 2008. Front cover. September 1.

Wilson, Zaphon. 1993. Gantt versus Helms: Deracialization confronts southern traditionalism. In *Dilemmas of Black politics*, ed. Georgia Persons, 176–93. New York: HarperCollins.

1   Meet the New Class
Theorizing Young Black Leadership in a "Postracial" Era[1]

Andra Gillespie

Introduction

By all accounts, Americans are being introduced to a third generation of Black elected leadership. Ironically, this new phase, like the phases that preceded it, is called "new Black politics." What distinguishes this new batch of leaders from their predecessors is their generation (i.e., they were born or came of age after the Civil Rights Movement), their education (they were educated in Ivy League and other White institutions), and their potential (they have realistic chances of holding higher executive and legislative positions more frequently than any other generation of Black leaders) (Reed and Alleyne 2002).

This latest wave of Black politicians is not immune from criticism. Not least among critics' concerns is whether these new Black politicians will advance the substantive and strategic policy goals of the African-American community. Yes, some of these women and men can realistically become senators and president, as Barack Obama has so aptly demonstrated, but at what price? Will they have to sell out Black interests to gain the electoral advantage needed to attain high office (Martin 2003)?

Implicit in this discussion of new Black politicians is their relative chance for success and the means by which they emerge onto the political spectrum. Is the emergence of this cohort of leadership an organic development emanating from Black communities, or are these politicians overly ambitious instrumentalists who are exploiting their racial background for political traction? What is more, does this cohort of elected leadership have a chance at developing a loyal base of Black voters, or are they being propped up by White elites seeking to divide and conquer Black communities?

The answers to these questions are important because the stakes are so high. The new cohort of Black elected officials receive such notoriety because their probability of attaining high office is greater than it has been for any generation of Blacks in the United States. If this cohort of elected leadership meets expectations, and continues to ascend in critical numbers to governors' mansions, the U.S. Senate, and the White House, what are the implications for Black communities? Clearly, these leaders will be in an unprecedented position to shape public policy. Thus, it seems that the big question is not just what pundits think about new Black politicians, but what constituents think about these candidates and whether the material conditions of African Americans will improve under their direction.

In the pages that follow, I trace the emergence of this new cohort of Black leadership. I draw on the Black leadership literature to see how scholars in the past defined and assessed would-be Black leaders. Indeed, they created multiple, yet similar typologies to evaluate leadership. I then use the basic demographic record of the current crop of young Black elected officials to introduce a new model of Black officials, which I in turn apply in describing the post-Civil Rights cohort.

New Black Politics Throughout History

So far, there have been three iterations of new Black politics in the post-Civil Rights era: the widespread election of the first Black elected officials in the 1970s; the successes of Black candidates in major elections in large, majority White jurisdictions in the 1980s; finally, the current rise of young, Black moderates, many of whom challenge members of the earlier wave of Black elected officials in majority Black cities and Congressional districts. Each wave of Black politicians is significant for the barriers that the politicians traversed. They are also important to study because the rise of each class of Black elected officials is concurrent with innovations in campaign strategy. However, despite the campaign innovations, scholars studying these waves of elected officials have been careful to question whether the programmatic agenda of these Black elected officials aligns with the interests of Black constituents.

New Black Politics: Phase I

Charles Hamilton notes that after the passage of Voting Rights Act, the focus of Black politics, in a literal and academic sense, shifted from the judicial to the legislative/electoral arena. Now that Blacks largely had the franchise, the goal shifted to channel that electoral power into legislative policies that would benefit Blacks (Hamilton, 1982). Putting Black officials in office was a key first step in achieving that agenda. Indeed, from 1965 to 1988, there was a more than thirteen-fold increase in the number of Black elected officials (Tate 1994, 1; see also Williams 1987, 112).

The elected officials of the first wave of new Black politics faced tremendous obstacles. As trailblazers coming on the heels of the Civil Rights Movement, they had to run in still racially tense environments. Furthermore, they had to reconcile with the White portions of their constituency that may have been skeptical of them as leaders (Smith 1990).

Moreover, these new Black elected officials had difficulty implementing their agenda. As Linda Williams notes, "urban Blacks today have reached city hall precisely at the moment when the real power to deliver jobs, money, education and basic services is migrating to higher levels of government and the private sector" (Williams 1987, 129). She observes that first wave Black politicians came to power during a period of national economic decline and decreased federal aid to cities. As a result, first wave Black mayors were hampered in their efforts to provide redistributive relief to their constituents. What little aid they were able to provide tended to focus on ameliorative policies such as affirmative action and set-asides, which disproportionately benefited middle class Black residents. What is more, Blacks ascended to the mayoralty in cities which severely proscribed their power, limiting some from having control over important functions such as taxation (Williams 1987, 128–29).

William Nelson further notes that the notion of new Black politics being the collective agent for improvement of the whole Black community is easier said than done. Using Cleveland as an example, he notes that uniting Blacks around a permanent agenda is difficult. Carl Stokes was able to unite Blacks under one political banner. However, that union dissolved when Stokes stepped down as leader of Cleveland's Black political organization. Diversity of opinion and ambition, then, undermined some attempts for political unity (Nelson 1982). Moreover, Robert Smith observes that the legislative record of these officials, with respect to their progressive, Black politics agenda, has been limited. They were only able to develop downtown space, implement municipal affirmative action, and respond to police brutality (Smith 1990).

New Black Politics: Phase II

One of the distinguishing features of each wave of new Black politics has been the new Black candidates' campaign style. While candidates in each wave of new Black politics have had some measure of crossover appeal, observers have attributed more crossover appeal to each subsequent generation of new Black political candidates. For example, Ardrey and Nelson (1990) note that Black elected officials elected in new Black politics' first wave, who were largely civil rights leaders, transferred the confrontational style from the movement to the electoral and legislative arena.

Many scholars viewed 1989 as a watershed year for Black politics. In November 1989, Blacks ascended to the mayoralty for the first time in Seattle (Norm Rice), New Haven (John Daniels), Durham (Chester Jenkins), and New York City (David Dinkins). Most notably, Douglas Wilder was elected Governor of Virginia, making him the country's first Black governor since Reconstruction. This cluster of elections is particularly important given that these men were elected in majority White jurisdictions with at least 40 percent of the White vote (McCormick and Jones 1993, 66, 68).

With their elections, Wilder and his peers ushered in the second wave of new Black politics. The second wave is characterized by the prevalent use of a deracialized campaign strategy. McCormick and Jones define a deracialized campaign as one being "...in a stylistic fashion that diffuses the polarizing effects of race by avoiding explicit reference to race-specific issues, while at the same time emphasizing those issues that are perceived as racially transcendent, thus mobilizing a broad segment of the electorate" (McCormick and Jones 1993, 76). McCormick and Jones (1993) go further to articulate this strategy by noting that candidates employing such a strategy convey *"a nonthreatening image"* (76, original emphasis), "avoid employing direct racial appeals in organizing the Black community" (76), and *"should avoid emphasis of a racially specific issue agenda"* (77, original emphasis).

Douglas Wilder clearly exemplifies the deracialized strategy. Strickland and Whicker note that Wilder, "adopted mainstream and even fiscally conservative positions. He was also able to avoid discussing overtly racial issues" (Strickland and Whicker 1992, 210). For example, Wilder's campaign theme was "the 'New Virginia Mainstream,'" and he made law and order, drug enforcement, and his support for the death penalty a key part of his platform (Jones and Clemons 1993, 140).

While this strategy may be electorally effective, some find it normatively troubling and wonder what the implications are for the pursuit of a pro-Black political agenda. Earl Sheridan (1996), in his article, "The New Accommodationists," implicitly likens such a strategy to Booker T. Washington's infamous Atlanta Compromise speech when he writes that instead of lauding Black elected officials who deemphasize race to get elected, "America needs Black leaders who will continue the legacy of the 1960's, not the 1890's—men and women who will call for meaningful change in our society" (Sheridan 1996, 169). He fears that in an attempt to gain office by any means necessary, these officials would abandon the issues of concern to the Black community to get votes and would shortchange Black interests to stay in power (Sheridan 1996, 165, 166).

McCormick and Jones are a little less fearful of the implications of using a deracialized electoral strategy, but they, too, brace for less progressive politics as a result of the strategy. They write that "In the absence of such demands from a politically organized African American community, there is little reason to expect African American elected officials who capture office in predominantly White political jurisdictions to be in the vanguard of articulating racially-specific policy issues" (McCormick and Jones 1993, 78). That being said, they proffer that even these politicians will occasionally have to make some explicitly racial overtures to their Black constituents, lest these officials lose an important base of support in their communities (McCormick and Jones 1993, 78).

However, much of the hand wringing over the implications of deracialization as a strategy of second-wave Black politicians was short-lived. Second wave politicians experienced a number of setbacks which prevented that cohort from making a long-term impact on the communities they represented. Some setbacks were structural. Doug Wilder, for instance, was constitutionally barred from seeking a second consecutive term as Governor of Virginia. Others, such as David Dinkins, had very short tenures in office due to poor public perceptions (see Kim 2000 for an example of Dinkins' alienation of Black constituents). However, a number of politicians in the second wave suffered electoral defeats that marked the end of their electoral pursuits. For instance, Harvey Gantt twice lost his bid to represent North Carolina in the U.S. Senate to Jesse Helms in what were racially vitriolic campaigns. Andrew Young[2] lost a bid to be Georgia's Governor by wasting time campaigning for White votes in southern Georgia at the expense of campaigning in his base in and around Atlanta. Thus, according to the various authors studying the rise of second wave politicians in the late 1980s and early 1990s, deracialized candidates overestimated racial goodwill outside of the Black community and paid a high electoral price for ignoring Black voters (Z. Wilson 1993; Davis and Willingham 1993; Pierannunzi and Hutcheson 1996).

Moreover, from an academic perspective, many authors challenged the notion that pure deracialization was even going on in the first place. Mary Summers and Phillip Klinkner, for instance, argue that John Daniels did not run a deracialized campaign in his successful bid to become New Haven's first Black mayor. They point to his progressive campaign platform, his integral role in introducing community policing to New Haven and his creation of a needle exchange program, in addition to his willingness to discuss his race on the campaign trail, as evidence that Daniels was not a deracialized candidate. Additionally, Lenneal Henderson studied Kurt Schmoke's ascendance to the mayoralty of Baltimore and reached similar conclusions. He contends that Schmoke's efforts at economic redevelopment were racially transcendent, but that Schmoke was not trying to distance himself from Black communities. Thus, Schmoke was a transracialized Black politician and not a deracialized Black politician (Summers and Klinkner 1996; Henderson 1996).

New Black Politics: Phase III

The current wave of new Black politics very much resembles the second wave in that this wave is characterized by ambitious politicians with more moderate politics. What distinguishes this group from its predecessors is its youth and connection to civil rights history. The figures associated with the third wave of new Black politics were born after 1960,[3] immediately before or after the passage of all the major civil rights legislation (Traub 2002). For example, Barack Obama was born in 1961; Cory Booker was born in 1969; Harold Ford Jr. and Kwame Kilpatrick were born in 1970. As a result, these figures benefited from the fruits of the struggle and were able to grow up in integrated neighborhoods and attend predominantly White schools from kindergarten to graduate school. However, their youth also means that some perceive this generation as being less likely to relate to the Civil Rights struggle (Bositis 2001, 3–11). While second wave new Black politicians were charged with deliberately not having been active in the Civil Rights Movement, they at least had the benefit of having been eyewitness to the monumental changes that took place in the 1950s and 1960s (Sheridan 1996, 166).[4] In addition, at the beginning of the twenty-first century, some could legitimately view this generation as being untested and unable to point to any record upon which to base their claims of being better legislators or government executives or to a clear agenda around which to organize their candidacies (Martin 2003).

This perceived lack of identification with the struggle is what raises so much skepticism among older Black elites when evaluating this emerging generation of leadership. In an interview with *Savoy* magazine, Ronald Walters voiced the suspicion that this new generation was merely a tool of White elites who wanted to replace more acerbic, older Black leaders with less threatening, younger Black leaders:

> [The White power structure] would rather supplant [the old guard] with a far more accommodating leadership. They are going to pit them against the so-called old leadership because they have been threatened by the interests and power of the Black leadership who really have the influence and control of Black people. (Walters, quoted in Martin 2003, 56)

In addition to having had their race consciousness questioned, this generation has also been accused of hubris. David Bositis acknowledged in an interview that young Black leaders "imagine themselves as governors, United States Senators, and even President" (Bositis, quoted in Martin 2003, 56). When Harold Ford Jr. ran to unseat Nancy Pelosi as House Minority Leader in 2003, his efforts were rebuffed even by members of the Congressional Black Caucus. Ford's attempted power grab failed, according to Walters, because he had not spent years currying favor and garnering support from his colleagues in the House Democratic Caucus. "To step out there because you've got a pretty face and no agenda," Walters said, "you're going to lose every time" (Walters, quoted in Martin 2003, 56).

If there is anything that does distinguish the third wave of new Black politics from the first two waves, it may be that it is the synthesis of the first and second waves. Where we witnessed civil rights activists turned legislators challenge the White power structure in the first wave, and where we witnessed second wave politicians attempt to join the White power structure, we now see third wave politicians who behave like second wave politicians and challenge first wave incumbents for power,[5] often in majority Black jurisdictions, and often with extensive mainstream media support. For instance, Alexandra Starr predicts that moderate politics would probably propel more Black candidates to national office (2002). James Traub goes so far as to say that the success of people like Cory Booker and Artur Davis against the Sharpe Jameses and Earl Hilliards of the world would be a "balm to White liberals, whose politics have been so heavily determined by an agonized sense of 'what Black people want,' as defined by the Black leadership class. And it will be a boon to the Democrats, for it will help heal the ideological rifts within the party" (Traub 2002, 1).

Analytical Concerns with Phases II and III of New Black Politics

The academy has not been immune from being infatuated with second and third wave new Black politics because of the nonthreatening dimension of their electoral strategy. Strickland and Whicker acquiesce to the reality of racism in

American society and propose a crossover model for Black electoral success. This model calls for espousing conservative positions on issues, deemphasizing race, and working outside the Civil Rights Movement. While they do all this, these candidates are supposed to excite and maintain a Black voting base (Strickland and Whicker 1992, 208, 209).

Strickland and Whicker acknowledge that catering to Whites while not alienating Blacks is easier said than done. However, their key mistake is assuming that Black voters will be loyal to any Black candidate. While that is a gross overgeneralization of Black voting preferences in and of itself, Strickland and Whicker fail to account for the situation when two Blacks would run against each other. Who should Black voters choose, then? In their study of congressional elections, Canon, Schousen, and Sellers (1996) studied the electoral success of Black candidates pitted against other Black candidates in majority minority districts. They argue that when first wave new Black politicians run against second or third wave new Black politicians, the second or third wave new Black politician will win if Whites, who should be a sizable minority of the constituency, vote as a bloc. They assume that Whites are more likely to support moderate Blacks. However, they do concede that if Blacks vote as a bloc, the first wave new Black politician has a better chance of winning.

This focus on which Black candidates appeal to White voters (as opposed to which Black candidates can best represent the interests of Black voters) is what is so troubling to students of Black politics. Ronald Walter's aforementioned quote captures this concern (Martin, 2003, 56). Indeed, it is this fixation with keeping Whites happy that seems to be anathema to Black self-determination, if only because the focus on this type of Black politics shifts the focus away from Blacks and their policy interests.

Critics must respond to the question, though, of whether these candidates are out of touch. Reed and Alleyne note that the hallmark of third wave new Black politics is their "philosophic mix of political pragmatism, pro-business sensibility, and social progressivism" (Reed and Alleyne 2002, 84). Martin notes that, "today's Black elected official may be more concerned with closing the digital divide, increasing economic opportunities for people of color, and school vouchers…" (Martin 2003, 54). Are these positions really out of touch with the policy preferences of Black constituents? David Bositis would have to concede that these candidates may not be so out of touch with their constituents. Reporting the results of the Joint Center's 2002 National Opinion Poll, he notes that a majority of Blacks were in favor of vouchers, that younger Blacks identified less with the Democratic Party, and that Blacks are far more concerned about the economy, foreign affairs, and education than they are about racism (Bositis 2002, 7, 6, 10). What is more, when the Joint Center compared the political attitudes of Black elected officials to the Black electorate, they found that generational differences in attitudes among Blacks generally paralleled generational differences among Black elected officials (Bositis 2001, 21).

Skeptics need also to consider the substantive critiques levied against older generations of Black leadership. While Walters chided the younger generation of Black elected officials for being overly ambitious but substantively unfocused and proclaimed that the older generation of Black leaders "really have the influence and control of Black people" (Walters, quoted in Martin 2003, 56), he has also acknowledged elsewhere that the earlier vanguard of leadership encountered institutional barriers that limited their effectiveness in providing benefits for Blacks (Walters and Smith, 1999, 135). His colleague, Robert Smith, argued that post-Civil Rights elected officials assumed power but were co-opted by the establishment and thus accomplished very little of the programmatic agenda to improve the lives of African Americans. The reality that even the first wave of Black politicians sold out to some degree led Smith to boldly proclaim in the title of his book that *We Have No Leaders* (Smith 1996). This reality begs the questions of whether younger, postracial candidates really can do more harm than good, relative to the previous generation of leadership, for the advancement of an African-American agenda?

Examining the Typologies of Black Leadership

The exercise of classifying a new, postracial cohort of leadership is deeply rooted in previous studies of Black leadership. In those studies, scholars went to great efforts to classify leaders. The classification scheme they chose varied on the margins, but all focus on identifying distinct leadership styles within the Black community based on the leaders' style in dealing with the White power structure.

The extant typologies of Black leadership go back to the late 1930s. In 1937, Guy Johnson defined Black leaders as either "gradualists" or "revolutionaries" (Ladd 1966, 148). As their names suggest, gradualists acquiesced to the realities of second class citizenship in the United States, and revolutionaries challenged the racial caste system. In the classic tome *An American Dilemma*, Gunnar Myrdal created the accommodationist/protest paradigm to classify Black leaders. Accommodationists are akin to Johnson's gradualists; and protesters are analogous to Johnson's revolutionaries (Ladd 1966, 148; see Myrdal 1944, 720).

Walters and Smith (1999) outline other major typologies created in the early 1960s to define Black leadership. James Q. Wilson, for instance, defined Black leadership styles on two dimensions. In his view, Black leaders were either militants or moderates, basing his typology on the methods these leaders used to achieve specific classes of civil rights goals. Militant leaders used direct action or protest techniques to achieve racial integration, which Wilson termed a "status" goal; moderate leaders, in contrast, tended to try to negotiate with Whites to achieve concrete, "welfare" goals for Black communities (Wilson 1960, 218, 235). Thus, a militant leader would lead a protest to achieve a measure of social accommodation for Blacks equal to Whites while moderate leaders might appeal to White power structures behind the scenes to achieve goals such as more goods and services targeted to Black communities (Wilson, chapter 9).

Drawing on Wilson's scholarship, Everett Ladd uses the notion of welfare and status goals, along with rhetorical style and tactics, to create his own typology of leadership. Like Wilson, he notes that conservatives and militants are at the extremes. However, he also notes that there is an intermediate class of leaders known as moderates. Militant leaders seek status goals using confrontational tactics and rhetoric. Conservative leaders seek welfare goals using acquiescent, nonconfrontational strategies and rhetoric (usually behind the scenes). Moderate leaders are a hybrid: they seek welfare and status goals depending on the situation using nonconfrontational rhetoric. However, they often take advantage of the presence of militants to achieve their goals. They are able to position themselves as the reasonable alternative to the militants and attempt to get access to dominant power structures along these lines (Ladd 1966, chapter 4).

In her study of Black politics in Durham, North Carolina, Elaine Burgess also extends the definition of Black leadership beyond the protest–accommodation binary to include other, intermediary types of leadership. In her typology, there were four types of Black leaders. On one end of the spectrum were conservative leaders, the old, established Black leadership who acquiesced to racial domination and with whom the White power structure was more comfortable. Moderates tended to be upper-class Blacks who did not devote their full time and energy to addressing racial issues. They tended to emerge to prominence working on nonracial issues, and they were committed to being part of biracial groups working to address city challenges. Liberals were those Black leaders, often from professional backgrounds, who were uncompromising in their commitment to achieving civil rights for Blacks. However, their tone was nonconfrontational, and they were perceived to be nonthreatening, especially in relation to radicals. Radicals were the leaders most prone to be outspoken and to engage in direct action to achieve civil rights. In Burgess's view, they were clearly inspired by Martin Luther King (Burgess 1962, 181–85; Walters and Smith 1999, 18).

While there are some clear differences in the typologies mentioned above, their similarities are striking. All of them use a linear continuum to judge a leader based on how radical he or she is. They judge the extent to which a person is radical based on the extent to which these leaders wish to work with powerful Whites and whether or not a leader tries to achieve his or her goals through protest or negotiation.

All of the aforementioned studies took place in the midst of the Civil Rights Movement and reflect the diversity of opinion about the efficacy of certain tactics. It would seem logical that in the wake of the legislative victories of the Civil Rights Movement that there would perhaps be some changes in how leadership was defined and categorized. For instance, at the time Burgess was writing, she noted that conservative leaders were losing their prominence in the Black community and even White leaders realized that this cohort's influence in the Black community was waning. It seemed to be that racial moderates would fill the role of racial conservatives (Burgess 1962, 181). Moreover, Robert Smith (1981) contends that in the wake of the Black Nationalist movement, many Black elites were radicalized. Thus, even some of the more conservative elements of the Black community would likely have been socialized into affirming some measure of race pride, whether through membership in a racially specific professional association or some other avenue of racial particularism.

Despite these radical social changes, our understanding of the basic types of Black leadership has not changed that much, though there has been some innovation. Walters and Smith acquiesce to the protest–accommodation paradigm in their book, *African American Leadership*. They concede that protesters are far less prevalent, and they contend that most leaders are now accommodationists. They do provide some innovation when they identify different ways Black leaders gain legitimacy. One can argue that Walters and Smith define leadership legitimacy on a two-dimensional scale, with White and Black acceptance being the x and y axes respectively. Leaders accepted by both Black and White communities are "consensus" leaders. Those embraced by the White community and not the Black community are called "external" leaders. Those embraced by the Black community and not the White community are called "community" leaders. Those who lack credibility in both Black and White communities are considered "auto-selected" leaders (Walters and Smith 1999, 217).

While Walters and Smith's two-dimensional rendering of racial acceptability is helpful, in reality, they are only judging legitimacy on racial acceptance. Still, others have continued to use the simple binary to define Black candidates and politicians. David Canon, Matthew Schousen, and Patrick Sellers (1996), for instance, used the terms *old style* and *new style* to describe Black candidates running against each other in majority-minority congressional districts. Old style candidates ran in the protest, confrontational spirit of the Civil Rights Movement and were thus the racialized candidates; new style candidates ran racially transcendent campaigns that were more palatable to some of the Blacks and the remaining Whites in these districts.

Lenneal Henderson (1996), in contrast, creates perhaps the most complex version of race leadership to date. While keeping with the one-dimensional model of racial radicalism (he defines Black leaders on a continuum from nonracial to hyperracial, with deracialized, racialized, and transracialized candidates as the intermediate points), he argues that both electoral and policy considerations should factor into how one categorizes Black politicians. Black candidates run differently when running against Whites and when running against other Blacks, and that should be taken into account. Moreover, race politics plays out differently in different parts of the policy process. An elected official could set the agenda for a policy in a racially transcendent tone, for instance, but once the policy was implemented, it could be judged to be highly beneficial for Blacks. Likewise, a policy could be introduced as explicitly helping Blacks, but by the time it was passed and implemented, might not achieve its intended purpose. Thus, Henderson suggests the importance of looking at the ends elected officials achieve in office rather than the means by which they get to office before judging them (Henderson 1996, 172–71). Unfortunately, Henderson's typology is very preliminary and in the end, still very unidimensional.

A Multidimensional Assessment Black Elected Leadership

Is there a better, perhaps more complex way to judge and examine Black leadership? For this new cohort of elected officials, I would like to proffer a new model of leadership that creates more complex typologies and presents a more nuanced, and I hope, more accurate picture of what we know about the post-Civil Rights cohort of Black leadership to date. While this model incorporates the traditional militant to moderate axis (under the rubric of crossover appeal), it also adds two more important dimensions: expected career trajectory (ambition) and preexisting connections to the Black establishment. These axes are far from simple, and in the next paragraphs, I will explain the criteria that go into determining a politician's position on these axes.

Crossover Appeal

As shown before, the militant–moderate continuum has figured prominently in studies of Black leadership for nearly seventy years (Walters and Smith 1999; Ladd 1966; Burgess 1962; J. Q. Wilson 1960; Canon, Schousen, and Sellers 1996). While it is extremely antiquated to judge Black politicians on whether they believe in acquiescing to second class citizenship for Blacks anymore (indeed, it would be hard to find a credible Black leader arguing for a rollback on the gains of the Civil Rights Movement), the dimension still has analytic merit. Politicians who run deracialized campaigns, for instance, would naturally be far less militant and more likely to have greater levels of crossover appeal than those who do run racialized campaigns.

Additionally, perceptions of moderation and militancy also spill over into policy issues. An elected official's degree of crossover appeal can affect his policy agendas or how she frames issues in the pursuit of achieving certain policy goals. For instance, a militant official, or one with less crossover appeal, may pursue the ending of police brutality and frame it as a racial issue. A moderate counterpart may either not address the issue entirely or frame it as being disadvantageous to the pursuit of law and order in order to maintain his or her crossover appeal. A more militant leader may champion affirmative action, while a moderate leader seeking crossover appeal may focus on more racially neutral issues such as traditional economic development.

It is important to acknowledge that crossover appeal is not necessarily synonymous with strong non-Black constituent support. It is easy to assume that candidates who garner a large share of the non-Black vote in their jurisdictions (especially the first time they run for office) or who win in majority non-Black jurisdictions are automatically deracialized and have high levels of crossover appeal. However, there may be some instances where non-Black voters are attracted to Black candidates who make strong racial appeals because of a commitment to liberal politics or because of a candidate's personal characteristics (i.e., they have a compelling personal story or are famous). Later in this chapter, we will see examples of Phase III Black politicians who do not neatly fit the stereotype of high crossover appeal.

Perceived Career Trajectory

If one reads the mainstream press, one can often find examples of Black politicians in the new cohort being touted as presidential material (Dionne 2004; Benson 2006). Clearly, there are members of this cohort besides Barack Obama who clearly aspire to be president one day and appear to be better positioned to achieve their goals than any other generation of Black politicians. However, there are members of this cohort who seem content to remain in the positions they currently hold for the foreseeable future.

The career trajectory dimension seeks to make distinctions between politicians who appear to be upwardly mobile (i.e., they could have credible aspirations for statewide or national office) and those who do not. Often, the personal backgrounds of politicians influence their ambitions. Pauline Stone studied the ambitions of Black elected officials in Michigan in the late 1970s. Using a typology developed by Joseph Schlesinger (1966, 10), she identified politicians with "progressive" ambitions (those who wanted to seek higher office), "static" ambitions (those who wanted to maintain their current positions), and "discrete" ambitions (those who wanted to step down from their current offices) (Stone 1980, 96). She found that politicians with discrete ambitions were more likely to have been drafted from the grassroots. In contrast, politicians with progressive ambitions were more likely to be young, well educated, and less committed to purely partisan politics (Stone 1980). For the purposes of this analysis, politicians with long trajectories will have progressive ambitions, while politicians with short trajectories will have static or discrete ambitions.

There are three factors that influence a politician's categorization as having a long or short career trajectory. First, a politician has to want (or appear to want) to pursue higher office. This is important for a number of reasons. Because these officials have not served in prominent office for a long period of time, their future ambitions figure prominently in popular evaluations of them because for now, we really cannot judge their record of achievement. Moreover, the perceived ambitions of these officials have been a point of criticism. Recall that Ronald Walters criticized this cohort of politicians for being too ambitious and for seeking higher office before they had paid their dues (Martin 2003, 56).

Second, the media also play a role in generating buzz about a Black candidate's future prospects. Adolph Reed Jr. noted in his analysis of Jesse Jackson Sr.'s 1984 presidential campaign that the mainstream media hyped Jackson's candidacy. Jackson had no chance of winning the Democratic nomination for president, yet because of the inordinate amount of media attention, he emerged from that campaign as the perceived spokesman for Black America, with no consideration of his actual legitimacy as a leader in the Black community (Reed 1986, chapter 8). It may very well be that some of these officials are media constructions; or conversely, the perception that some of these candidates are mere media constructions could have a very negative impact on their legitimacy in Black communities (Walters and Smith 1999, 217).

Finally, there are structural and political considerations that do impact the future career trajectories of some of these officials. Black elected officials representing majority-minority enclaves in overwhelmingly White states may have difficulty winning statewide elections. Similarly, ambitious Black elected officials living in the District of Columbia, such as Mayor Adrian Fenty, would have to move to a state to pursue higher political office. Finally, elected officials who fail to achieve policy goals in office or get mired in scandal jeopardize their chances to make credible runs for higher political office.

Connections to the Black Establishment

The final dimension of the model assesses the strength of young Black politicians' connections to the Black establishment. Part of this analysis looks at political socialization. Some young Black politicians have clear connections to traditional centers of Black political power. They are either the scions of political or activist families (i.e., Harold Ford Jr. and Jesse Jackson Jr.) or have been politically socialized in traditional Black institutions, whether it be serving on the staff of an established Black politician or working with prominent legacy civil rights organizations such as the NAACP. Others are clearly new players to the body politic and lack the traditional political connections to the Black establishment. Having connections to traditional Black centers of power can be invaluable. Those with access to the establishment could gain a fundraising or endorsement advantage, while those without those establishment ties have to raise money or win endorsements from scratch.

Being part of the establishment or being a newcomer to the political scene could have significant implications for the types of agendas young Black politicians advance and the tone they use to advance those agendas. Someone who is a newcomer to the political scene may be more likely to ruffle feathers or to challenge the elders. Those with establishment connections may be less likely to challenge their elders, who literally could have raised them or their childhood friends. This decreased likelihood to challenge the system could have significant consequences for the advancement of Black politics and the improvement of the material lives of Black people. Those less likely to challenge the status quo may in fact be less likely to provide the needed innovations to advance African-American interests.

Assessing linked fate also figures prominently into evaluations of a young Black politician's connections to the Black establishment. Michael Dawson (1994) noted that middle-class Blacks, who may physically remove themselves from core Black communities when they gain affluence, often maintain physical and psychic connections to Black communities through a number of means. They can return to these communities for things as mundane as church and hair appointments, and they may still have relatives who still live in these core communities, which solidifies their connections to these communities. Finally, the

Table 1.1 Typologies of Third Phase Black Politicians

Typology	Cross-over Appeal	Ties to the Black Establishment	Perceived Trajectory	Example	Political Opportunity Structure	Challenges Facing This Sub-Cohort
Ivy League Upstarts	High	Weak	Long	Booker, Davis, Obama	Systemic failure in their Jurisdiction	They have to answer the charge that they are racially inauthentic and only seek to exploit Black communities for their personal political gain.
Local Kids Made Good	High	Weak	Short	Brown, Fenty, Johnson, McTeer-Hudson, Richardson	Open Seats	Some in this sub-cohort choose not to pursue higher office. thers are deterred either because of structural constraints or unresolved racial tension.
Rebrands of Their Parents	High	Strong	Long	Ford	Generational Succession + Long Term Dynastic Planning	Their ties to the Black establishment, and their parents' racialized political records could undermine their crossover appeal.
Deracialized Sequels	High	Strong	Short	Mallory, Mitchell	Generational Succession + Demographic Shift Privileging Non-Blacks	This group largely limits themselves deliberately from attaining higher office.
Chips Off the Old Block	Low	Strong	Short	Carson, Clarke, Kilpatrick	Their Parents Pave the Way	This group may face the most pressure to maintain the political status quo, even if that hurts Black advancement.
New "Old Standard Bearers"	Low	Strong	Long	Jackson, Meek	Open Seat + Demographic Shift Favoring Blacks	In order to have viable long term career trajectories, they have to cultivate crossover support.

Dominant Characteristic: Strong Credentials

Dominant Characteristic: Strong Connections To Black Establishment

Dominant Characteristic: High Levels of "Street Credibility"						
New Activists	Low	Weak	Long	Ellison	Rising Internal Class Warfare; Increased Lower Class Participation; Novelty Candidacies	It is extremely difficult to maintain a long career trajectory without cultivating crossover appeal and establishment ties.
Rebels Without A Chance	Low	Weak	Short	Hutchins, Powell	Most Likely To Emerge as the Result of a One-Time Disturbance	The emergence of successful candidates from this cohort is unlikely without the cultivation of other resources.

Source: Author's compilation.

fact that middle-class Blacks still experience racial discrimination still plays a radicalizing force. These factors combine to give middle-class Blacks a sense that their fate is tied to the fate of other Blacks, which in turn leads them to support policy positions (such as welfare spending) that non-Blacks of the same class status are far less likely to support. Thus, some young Black politicians with no roots in traditional Black communities at all may be far less likely to advance a political and policy agenda that would advance the interests of Black communities.

Typologies of Phase III

Having articulated the factors that contribute to the political identities of young Black elected officials and aspirants of the post-Civil Rights generation, it is important to see how those factors interact and how this affects the classification of young Black politicians.

If we look at the three definitional axes (crossover appeal, perceived career trajectory, and connections to the Black establishment), and scale them on a binary (ranking people as low or high relative to each other on the scales), this yields eight possible archetypal permutations, as shown in Table 1.1. For the rest of this section, I will provide a thumbnail sketch of these typologies, devoting most of the attention to the observed archetypes.

New Black Politicians with Strong Credentials

The first set of Phase III Black politicians are largely characterized by two of the three dimensions. They actively employ deracialization as a campaign and governance strategy, and they have weak ties to the Black political establishment. The combination of the resources these politicians have at their disposal usually lead to these politicians being defined by their training. Indeed, politicians in the first two categories emphasize their newness and their stellar credentials when running for office.

Ivy League Upstarts

The Ivy League Upstarts, which include President Barack Obama, Alabama Congressman Artur Davis, and Newark, New Jersey Mayor Cory Booker, are among the most visible of the post-Civil Rights cohort of Black elected leadership. This subset is defined by high crossover appeal, high levels of ambition, and weak ties to the Black political establishment. This subcohort tends to be highly educated, graduating with advanced degrees from prestigious, majority-White institutions. For example, Obama graduated from Columbia and Harvard Law School. Davis, whose Harvard Law School career overlapped with Obama's, also earned his bachelor's degree from Harvard. Booker graduated from Stanford, Oxford University (as a Rhodes Scholar), and Yale Law School. They also receive a lot of buzz in the mainstream media and appear to be anointed as the next wave of Black leaders because of their credentials. For instance, a month before

Barack Obama delivered his now-famous keynote address to the 2004 Demo-cratic National Convention, columnist E. J. Dionne dubbed Obama, "a media darling in this year's election.... Already there's speculation that he may be the first African American president of the United States—and he's only a state sena-tor" (Dionne 2004, A29). The week after Cory Booker won his election to lead New Jersey's largest city, *New York Times* reporter Josh Benson noted that people were already discussing Booker's next political office (Benson 2006). Indeed, these gentlemen receive a lot of attention for their poise and for projecting a nonthreatening image, similar to the deracialized candidates of Phase II. For his part, Davis is planning a 2010 gubernatorial candidacy (Evans 2007).

However, these candidates were also embattled, at least at first, in Black com-munities. All three of these men suffered defeats early in their careers, when they challenged established longtime Black incumbents for political power. Those campaigns were marked by noticeably high levels of racial vitriol, where they were condemned for not being culturally Black enough and for being interlopers who at best did not know enough about the communities they aspired to lead and at worst were insincere instrumentalists who planned to exploit and gen-trify their communities for political gain (Curry 2005; Lawrence 2000; Harnden 2002). While Ivy League Upstarts typically rebound from these initial defeats, their emergence onto the political scene raises important normative questions about class, racial authenticity, and linked fate.

In addition to the normative debate surrounding these candidates about linked fate and their ability to hold the best interests of Black communities at heart is the inherent pressure to perform. These candidates often run on good government platforms, in response to what they perceive to be failures of previous administrations to deliver goods and services effectively to their communities. When they get elected to office, they are expected to produce results immedi-ately, and if they do not produce, then their constituents may be less forgiving at the next election.

Local Kids Made Good

The Local Kids Made Good, include Washington, DC Mayor Adrian Fenty, Sacramento, California Mayor Kevin Johnson, Greenville, Mississippi Mayor Heather McTeer Hudson, Maryland Lieutenant Governor Anthony Brown, and California Congresswoman Laura Richardson. They are very similar to the Ivy League Upstarts, but they receive far less attention. They, like the Ivy League Upstarts, are extremely well educated, have crossover appeal, are committed to good government, and are generally political newcomers (i.e., they are not the scions of political families), but they are perceived to have shorter progressive political ambitions. Some, like Laura Richardson, who won a special election to replace the late Congresswoman Juanita Millender-McDonald, assumed her post in the middle of 2007; thus, she has not been in office long enough to start talking about the next political office. Similarly, Anthony Brown is only in his first term as lieutenant governor. If he were to run for Governor of Maryland, he would likely defer to Gov. Martin O'Malley (who is eligible for reelection in 2010) and not run until 2014, at which point, we could start calling him an Ivy League Upstart. Others, such as Adrian Fenty, are structurally impeded from pursuing higher office. As a resident of Washington, DC, Fenty does not have the option of running for governor or being able to run to be a voting member of Congress. Thus, barring Washington, DC obtaining statehood, the DC delegate earning full voting privileges in Congress, or Fenty moving to a state, his elected political career is probably limited.

Heather McTeer Hudson, on the other hand, is potentially constrained by the political and racial conditions in her state. Hudson is notable because unlike Fenty, she was the first Black person to be elected to her post. In fact, Hudson is the first Black mayor in the Mississippi Delta, which is 70 percent Black (Byrd 2004). As such, her obstacles relate to larger issues of political incorporation. In her analysis of racial politics on the Mississippi Delta, Sharon Wright Austin notes that while Mississippi has the largest number of Black elected officials of any state in the United States, Blacks are still not fully incorporated politically. Blacks are still underrepresented in county government, and Black–White political coalitions have yet to form. As such, it will be very difficult for a Black politician to develop a statewide profile for the foreseeable future (Austin 2006, chapter 5). With Blacks in her region being largely unable to translate their numerical dominance into political power, it is difficult to project that Hudson would be able to easily win higher political office.[6]

Some may question the inclusion of Kevin Johnson as a Local Kid Made Good. Johnson, a former point guard for the Phoenix Suns, could easily be racialized because of his previous occupation. Moreover, allegations that Johnson had engaged in sexual misconduct with minors and had criminally mismanaged money in a non-profit organization he ran (at the time of this writing, Johnson has not been charged with any crime) could have reinforced stereotypes about Blacks that would have implications for his electoral viabililty. Despite this, Johnson very much fits the profile because he parlayed his post- NBA career as a charter school advocate into a political career where he ran for mayor on a good government platform (Marshall 2008; Chawkins 2008; Bailey 2008; Associated Press 2009; Chavous 2008; "Day One" 2008).

New Black Politicians with Strong Ties to the Black Establishment

The next subset of young, Black politicians is extremely diverse, and includes four of the eight types. Their common attribute is their connection to the Black political establishment. Phase III Black politicians who have strong ties to the Black political establishment have different relationships with Black constituents, approach Black politics from a different perspective, and make different strategic decisions when running for high profile offices. All of the politicians in the next four categories have strong ties to the Black political establishment. While every politician profiled here is the son or daughter of a prominent Black activist or politician, it is also possible to have strong ties to the Black political establishment through intensive mentoring by Phase I or II Black elected officials or activists.

Chips off the Old Block

The Chips off the Old Block are the children of prominent Black politicians or civil rights leaders who used their lineage as a steppingstone to a political career. This subcohort includes people such as Indiana Congressman André Carson, New York Congresswoman Yvette Clarke, and Detroit Mayor Kwame Kilpatrick, all children or grandchildren of prominent politicians (the late Congresswoman Julia Carson, former New York City Councilwoman Una Clarke, and Congress-woman Carolyn Cheeks-Kilpatrick respectively). This subcohort is probably most diverse in terms of its orientation. While most of them espouse more moderate politics than their parents, they are perceived to have less crossover appeal than their counterparts who are largely defined by their credentials and who lack politi-cal lineages. These politicians clearly have connections to the Black establishment and are thus less likely to have their commitment to Black communities called into question. They may even, as we will see in chapter 5, embrace Black youth culture as a cultural affirmation. However, they are less likely to be perceived as having a long career trajectory. For those serving in the House of Representatives, if they continue their congressional careers, they are likely to gain seniority and committee chairmanships, but as of yet, they do not appear likely to take the risk of running for statewide or national office. Or, in the case of former Mayor Kilpatrick, they may have been implicated in political scandals that circumscribe future political opportunities (see Star News Services 2005).

Rebrands of Their Parents

Rebrands of Their Parents are a different breed of Black dynastic heirs. They have high crossover appeal, strong ties to the Black establishment, and long perceived career trajectories. Rebrands are very similar to Ivy League Upstarts, but they differ on the establishment dimension. Because these politicians have ties to the Black establishment—indeed, they are often children of Phase I and II politi-cians they tend to be less susceptible to the charges of racial inauthenticity that are levied at Ivy League Upstarts.

Former Tennessee Congressman Harold Ford Jr. typifies this category. Ford assumed the Memphis congressional seat held by his father in 1996, but he clearly had higher political ambitions and cultivated a more conservative national political presence. Al Gore chose him to deliver one of the keynote addresses at the 2000 Democratic National Convention because "He's a rising star. He has a bright future. And he's from Tennessee" (Gore, quoted in Brosnan 2000). After the 2002 midterm elections, Ford made an unsuccessful bid to be Minority Leader of the House of Representatives. In 2006, Ford came within 3 percent-age points of becoming Tennessee's first Black U.S. Senator. Therefore, unlike the Chips off the Old Block, who currently do not publicly evince an interest in seeking office beyond the posts they currently hold, Rebrands of Their Parents use their parents' old seats as springboards to seek high offices that their parents could only dream of attaining.[7]

However, because Rebrands got their political starts at their parents' knees, they could be constrained by their families no matter how hard they try to escape the proverbial apple tree. If a family's reputation is mixed, it can cause problems for the Rebrand candidate. When Ford ran for the Senate in 2006, his family's ethical issues became a campaign obstacle. For instance, his opponent, Bob Corker, ran an ad ("Family Ties"), which charged that Harold Ford Jr. was a puppet for his father (Strategic Perception 2006). This ad clearly was meant to prime antipathy for members of the Ford family, which has had more than its share of ethics charges levied against them (Davis and Sher 2006).

New "Old Standard Bearers"

Congressmen Jesse Jackson Jr. of Illinois and Kendrick Meek of Florida fit the archetype of a New "Old Standard Bearer." Jackson, like Harold Ford Jr., harbors progressive political ambitions, as evidenced by his lobbying to be appointed to replace Barack Obama in the U.S. Senate in 2008 (Mihalopolous 2008). However, Jackson lacks the same crossover cachet as Ford. Given Jackson's relative lack of crossover appeal, his path to progressive power is different from that of a Rebrand. Jackson may find it even more difficult than Ford did to cultivate non-Black support or support outside of Chicago. As such, having an alternate path to power becomes even more important for him. If he had been appointed to Barack Obama's Senate seat, he could have run as the de facto incumbent, which would have given him an advantage in the 2010 election that he may have had difficulty cultivating on his own.

Kendrick Meek, a 2010 candidate for Florida's U.S. Senate seat, faces the same challenge that Jackson faced in 2008. Meek chose to seek his party's nomination for the Senate after incumbent Mel Martinez chose to retire. By not challenging an incumbent, Meek and Jackson exercised caution and strategic insight in making a bid for a higher office (Jacobsen and Kernell 1983). This contrasts to some of their Ivy League Upstart peers, who cut their political teeth challenging entrenched incumbents for powers (see chapters 2–3).

New Old Standard Bearers like Meek, who run for their seats, have to adopt other strategies to ensure victory. When New Old Standard Bearers run for office, they have to generate enough crossover appeal to effectively split the White vote, thus making Black voters the crucial swing vote in their particular contest. In any case, Blacks must make up a decisive portion of the electorate in order for New Old Standard Bearers to have a viable chance at nomination and victory.

Deracialized Sequels

Deracialized sequels are like Rebrands of Their Parents in that these politicians have high crossover appeal and strong ties to the Black establishment. However, unlike Rebrands of Their Parents, they have shorter career trajectories. A Deracialized Sequel politician is most likely to emerge in an area accustomed to Black leadership but with a large enough non-Black population that requires Black candidates to reach out to non-Black constituents in order to be politically viable.

Cincinnati Mayor Mark Mallory and former Baltimore City Councilman and mayoral candidate Kieffer Mitchell provide examples of Deracialized Sequels. Mallory's father, William Mallory, served as Majority Leader of the Ohio House of Representatives. The younger Mallory replaced his father in the Ohio House and then won a State Senate seat in 1998. In 2005, Mallory ran for mayor. He won the nonpartisan primary largely on the backs of Black votes—43 percent of the city's residents were Black. Nevertheless, Mallory made a point to campaign among White voters. Mallory went on to beat the Cincinnati City Council President David Pepper by 4 percentage points. Mallory's tenure in office was not without controversy. In his first term, the Cincinnati NAACP gave Mallory a vote of no-confidence because they contended that Mallory had not done enough to ensure that minority-owned businesses got a fair share of city contracts. The civil rights organization threatened a recall effort but at the time of this writing, had not followed through on that threat. Mallory is running for reelection in 2009. His showing in this race will reveal his future prospects for public office should he develop an interest in higher office (Ifill 2009, 132–35; "Mayor's Biography" n.d.; "New Mayors…" 2005; Korte 2005; Kinney 2005; Prendergast 2009a, 2009b, 2009c).

Mitchell, the grand-nephew of the late Maryland Congressman Parren Mitchell and scion of a legendary Black activist family in Maryland, served on Baltimore's City Council for eleven years before running for the Democratic nomination for Mayor of Baltimore in 2007. Mitchell represented a diverse city council ward and was comfortable reaching across racial and class lines. Mitchell clearly attempted to capitalize on his family's reputation to be elected Mayor of Baltimore. However, Mitchell publicly acknowledged that he had no intention of seeking higher office beyond the mayoralty. At an August 14, 2007 debate (which the author attended), Mitchell announced that he had no intention of running for higher office after serving as mayor.

Despite Mitchell's pledge to devote his career to Baltimore politics, his campaign efforts were hampered in part because of family drama. Mitchell's father, who initially served as treasurer of his campaign, was forced to resign after it was alleged that he had used campaign funds for noncampaign expenses. Mitchell's father then evicted his son's campaign out of office space he rented to them. By the time that this scandal emerged, Mitchell already trailed the eventual nominee and winner, Sheila Dixon,[8] in polling by double digit margins. The scandal, though, presented a new distraction at best and further hampered his efforts. In a *Baltimore Sun* poll taken weeks before the September 11 primary, 16 percent of voters said that the scandal did make it less likely for them to vote for Kieffer Mitchell (Brewington 2007).

New Black Politicians with Street Credibility

The final two typologies are largely defined by their relative lack of crossover appeal and few ties to the Black political establishment. These resource paucities make it very difficult for politicians adopting this posture to gain electoral success. Despite these challenges, some young Black politicians can be successful when they adopt this posture. Local conditions have to be absolutely perfect in order for politicians to emerge in this type. They often have to take advantage of exogenous shocks to mobilize Black voters in the hopes of reviving and updating the Civil Rights Movement. Thus, politicians adopting this posture emphasize their street credibility to offset the deficits of not always being guaranteed mainstream or Black establishment support.

New Activists

New Activists are characterized by low crossover appeal, weak ties to the Black establishment, and long perceived trajectories. Because of the low crossover appeal and weak ties to the Black establishment, I argued elsewhere (Gillespie 2009, 154–55) that it would be difficult to conceive that any successful, young Black politician would emerge who fits this type. However, upon further examination, I came to the conclusion that Congressman Keith Ellison of Minnesota fits the characteristics of a New Activist. At a first glance, Ellison appears to be a Local Kid Made Good. Because he represents a diverse, but overwhelmingly White district from Minnesota, it is easy to automatically assume that he is deracialized. However, a deeper examination of Ellison's background reveals that he is far more racialized than any of the Ivy League Upstarts or Local Kids Made Good (Gillespie 2009, 152). By vocation, Ellison is a criminal defense attorney who specializes in criminal defense for poor, largely minority clients. He has been active in the Minneapolis environmental justice movement, working to ensure that toxic waste sites and landfills are not disproportionately located in minority communities. When Ellison first ran for Congress in 2006, he won the support of Phase I Black politicians such as Jesse Jackson and John Conyers.[9] In addition, Ellison, who is Muslim, initially converted to his faith by way of the Nation of Islam, which proved to be extremely controversial during his congressional campaign ("The New Members" 2006; Ellison 2008). Cumulatively, these characteristics suggest that Ellison was not deracialized, despite his success in reaching beyond the Minneapolis Black community to attract non-Black voters. In fact, it appears that at least some non-Black voters in his liberal district may have been attracted to Ellison in part because of his background. For instance, an Associated Press reporter quoted a Minneapolis voter who voted for Ellison because of his liberal policy stances. The voter also noted that while religion did not factor into his vote choice, he was "happy to send a Muslim to Congress" (Condon 2006). Similarly, a lawyer for the local Democratic Party went on record in 2006 saying that sending a Muslim to Congress at the height of opposition to the Iraq War sent a powerful message to the Bush Administration (Olson 2006). Thus,

Ellison was successful because he had the right background for the right district at the right moment in history to be electorally successful.

Rebels Without a Chance

Rebels Without a Chance are characterized by low crossover appeal, weak ties to the Black establishment, and a short career trajectory. Because Rebels Without a Chance lack the conventional resources that are needed to win elections (i.e., support from Black elites and non-Black voters), they only succeed in cases where they have massive grassroots support among largely disaffected Black voters who would almost certainly have to comprise a majority of the electorate. Given the structural obstacles impeding Rebels Without a Chance, it is difficult for a successful Phase III Black politician to emerge in this mode. That is, they may not have majority support in their constituency depending on the demographic makeup of their jurisdiction; they may not have access to the resources needed to run campaigns, such as money or professional staff; and they have the difficult task of trying to mobilize potentially discouraged and inefficacious voters.

Despite the long odds of success, Rebel Without a Chance candidates have emerged recently. Markel Hutchins, an Atlanta minister, rose to prominence as the spokesperson for the family of Kathryn Johnston, a 92-year-old Atlanta woman who was shot to death by police during a bungled no-knock warrant arrest in 2006. In February 2008, Hutchins challenged Congressman John Lewis for the Democratic nomination for Georgia's Fifth Congressional District. Clearly, Hutchins was attempting to translate his stature as a young activist into political power. He also hoped to tap into voter disappointment with Lewis's original endorsement of Hillary Clinton over Barack Obama in the 2008 presidential primaries. However, he was unable to unseat Lewis, who won nearly 70 percent of the vote in a three-person field. Hutchins only garnered 16 percent of the vote (Galloway 2008; Smith 2008).

Kevin Powell, a reality TV star turned author/activist, challenged Brooklyn Congressman Edolphus Towns for the Democratic nomination in New York's 10th Congressional District in 2008. Towns, a thirteen-term congressman, won his 2006 primary against New York City Councilman Charles Barron with only a plurality of the vote in a three-person field. This showing, on the heels of narrow primary wins in 1998 and 2000, suggested that he was politically vulnerable. Towns also made a big strategic misstep when he endorsed Hillary Clinton in the 2008 Democratic presidential primary. Powell hoped to use all of these vulnerabilities, plus his own assertion that Towns was unresponsive to the needs of his constituents, to gain a foothold in the congressional primary. Despite his notoriety as an original cast member of MTV's *The Real World* and his potential appeal to young people, though, Powell was not successful. Towns eventually beat Powell by a two-to-one margin in 2008 (Hicks 2008a, b; Hernandez 2008).

It is important to note the differences between politicians like Ellison and politicians like Hutchins or Powell (particularly Hutchins). Ellison had a long track record of community organizing and service in elective office (he was a state legislator before running for Congress, while Hutchins, in his causes and cadence, assumes the role of a classic civil rights leader. This framing may put Hutchins at a disadvantage (even in Atlanta) if voters prefer more moderate Black candidates (See Canon et al. 1996). In contrast, Ellison has been able to juggle his many identities to be electorally successful at the state and federal level. Though Ellison's future political plans are unclear (He told me in an interview he is content in his current role), the fact that he made it to Congress via this unconventional path, provides a stark contrast with aspirants such as Hutchins, who have found it extremely difficult to get elected (Ellison 2008).

Analysis and Further Questions

The typologies listed above serve a twofold purpose. First, they are designed to show the diversity among this class of individuals—a diversity that is often obscured in the popular press with their preoccupation with a few of these elected leaders. Moreover, the typologies help to organize our assessment of these leaders and give us some uniform metrics by which to judge them.

The typologies are not meant to be a monolith, though. There are other important considerations that the typologies do not take into consideration. I would like to briefly touch on these points.

Where Are the Women?

One of the interesting and troubling aspects of this research into the third wave of Black elected officials is the relative absence of women on the national scene. Not until Yvette Clarke's election in November 2006 had any Black woman born after 1960 achieved any measure of prominence by being elected to a federal office (she has since been joined by Congresswoman Laura Richardson, who replaced the late Juanita Millender-McDonald. Donna Edwards, who was born in 1958, beat Albert Wynn to represent Maryland's Fourth Congressional District in 2008). At the state and local level, three young women stand out. San Francisco District Attorney Kamala Harris has announced her bid for the Democratic nomination for California Attorney General in 2010 (Marinucci 2008). Louisiana State Representative Karen Carter Peterson challenged embattled former Congressman William Jefferson in 2006. She recently announced that she would not run for Mayor of New Orleans, feuling speculation that she may run for Jefferson's old congressional seat in 2010 (Donze 2009). And Heather McTeer Hudson is an example of a young, Black, female mayor. Hudson does not lead a major city, though; her city has a population of less than 50,000 residents (U.S. Census Bureau 2007).

There could be a reason to explain this apparent dearth of young, female Black politicians. Jennifer Lawless and Richard Fox (2005) have found that women who are well situated professionally to run for political office (i.e., they come from the pipeline professions of law, education, politics, or business) are less likely to consider running for office and less likely to actually run for office once they have considered the possibility. Moreover, when they do consider running for office, women are more likely to consider running for a lower level office than men (i.e., local government as opposed to state government). On a small scale, Lawless and Fox's findings mirror what we observe in the cohort of young Black politicians. The women who are running for office are concentrating their efforts at the state and local level. Yvette Clarke started out as a city councilwoman; Heather McTeer Hudson is mayor of a small city. Similarly, Alicia Thomas Morgan of Georgia, Jennifer McClellan of Virginia, Jill Carter of Maryland, and Grace Spencer of New Jersey are examples of Phase III female elected officials who serve as state legislators. These women stand in contrast to Harold Ford and Jesse Jackson Jr., whose first elections were for congressional seats. However, only time will tell if these observations are temporary and these women use these first seats as steppingstones to higher political office.

Phase 2.5

In addition, there are also some elected officials who by virtue of their age, will not define the new generation of Black politicians. In popular parlance, Black politicians who were born at the tail end of the Baby Boom but who did not emerge as prominent political players until the late 1990s and early- to mid-2000s are often mentioned alongside their Generation X peers. Yet, it is the Xers who largely define this new phase of Black politics and by virtue of their relative youth, will likely have the most lasting impact on American politics generally and Black politics specifically. Because of this, we focus primarily on Generation X politicians in this volume. However, we do make a couple of exceptions and will cover Deval Patrick in chapter 8 and Michael Steele in chapter 11.

Some may question the decision to use a 1960 birthdate as a cutoff for Phase III. How different is a politician born in 1955 from one born in 1960? The differences are small, but significant. Take Massachusetts Governor Deval Patrick, for example. Born in 1956, Patrick is technically too old to be considered part of the post-Civil Rights cohort, but he has the profile and politics of an Ivy League Upstart (he is Harvard educated and worked in the Clinton administration). In many ways, Patrick's personal narrative draws on the themes of being on the racial vanguard characteristic of previous phases of Black leadership and melds it with the postracial pragmatism of some of the Phase III leadership. He is from the South Side of Chicago and was one of the first Blacks to be afforded a prep school education through a program targeted to poor students of color. As a young lawyer, he worked in Darfur and for the NAACP Legal Defense Fund. He followed that with a stint in the Clinton Justice Department (Civil Rights Division) and work in the private sector (Anderson 2006). Thus, because of the breadth of his experience that comes with age, Patrick and those like him are able to appeal to both Blacks and Whites, apparently without the same need to prove their racial authenticity in the ways that their Ivy League Upstart counterparts have had to prove.

Another important reason to make distinctions between politicians born in the late 1950s and those born in the 1960s and 1970s is that there is considerable diversity among politicians and activists born in the 1950s. Some, such as Congresswoman Sheila Jackson Lee (D-TX), former Congresswoman Cynthia McKinney (D-GA), and 2004 presidential candidate Al Sharpton, have had very long careers in high profile elective office or activism. Because they began cultivating their national political careers in the late 1980s and early 1990s, they adopted the policy platforms and campaign styles of their Phase I and Phase II forebears. As such, they should be classified with Phase I and Phase II politicians (Lee is Phase II; while McKinney and Sharpton are Phase I). Phase 2.5 politicians, however, did not start running for high profile political offices until very recently. Because their ascendance coincides with the rise of Generation X Black politicians, it is helpful to think about them alongside Phase III politicians.

Other Phase 2.5 politicians mirror other types of Phase III Black politicians (as shown in Table 1.2).[10] Philadelphia Mayor Michael Nutter and Buffalo, New York Mayor Byron Brown share similarities with Local Kids Made Good. They won their elections with high levels of White support. Nutter won the highest share of the White vote of any Black Democratic primary contender in the city's history when he won his seat in 2007 (Matza 2007). Brown, who is Buffalo's first Black mayor, broke a glass ceiling that six predecessors had been unable to crack. Analysts attribute his success to having previously represented a majority White state senate district and having garnered union support (Hicks 2005). Both of these men cultivated reputations for good government and assumed office in times of crisis: Nutter succeeded embattled Mayor John Street; New York State placed Buffalo into receivership two years before Brown was elected (Fagone 2008; Staba 2005).

Congressman William Lacy Clay of Missouri is similar to a Chip Off the Old Block. Clay, the son of former Congressman William "Bill" Clay, succeeded his father in Congress after serving nearly two decades in the Missouri legislature. As a Congressman, the younger Clay has maintained the advocacy tradition of his father, a founding member of the Congressional Black Caucus. The younger Clay's congressional Web site boasts his numerous commitments to minority constituents (i.e., his efforts to protect voting rights, promote minority home ownership, and the mandatory inclusion of Black history in K-12 school curricula) (Clay, n.d.).

Table 1.2 Approximate Typology of Selected Phase 2.5 Black Politicians

Approximate Typology	Representative Politician
Ivy League Upstarts	Deval Patrick
Local Kids Made Good	Michael Nutter, Byron Brown
Chips Off the Old Block	William Lacy Clay
New Activists	Donna Edwards, Chaka Fattah
Rebel Without a Chance	Ray Nagin

Source: Author's compilation.

Congresswoman Donna Edwards of Maryland and Congressman Chaka Fattah of Pennsylvania share similarities with New Activists. Edwards rose to prominence as an anti-war advocate who challenged incumbent Congressman Albert Wynn in the DC suburbs in 2006 and 2008. Wynn supported the War in Iraq, and Edwards sensed that this weakened him politically. While Edwards was unsuccessful in her 2006 challenge, she successfully mobilized progressive, left-wing surrogates to raise money for her, and she succeeded in winning the nomination and the office in 2008. Fattah, the son of local community organizers, ran unsuccessfully for Congress in 1991. When he won his seat in 1994, he beat a powerful black incumbent who had the support of Philadelphia's political establishment (Lucien Blackwell) by gaining the support of grassroots black leaders (Wiggins 2006; Helderman, Wan and Wiggins 2008; Helderman 2008; Williams 1994a, b).

New Orleans Mayor Ray Nagin is an interesting case. Currently, he is a Rebel Without a Chance, but really, his political style evolved over the course of his tenure in office. Nagin, a former cable executive, started out as a Local Kid Made Good. When he first ran for office in 2002, he ran as a pro-business reformer and won the support of whites and middle class blacks. However, in the aftermath of Hurricane Katrina, Nagin lost significant white support, and his rhetoric became increasingly racialized. For instance, Nagin famously declared that he wanted post-Katrina New Orleans to remain a "chocolate city" (Nossiter 2006). When he ran for reelection in 2006, Nagin's electoral coalition was markedly different. This time, blacks were the overwhelming majority of his base (Firestone 2002; Nossiter 2006).

Conclusion

To be sure, despite the election of Barack Obama as President of the United States, the younger generation of leadership has not amassed enough power or seniority as a whole to affect widespread change in the Black community. Thus, it remains to be seen whether their strategies and agenda produce favorable or unfavorable outcomes for Blacks. However, we can apply what we now know about this emerging generation of Black leadership to developing important questions to guide future research. I conclude with three of these questions, which I hope will lead to more questions and further lines of inquiry on this topic.

First, we know that the new crop of young, Black elected officials is more diverse than it would appear to be in the mainstream media, who focus mostly on those with Ivy League credentials and high crossover appeal. Indeed, a significant number of young Black politicians were socialized into politics at their parents' knee. Will the exodus of Phase I and II Black politicians from the scene free this subcohort to be innovative in Black politics? Or will the dynastic heirs assume the oppositional mantle of their parents and vie for influence with their popular peers who have fewer ties to the Black establishment?

Second, the age, class status, and upbringing of these politicians raise larger questions for the study of Black public opinion. Does this new generation of leadership reflect the larger generation that they came from, or are their prefer-ences artifacts of calculated political ambition? If the values, perspectives, and policy preferences of these politicians reflect the values of their cohort of Blacks generally, as Bositis (2002) suggests, then this means that we have to reevaluate conventional wisdoms about how Blacks develop linked fate and about how they choose parties, candidates, and policy preferences. Further study of this cohort may provide further credence to Adolph Reed's argument that class differences within the Black community betray multiple Black agendas (Reed 2000, chapter 1).

Finally, we will eventually have to ask whether the campaign, legislative, and governing approach of this new generation of politicians will actually be more successful in delivering goods and services to African-American communities. This question becomes especially important as more minority groups make legitimate claims for recognition, representation, and scarce resources. Moreover, the question reflects the nearly 20-year skepticism over deracialization gener-ally. Robert Smith gloomily predicted that deracialization "…is not likely to be able to arrest and reverse the decline of the Black community, and…it suggests that even Black leadership itself may be turning away from the problem" (Smith 1993, 220). If the new generation of Black leaders turns away from problems that face the Black community or is unable to deliver on their promises, then this could have a negative impact on already deep divisions within Black communi-ties. Moreover, it could lead to a deeper secondary marginalization of Blacks deemed less socially desirable even within the Black community (Cohen 1999). By reflecting on these issues sooner rather than later, this line of research can use lessons from the past forty years of Black elected leadership to chart a course for greater policy advancement in the future.

Notes

1. This is adapted with permission from Andra Gillespie. 2009. The Third Wave: A Theoretical Introduction to the Post-Civil Rights Cohort of African American Leadership. *National Political Science Review* 12:139–161.
2. Andrew Young, like Jesse Jackson Sr., represents an interesting case of Phase I Black politicians who attempted to adopt a Phase II posture in order to pursue high elective office. Their evolution evinces the possibility that older Black politicians can shift phases depending on changes in their personal philosophy or in the office they were pursuing (for further discussion, see Pierannunzi and Hutcheson 1996; Davis and Willingham 1993; Tate 1995, 8–15). In general, though, most politi-cians maintain a particular posture throughout their careers.
3. My discussion of Phases I and II deliberately avoided defining the Phases by gener-ation. That is because there is a generational overlap between Phases I and II. While most Phase I politicians were members of the Greatest (or World War II) Genera-tion, there are some Baby Boomers who adopted a Phase I posture (e.g., Jesse Jack-son Sr. in 1984). Similarly, while most Phase II Black politicians are members of the Silent and Baby Boom Generations, there were older Phase II politicians (e.g., Tom Bradley).
4. Sheridan uses Douglas Wilder as a example of a second wave politician who refused to identify with the civil rights struggle, saying that he opted to make money rather

than advocate for change in the 1960s. Whatever one can say about Wilder's personal politics, given his age, no one can argue that he missed being personally affected by Jim Crow growing up in Richmond, Virginia (Sheridan 1996, 166).

5. To be sure, there are earlier examples of young, moderate Blacks challenging leaders from the older, Civil Rights generation. Ardrey and Nelson note that Michael White challenged the combative, divisive tactics of George Forbes and beat him for the mayoralty of Cleveland. There are other early examples of Black politicians competing against other Black politicians, such as former Detroit Mayor Dennis Archer (Ardrey and Nelson 1990; Nordlinger 2002).

6. McTeer Hudson has expressed interest in running for statewide office in 2011.

7. Please refer to page 30 for a definition of high office. If I define a Rebrand or New Old Standard Bearer broadly as someone who wins his or her parent's seat and then seeks higher office, then Congresswoman Yvette Clarke qualifies as a New Old Standard Bearer. She took over her mother's New York City Council seat. Winning a congressional seat could qualify as a step up. However, because this analysis defines high offices as offices higher than congressional seats, Congresswoman Clarke is classified as a Chip off the Old Block until she pursues a U.S. Senate seat, the New York Governorship, or the Presidency of the United States.

8. Dixon was recently indicted on corruption charges, and personal sources indicate to me that Mitchell will run again for mayor.

9. Earning the endorsement of Phase I or II Black politician does not constitute having strong familial or mentoring ties to the Black political establishment. However, that these politicians supported his candidacy suggests that Ellison was not deracialized, especially when we consider that they have been critical of some of Ellison's contemporaries who were clearly deracialized.

10. To some, Governor David Patterson of New York will seem noticeably absent from this list. Every politician listed in Table 1.2 was born after 1955. Patterson was born in 1954 and is thus not a Phase 2.5 politician.

References

Anderson, Lisa. 2006. Chicago-born, leading in Mass: Deval Patrick rose from poverty, bids to be state's 1st Black governor. *The Chicago Tribune*, October 29.

Ardrey, Saundra C., and William E. Nelson. 1990. The maturation of Black political power: The case of Cleveland. *PS: Political Science and Politics* 23(2): 148–51.

Associated Press. 2009. FBI investigating Kevin Johnson's Calif. non-profit, http://www.azcentral.com/news/articles/2009/06/17/20090617kj-probe0617-ON.html (accessed August 19, 2009).

Austin, Sharon Wright. 2006. *The transformation of plantation politics: Black politics, concentrated poverty and social capital in the Mississippi Delta*. Albany: SUNY Press.

Bailey, Eric. 2008. US suspends funding of non-profit run by Sacramento mayoral candidate. *The Los Angeles Times*. September 26, 2008, http://articles.latimes.com/2008/sep/26/local/me-kevin26 (August 19, 2009).

Benson, Josh. 2006. Next for Booker? (Get used to the question). *The New York Times*, sec. 1, May 14.

Bositis, David A. 2002. *2002 National opinion poll: Politics*. Washington, DC: Joint Center for Political and Economic Studies, http://www.jointcenter.org.

———. 2001. *Changing the guard: Generational difference among Black elected officials*. Washington, DC: Joint Center for Political and Economic Studies.

Brewington, Kelly. 2007. Mitchell, father renew their feud. *Baltimore Sun*. http://www.baltimoresun.com (accessed September 24, 2007).

Brosnan, James W. 2000. Youngest congressman to speak to Democrats. *Cleveland Plain Dealer*, August 6.

Burgess, M. Elaine. 1962. *Negro leadership in a southern city*. Chapel Hill: University of North Carolina Press.

Byrd, Veronica. 2004. My generation can't just complain. We have to get involved. *Essence*. October. http://www. findarticles.com (accessed June 14, 2007).

Canon, David T., Matthew Schousen, and Patrick Sellers. 1996. The supply side of congressional redistricting: Race and strategic politicians, 1972–1992. *The Journal of Politics* 58, no. 3: 846–62.

Chawkins, Steve. 2008. Former NBA Star Kevin Johnson elected Sacramento's mayor. *The Los Angeles Times*. November 6, 2008. http://articles.latimes.com/2008/nov/06/local/me-state6 (accessed August 19, 2009).

Clay, W. L. n.d. Biography. Web site of Congressman William Lacy Clay Jr. http://lacy-clay.house.gov/biography.shtml (accessed April 19, 2009).

Cohen, Cathy. 1999. *The boundaries of Blackness: AIDS and the breakdown of Black politics*. Chicago: University of Chicago Press.

Condon, Patrick. 2006. First Muslim in congress is reluctant trailblazer. *Associated Press State and Local Wire,* November 9.

Curry, Marshall, dir. 2005. *Street fight* [DVD]. United States: Marshall Curry Productions.

Davis, Marilyn, and Alex Willingham. 1993. Andrew Young and the Georgia state elections of 1990. In *Dilemmas of Black politics*, ed. Georgia Persons, 147–75. New York: Harper Collins.

Davis, Michael, and Andy Sher. 2006. State GOP mailing focuses on Ford family. *Chattanooga Times Free Press*, November 2, B2.

Dawson, Michael C. 1994. *Behind the mule*. Princeton, NJ: Princeton University Press.

Day One: Kevin Johnson's plan for Sacramento, A city that works for everyone. 2008. [Campaign Brochure]. Sacramento: Kevin Johnson for Mayor. http://www.cityofsacramento.org/mayor/KJ_day_one.pdf (accessed August 19, 2009).

Dionne, E. J. 2004. In Illinois, a star prepares. *The Washington Post*, A29, June 25.

Donze, Frank. 2009. Another contender out: Karen Carter Peterson won't run for mayor. *New Orleans Times-Picayune*. September 23, 2009. http://www.nola.com/politics/index.ssf/2009/09/httpwwwyoutubecomwatchvtvoqa-l.html (accessed October 9, 2009).

Ellison, Keith. 2008. Personal interview. March 7, 2008.

Evans, Ben. 2007. Davis won't challenge sessions for senate seat in 2008. *Associate Press State and Local Wire,* January 8.

Fagone, Jason. 2008. Michael Nutter's dilemma. *Philadelphia Magazine*, January 15. http://www.phillymag.com/scripts/print/article.php?asset_idx=198252 (accessed April 21, 2009).

Firestone, David. 2002. TV executive defeats police chief to become mayor of New Orleans. *The New York Times*. http://www.nytimes.com/2002/03/03/us/tv-executive-defeats-police-chief-to-become-mayor-of-new-orleans.html?scp=2&sq=ray%20nagin%20tv%20executive&st=cse"http://www.nytimes.com/2002/03/03/us/tv-executive-defeats-police-chief-to-become-mayor-of-new-orleans.html?scp=2&sq=ray%20nagin%20tv%20executive&st=cse (accessed August 28, 2009).

Galloway, Jim. 2008. Hutchins to seek Lewis' seat. *Atlanta Journal-Constitution*. February 23, 2008, http://www.lexis-nexis.com (accessed August, 19, 2009).

Gillespie, Andra. 2009. The third wave: Assessing the post-civil rights cohort of Black elected leadership. *The National Political Science Review* 12: 139–61.

Hamilton, Charles V. 1982. Foreword. In *The new Black politics: The search for political power,* ed. Michael B. Preston, Lenneal J. Henderson Jr., and Paul Puryear, xvii–xx. New York: Longman.

Harnden, Toby. 2002. Dream coming true for gifted Black politician: Times are changing in the Deep South, reports Toby Harnden in Aliceville. *The Daily Telegraph (London)*, June 25, 13.

Helderman, Rosalind. 2008. Edwards overpowers Wynn: 8-term congressman concedes after heated race; Gilchrest in tough fight. *The Washington Post*, February 13, A21.

———. William Wan, and Ovetta Wiggins. 2008. Rare dual losses in Md. put incumbents on notice. *The Washington Post*, February 14, A1.

Henderson, Lenneal J. Jr. 1996. The governance of Kurt Schmoke as mayor of Baltimore. In *Race, governance, and politics in the United States*, ed. Huey L. Perry, 165–78. Gainesville: University of Florida Press.

Hernandez, Raymond. 2008. New campaign charge: You supported Clinton. *The New York Times*, July 1, 2008. http://www.nytimes.com/2008/07/01/us/politics/01dems.html?scp=8&sq=kevin%20powell&st=cse (accessed October 9, 2009).

Hicks, Jonathan. 2005. Race plays silent role in campaign for mayor of Buffalo. *The New York Times*, October 13, B6.

Hicks, Jonathan P. 2008a. Brooklyn congressman and veteran of tough primaries faces new fight. *The New York Times*. April 28. http://www.nytimes.com/2008/04/28/nyregion/28brooklyn.html?_r=1&scp=5&sq=kevin%20powell&st=cse (accessed April 1, 2009).

Hicks, Jonathan P. 2008b. Towns's challenger vows to run again. *The New York Times City Room Blog.* [Online Source]. September 16, 2008. http://cityroom.blogs.nytimes.com/2008/09/16/townss-challenger-vows-to-run-again/?scp=11&sq=kevin%20powell&st=csettp://cityroom.blogs.nytimes.com/2008/09/16/townss-challenger-vows-to-run-again/?scp=11&sq=kevin%20powell&st=cse (accessed April 1, 2009).

Ifill, Gwen. 2009. *The breakthrough: Politics in the age of Obama.* New York: Doubleday.

Jacobson, Gary C., and Samuel Kernell. 1983. *Strategy and choice in congressional elections* (2nd ed.). New Haven, CT: Yale University Press.

Janofsky, Michael. 1998. Marion Barry isn't running for a fifth term. *The Washington Post,* May 22, final edition, sec. A, 14.

Jones, Charles E., and Michael Clemons. 1993. A model of racial crossover voting: An assessment of the Wilder victory. In *Dilemmas of Black politics*, ed. Georgia Persons, 128–46. New York: HarperCollins.

Kim, Claire. 2000. *Bitter fruit: The politics of Black–Korean conflict in New York City.* New Haven, CT: Yale University Press.

Kinney, Terry. 2005. New Cincinnati mayor vows to reform city government, reduce crime. *Associated Press State and Local Wire.* December 1.

Korte, Gregory. 2005. Racial pattern seen in primary. September 15. http://news.cincinnati.com/apps/pbcs.dll/article?AID=20050915 (accessed March 31, 2009).

Ladd, Everett C. 1966. *Negro political leadership in the south.* Ithaca, NY: Cornell University Press.

Lawless, Jennifer, and Richard Fox. 2005. *It takes a candidate: Why women don't run for office.* New York: Cambridge University Press.

Lawrence, Cynthia. 2000. Rush wins in 1st: Did Obama deliver a wake-up call to Rush? *Chicago Sun-Times*, March 22. http://www.jessejacksonJr..org/creadpr.cgi?id=971 (accessed June 14, 2007).

Marinucci, Carla. 2008. D. A. Harris plans run for attorney general. *San Francisco Chronicle*, November 12. http://www.sfgate.com/cgi-in/article.cgi?f=/c/a/2008/11/12/MNF1142KCH.DTL (accessed June 4, 2009).

Marshall, Carolyn. 2008. Ex-NBA Star adds glitz to Sacramento's mayoral race. *The New York Times,* June 9, 2008. http://www.nytimes.com/2008/06/09/us/09sacramento.html?_r=1 (accessed August 19, 2009).

Martin, Roland. 2003. Ready or not.... *Savoy* March, 52–56.

Matza, Michael. 2007. How Nutter's win made history. *The Philadelphia Inquirer*, May 17, A13.

Mayor's biography. n.d. City of Cincinnati. http://www.cincinnati-oh.gov/mayor/ (accessed April 19, 2009).

McCormick, Joseph II, and Charles E. Jones. 1993. The conceptualization of deracialization: Thinking through the dilemma. In *Dilemmas of Black politics*, ed. Georgia Persons, 66–84. New York: HarperCollins.

Mihalopoulos, Dan. 2008. Rep. Jesse Jackson Jr. touts senate credentials to Blagojevich. *The Clout (The Chicago Tribune)* [Blog]. December 9.http://newsblogs.chicagotribune.com/clout_st/2008/12/rep-jesse-jacks.html (accessed December 22, 2008).

Myrdal, Gunnar. 1944. *An American dilemma.* New York: Harper and Brothers.

Nelson, William E. 1982. Cleveland: The rise and fall of the new Black politics. In *The new Black politics: The search for political power,* ed. Michael B. Preston, Lenneal J. Henderson Jr. and Paul Puryear, 187–208. New York: Longman.

———.2005. New mayors in Cleveland and Cincinnati. *United Press International*, November 9.

———. 2006. The new members of the House. *Roll Call*, November 13.

Nordlinger, Jay. 2002. Some "dissident." Doin' the skin-color nasty. A bit of righteous kvetching. etc. *National Review Online* May 28. LexisNexis Academic Universe. http://www.web.lexis-nexis.com/universe (accessed January 20, 2003).

Nossiter, Adam. 2006. Nagin re-elected as New Orleans mayor. *The New York Times*, May 21. http://www.nytimes.com/2006/05/21/us/21election.html?_r=1&sq=ray%20nagin&st=cse&adxnnl=1&scp=7&adxnnlx=1255059611-F+HLkzKKGHOvXZHmTJA4Uw (accessed October 9, 2009).

Olson, Rochelle. 2006. Tammy Lee endorsed by 12 local officials of various parties. *Star Tribune*, November 1, B4.

Pierannunzi, Carol A., and John D. Hutcheson Jr. 1996. The rise and fall of deracialization: Andrew Young as mayor and gubernatorial candidate. In *Race, governance, and politics in the United States*, ed. Huey L. Perry, 96–105. Gainesville: University of Florida Press.

Prendergast, Jane. 2009a. NAACP: No confidence in Mallory. February 26. http://news.cincinnati.com/apps/pbcs.dll/article?AID=2009226 (accessed March 31, 2009).

———. 2009b. NAACP delays vote on recall initiative. March 26. http://community-press.cincinnati.com/apps/pbcs.dll/article?AID (accessed March 31, 2009).

———. 2009c. Mallory declares his impact "undeniable." March 12. http://news.cincinnati.com/apps/pbcs.dll/article?AID=2009312/ (accessed March 31, 2009).

Reed, Adolph. 2000. *Class notes.* New York: The New Press.

Reed, K. Terrell, and Sonia Alleyne. 2002. What it takes to win. *Black Enterprise* November: 82–95.

———. 2006. Rep. Jesse Jackson Jr.. won't run for Chicago mayor. *Jet,* November 27.

Schlesinger, Joseph. 1966. *Ambition and politics: Political careers in the United States.* Chicago: Rand McNally.

Sheridan, Earl. 1996. The new accommodationists. *Journal of Black Studies* 27(2): 152–71.

Smith, Robert. 1981. Black power and the transformation from protest to poltics. *Political Science Quarterly* 96(3): 431–443.

Smith, Robert C. 1990. Recent elections and Black politics: The maturation or death of Black politics? *PS: Political Science and Politics* 23(2): 160–62.

Smith, Robert C. 1993. Ideology as the enduring dilemma of Black politics. In *Dilemmas of Black politics,* ed. Georgia Persons, 211–25. New York: HarperCollins.

———. 1996. *We have no leaders.* Albany: SUNY Press.

Smith, Ben. 2008. Election results: US House and Senate; US House: Incumbents win all primary races: Lewis avoids runoff despite two ppponents. *Atlanta Journal-Constitution,* http://www.lexis-nexis.com (accessed August 19, 2009).

Staba, David. 2005. Buffalo elects first Black mayor, who claims mandate. *The New York Times,* November 9, B10.

Star News Services. 2005. Kwame's woes: Conflict follows Detroit mayor in his battle for a second term. *Windsor (Ontario) Star,* July 16.

Starr, Alexandra. 2002. We shall overcome, too. *Business Week,* July 15. LexisNexis Academic Universe http://www.web.lexis-nexis.com/universe (accessed January 20, 2003).

Strategic Perceptions, prod. 2006. Family ties. [Political Advertisement]. Hollywood, CA: Strategic Perceptions. http://nationaljournal.com/members/adspotlight/2006/11/1106tnsen2.htm (accessed June 14, 2007).

Strickland, Ruth Ann, and Marcia Lynn Whicker. 1992. Comparing the Wilder and Gantt campaigns: A model for Black candidate success in statewide elections. *PS: Political Science and Politics* 25(2): 204–12.

Stone, Pauline Terrelonge. 1980. Ambition theory and the Black politician. *The Western Political Quarterly* 33(1): 94–107.

Summers, Mary, and Phillip Klinkner. 1996. The election and governance of John Daniels as mayor of New Haven. In *Race, governance, and politics in the United States,* ed. Huey L. Perry, 127–50. Gainesville: University of Florida Press.

Tate, Katherine. 1994. *From protest to politics: The new Black voters in American elections.* New York and Cambridge, MA: Russell Sage Foundation/Harvard University Press.

Traub, James. 2002. The way we live now: 9-8-02; The last color line. *The New York Times Magazine* September 8. LexisNexis Academic Universe. http://www.web.lexis-nexis.com/universe (accessed January 20, 2003).

U.S. Census Bureau. 2007. American factfinder: Greenville, Mississippi. http://factfinder.census.gov (accessed June 14, 2007).

Ronald Walters, and Robert C. Smith. 1999. *African American leadership.* Albany: SUNY Press.

Wiggins, Ovetta. 2006. As ballots are counted, Wynn's unbeatable status is questioned. *The Washington Post,* September 15, B1.

Williams, Linda. 1987. Black political progress in the 1980's: The electoral arena. In *The new Black politics: The search for political power.* 2nd ed., ed. Michael B. Preston, Lenneal J. Henderson Jr., and Paul Puryear, 97–136. New York and London: Longman.

Williams, Vanessa. 1994a. Blackwell and Fattah keeping campaign hot as election nears. *The Philadelphia Inquirer.* May 3, B1.

Williams, Vanessa. 1994b. Ambition, persistence paid off for Fattah. *The Philadelphia Inquirer*. May 12, B1.

Wilson, James Q. 1960. *Negro politics: The search for leadership*. Glencoe, IL: Free Press.

Wilson, Zaphon. 1993. Gantt versus Helms: Deracialization confronts southern traditionalism. In *Dilemmas of Black politics*, ed. Georgia Persons, 176–93. New York: HarperCollins.

Part I

Creating Opportunity

How Young Black Politicians
Break Into the Political Scene

In the early 1980s, political scientists Gary Jacobson and Samuel Kernell outlined the theory of strategic campaigning. American lawmakers, particularly at the congressional level, enjoy a huge incumbency advantage. This makes it difficult for new candidates to get elected. In light of this reality, Jacobson and Kernell argue that smart political candidates wait for favorable conditions before running for office. They rarely challenge incumbents for their seats because it is often futile to do so. Instead, they wait to run for open seats after incumbents die or retire. If they do run against incumbents, they wait until an incumbent has proved vulnerable before they mount a challenge. Scandal or weak electoral showings in recent elections all suggest an incumbent's vulnerability and make them more attractive targets for their would-be opponents. Incumbents often realize their vulnerability and drop out of races before they begin, rather than risk defeat (Jacobson and Kernell 1983).

Jacobson and Kernell developed their theory to explain the high turnover in Congress in the wake of the Watergate scandal. Democrats gained congressional seats in the wake of the scandal as citizens lost confidence in Republican lawmakers (Jacobson and Kernell 1983). This theory is also applicable to more recent elections. Personal and political scandals, the war in Iraq and the 2008 stock market crash all made once invincible Republican lawmakers vulnerable in 2006 and 2008. Some lawmakers were forced to retire, while others lost their seats.

Historically, African-American lawmakers have enjoyed a huge incumbency advantage as well. For instance, Black members of Congress enjoy some of the highest seniority rates, and many have faced only token challenges over the course of their careers (Gerber 1996; Gillespie 2005, 125–28).

If a candidate in a majority Black jurisdiction were to follow Jacobson and Kernell's prescription, they could wait decades before a seat opened up. Some people just do not have that much time to wait. As such, they may take risks that appear quixotic or hubristic to outside observers.

Part I recounts the experiences of two Third Phase Black politicians who took risks to launch their political careers. Instead of waiting for incumbents to retire or die in office, they chose to challenge their predecessors at the apparent apex of their power. While neither of them was successful in their first attempt, their efforts did reveal vulnerabilities in their incumbent opponents that had previously gone unnoticed. As a result, both new candidates were well positioned to win the next election. At the end of the day, those initial challenges may not have been as far fetched as they initially seemed.

References

Gerber, Alan S. 1996. African Americans' congressional careers and the Democratic House delegation. *Journal of Politics* 58: 831–45.

Gillespie, Andra. 2005. *Community, coordination and context: A black politics perspective on voter mobilization*. PhD diss., Yale University.

Jacobson, Gary C., and Samuel Kernell. 1983. *Strategy and choice in congressional elections*. 2nd ed. New Haven, CT: Yale University Press.

2   Racial Authenticity and Redistricting

A Comparison of Artur Davis's 2000 and 2002 Congressional Campaigns[1]

Andra Gillespie and Emma Tolbert

In 2000, a young former U.S. Attorney, Artur Davis, challenged four-term incumbent Congressman Earl Hilliard for the Democratic nomination in Alabama's Seventh Congressional District. Davis perfectly fit the profile of an Ivy League Upstart: articulate, Harvard educated, and from Montgomery.

Hilliard beat Davis by a two-to-one margin in the 2000 primary. Some opponents would have recoiled in embarrassment, never to challenge the incumbent again. Davis, however, regrouped and resumed his challenge in 2002. This time, though, he beat Hilliard and went on to win the general election in November 2002.

How was Davis able to turn a stunning defeat into a solid victory? Did he change his campaign strategy? Cultivate a new image? Tone down his crossover appeal with non-Black voters? In this chapter, Andra Gillespie and Emma Tolbert examine Artur Davis's political transformation from loser to victor. Using in-depth interviews, redistricting data, and internal polling data, they find that while Davis did not change his political style between 2000 and 2002, he did make some key strategic changes that enabled him to better position himself against Hilliard. More important, though, Davis benefited from a decennial redistricting effort—endorsed by the incumbent himself—that introduced new voters into the district who had no loyalties to Earl Hilliard and who were more receptive to Artur Davis's message.

In 2000, a little known Birmingham lawyer named Artur Davis challenged Earl Hilliard, a titan of Alabama's Black political establishment and the state's only Black congressman. It seemed like a classic David vs. Goliath battle: popular incumbent faces earnest neophyte. Unlike the biblical account, though, this Goliath won in a landslide.

Given the extent of the landslide, it would have been completely understandable for someone in Davis's position to retire to a quiet life in the private sector. Instead, Davis regrouped and staged a comeback two years later, beating Hilliard in the Democratic primary runoff and cruising to victory in the general election.

In this chapter, we chart Davis' comeback victory. Some might think that it took a lot of guts for Davis to challenge Hilliard in the first place, much less twice. Others would think it was downright crazy. Indeed, there are longstanding political science theories which suggest that it would be reckless to challenge a strong incumbent like Hilliard. However, Davis and other young, Black politicians like Barack Obama, Cory Booker, and Donna Edwards cut their political teeth on challenging popular incumbents. They lost their first major elections, but they used those defeats as steppingstones to develop successful political careers later.

How did Davis do it, then? We examine the role that the candidates's campaign strategies played in both Hilliard's 2000 and Davis's 2002 primary victories. In particular, we ask what changed between 2000 and 2002? We find that Davis was able to capitalize on key political changes in the two-year period between those elections. Specifically, Davis was able to leverage redistricting changes and the post-September 11 political environment to his advantage.

In the pages that follow, we present a brief overview of the strategic campaign and redistricting literatures. Then, we apply the theories presented in those literatures to the Alabama case. Using interview, archival and survey data, we show that Davis benefited from an influx of new, White voters who were unfamiliar with Earl Hilliard and more attracted to Davis' personal style.

Why Strategic Campaigning Has Not Always Worked for Black Political Aspirants

In the early 1980s, Gary Jacobsen and Samuel Kernell revolutionized the study of congressional elections when they proffered the theory of strategic campaigns. They argued that congressional aspirants were very deliberate in timing their candidacies. Instead of running whenever there was an election, quality challengers (i.e., challengers with previous political experience) timed their bids to coincide with open seat contests or with changes in the national political climate that favored their party. Incumbents, in turn, are more likely to retire if they think they might lose or if their party is likely to perform badly, thus preventing the incumbent from gaining a coveted leadership position such as a committee chairmanship (Jacobsen and Kernell 1983, chapters 3 and 5).

To Jacobsen and Kernell, good challengers view their campaigns as finite resources. Smart challengers know not to waste their time, their money, and their supporters' patience on quixotic political campaigns. So, they wait until conditions are most favorable before they run for office. The ideal time is when one does not have to run against an incumbent, but other conditions can prove favorable. For instance, if an incumbent is plagued by scandal, or if the incumbent's party is unpopular and likely to lose seats in the upcoming election, that may be a good time for a challenger to launch a campaign (Jacobsen and Kernell 1983, 32–33).

The implicit advice Jacobsen and Kernell offer—wait for an open seat, scandal, or incumbent party backlash—seems like good advice for any serious political aspirant, regardless of race or prior political experience. However, for Black political aspirants, this may not be so clear cut. Historically, Black congressional aspirants have faced additional barriers to winning office. These barriers have caused some potential challengers, like Artur Davis, to use slightly unorthodox methods to break into the electoral arena.

Jacobsen and Kernell's strategy assumes robust partisan competition in a congressional district. However, majority or near-majority Black districts are generally very Democratic (Tate 1995; Cameron, Epstein, and O'Halloran 1996). As such, serious political aspirants have to challenge fellow Democrats during party primaries for seats. This means that the notion of an aspirant being able to take advantage of national conditions that disadvantage the opposite party rarely applies to Black districts.

Moreover, the historic glass ceiling has created a bottleneck of Black members of Congress who, under other conditions, may have mounted bids for higher offices. While many incumbents strategically retire because they think they will lose or that their victory will not contribute to a House or Senate majority for their party, others retire to pursue even higher offices. House members could run for a Senate or gubernatorial seat; senators could run for president (Jacobsen and Kernell 1983, 24–25).

Jacobsen and Kernell argue that most ambitious incumbents use the same strategic calculus to decide whether to abandon one seat for another. As such, many incumbents are risk averse and choose to stay in their current office (Jacobsen and Kernell 1983, 24–25). Black congressional incumbents may be even more risk averse than their White counterparts when it comes to giving up one seat to run for a more prestigious seat. Despite the recent breakthrough success of Barack Obama at the national level, as of 2008, only five Blacks (Obama, Deval Patrick, Douglas Wilder, Carol Moseley Braun, and Edward Brooke) had ever won statewide office in an election (governor or U.S. Senate) after Reconstruction. Given the historic difficulty Black members of Congress faced getting elected to higher offices, many Black congressmen and congresswomen were led to strategically calculate that they should hold on to their current seats. And their Black constituents appeared willing to oblige them. Carol Swain, for instance, observed that "grumblings alone are unlikely to cost Black representatives from historically Black districts many votes. Disapproving Black constituents are more likely to stay home than go to the polls and 'vote the rascal out'" (Swain 1995, 70).

In reality, it is less likely that voters were lazy. Rather, they often lack options. In the overwhelming majority of general election matchups featuring Black congressional incumbents between 1964 and 1992, incumbents beat their challengers by margins of 60 percentage points or more in nearly two-thirds (64 percent) of the contests. Overall, 14 percent of races were uncontested. Only 10 percent of these races were even marginally close (with margins of less than 20 percentage points) (Gillespie 2005, 126).

That incumbents have a tremendous advantage when they run for reelection is not unique to Black politicians; this has been a feature of American congressional elections for well over a century (Jacobsen and Kernell 1983, 26). However, because Black members of Congress are less likely to relinquish a congressional seat for unlikely-to-be-fulfilled, progressive political ambitions, they enjoy some of the highest seniority rates in Congress (Gerber 1996). The upside of this is that when Democrats took control of the House and the Senate in 2006, this propelled a number of long-serving Black members of Congress into key committee chairmanships (Naylor 2007). The downside, though, is that this means that strategic open seat opportunities may be even more limited for Black political aspirants running for office in majority Black districts.

Creating Opportunity

The serious Black challenger facing an entrenched incumbent may have to create political opportunities for him- or herself. Instead of waiting years, even decades, for an incumbent to retire, Black challengers may choose to challenge well-regarded incumbents for their seats during primaries. To some, this effort will seem quixotic, even hubristic. If the challenger loses, then the incumbent may even feel vindicated. However, a challenger may be able to use that initial loss as a platform for a future campaign. Some, like Barack Obama, may abandon a future challenge against a popular Black incumbent to make a more traditionally strategic run for another open seat. Others would make a respectable or even strong showing against a Black incumbent and use that as a platform to challenge that incumbent again. For instance, Cory Booker lost his first mayoral bid to Sharpe James in Newark, New Jersey by 7 percentage points. When he ran again in 2006, James chose to drop out of the race rather than risk defeat (see chapter 3). In 2006, Donna Edwards narrowly lost to Congressman Albert Wynn in the Democratic primary for Maryland's Fourth Congressional District. Edwards resumed her challenge in 2008 and beat him (Helderman and Wan 2008).

We should not discount the importance of those failed challenges. While these candidates had to endure the embarrassment of defeat, they laid the groundwork for future candidacies. Often, voters suggested that they did not support the challengers the first time around because they were less familiar with them and more familiar with and confident in the incumbent. This was clearly the case when voters in the Illinois First Congressional District repudiated Barack Obama in 2000. In a 2004 *New Yorker* article, Obama intimated to William Finnegan that voters told him that "he seemed like a nice fellow with some good ideas. 'But Bobby ain't done nothing wrong'" (Finnegan 2004). Voters clearly valued familiarity.

After a challenger runs unsuccessfully for office, especially if she does better than expected and is a charismatic campaigner, she will not be the unknown quantity the second time around that she was before. The second time around, she will enjoy higher name recognition. Moreover, if she performed strongly in her first bid, she could be well-positioned to run again, especially if her opponent had previously been perceived as invincible. If an incumbent narrowly wins after a challenge, some could easily interpret that as a vulnerability. Such weakness may make it easier for challengers to mobilize resources to challenge the incumbent again.

The Personal Vote

If a challenger chooses to run against an incumbent, it may make sense to wait until after decennial redistricting to mount that challenge. The literature on redistricting suggests that incumbents are most vulnerable in the election immediately following congressional redistricting. Even strong incumbents see their margins shrink in that first election. Scholars attribute this shrinkage to a decline in what they call the "personal vote" (Desposato and Petrocik 2003, 18). Members of Congress develop a rapport with their constituents over the course of a decade. In the very least, the name of the incumbent becomes familiar to voters during that time (Desposato and Petrocik 2003; Ansolabehere, Snyder, and Stewart 2000).

After decennial redistricting, congressional district lines are redrawn to reflect population shifts and the potential gain or loss of a state's congressional seats. The new districts that emerge from this process contain parts of the incumbent's old district, but also new territory and new constituents. Additionally, the incumbent has also probably lost territory that was once part of his district. Consequently, every ten years, members of Congress must sell themselves anew to a different set of constituents. Until a member of Congress establishes him- or herself with the new voters, he or she is likely to perform relatively poorly in those new parts of the district. A number of recent studies reveal that in that first postredistricting election, incumbents get disproportionately more votes from the older, more familiar parts of the district than from the newer parts of the district (Desposato and Petrocik 2003; Ansolabehere et al. 2000; Hetherington, Larson, and Globetti 2003).

Given the electoral vulnerabilities inherent in redistricting and the congressional imperative to get reelected (Mayhew 1974), one would assume that members of Congress would be somewhat resistant to the process and would attempt to peddle influence with the state lawmakers drawing the district lines to ensure the most electorally friendly district possible. The irony is, incumbents often willingly sacrifice a portion of their reliable base for statewide partisan advantage. For example, in their study of post-1980 redistricting, Goppian and West (1984) found that party leaders may try to maximize the number of congressional seats they can win by not concentrating partisans in a few districts. By spreading the partisan vote share across many districts, the party hopes to be competitive in many districts, as opposed to being safely elected in only a few districts.

Hypotheses

The extant literature review helps to frame our understanding of what took place in Alabama's Seventh Congressional District. We believe that the historical and empirical record shows that a combination of strategic and not-so-strategic decisions allowed Artur Davis to rebound from his 2000 primary defeat. The 2000 campaign cannot be viewed as a strategic campaign; Davis would not be considered a quality challenger because of his lack of prior office holding, and most people would have waited for Hilliard to retire before running for the seat. However, Davis used that first foray into electoral politics to establish a platform from which to launch a second bid for office. The second time around, Davis was able to capitalize on redistricting and other changes to best Hilliard.

Data and Methods

To further explore these questions and test these hypotheses, we use a variety of research methods. We use secondary news sources and in-depth interviews with Artur Davis, Earl Hilliard, and other key Alabama political players to provide historical perspective. We also conducted archival analysis of the post-2000 redistricting process, which we supplement with interview data. Finally, we include quantitative data from Congressman Davis's own internal polling.

Congressman Davis graciously granted us access to his 2002 polling data. Unfortunately, there is no polling data available from 2000. Democratic pollster Mark Mellman[2] served as Davis's pollster in 2002, and conducted two polls for the campaign in 2002: one before the May primary election and one just before the June runoff election. Both polls conducted a cluster sampling of 400 likely Democratic primary voters each in the Seventh Congressional District. For this analysis, we will focus our attention on the second poll, taken before the runoff primary.

Using a candidate's personal polling data presents a number of empirical testing opportunities that would not usually be available to scholars studying elections on the local level. Most of the time, we would be limited to examining election results by precinct, city, or county and looking for regional trends. For Southern states like Alabama, which is covered by the Voting Rights Act, we might be able to make additional ecological inferences on the racial effects of voter preference because we know the racial demographics of the precincts. Short of having exit poll data (which is rare for this kind of primary), it would be difficult to determine how voter preconceptions of the candidates relate to their voting preferences. While voter attitudes no doubt changed between the time that this survey was taken and the actual votes were tabulated, this data set provides much richer opportunities to examine why voters selected the candidates they did.

It is highly unusual for a candidate to release his or her polling data to academic researchers. As such, we had to make certain concessions to protect the candidate's campaign secrets. We have slightly altered the wording of certain questions to protect proprietary secrets. In other places, we only report approximate ranges of figures for the same purpose.[3]

Table 2.1 below lists the basic weighted demographic characteristics of each sample. In the survey, Mellman and his team tracked how voters planned to vote, and they tested positive and negative messages for both Davis and Hilliard. These messages would be incorporated into Davis's direct mail pieces and television outreach.

Table 2.1 Weighted Demographics from Artur Davis' Internal Polls

	April 2002 Poll	June 2002 Poll
Men	44%	41%
Women	56%	59%
Age 18-29	4%	8%
Age 30-39	12%	11%
Age 40-49	29%	23%
Age 50+	19%	16%
Age 60+	33%	36%
Republican (incl. leaners)	4%	5%
Independent	10%	13%
Democrat (incl. leaners)	83%	78%
High School or Less	38%	40%
Some College	33%	30%
College Graduate +	29%	28%
African American	59%	62%
White	39%	36%
Under $40K/year	45%	53%
$40-under $60K/year	16%	15%
$60K+/year	15%	13%

Source: Alabama 7th Congressional District Poll (N=400; Release Date April 24, 2002 and
N=400; Release Date June 9, 2008). The Mellman Group, Inc.

The demographics of the polling sample do not differ tremendously from
the overall district demographics at the time. According to the U.S. Census, in
2000, the Seventh Congressional District was 47 percent male; 62 percent African American; 36 percent White (U.S. Census Bureau 2000). In 1998, *National
Journal's Almanac of American Politics* listed the district's median income as $16,
560, and noted that 32 percent of the district's voters had a college education
("Alabama: Seventh District" 1998). As is not terribly unusual, older voters are
overrepresented in this sample, as older people tend to be more likely to vote than
younger people (Verba and Nie 1972).

History of the 2000 Democratic Primary

Artur Davis announced his bid to challenge Earl Hilliard in the summer of 1999
(Temple 1999). Davis, a Harvard-trained lawyer who had previously worked for
the Southern Poverty Law Center and as an Assistant U.S. Attorney, had no prior
elective experience. Hilliard, in contrast, was a seemingly popular four-term

incumbent who had previously served as a state representative (including a stint as Chairman of Alabama's Legislative Black Caucus) and state senator. As a college student, Hilliard had become active in the Civil Rights Movement, participating in sit-ins and joining the Southern Christian Leadership Conference while he was a student at Morehouse College ("Representative Earl Hilliard" 2002; Hilliard 2007).

Hilliard had enjoyed the long-term backing of three prominent Black political organizations in Alabama: the Alabama Democratic Conference (ADC), the Jefferson County Citizen's Coalition (JCCC), and the New South Coalition. These organizations were essentially regional Black political machines that had helped launch the careers of Black Alabama legislators, including Earl Hilliard. The JCCC, which was controlled by Richard Arrington, Birmingham's first Black mayor, was the dominant force in the Birmingham metropolitan area. State Senator Hank Sanders, representing Selma, controlled the New South Coalition. The ADC, which is led by Joe Reed, is dominant in Montgomery. Together, these three organizations were instrumental in launching the careers of a generation of Black politicians. Usually, when Black politicians wanted to run for office in Alabama, they needed the support of these organizations. For a prominent seat such as a congressional seat, it was assumed that a candidate would need the support of all three organizations. In 2000, Hilliard easily won the support of all three machines. Davis's campaign, then, appeared to be doomed unless he could garner the support of one of these legendary Black bosses (McClure and Gordon 2002; Haeberle 1997; Reed n.d; Murray 2007).

However, there were signs that the three Black political machines were not as strong as they once were. Both Reed and Arrington suffered huge psychological and political blows leading up to the Seventh Congressional District primary in 2000. Arrington, who retired from his mayoral post before completing his term, had backed his hand-picked protégé, William Bell, to be his permanent successor. Bell lost to Bernard Kincaid, a moderate Black in 1999. Similarly, Joe Reed, who in addition to serving as Chairman of the ADC was also a Montgomery city councilman, lost his city council seat (McClure and Gordon 2002).

Despite these political changes, Hilliard had the clear advantage. He was a four-term incumbent; he had vanquished all of his previous primary and general election opponents (see Table 2.2 below); he had the backing of the major Black political machines in the state; and he held a tremendous name identification and fundraising advantage. Davis was aware that he was heavily favored to lose this election; yet, he felt compelled to run anyway (Davis 2007).

A number of factors contributed to Davis's decision to run. He believed that Earl Hilliard had been an unproductive Congressman. He argued that Hilliard was not

> effective as a member of Congress in terms of passing legislation, getting support or building alliances within the institution. He certainly was not effective in the conventional ways, in terms of bringing resources to the district or launching initiatives within the district. I followed his career closely

Table 2.2 Earl Hilliard's Election Performance 1992–1998

Year and Election	Hilliard's Vote Share	Margin (From Closest Competitor)
1992 primary runoff	50.5%	1 percentage point
1992 general	69.5%	52 percentage points
1994 general	77%	54 percentage points
1996 primary	100%	unopposed
1996 general	71%	44 percentage points
1998 general	100%	unopposed

Source: "Alabama: Seventh District. Rep. Earl Hilliard." *Almanac of American Politics.* 2000 and 2002 Editions. Alabama Secretary of State. Elections Results Archive-US House of Representatives 1986-2002. Retrieved from www.state.al.us/downloads/dl2.aspx?div1=ElectionsDivision&types=Data

through the '90's, and my assessment was that he was very much an underperformer. (Davis 2007)

We asked Hilliard to list his own accomplishments as congressman, he cited three major accomplishments: an additional Job Corps center in his district; two Enterprise Zones; and infrastructural changes that built bridges and underpasses in the district. Hilliard was especially proud of his political maneuvering to get those resources for his district. He won the Job Corps Center in exchange for his vote for the Clinton balanced budget plan, and he won the Enterprise Zones in exchange for his support of NAFTA (Hilliard 2007).

Despite Hilliard's record of accomplishment and ease getting elected, Davis suspected that Hilliard might be weaker than he looked. Davis recounted:

Substantively, I felt that I could do the work, and I felt that I could do it better than he was doing it. Secondly, I thought politically that there was an opening, I thought that his support was not terribly deep and that a great many people didn't know who he was much less about his work or his record. I thought that he had been a somewhat polarizing figure. There were large pockets of voters that were resistant to him because of his style. I felt that he was not nearly as strong even in his political base as he thought he was. Birmingham is his base. One of the first things that I noticed, Earl Hilliard explored running for mayor of the city in 1999, and the perception was that he'd be very strong—you know, this guy's been a Congressman for seven years. There was the idea that if he ran for mayor, he'd be a very serious force. But he didn't come out in the polling, his numbers were consistently below 10 percent, and it struck me that someone who had near 100 percent name recognition in Birmingham, who'd represented part of Birmingham for 18 years, represented all of Birmingham at some point, at least Black Birmingham—it struck me as interesting that his numbers were so low. And my theory is that if people like you, they usually want to see you advance. They want to see you be in a job where you can do even more for them. It was notable to me that his numbers were so poor in the mayor's race. That data as much as anything else, if there's anything else empirical, [was what] convinced me that a serious campaign against him could be successful. Mind you that he'd never been opposed in a Dem[ocratic] primary, he had drawn only marginal Republican opposition. I believe that most of those who voted against him in the general didn't even vote in the Dem[ocratic] primary, so that didn't tell me anything. The only thing that I had to draw from was just my sense of his work and that data of the polling in the mayor's race. But it led me to think that there was a major opening, and I moved to start campaigning in 1999, it was very clear that he had not made a good impression on the district. It was very clear that people knew there was a Black Congressman named Earl Hilliard but people didn't have any real sense of his work. It became very clear that there was just a real absence of a foundation for his support. That encouraged me as I moved through those first few months. (Davis 2007)

Davis's analysis evinces the careful deliberation he undertook before deciding to run in 2000. While Hilliard appeared to have a safe congressional seat, political developments in the local area suggested that Hilliard and the generation that he represented may not have been omnipotent. Davis interpreted all of those events as ample justification for entering the 2000 primary as a dark horse.

Just because Davis noticed Hilliard's vulnerabilities, though, does not mean that the 2000 primary was destined to be his victory. Hilliard still had name recognition, incumbency advantage, a war chest, and previous electoral experience. Davis was quite candid about his disadvantages in 2000. In newspaper reports, he acknowledged his fundraising deficiencies in particular. Davis noted that some potential donors, while sympathetic to him, were reluctant to give to him, presumably because they did not foresee a return on their investment (Johnson 2000).

Davis's reluctant supporters had a right to be skeptical in 2000. In the end, Hilliard won 58 percent of the vote in the Democratic primary that year, compared to approximately 34 percent for Davis. Both Davis and Hilliard reflected on the results of that race. Both of them noted that Hilliard outspent Davis. Hilliard noted that he had the support of the major Black political machines (Davis 2007; Hilliard 2007). Davis acknowledged that he was unable to overcome those huge deficits:

Gillespie: In the end, why do you think you lost in 2000? Was it all money or were there other factors?
Davis: Not enough people knew me, couldn't reach enough people. I came into it with zero name rec[ognition] and I wasn't able to get substantially beyond 40 percent name rec[ognition]. Obviously we didn't have the benefit of any advance polling, but my guess is that among the people who voted on Election Day in 2000, that we probably got three-quarters of the people who

knew who I was. It was a low turnout race. Between 55,000 and 60,000 voted in 2000. People didn't know who I was…it was very, very difficult to campaign without resources. That was honestly the biggest impediment we encountered. When people heard what I had to say, especially by the end of the campaign, people were very responsive to that. People definitely wanted a different style of representation. People definitely wanted a more effective representation. But ultimately we couldn't reach enough people to make the sale. And frankly we never got a massive break in the 2000 campaign, we didn't have any external event occur which changed the way voters thought about the race. There was no interest from anyone outside the state. There was not significant media coverage. We struggled really for every story that we got during the 2000 campaign. (Davis 2007)

Political Changes in the 2002 Primary Election

Davis made the decision to run again almost immediately. He believed that Hilliard's winning less than 60 percent of the vote in the 2000 primary was evidence of his vulnerability. Davis believed that if he resumed his efforts, continued to keep his name in the public eye, and met more people, he would be well-positioned to beat Hilliard in 2002. As such, he started doing television commentary for a local news station and began actively campaigning again as early as February 2001 (Davis 2007).

Davis also identified fundraising as one of his biggest weaknesses in 2000, so he redoubled his efforts in that vein. Davis knew early on that without the support of the local political establishment, it would be very difficult for him to fundraise in Alabama. So, he set his sights outside the state (Davis 2007).

In the wake of September 11, Jewish donors proved to be a reliable fundraising base. Earl Hilliard had generated some controversy by speaking out publicly against Israel in the Israeli–Palestinian conflict and by voting against a House resolution which condemned suicide bombings and expressed support for Israel. Additionally, Hilliard visited Libya while the U.S. government still classified the country as a state sponsor of terror (Halbfinger 2002; Schneider 2002; Orndorff 2002a). Davis was able to use Hilliard's foreign policy positions to attract new donors to his base. One such donor was Donald Hess, who had been a high ranking executive with the Birmingham-based Parisian Department Store chain. Hess introduced Davis to officials at the America-Israel Public Affairs Committee (AIPAC), the nation's largest pro-Israeli lobbying group. From there, Davis was able to raise money in places such as New York and Washington (Halbfinger 2002; Orndorff 2002b).

Not to be outdone, Hilliard also went outside of Alabama to raise funds. In fact, Hilliard had more out-of-state donors than Davis. Hilliard received support from colleagues in Congress such as Nancy Pelosi, Charles Rangel, and the Congressional Black Caucus. As a counter to AIPAC's support of Artur Davis, Arab American donors, including James Zogby, the President of the Arab American Institute, donated to Hilliard (Bailey 2002; Orndorff 2002c).

Foreign policy issues would also be a key theme of the campaign. Davis's fundraising tactics had clear synergies with his campaign rhetoric. Concerns about national security in America in the wake of September 11 provided Artur Davis with both substantive and strategic opportunities to gain a foothold against Earl Hilliard. Davis's internal polling reveals that Davis considered four primary criticisms of Hilliard: that he had ethical lapses—this stemmed from a House Ethics Committee inquiry into his campaign spending (McMurray 2001); that Hilliard supported terrorist nations like Libya and Iraq; that local clinics and hospitals closed under his watch; and that Hilliard was a do-nothing congressman (The Mellman Group 2002a). These attacks were presented to voters in dyads where they were asked to pick the candidate against whom they would be more likely to vote. Voters were given two choices per question and asked to pick the statement that would turn them off to a candidate the most. The pollster then analyzed this data using a technique called conjoint analysis. In conjoint analysis, the pollster aggregates the dyad results to see which statement is the overall best choice. We present the aggregate rankings in Table 2.3. The table shows that voters indicated an inclination to vote against a congressman who supported terrorist countries more than any other kind of congressman. When voters were asked whether they would vote against a congressman who supported terrorist countries or a congressman with ethical problems, respondents indicated that they would vote against the supporter of terrorists by a more than 20 percentage point margin. Respondents said that they would vote against a supporter of terrorist nations over a congressman with no record of achievement by a more than 30 percentage point margin. Finally, voters indicated that they would oppose a congressman who supported terrorist countries over one who did not stop the closing of health care facilities by a more than 25 percentage point margin (The Mellman Group 2002a).

Armed with this data, Davis's campaign hit hard on foreign policy. Davis publicly questioned Hilliard's judgment in going to Libya and wondered how such a visit was relevant to the voters of the Seventh Congressional District. In doing so, he implied that Hilliard was shirking his responsibilities at home. Davis also ran an ad where Hilliard's picture was juxtaposed to a picture of Osama bin Laden. In the ad, Davis criticized Hilliard for his support of ending unilateral

Table 2.3 Conjoint Analysis Ranks for Voter Opposition in the 2002 Alabama 7th District Primary

Would Voters Rather Not Vote For A Congressman:	*Conjoint Rank*
Who Supports Terrorist Countries Such As Iraq and Libya	1
Who Had Ethical Problems	2
Who Did Not Keep Hospitals and Clinics From Closing	3
Who Has Not Accomplished Much In Office	4

Source: Alabama 7th Congressional District Poll (N=400; Release Date April 24, 2002). The Mellman Group, Inc.
Phrasings are slightly paraphrased for confidentiality purposes

sanctions against rogue nations and starting negotiations with these countries (Orndorff 2002c).

Davis was able to use these vulnerabilities to finish a close second to Hilliard in the May 2002 Democratic Primary. There was a third candidate on the ballot who won 11 percent of the vote. Given the close nature of the race between Hilliard and Davis, and given the fact that Alabama elections law requires that candidates win primaries with a clear majority of the vote, Davis would have one more chance to best Hilliard in a June runoff (Alabama Secretary of State 2008).

Redistricting Changes between 2000 and 2002

Davis was able to leverage geographic changes in the district to win the race in the runoff. Some of the biggest changes in the Seventh Congressional District happened as a result of the 2000 census. While Alabama did not gain or lose a congressional district as a result of that enumeration, the Alabama State Legislature still had to redraw congressional district lines to account for population shifts within the state. In particular, the Seventh Congressional District needed to be redrawn because it had approximately 100,000 fewer residents than the other congressional districts (Black 2008).

State legislatures are responsible for redrawing district lines every ten years. However, members of Congress do have a say in how their districts will eventually look. The Alabama congressional delegation did offer their own redistricting suggestions, but they were ignored by the state legislature (Black 2008).

State lawmakers did want to increase the number of Democrats in the U.S. Congress. The dispersion of Black voters throughout those congressional districts would be key to achieving that goal. Because African Americans are the most reliable Democratic voting bloc in the United States (Tate 1995), districts that are majority Black tend also to be reliably Democratic. In 1996, Cameron, Epstein, and O'Halloran found that concentrating Black voters in majority-minority districts had a negative impact on Democrats' ability to win in nonminority-majority districts. When Black voters are concentrated in supermajority Black districts, the adjacent districts are not only Whiter, but also more Republican. Cameron et al. contended that as a result of the creation of a number of majority Black districts after the 1990 redistricting, Republicans were well-positioned to gain a majority in the U.S. House and Senate in 1994 (Cameron et al. 1996).

While Democrats only held two of seven congressional seats, they did control the state's legislative and executive branches. State Democratic leaders wanted to create a third Democratic district in time for the 2002 congressional elections. In order to do that, the Seventh Congressional District would need to sacrifice some of their reliable Black Democratic voters. According to State Representative Marcel Black, the Co-Chairman of the Reapportionment Committee, "Our thinking was that if we could carve 8 or 10 percent out of that District, we could move some of that to places to create a more advantageous seat for a White Democrat. When you've got 70 percent Black districts, you're creating a Republican district just about every time" (Black 2008). Thus, legislative Democrats adopted the goal of making the adjacent Third Congressional District more competitive for a Democratic candidate (Black 2008).

Table 2.4 outlines the racial composition of Alabama's congressional districts in 2000 and the racial composition of the proposed redrawn districts in the primary redistricting plans.[4] In 2000, the Seventh Congressional District was 70 percent Black. Every proposed redistricting plan would increase the number of White voters in the Seventh Congressional District.

State Senator Hank Sanders presented the Modified Enfinger Congressional Plan (Proposed Plan I) for the first time on January 1, 2002. This plan included extending the Seventh Congressional District further into Jefferson County and adding Bibb and parts of Shelby Counties. Under this plan, Pickens and Montgomery Counties would be removed from the district while Lowndes County would remain. As a result of these changes, the Black composition of the Seventh District would fall from 70 percent Black to just over 61 percent Black, while the White proportion of the district would increase from nearly 29 percent to 37 percent. This would help to increase the Black population in the Third Congressional District from 25 percent to 35 percent.

After deliberations by the Senate Elections Committee, the plan was amended and renamed. It was presented to the floor of the Alabama State Senate on January 22, 2002 as the Compromise Congressional Plan (Proposed Plan II). This plan included extending the Seventh Congressional District into Jefferson County, and removing Lowndes and Montgomery from the district completely. In the Compromise Plan, Shelby and Bibb Counties remained a part of the Sixth Congressional District, while part of Pickens County remained in the Seventh Congressional District. Additionally, Montgomery County moved almost entirely into the Third Congressional District. The Second Congressional

Table 2.4 Racial Composition of Proposed Alabama Congressional Districts, 2002

District	Original District Composition		Proposed Plan I: Modified Enfinger Plan		Proposed Plan II: Compromise Congressional Plan I		Final Plan: Compromise Congressional Plan II	
	% White	% Black	% White	% Black	% White	% Black	% White	% Black
1	68	28.6	68.5	28.4	68.5	28.4	68.5	28.4
2	69.3	28	71.1	26.6	67.5	30.2	67.7	30.0
3	72.6	25.3	63.4	34.9	65.9	32.3	65.5	32.7
4	90.3	6.3	89.8	7.3	91.5	5.5	91.7	5.3
5	79.9	16.2	78.9	17.2	78.9	17.2	78.8	17.4
6	82.1	14.9	89.0	8.5	89.5	8.1	89.7	7.9
7	28.7	70	37.3	61.2	36.0	62.4	36.0	62.4

Source: Alabama Apportionment Office Archives.

District absorbed the remainder of Montgomery County as well as Lowndes County. Under this plan, the Black population in the Second Congressional District would increase by 2 percentage points, and the Black population in the Third Congressional District would increase by 7 percentage points. This would leave the racial composition of the Seventh Congressional District at approximately 62 percent Black. The first Congressional Compromise Plan, though, met significant opposition from the Republican incumbent who represented the Third District, and was tabled.

The Congressional Compromise Plan I was amended on the floor and became the Congressional Compromise Plan II. With this plan, more of Jefferson and Tuscaloosa Counties was included in the Seventh Congressional District. Lowndes County moved into the Second District, and Montgomery County was split between the Second and Third Districts. This plan was very similar to the original Compromise Congressional Plan in terms of racial composition of the Districts. However, the second compromise plan shifted Democrats' attention from trying to increase the number of Democrats in the Third Congressional District to trying to use the numbers of Democrats in the Second Congressional District, where the incumbent congressman was retiring. This plan was passed by the Senate on January 24, 2002.

The House Elections Committee made attempts to revise the Compromise Congressional Plan II, but on January 31, 2002, the plan was passed as it had been originally presented with a 60 to 38 vote. All the Black members of both the House and Senate who were present for the vote supported the plan, including John Hilliard, Earl Hilliard's brother.

The new demographic composition of the Seventh Congressional District would have serious consequences for Earl Hilliard. According to the ADC's Dr. Joe Reed, "Earl Hilliard agreed to give up Montgomery and Lowndes Counties to help the 3rd District, and the ADC supported him, but that was the big mistake for Earl" (Reed 2008). Dr. Reed further contended, "If Earl had kept Montgomery and Lowndes Counties, he would have won in spite of the money that Artur had" (Reed 2008). In the end, it seems that Earl Hilliard made a move to work with and try to advance his party, but his efforts did not produce the desired effect for the party or for him personally. As Hilliard's son, State Representative Earl Hilliard Jr., commented, "You can't use incumbency in a 50 percent new district; people have never worked with you before. You basically get what the news says instead of what the people have had firsthand" (Hilliard 2008). For his part, Earl Hilliard recognized that he would lose a little of his incumbency advantage as a result of the redistricting process, but he thought that he would still be able to beat Davis handily (White 2002).

At the time of the redistricting, Davis publicly acknowledged that the new boundary lines would work to his benefit because new voters would be especially resonant to the idea of new leadership (White 2002). However, when we spoke with him in 2007, Davis minimized the effect of redistricting on the eventual primary outcome. He said:

It [redistricting] mattered a bit, but not as much as people think. Frankly, I believe that if Montgomery County had remained in the District, we would have been the kind of a turn around in Montgomery County that we had in Sumter and Greene [Counties], or Sumter in particular because we actually won Greene in 2000. We lost Sumter 74-21 and we lost Montgomery 75-22. I believed that if Montgomery had stayed in the District, we would have got 60 percent of the vote there in 2002. I bet that to this day that if we'd been able to run TV ads down there, which we would have, that Montgomery would have turned around. So I don't think redistricting mattered as much as some people perhaps think. It certainly did affect the boundaries a little bit. It meant there was more of Jefferson County, that had a strategic impact because it meant we could focus more here than we had planned to before. It meant that there was more of Tuscaloosa, and we had done well in Tuscaloosa, so that was helpful to us to get more of an area where we had done well. But honestly, once we had the resources, there was no portion of this District or the old District that would've been off limits in my opinion. (Davis 2007)

A systematic examination of voter attitudes in the new and old parts of the Seventh Congressional District will help to shed light on the actual impact of redistricting on voter preferences. To do this, we focus our attention on the June 2002 poll that The Mellman Group conducted for Artur Davis just before the June runoff election.

The primary runoff presented a number of challenges and opportunities for the candidates. If our hypothesis is correct, then Davis should have an advantage among voters who were new to the Seventh Congressional District in 2002. They would be less familiar with Earl Hilliard and might be more willing to vote for a new person. If Canon et al. (1996) are correct, Davis, as the moderate candidate, should have an advantage with White voters as well. In order for Davis to win, he must split the Black vote with Hilliard and win the lion's share of the White vote.

Polling Data Analysis

When The Mellman Group surveyed voters, they did collect enough personal information (i.e., zip codes, precinct place, and county and city of residence) to be able to distinguish between voters in the new and old parts of the district. Using zip code data from the Congressional Directories for the 106th and 108th Congresses, we were able to determine which zip codes had fallen into the old (pre-2002 redistricting) and new (postredistricting) Seventh Congressional Districts. There were times when parts of some zip codes had fallen into the old part of the district and then were completely included in the district in 2002. For those voters, we relied on precinct data (obtained from the Alabama Secretary of State's Web site and American University's Center for Congressional and Presidential Studies Federal Elections Project) to determine whether they were part of the old or new parts of the district.

The data we use is not perfect. Because of the problem of zip codes overlapping both old and new parts of the district, we also had to rely on precinct information to properly classify about 45 percent of the voters in the dataset. Nearly all of these voters were in the district's two largest counties: Tuscaloosa and Jefferson, which made the task somewhat easier. However, because of diffuse or inadequate recordkeeping, it was still extremely difficult to classify voters by precinct in those counties, as the state and the counties sometimes used different precinct codes for the same polling place or district. Despite these challenges (and with help from local officials), we still managed to figure out how to code all of the respondents. Given our level of uncertainty in coding, we decided to err on the side of caution. When we were not sure, we coded respondents as being part of the newly redistricted portion of the district. If we inadvertently miscoded a respondent, then, it should bias our results in favor of our null hypothesis, that Hilliard should perform equally well in the new and old parts of the district. A local official in Alabama intimated that those codes will be standardized in the near future. As soon as updated information is available, we will update this analysis.

After recoding the data to reflect voters' designation as an old or new constituent, we ran a series of bivariate analyses (i.e., crosstabs) to gain a sense of the electoral dynamics at the heart of this election. Those results are presented below in Table 2.5.

Table 2.5 Bivariate Analysis of the Relationship between District Tenure and Candidate Favorability/ Preference, Alabama 7th District

		Old District Voters	New District Voters	Total
Hilliard Favorability	Favorable	53%	44%	51%
	Unfavorable	27%	41%	31%
	DK/Never Heard of	20%	16%	19%
Davis Favorability	Favorable	44%	52%	46%
	Unfavorable	10%	10%	10%
	DK/Never Heard of	47%	48%	44%
Hilliard Job Performance	Excellent/Good	34%	27%	32%
	Fair/Poor	47%	57%	50%
	DK	18%	17%	18%
Vote	Hilliard	40%	30%	37%
	Davis	37%	50%	40%
	Undecided	23%	20%	22%
Total		284	115	399^

Source: Alabama 7th Congressional District Poll (N=400; Release Date June 9, 2002; unweighted). The Mellman Group, Inc.
^Sample size is due to rounding error.

The data indicate that while a majority of voters had a favorable opinion of Earl Hilliard, nearly a third of voters had an unfavorable opinion. However, voters had a negative impression of Hilliard's job performance ratings. Half of the sample indicated that they thought that Hilliard was doing a fair or poor job as congressman. While Davis was still combating low name recognition in the weeks before the runoff election, his instincts that voters were dissatisfied with Hilliard's job performance seem to be substantiated.

The internal polls indicate that overall, the race was a statistical dead heat. Davis led Hilliard by 3 percentage points in a poll with a margin of error of +/-6 percentage points. However, the data also indicate that Davis had a clear advantage with voters from the newly redistricted parts of the district. Voters in the new part of the district were significantly (p<.05) more likely to have an unfavorable view of Hilliard than voters in the older part of the district. And voters in the newer part of the district were significantly more likely to indicate that they were voting for Davis (p<.10).

An analysis of Black and White voters in the old and new parts of the district reveals even deeper polarity. Black voters in both the old and new parts of district gave both Hilliard and Davis similar favorability and job performance scores, while Whites in the new part of the district were noticeably (though not signifi-

Table 2.6 Bivariate Analysis of the Relationship between District Tenure* Race and Candidate Favorability/ Preference, Alabama 7th District

		Old District Voters		New District Voters		Total
		Black	White	Black	White	
Hilliard Favorability	Favorable	59%	41%	58%	29%	51%
	Unfavorable	20%	40%	24%	58%	31%
	DK/Never Heard of	20%	18%	18%	14%	19%
Davis Favorability	Favorable	41%	47%	47%	58%	46%
	Unfavorable	9%	10%	6%	14%	`10%
	DK/Never Heard of	50%	43%	47%	29%	44%
Hilliard Job Performance	Excellent/Good	36%	30%	35%	19%	32%
	Fair Poor	45%	53%	53%	62%	50%
	DK	19%	17%	13%	19%	18%
Vote	Hilliard	42%	40%	46%	15%	37%
	Davis	31%	47%	32%	68%	40%
	Undecided	28%	13%	21%	17%	22%
Total		190	87	56	59	392^

Source: Alabama 7th Congressional District Poll (N=400; Release Date June 9, 2002; unweighted). The Mellman Group, Inc.
^Sample does not include seven voters who refused to reveal their race or who were not Black or White.

Table 2.7 June 2002 Runoff Election Results by New/Old District, Alabama 7th District

	Old District Voters	New District Voters	Total
Hilliard	46%	39%	45%
Davis	54%	61%	55%
Total	103293	19358	122651*

Source: Author's compilation from Alabama Secretary of State Data
*These totals code all absentee ballots as old district voters because absentee ballots are aggregated and not counted by precinct. This explains the slight deviation from "Alabama: Seventh District 2002."

cantly) more anti-Hilliard. While 41 percent of White voters in the old part of the district gave Hilliard a favorable rating, only 29 percent of White voters in the new part of the district did so. And though Davis and Hilliard were roughly equally matched among Blacks in the new and old parts of the district, the divergence between Whites was significant. Forty percent (40 percent) of Whites in the old part of the district indicated that they would vote for Hilliard, but only 15 percent of White voters in the new part of district indicated that they would vote for Hilliard (p < .05).

Based on our analysis, then, it seems as though race and tenure in the district correlate with preference for Artur Davis in 2002. Voters in the newly redistricted parts of the district were more likely to support Davis, and White voters in the new part of the district were especially likely to support Davis. As long as Davis could hold his own against Hilliard in the older parts of the district, Davis would be in a good position to win.

By all accounts, Davis did more than hold his own against Earl Hilliard. In the final analysis, Davis defeated Hilliard 56 percent to 44 percent ("Alabama: Seventh District" 2002). A breakdown of the vote by new and old parts of the districts[5] reveals that Davis performed strongly in both parts of the district. Davis clearly performed more strongly in the new part of the district, but voters in that part of the district were only about 16 percent of the total runoff electorate. This means that Davis won largely because he beat Hilliard decisively in the old part of the district, too.

Conclusions

We will never know if Artur Davis would have improved his margins in Montgomery and Lowndes Counties (Hilliard's base) if those counties had remained in his district. However, we do know that Davis improved his margins in both the new and old parts of the Seventh Congressional District when he challenged Earl Hilliard for the second time.

The results of the 2002 primary runoff do confirm the extant literature on the impact of the personal vote. Davis posted his strongest showings in the new parts of his district, where he and Earl Hilliard both had to cultivate relationships with new voters. However, it is important to know that Davis won because he beat

Hilliard in the old part of the district. Davis's intuition was absolutely right: voters liked Hilliard, but they were dissatisfied with his service. In the final analysis, Davis's quixotic run does not seem so crazy.

One of the most interesting findings of this study was the intersection between race and tenure in the district. White voters from the new part of the Seventh Congressional District were far more likely to support Artur Davis than Black voters from the new part of the district. Given the fact that Davis was the more racially moderate of the two candidates, these findings underscore Canon, Schousen, and Sellers' (1996) findings that when moderate and less moderate Blacks compete in congressional elections, the moderate Black candidate wins by splitting the Black vote and winning the White vote outright. The findings in this district suggest that new White voters are the most receptive to moderate Black candidates, though.

These preliminary findings warrant further study. No one has attempted to replicate Canon et al. since it was first published in the mid-1990s. It is certainly advisable to replicate that study and improve upon the original study by controlling for the interaction of voters' race and whether they were recently incorporated into a new congressional district.

Notes

1. The authors would like to thank officials at the Alabama Apportionment Office and the Secretary of State's Office for their assistance in this project. Special thanks go to David Perkins of the Tuscaloosa County Registrar's Office for his help beyond the call of duty.
2. It should be noted that one of the authors (Gillespie) worked for Mellman about two years after Davis was a client of the firm.
3. We also had to promise to not release the polling data to outside researchers.
4. We used archival data in this section. There were other proposed plans, but because they were not given serious consideration, we exclude them from the analysis.
5. This breakdown approximates new and old parts of the district based on Secretary of State precinct codes and actual precinct names. Alabama sometimes splits voters in a single precinct between congressional districts. Thus, if a precinct was partially included in a congressional district in 1991 and then fully included in 2001, then we count that precinct as part of the old district. These figures also do not account for minor precinct boundary changes that were in process in 2002.

References

Alabama Secretary of State. 2008. Elections results archive—US House of Representatives 1986–2002. http://www.state.al.us/downloads/dl2.aspx?div1=ElectionsDivision &types=Data (accessed December 6, 2008).
———. 1998. Alabama: Seventh District: Representative Earl Hilliard. *Almanac of American Politics 1998*, ed. Michael Barone. Washington, DC: The National Journal Group. http://www.nationaljournal.com/almanac/1998/al07.htm (accessed December 6, 2008).
———. 2002. Alabama: Seventh District: Representative Earl Hilliard. *Almanac of American Politics 2002*, ed. Michael Barone. Washington, DC: The National Journal

Group. http://www.nationaljournal.com/almanac/2002/states/al/al07.htm (accessed December 6, 2008).

———. 2002. Representative Earl Hilliard (D): Alabama: Seventh District. *Almanac of American Politics 2002*, ed. Michael Barone. Washington, DC: The National Journal Group. http://www.nationaljournal.com/almanac/2002/people/al/rep_a.htm (accessed December 6, 2008).

Ansolabehere, Stephen, James M. Snyder Jr.. and Charles Stewart III. 2000. Old voters, new voters and the personal vote: Using redistricting to measure the incumbency advantage. *American Journal of Political Science* 44 (1): 17–34.

Bailey, Stan. 2002. Hilliard, backers rap Davis at bridge. *The Birmingham News*, June 19.

Black, Marcel. 2008. Personal interview. March 12.

Cameron, Charles, David Epstein, and Sharyn O'Halloran. 1996. Do majority-minority districts maximize substantive Black representation in Congress? *American Political Science Review* 90 (4): 794–812.

Canon, David T., Matthew Schousen, and Patrick Sellers. 1996. The supply side of congressional redistricting: Race and strategic politicians, 1972–1992. *The Journal of Politics.* 58 (3): 846–62.

Davis, Artur. 2007. Personal interview. September 12.

Desposato, Scott W., and John R. Petrocik. 2003. The variable incumbency advantage: New voters, redistricting and the personal vote. *American Journal of Political Science* 47 (1): 18–32.

Finnegan, William. 2004. The candidate: How the son of a Kenyan economist became an Illinois everyman. *The New Yorker*. May 31, 32–38.

Gerber, Alan S. 1996. African Americans' Congressional careers and the Democratic House Delegation. *Journal of Politics* 58: 831–45.

Gillespie, Andra. 2005. *Community, coordination and context: A Black politics perspective on voter mobilization.* PhD diss., Yale University.

Goppian, J. David, and Darrell M. West. 1984. Trading security for seats: Strategic considerations in the redistricting process. *The Journal of Politics* 46 (4): 1080–96.

Haeberle, Steven H. 1997. Exploring the effects of single-member districts on an urban political system: A case study of Birmingham, Alabama. *Urban Affairs Review* 33 (2): 287–98.

Halbfinger, David. 2002. Generational battle turns nasty in Alabama primary. *The New York Times*. June 3.

Helderman, Rosalind S., and William Wan. 2008. Md. challenger Edwards wins stunning victory over long-time incumbent Wynn. *The Washington Post*, February 13.

Hetherington, Marc J., Bruce Larson, and Suzanne Globetti. 2003. The redistricting cycle and strategic candidate decisions in US House races. *The Journal of Politics* 65 (4): 1221–34.

Hilliard, Earl Jr. 2008. Personal interview. March 12, 2008.

Hilliard, Earl Sr. 2007. Personal interview. October 19, 2007.

Jacobson, Gary C., and Samuel Kernell. 1983. *Strategy and choice in congressional elections.* 2nd ed. New Haven, CT: Yale University Press.

Johnson, Bob. 2000. Hilliard wins nomination in 7th District. *Associated Press State and Local Wire,* June 7.

Mayhew, David. 1974. *Congress: The electoral connection.* New Haven, CT: Yale University Press.

McClure, Vicki, and Tom Gordon. 2002. Davis' win seen as sign voters more independent: Historically influential Black groups backed Hilliard. *The Birmingham News,* June 27.

McMurray, Jeffrey. 2001. Hilliard rebuked for campaign violations. *Associated Press State and Local Wire*, June 22. http://www.lexis-nexis.com (accessed August 20, 2009).

The Mellman Group. 2002a. Alabama 7th Congressional District poll (N = 400); Release date April 24.

———. 2002b. Alabama 7th Congressional District Poll (N = 400); Release date June 9.

Murray, Shailagh. 2007. Ala. Black group endorses Obama. *The Trail*. December 1. http://voices.washingtonpost.com/the-trail/2007/12/01/obama_collects_key_ala_backing.html (accessed December 22, 2007).

Naylor, Brian. 2007. Black power on display in new Congress. *NPR's Morning Edition* [Transcript]. January 19. http://www.npr.org/templates/story/story.php?storyId=6915852 (accessed December 22, 2008).

Orndorff, Mary. 2002a. Davis ousts Hilliard: 34-year-old lawyer beats 5-term congressman. *The Birmingham News*, June 26.

———. 2002b. Donors sought Jewish-Black unity, Davis says. *The Birmingham News*, June 27.

———. 2002c. Hilliard revs up fund raising, ads $30,000. *The Birmingham News,* May 31.

———. 2002d. Ad watch. *The Birmingham News*, June 1.

Reed, Joe. n.d. Chair's message. Alabama Democratic Conference. http://www.alabama-democraticconference.org/content/view/15/30/ (accessed December 6, 2008).

———. 2008. Personal interview. March 12, 2008.

Schneider, William. 2002. Israel via Alabama. *National Journal* 34(27): 20–46.

Swain, Carol. 1995. *Black faces, Black interests: The representation of African Americans in Congress*. Cambridge, MA: Harvard University Press.

Tate, Katherine. 1995. *From protest to politics: The new Black voters in American elections*. Enlarged ed. New York: Russell Sage Foundation.

Temple, Chanda. 1999. Davis to seek Hilliard's seat. *The Birmingham News*, August 1.

U.S. Census Bureau. 2000. Congressional District 7, Alabama-fact sheet. *U.S. Census Bureau: Fast facts for Congress,* http://fastfacts.census.gov/servlet/CWSFacts?_event=ChangeGeoContext&geo_id=50000US0107&_geoContext=01000US|04000US01&_street=&_county=&_cd=50000US0107&_cityTown=&_state=04000US01&_zip=&_lang=en&_sse=on&ActiveGeoDiv=&_useEV=&pctxt=fph&pgsl=040&_content=&_keyword=&_industry= (accessed August 20, 2009).

Verba, Sidney, and Norman Nie. 1972. *Political participation in America*. Chicago: University of Chicago Press.

White, David. 2002. Hilliard sees new district as a threat. *The Birmingham News*, February 3.

3 Losing and Winning

Cory Booker's Ascent to Newark's Mayoralty

Andra Gillespie

In 2002, Cory Booker, a one-term city councilman, Yale-trained lawyer, and former Rhodes Scholar, challenged four-term incumbent Mayor Sharpe James for the mayoralty in Newark, New Jersey. The election drew national attention and became New Jersey's most expensive municipal election to date.

There were many reasons why Newark's 2002 mayoral election garnered national attention. The matchup between James, the seasoned and flamboyant incumbent, and Booker, the telegenic newcomer with famous friends, made for a compelling story that sold papers and increased television ratings. James also successfully made the 2002 mayoral election a referendum on whether Booker was authentically Black enough to lead a majority-minority city. James's strategy appeared to work, as he narrowly won the election by posting decisive victories in the city's Black wards.

For his part, Booker vowed to fight again for the mayoral seat in 2006. In order to be successful, though, he would have to address the concerns about his ability to lead a majority-minority city. How could Booker address those concerns without capitulating to race-baiters? This is the story of this chapter.

The year 2002 was a challenging one politically for Cory Booker. While his political and generational peers Artur Davis and Kwame Kilpatrick had recently scored stunning electoral victories in Alabama's Seventh Congressional District and Detroit's mayoralty, respectively, Booker suffered a narrow but nationally publicized defeat in his quest to become mayor of Newark, New Jersey. Booker's loss to then-sixteen-year incumbent Sharpe James was particularly stinging given the racial vitriol of the campaign. James attacked Booker's racial authenticity, labeling Booker a "faggot White boy" and claiming that he had received campaign donations from Jews, the Ku Klux Klan, and the Taliban (Curry 2005). James went on to win the election by soundly beating Booker in all three of Newark's predominately Black wards, including Booker's own Central Ward.

In January 2006, it appeared that there would be a rematch between Booker and James. Booker announced his candidacy, and many expected that James would attempt to run for an unprecedented sixth term. Some assumed that should a Booker–James rematch take place, the race would be close at best. The Associated Press quoted political scientist David Rebovich, who predicted that "It will be an uphill battle for Booker if James runs" (Anderson 2006).

A Booker–James rematch was not to be, though. On March 27, ten days after filing for candidacy in a very public spectacle, James pulled out of the race, leaving Booker to face State Senator and Deputy Mayor Ronald Rice Sr. and two minor candidates in the May 9 municipal election. Booker would go on to soundly defeat his opponents, garnering more than 70 percent of the vote. And by June 13, Booker's running mates or supporters had managed to secure every seat on Newark's Municipal Council, beating long-time incumbents and even Sharpe James's own son, who was running for an open seat representing the South Ward.

Why did Booker's 2006 fortunes differ from those of 2002? Much of the extant literature states that Booker lost because his deracialized campaign tactics fell flat with Black voters. Their theories and evidence suggests that in order for deracialized Black candidates to win after a defeat, it is necessary for these candidates to racialize themselves. I argue that different circumstances were at work in Newark in 2006. Cory Booker would be hard pressed to mount a credible racialized campaign. However, he could make subtle changes to his racial appeal and leverage new political developments to position himself for victory.

Data, Methods, and Chapter Outline

The pages that follow illumine and answer the aforementioned issues and questions in greater detail using ethnographic data, interviews with Newark political elites, and election returns. After presenting a brief overview of the literature on deracialized campaigns, I present ethnographic and interview data. I collected the ethnographic data and recollections as a participant observer in the Booker campaign from March to July 2006. I conducted turnout experiments in Newark's 2002 municipal elections for my doctoral dissertation (Gillespie 2005). At that time, I volunteered on Booker's first mayoral campaign. I maintained contact with Booker, his teammates (particularly Ronald Rice Jr., the West Ward candidate), family, and staff after the 2002 election, so my presence in 2006 was not unusual. I leveraged the relationships I had developed in the previous four years to obtain informed consent from Booker's campaign manager to conduct ethnographic research on the 2006 campaign. In exchange for access to the campaign, I performed a variety of tasks for the campaign, including canvassing for Booker and his council teammates in the Central, South, and West Wards, conducting opposition research and analyzing turnout results from May 9 to strategize for the June 13 runoff.

For two years after the 2006 election, I conducted in-depth, semistructured interviews with key members of Booker's staff and Booker's political opposition. These interviews were audiotaped and lasted anywhere from 45 to 120 minutes.

After briefly acquainting the reader with the issues, results and theoretical context of the 2002 election, I move to a discussion of Booker's strategy in the interim period between 2002 and 2006. I then turn to an examination of the structural issues that hampered Ronald Rice Sr.'s ability to mount a strong challenge to Booker. After that, I examine the role race and class played in this campaign by conducting a demographic analysis of the vote returns.

The Efficacy of Deracialized Campaign Tactics in Majority Black Communities

There has been a spirited debate about the general efficacy of deracialization. On the one hand, there is evidence suggesting that candidates who use deracialized campaign tactics are successful; this evidence extends well before Barack Obama's successful use of the strategy in his 2008 presidential bid. For instance, in their analysis of the electoral fortunes of 1992 congressional candidates in majority-Black districts, Canon, Schousen, and Sellers (1996) handicapped the electoral fortunes of racialized and deracialized Black candidates. They found that any Black candidate was likely to win against a White candidate in a one-on-one race.[1] However, when a racialized Black ran against a deracialized Black, the deracialized candidate usually won; the two candidates would split the Black vote, and the deracialized candidate would attract the lion's share of the White vote.

Given the projected efficacy of deracialization, it is not surprising that deracialization has become a standard tool for Black elected officials. In their survey of Black elected officials in California, Byron D'Andra Orey and Boris Ricks found that most Black elected officials surveyed embraced some form of deracialization. The majority of officials described themselves as either racially moderate or racially neutral. Clearly, these officials saw the utility in not emphasizing racial issues (Orey and Ricks 2007).

It is important to note, though, that there is also a body of literature suggesting that deracialization is not a fool-proof strategy. In the 1990s, deracialized Black candidates such as Andrew Young and Harvey Gantt lost their bids for statewide office. Despite the fact that both of these men deemphasized racial issues in their campaign and made extensive overtures to White voters, White voters were still reluctant to vote for them. In Gantt's case in particular, his White opponent, Jesse Helms, inflamed racial passions with an anti-affirmative action campaign ad to solidify his base of support among White voters (Davis and Willingham 1993; Wilson 1993).

There are also examples of potential deracialized candidates choosing not to run deracialized campaigns. In her study of electoral politics in Memphis, Sharon Wright found that while Willie Herenton pledged to run a deracialized campaign for mayor in 1991, in reality, he ran to his base and ran a racialized campaign. While the voting in that election was the most racially polarized voting ever seen in a mayoral election featuring a winning Black candidate—Herenton only got 3 percent of the White vote—Herenton was able to win. Wright concludes that given Memphis's racially polarized politics, it was expedient for Herenton to run a racialized campaign, regardless of any normative desire to transcend race (Hajnal 2007, 175; Wright 1996).

Byron D'Andra Orey had similar findings in his study of mayoral politics in Jackson, Mississippi. In that study, Orey charted the political fall and rise of Harvey Johnson, the city's first Black mayor. Johnson first ran for the Democratic nomination for mayor in 1993. He lost. In 1997, Johnson retooled his campaign and won. Orey argues that in that first mayoral attempt, Johnson employed a deracialized campaign strategy to try to reach out to White voters. Johnson refused to seek the endorsement of local Black activists, who wanted to coalesce around one Black candidate so as not to divide the Black vote. They ended up endorsing another Black candidate. Moreover, Johnson's campaign platform, while it included a race relations plank, also focused on crime and economic development. Using ecological inference, Orey argues that Johnson's attempts to woo White voters had little effect; he estimates that Johnson won only 7 percent of the White vote. However, he also only won 46 percent of the Black vote, which put him in third place. The eventual winner, incumbent Kane Ditto, won a quarter of the Black vote and 41 percent of the White vote. This gave Ditto a first place finish in the primary, which put him in a runoff which he easily won (Ditto ran against another White candidate in the runoff) (Orey 2006, 822–26).

Johnson did a 180 degree turn in his 1997 attempt for the Democratic mayoral nomination. Instead of trying to reach out to White voters, Johnson devoted most of his energies to reaching out to Black voters. He distanced himself from racially transcendent sentiments in this election, acknowledging the fallacy of colorblindness. He pledged to help grow Black businesses. He successfully sought the endorsement of the Black political establishment. He won the endorsement of the *Jackson Advocate,* the city's largest Black newspaper, and of Bennie Thompson, the state's only Black member of Congress. Thompson even loaned Johnson one of his staffers for the campaign. As a result of Johnson's efforts, Johnson won the primary outright. He won 77 percent of the Black vote and 19 percent of the White vote. Johnson went on to easily win the general election, garnering 70 percent of the vote (Orey 2006, 826–31).

Orey uses the results of these two elections to draw some of the same conclusions that previous scholars (Davis and Willingham 1993; Wilson 1993) had drawn: deracialized campaign strategies do not guarantee greater White support and can alienate Black voters. However, there are other factors to keep in mind which confound Orey's analysis and probably significantly contributed to Johnson's defeat. Based on Orey's description of events, Johnson's first campaign was poorly run. For instance, he cites a newspaper article in which a local college professor, Mary Coleman, noted that "'[t]he campaign for Johnson is a week late on everything…some would say a year late'" (Coleman cited in Howard cited in Orey 2006, 825). Moreover, the campaign was underfunded. In fact, Johnson's campaign was so strapped for cash that it could afford to print only a few signs and could not print palm cards with the candidate's name to distribute to voters. Orey also reports that Johnson's get-out-the-vote efforts were also limited to Black church visits. An underfunded campaign which eschews basic, effective mobilization methods such canvassing and phone calls was likely doomed to failure from the beginning (Orey 2006, 825; Green and Gerber 2004).

So, while Johnson's initial campaign strategy may not have been ideally suited to reach out to Jackson's racially polarized electorate, Johnson's first campaign had amateurish elements that also contributed to its defeat. When Johnson ran a second time, he learned from his mistakes, attracted qualitatively better endorsements, and ran a strategically smarter campaign.

Hypotheses

I contend that a defeated deracialized candidate need not necessarily abandon a racially transcendent campaign strategy in order to subsequently win in a majority Black city. He or she should be mindful of not alienating Black voters. However, a losing candidate who performs well in an election lays the groundwork for a future electoral bid. He establishes name recognition. He earns the respect of potential supporters. And he learns the mistakes of his failed bids and is able to use them to mount better campaigns in the future.

Cory Booker's first and second mayoral campaigns illustrate the efficacy of a deracialized candidate essentially staying the course for his second campaign. Like Harvey Johnson, Booker lost a deracialized campaign only to win on his second try. In that first campaign, Booker, like Johnson, made some amateur mistakes and alienated his city's Black political establishment. Booker's second campaign was more politically sophisticated than his first, as was Johnson's. However, Booker ran an essentially deracialized campaign the second time around as well. Given his disposition and worldview, he would have been hard pressed to run a credible racialized campaign. So why did he still win? Booker clearly benefited from the incumbent's decision to not run; but he was able to force the incumbent out of the race in part because of his political savvy and in part because between his first and second elections, voters became more comfortable with the idea of his leadership.

The 2002 Election

Newark's 2002 mayoral campaign epitomized the tensions between the racialized Civil Rights and deracialized, newer generations of Black leadership, albeit in a crude way. Incumbent Sharpe James, who was first elected to Newark's Municipal Council in 1970, first made a name for himself as a community leader during the 1967 riots. In 1986, he successfully challenged Newark's first Black mayor, Kenneth Gibson for the mayoralty. As mayor, he became Newark's chief booster and was credited with attracting corporations such as Verizon and IDT to the city, as well as building a multimillion dollar performing arts center that was a central component of downtown redevelopment. Despite these successes, some of James's associates, particularly his former chief of staff, had been convicted on corruption charges (Jacobs 2002).[2]

It was in this environment that Cory Booker emerged as a contender for Newark's mayoralty. Born in Washington, DC and raised in Harrington Park, New Jersey (a mostly White, Bergen County suburb of New York City), Booker was an All-American tight end at Stanford. He won a Rhodes scholarship in 1992, and went on to receive his law degree from Yale in 1997. While at Yale, he moved to Newark, and after graduation, he took a fellowship where he worked as a tenants' rights lawyer. As a result of his tenants' rights work, he developed a base to launch a campaign for the Central Ward Council seat in 1998. Booker beat a sixteen-year incumbent in a runoff to become Councilman that year (Booker n.d.).

Booker is a natural deracialized candidate. As the product of a majority White community and elite White schools, Booker was imminently comfortable with White audiences. Moreover, Booker espouses a worldview that is quintessentially multicultural. In a personal interview with Booker, I asked him if he had linked fate with other Blacks, or if he believed that what happened to other Blacks affected him (Dawson 1994). Booker responded that he had linked fate with everyone, not just Blacks (Booker 2008).

Booker chose to challenge Sharpe James for Newark's mayoralty in 2002. That year, Booker ran on a general reformist platform. His campaign slogan proclaimed him "the change we want; the leadership we need." In kaffeklatsches and campaign speeches, Booker touted his plans to reform government, provide better public services, and ensure that neighborhood redevelopment did not come at the expense of downtown redevelopment (Sharif 2006). Booker also made light of sobering statistics, which he believed proved that James had not done enough to improve the quality of life of Newark residents. In a campaign video distributed to undecided voters the week before the election, Booker cites high unemployment and high school dropout rates as one of the key reasons James did not deserve a fifth term in office (Booker n.d.).

While Booker attempted to run on a reformist platform, James quickly and deftly made the election a question of racial and geographic authenticity. Having originally chosen "Let the Work That I've Done Speak for Me" as his campaign slogan, James was persuaded by campaign advisors to proclaim himself "The Real Deal" (Curry 2005; James 2006; "Bill Clinton Was the Comeback President" n.d.). Oscar James Sr., who was Sharpe James's (no relation) Field Director in 2002 and Booker's Central, South, and West Ward Field Director in 2006, recalls that the slogan was not explicitly intended to imply James's racial authenticity (James 2006). However, the vernacular use of the slogan has unmistakable racial connotations. In my analysis of the 2002 election, I conducted a focus group of Black voters in Newark's West Ward. I asked them specifically about what they thought "The Real Deal" meant. One respondent answered "Yeah, he [Sharpe] meant he was the 'real deal' that he was the real Black man" (Gillespie 2006, 35). Others indicated that they thought that "The Real Deal" indicated that he was a real Newarker (Gillespie 2006, 35). Additionally, Steve DeMicco, a noted New Jersey campaign media consultant who worked for James in 2002 and Booker in 2006, acknowledged that the campaign hoped to prime feelings of Black racial solidarity with the term *real deal* (DeMicco 2008).

Booker's upbringing in Bergen County, New Jersey and his perceived status as an outsider was a huge issue in this election, one that was sometimes inextricably linked to issues of racial authenticity and class difference. For instance, in his campaign literature, James attacked Booker for his support of school vouchers. In one piece in particular, James suggests that if Booker were actually from Newark, he would know better than to support such a policy that would hurt Newark schoolchildren ("Maybe If Cory Booker Came From Newark, He'd Understand" n.d.). In doing so, he cast Booker as an elitist outsider who was out of touch with the needs of everyday residents.

For his part, Booker and his campaign did not effectively address the race and class issues that emerged in the campaign. They miscalculated and did not attack the charges head on, thus neutralizing the issues. By doing so, they allowed James to define Booker, thus putting him on the defensive (Sharif 2006).

Additionally, Booker's surrogates and staffers perhaps unwittingly contributed to the perception that Booker was out of step with everyday Newarkers. Booker received unsolicited praise in the national press from commentators such as George Will (2002). This led Harvard Professor Emeritus Martin Kilson to dub Booker "an errand boy Black politician for conservative Republican power-class penetration of governing control of Black Newark..." (Kilson 2002, 3). For Kilson, anyone that conservative Will liked could not have the best interests of the Black community at heart (Kilson 2002, 1).

Surrogates closer to home also made critical errors, which corroborated the perception that Booker was a Republican outsider. The group Citizens for a Better Essex County, which was based in Montclair, mailed literature to Newark residents that all but called him a Republican. In one piece, Booker is called a fiscal conservative. In another piece, they positively compared Councilman Booker's efforts to make government more efficient to Mayor Rudolph Giuliani's efforts to do the same in New York City ("Cory Booker: Restoring Newark's Promise" n.d.; "Cory Booker: Fiscal Responsibility for Newark" n.d.).

These missteps were compounded by the demographic makeup of Booker's 2002 staff. The main campaign headquarters was located in an obscure factory in the East Ward, Newark's smallest ward with a majority Portuguese population. The staffers in that headquarters were largely White and from out of town. In hindsight, Booker's 2006 staffers acknowledge that this contributed to the perception that Booker was insensitive to Black residents. Carl Sharif, Booker's 2006 Campaign manager, noted that it was hard to combat the perception that Booker was not planning to gentrifying Newark and kick all the Black people out when one looked at the 2002 staff. In one clear example, he cited a rally held in the heart of Newark's South Ward, home to the Black political elite of the city. Sharif noted that there were campaign photos taken of Booker and his White staff. The only other Black person in the picture was Ronald Rice Jr., one of Booker's city council running mates. Sharif acknowledged that that type of staffing myopia contributed to Black voter mistrust of Booker in 2002 (Sharif 2006). Even Booker's White staffers in 2006 acknowledged the staffing myopia. *Kevin Morris,*[3] who worked on both the 2002 and 2006 campaigns, questions his own public role in the 2002 campaign, where he assisted press secretary Jennifer Bluestein. In personal conversations with me and in his formal interview, he noted that in an election when Booker was being pejoratively labeled as a tool of White, Jewish interests, having two Whites who happened to be Jewish as the public face of the campaign only exacerbated these admittedly bigoted perceptions of Booker (Morris 2006).

In the end, Booker lost the election because he failed to convince enough Black voters, who were estimated by the *Newark Star Ledger* to be 52 percent of the electorate. While Booker won in predominantly White (62 to 37 percent) and Latino precincts (57 to 42 percent), they argued that he lost in the majority Black precincts by nearly 20 percentage points (40 to 59 percent) ("How Turnout…" 2002).

The Interim Period (2002–2005): Settling in and Building Bridges

After losing in 2002, Booker maintained his commitment to Newark. He continued to live in Brick Towers, a housing project in the Central Ward. He became a partner in a West Orange law firm. He also opened an office in Newark, founded a nonprofit organization called Newark Now, which provides training and assistance to local community organizations and sponsors high profile activities such as an annual Easter Egg hunt, a Thanksgiving Turkey giveaway, and a Holiday Toy Drive.

Booker also vowed to fight again for his seat. The day after losing to James, Booker vowed to try again for the mayoralty (Jones 2002). This time, though, Booker would run as a little less of a maverick. In the period between 2002 and 2005, Booker would reach out to selected members of Newark's old guard in a series of key tactical decisions that would solidify his position as a force to be reckoned with in Newark politics.

In the years between 2002 and 2006, James's chokehold on the Municipal Council loosened to some degree. In 2003, James proposed privatizing the water system in Newark. The administration argued that the arrangement would be similar to one in Passaic County and would benefit the community. Opponents, including future West Ward Councilman Ronald Rice Jr., contended that the optimization plan was merely another way for James and his cronies to benefit financially at the expense of taxpayers. They contended James and members of the Municipal Council would serve on the board of the private water board (for which they would be paid) and would likely be able to set their terms such that they would guarantee themselves seats on the boards after they retired from elective office.

It was during the water optimization debate that Councilman-at-Large Luis Quintana and East Ward Councilman Augusto Amador emerged as critics of Sharpe James. Actually, the water optimization proposal was one of many issues that pitted Quintana and Amador against Sharpe James in the early part of his last term. James's relationship with Quintana suffered after he blamed Quintana for not delivering the Latino vote to him. Furthermore, just before the water optimization, the City of Newark adjusted property taxes. Taxes in the predominately Latino and Portuguese North and East Wards tripled in some cases, while property taxes in the predominately Black South Ward sometimes decreased (Quintana 2007; Amador 2007).

It was in this climate that Booker was able to forge an alliance with Quintana, Amador, and Councilman-at-Large Donald Tucker. Quintana, with Booker's support, challenged Sharpe James for the Democratic nomination for State Senate (James was also a State Senator) in 2003. Donald Tucker's endorsement of Quintana signaled his public support of Booker. To be sure, Carl Sharif, Booker's campaign manager, notes that Tucker, who died in 2005, had never been a James ally and had never publicly upbraided Booker or opposed anything he had proposed while Booker represented the Central Ward (Sharif 2006).

Booker's staff also tried to appeal to others aligned with James, with mixed success. In 2004, Carl Sharif approached Oscar James Sr., who had worked for Sharpe James or his administration since 1979—to coordinate Booker Team field activities for the Central, South, and West Wards. I asked Mr. Sharif about that decision; why would Booker hire someone who had worked against him in the previous election? Sharif explained that he and Oscar James had always had a good working relationship and that he trusted that Oscar would be loyal and would work hard to elect Booker. Moreover, Sharif was strategic. He figured that as long as Oscar James was working for Cory Booker, he was not working for anyone else. Apart from any consideration of his skills as a field operative, this was reason enough to invite James to be part of the team (Sharif 2006).

Oscar James Sr. has a complementary but somewhat different version of the same events. When I asked him why he switched sides between 2002 and 2006, he told me that he had always admired Cory Booker, but did not think that he was a viable candidate in 2002. However, by 2004, he believed that Booker could beat Sharpe James in a head-to-head matchup. He noted that he had a meeting with Sharpe James about Booker's electoral prospects in early 2004. Sharpe James truly believed that he could still beat Cory Booker. Oscar James indicated to me that Sharpe James's delusional conviction on the matter was what compelled him to join the Booker Team (James 2006).

Incidentally, another event may have helped influence Oscar James to join the Booker Team. Oscar James Sr.'s son Sidney in 2006 (or Oscar S. James II) ran with Booker as the candidate for South Ward Council. Sidney graduated from Villanova with a degree in political science in 2004. He took an African-American politics class at Villanova, where his professor challenged him to think critically about the failed political agendas of the Civil Rights generation of leadership. After taking the class, both Oscar and Sidney James in separate accounts recall a conversation between the two of them where Sidney announced that he could never support Sharpe James again, presumably because he represented failed leadership. After graduating from college and returning to Newark, Sidney started driving for Booker and eventually became the South Ward Councilman[4] (James 2006; Oscar Sidney James 2007).

Booker's campaign also tried to recruit West Ward Councilwoman Mamie Bridgeforth. Carl Sharif had helped Bridgeforth, a social work professor at Essex County College, get elected to her seat in 1998. However, once on the Municipal Council, she supported most of Sharpe James's agenda. Many in the Booker camp assumed that Bridgeforth had just acquiesced to the pressure of James's power and had been overwhelmed by the number of James supporters on the Municipal Council. They believed that if progressive, reformist politicians made up a majority of the Council, she would support them (Sharif 2006).

Booker's pursuit of Mamie Bridgeforth was significant because her presence on the Booker Team would have strategic consequences for Ronald Rice Jr., the son of Booker's eventual opponent in 2006 and a longtime Booker supporter. Rice Jr. ran and lost on the Booker Team for an at-large council seat in 2002. Given the difficulty of running city-wide, he considered running for the West Ward seat in 2006 (his father held that seat from 1982 to 1998, and he thought he could more easily win the seat). Booker wanted Rice Jr. to run at-large again, though, so that Bridgeforth could run as an incumbent on the Booker Team. There was some friendly tension between Rice Jr. and Booker over this matter. Rice Jr. was determined to run for the ward seat and made it clear that he would mount an independent campaign if Booker chose Bridgeforth as his teammate. Meanwhile, Bridgeforth hesitated in making her decision to join the Booker Team. Understanding that Rice Jr.'s threats were serious, the Booker Campaign gave Bridgeforth a deadline to decide whether to join the ticket. She did not meet the deadline, so they invited Rice Jr. to the ticket as the West Ward candidate (Sharif 2006).

Booker's political dealings between the 2002 and 2006 elections show a level of political sophistication and realism that observers had not previously witnessed in Booker. Sharif, Booker's longtime political mentor, noted that Booker became more realistic between 2002 and 2006, and realized that one cannot dismiss everyone within the established power structure to achieve political change. Booker's political rapprochement with some members of the Municipal Council reflects this pragmatism.

The 2006 Election

Booker officially announced his candidacy in January 2006. For this election, he ran on a crime, kids, economic development, and efficient government services platform. Carl Sharif noted that the focus group data they gathered indicated that crime was the foremost concern of residents (Sharif 2006). This information, coupled with a rash of teenage homicide victims in the previous year, strongly influenced the Booker campaign to run on an anti-crime platform. They then linked crime to children and family issues by arguing that addressing crime would make it safer for kids to walk home from school. Moreover, Booker proposed increasing recreation funds for the city as a deterrent to gang recruitment.

Booker took a populist stance on economic development, one that would appeal to local residents and perhaps cast the James administration as being so corrupt as to be economically damaging to the city. In public comments, Booker would often address the explosion in new housing construction in the city. However, he would also note that the developers who received these contracts (1) did not live in the city of Newark; (2) were mere friends and supporters of Sharpe James; and (3) received heavy discounts for the lots they purchased from the city. A common refrain throughout the campaign was that these developers got property for $4/square foot when the market value was $60 to $70/square foot.[5] Moreover, Booker noted that non-Newarkers were often the construction workers, and that this was unacceptable, given the discounts the developers received and Newark's high unemployment rate.

Booker's embrace of populism on the housing issue as it relates to economic development served a couple of purposes, intentionally and unintentionally. The housing kickbacks clearly demonstrated how corruption in the James administration hurt Newark financially. Furthermore, by embracing a Newark first policy in hiring, Booker demonstrated his commitment to the city, potentially neutralizing criticism that he was a carpetbagger who was bringing New Yorkers to take over the city.

However, my conversations with voters while canvassing indicate that some of them may have had a different perspective on the situation. Voters were clearly concerned about the rate of housing growth. They were particularly concerned that the new housing was overpriced and substandard. (The new three-family houses reportedly ranged in price from $400,000 to $750,000; rents could run from $1,000 to $1,500, depending on the size of the apartments.) At a March 15, 2006 Municipal Council meeting, residents complained about new substandard housing: exposed live wires and thin walls. There was a genuine concern in the community that the new houses were destined to fall apart in a couple of years.

However, many Black residents are also concerned that they were being shut of the new housing on account of race. On more than one occasion while canvassing, Black voters, particularly in the Central and South Wards, would complain that Latinos were shutting them out of the new housing. On one afternoon in the South Ward, residents were complaining that Whites from New York were flipping properties and driving up the values of houses in their neighborhood so that Blacks could not purchase homes in these communities. So while Booker may have embraced housing as an issue to burnish his credentials as being concerned about Newarkers first and foremost, some residents may have been concerned about this issue from a racialized, ethnicized, or just plain prejudiced perspective.

Government services also became a primary component of the Booker platform. On 2002, Booker tried to run on the same plank. He would note that none of his then-council colleagues could read spreadsheets (for this reason, he invited Carlos Gonzalez, a certified public accountant, to join his team as an at-large council candidate), thus making it difficult for them to do their primary job of passing the city's budget (which was never passed on time). He also noted that in 2002, it did not make sense that residents could not pay bills and fines online. He wanted to streamline government services to update them and make them easy to use.

Booker shifted the focus of his government proposals in 2006 to focus less on process and more on customer service. Marilyn Gaynor, the 2006 West Ward Field Director, constantly referred in passing to City Hall under the James Administration as "Silly Hall" because of the poor quality of customer service. The platform was probably best articulated by Terrance Bankston, the South Ward Field Director and later Director for Constituent Services. At a March 2006 rally in the South Ward, Bankston urged supporters to vote for Booker if they wanted to call City Hall and actually have someone answer the phone. Or if someone did answer the phone, to ensure that they would not be rude.

Staffing Decisions

In addition to modifying the platform to make it more personally relevant to everyday voters, the Booker campaign made staffing decisions that were more sensitive to the racial concerns of residents. The demographic makeup of Booker's staff in 2006 was noticeably different from 2002. Many of Booker's young, White, just-out-of-college and not-from-Newark staff were absent in 2006 (to be sure, there were still Whites, non-Newarkers, and young people represented on his staff). Instead, there were Blacks or Newarkers represented in key positions. In particular, his press secretary was Sakina Cole, an African-American woman. The campaign took care to send White and out-of-town volunteers to work in the North and East Ward, where they would stand out less (Morris 2006). Both Carl Sharif and Oscar James Sr. contended that this level of racial matching was necessary in order to avoid the negative perceptions about the Booker campaign that pervaded the 2002 race (Sharif 2006; James 2006).

More Subtle Racial Cues

There were even discussions throughout the campaign about how to make Booker more "hip." Voters and even some of the people I spoke with acknowledged that Sharpe James's style fit Newark residents better than Booker's style. Voters and elites recalled James dancing at parties and relating to people on a personal level. After the 2002 elections, voters I spoke with negatively perceived Booker to always be campaigning (Muhammad 2006; Gillespie 2006). Carl Sharif even admitted that Booker's love of discussing policy constantly could be off-putting at times, but that after becoming more familiar with Booker, residents started to warm up to him (Sharif 2006).

The Booker campaign avoided obvious attempts at pandering to make Booker more urban, more hip. Sharif noted that someone had proposed hiring an image consultant to spruce up Booker, but everyone agreed that was too extreme a move. However, there were some subtle changes in 2006. I, for one, noticed that Booker's wardrobe changed. Instead of wearing the same black suit, blue shirt, and red tie, he incorporated more color into his wardrobe. I casually asked a friend of Carl Sharif the day before the election if the wardrobe change was deliberate. He burst out laughing and said that Elnardo Webster, one of Booker's confidants and his campaign treasurer, pulled him aside and told him that he was dressing like "a goddammed White Republican." This friend had apparently helped Booker incorporate more color into his wardrobe.

I asked both Webster and Booker himself to corroborate the story. Webster said that he did not remember being so emphatic or mentioning Republicans, but he acknowledged that he had approached Booker about his wardrobe and appearance. While he said that Blacks probably pay more attention to wardrobe than other groups, Webster claimed that he would have had the same talk with Booker if he had been running in a majority-White city. To him, it was about brand development and making sure that the message and the man corresponded to each other (Webster 2007).

For his part, Booker also did not recall having his wardrobe challenged on racial grounds. According to him, it was a White staffer who called him on his wardrobe and, in his words, "introduced me to Barney's [New York]" (Booker 2008).

Booker's famous Black friends also moved into the spotlight during this campaign in ways they had not before. In 2002, Barbara Streisand and Bobbi Brown were highlighted as strong Booker supporters. In this election, Oprah Winfrey was the booster of choice. Moreover, Winfrey's friend Gayle King made appearances in Newark on Booker's behalf, fueling speculation that Booker and King were dating (they were not).

Why Sharpe James Dropped Out

In addition to all of the aforementioned strategic changes from 2002 to 2006, the Booker Team was determined to run an offensive campaign. To do that, they seized upon a proposal by Sharpe James about how to spend part of a $450 million (Cave 2006c) settlement from a dispute over rents from the Port Authority for Newark Liberty International Airport. James proposed privatizing $80 million of the settlement for redevelopment. Fifty million would go into a fund for core/downtown development, and each ward would receive $6 million for neighborhood redevelopment. The structure of the private corporations overseeing the funds would be similar to the proposed water optimization board. James and the members of the Municipal Council would all have seats on the board, and their terms on the board would outlast their terms in elective office.

The Booker campaign quickly attacked the core downtown proposal[6] as a scheme by Sharpe James to make money off of taxpayers. The campaign issued a mailing titled "Scheme Machine," which was tailored for the Central, South, and West Wards. The piece attacked James and the appropriate ward member of the Municipal Council and accused them of trying to use the plan to fund their retirement. Inside the piece, the at-large members of the Municipal Council were also shown and accused of being a part of this scheme. The piece also showed members of the Booker Team expressing their outrage and calling for a change in leadership ("Scheme Machine" n.d.). The piece contributed to a sense of outrage in the local community. At the March 15, 2006 Municipal Council Meeting, residents spoke angrily against the privatization plan.

The piece did garner criticism from council members and their supporters. From the dais, Councilwoman Mamie Bridgeforth announced that she would be seeking a $25 million in libel damages from the Booker Team for this piece; other Council members said that they would join the suit as well. Poet Amiri Baraka, whose son Ras was a Councilman-at-Large, got up and protested the fact that only Black officials were attacked in the piece (because the Booker Team was not fielding a candidate in the North Ward, Hector Corchado was not criticized in the piece). "They're trying to divide us [Blacks and Hispanics]," Amiri Baraka contended. He went on to note that Newark did not need any "buppies, yuppies, puppies or closet Republicans" in power, implying his disdain for Booker and his teammates.

The Port Authority settlement privatization scheme clearly evoked a viscerally negative impact in the community. Sharpe James suffered another defeat when he lost the endorsement of SEIU Local 617 on or about March 18. Local 617 represented many city workers, and had been a longtime supporter of Sharpe James. By 2006, though, the union leadership believed that James had become greedy and power hungry at the expense of being a good leader. They decided to endorse Booker instead. This endorsement, according to Rahman Muhammad, President of Local 617, meant that James would lose a significant number of his Election Day workers. This, in Muhammad's estimation, was the proverbial nail in the coffin of Sharpe James's municipal career. Muhammad argued that before Local 617 refused to endorse James, everyone else had been afraid to defy James for fear of retribution. Once one group was willing to stand up to James, other groups felt empowered to not go along with him as well (Muhammad 2006).

Despite the controversy surrounding the Port Authority settlement money and the loss of a crucial union endorsement, Sharpe James made a very public entry into the mayoral race on March 17. Donning a track suit and straw hat and riding a bike hitched to a wheelbarrow of petitions, James made the deadline to appear on the ballot. Ten days later, he quietly withdrew from the race. His stated reason was to concentrate on being a state senator (Cave 2006a).

James's exit from the race left State Senator and Deputy Mayor Ronald Rice Sr. as Booker's primary competitor. Rice Sr., the first Black councilman from Newark's West Ward, had more than twenty years of experience in elective office. He had also run for mayor before, against Sharpe James in 1998. By all accounts, Rice Sr. had expected for years to be James's heir apparent, and as his son told me during the ethnographic portion of my project, James had all but promised to step down as mayor and endorse him in 1998. After losing to James that year, Rice Sr. became his campaign chairman in 2002, in the hopes of securing his endorsement to run for mayor in 2006.

Unfortunately, Rice Sr.'s strategy did not work as planned. Rice Sr. was hesitant to begin his 2006 campaign in earnest until Sharpe James made his final decision about whether to run. By dropping out on March 27, Rice had six weeks to organize a campaign. With James out of the race, it was assumed that James would endorse Rice and provide him with financial and personnel support. However, James did not endorse Rice until the last week of the campaign, having skipped the event where he was to formally endorse Rice because he heard that there were no photographers at the event (Cave and Benson 2006).

Rice also suffered from an extreme fundraising disadvantage. Booker amassed more than $6 million in campaign contributions for himself and his teammates. In contrast, Rice Sr. only raised about $150,000 (Cave 2006b).

Despite the obvious disadvantages he faced, Rice Sr. joined forces with incumbents Ras Baraka, Mamie Bridgeforth, Charlie Bell, Bessie Walker, civil servant Norma Gonzalez, and John Sharpe James, the mayor's son, to run as the "Home Team." As the "Home Team," they and their surrogates attempted to attack Booker as an inexperienced outsider who was being funded by outside interests. In one of Rice's pieces, he attacked Booker for having no record, and said that his only claim to fame was that "he attended college on a scholarship" ("Good News for Newark Residents" n.d.). A flyer distributed by Activists Concerned for Newark noted that approximately ten of Booker's contributors, including singer Stephanie Mills and Circuit City Chairman Richard Sharp, had also made contributions to George W. Bush in 2004 ("Why Are They Buying Your City?" n.d.).

The Home Team's attacks on Booker were to no avail. Despite their efforts, they could not make up for the resource disparity. On May 9, Booker won in a landslide, securing more than 70 percent of the vote.

On the surface, it would seem that Booker effectively neutralized the attacks on him for being a carpetbagger who did not understand the plight of poor people of color, particularly Blacks. I asked Carl Sharif if the 2006 campaign had settled those issues in the minds of voters. Sharif was skeptical that these issues were entirely dead. He firmly believed that voters, particularly Blacks, had begun to warm to Booker. However, he acknowledged that there was still some skepticism about Booker. In his estimation, they were willing to give Booker a chance, but that they might be quick to crucify him, so to speak, if he did not deliver change quickly (Sharif 2006).

A basic analysis of the election returns suggests that Carl Sharif's interpretation is at least plausible. Booker's support was weakest in overwhelmingly Black precincts. I mapped precinct results by 2000 Census demographic precinct data and present the results in Table 3.1. While the data does not allow me to make voter level inferences about voter turnout and voter preference, I can make precinct-level inferences. While the data does not show a correlation between the proportion of Blacks in a precinct and voter turnout, there does appear to be a negative correlation between the concentration of Blacks in a precinct and Booker's average share of the vote in those precincts. Booker's performance was strongest in precincts where fewer than 25 percent of the residents were Black, and weakest in precincts where more than 75 percent of the residents were Black (a majority of the city's precincts).

Analysis/Conclusion

In many ways, the election returns from Newark's recent mayoral election reflect Canon, Schousen, and Sellers' (1996) predictions of what happens when moderate

Table 3.1 Turnout Rates By Ward, 2006 Newark Municipal Election

% Non-Hispanic Black Precinct Composition	# Precincts	2006 Turnout	Booker % (All Candidates)	Booker % (Booker vs. Rice Only)
Less than 25% Black	48	39.17%	88.97%	92.91%
25–75% Black	38	33.38%	75.12%	78.59%
More than 75% Black	93	36.99%	59.75%	62.84%
Citywide	179	36.81%	70.85%	74.25%

Source: Compiled by the author, using 2000 U.S. Census Data and 2006 election returns from Newark City Clerk's Office. This data does not include absentee or provisional votes.

and more civil-rights oriented or militant Black candidates face each other in Congressional elections. In their article, Canon and his colleagues predicted that the moderate Black candidate would win a majority of the non-Black vote and split the Black vote, creating enough of a rainbow coalition to win. This strategy clearly did not work for Booker in 2002, when he did not win a large enough share of Newark's large Black electorate to win. However, by 2006, Booker had become enough of a known player in Newark politics that he was able to attract more than enough Black support to be able to decisively win the election.

Booker's deracialized campaign tactics appear to have had little effect on his political fortunes in 2006. In the years leading up to 2006, Booker and his campaign staffers made key strategic moves to put themselves in the frontrunner position for 2006. While Booker was more racially sensitive to Black voters in his second mayoral campaign, he essentially maintained the same deracialized style from his previous election. In the final analysis, Booker needed more time—not a racialized makeover—to convince Newarkers to vote for him.

Notes

1. When two Black candidates ran against a White candidate, the White candidate had the advantage. Presumably, the Black candidates would split the Black vote, allowing the White candidate to win a plurality of the vote (Canon et al. 1996, 851).
2. In 2008, James was convicted and sentenced to federal prison for arranging the sale of city owned property to a mistress who flipped the property for profit without making the required improvements (see Miller and James 2008).
3. Kevin Morris is a pseudonym, given to protect the respondent's identity. I italicize all pseudonyms.
4. There were certainly some people with whom I spoke during the ethnographic portion of this project who believed that Oscar James procured a position for his son on the ballot as a part of his agreement to work for Booker. However, Oscar James insists that Sidney James appealed to Booker on his own accord to be placed on the ballot, and his son confirms this (James 2006; O. James 2007). Carl Sharif did not provide me with any evidence to contradict Oscar James's version of events. In any case, it is important to note that Sidney James was not expected to win the South Ward seat in the first place. That seat was previously held by Donald Bradley, the Municipal Council President. Bradley was perceived to be too powerful and too

popular to be ousted, even by someone of Cory Booker's choosing. However, after being investigated in the spring of 2006 on corruption charges stemming from the scandal embroiling the University of Medicine and Dentistry in New Jersey (Bradley served on the Board and is alleged to have illegally procured jobs for friends and family), Bradley had to pull out of the race (see Benson 2008).

5. To be sure, Booker's political opponents and former Municipal Council colleagues pointed out that Booker voted for the $4 rate as a City Councilman. They contend that they set the price so low because that was all buyers were willing to pay and they wanted to encourage development (Bell 2007; Bridgeforth 2007)

6. The Scheme Machine leaflet only attacked the Core/Downtown corporation because Quintana and Amador initially voted for the neighborhood corporations. At the March 15 Municipal Council meeting, Quintana and Amador tried to rescind their vote, but lost on the motion to do so. The state enjoined the corporation until after the new Council members took office on July 1, 2006. At their first regular council meeting, they voted to rescind the corporations.

References

Amador, Augusto. 2007. Personal interview. October 5.

Anderson, Andrea. 2006. Booker says Newark's race will be no "street fight." *Associated Press and Wire,* February 12.

Bell, Charles, 2007. Personal interview. July 14.

Benson, Josh. 2008. Rare power vacuum in Newark. *New York Times,* May 8. http://www.nytimes.com/2006/05/08/nyregion/08council.html?_r=1 (accessed September 28, 2009).

Bill Clinton was the "comeback" president. n.d.. Direct mail leaflet. Paid for by Citizens to Elect Sharpe James, Newark, NJ.

Booker, Cory. 2008. Personal interview. August 3.

Booker, Cory for Mayor. n.d. [Campaign video].

Canon, David T., Matthew Schousen, and Patrick Sellers. 1996. The supply side of congressional redistricting: Race and strategic politicians, 1972–1992. *The Journal of Politics* 58 (3): 846–62.

Cave, Damien. 2006a. After 5 terms as Newark mayor, James opts not to run again. *New York Times,* March 28.

———. 2006b. On second try, Booker glides in as Newark's mayor. *New York Times,* May 10, A1.

Cave, Damien, and Josh Benson. 2006. Newark mayoral candidate tries to escape shadows. *New York Times,* May 5, B1.

Cory Booker: Restoring Newark's promise. n.d. Direct-mail leaflet. Paid for by Citizens for a Better Essex County, Montclair, NJ.

Cory Booker: Fiscal responsibility for Newark. n.d. Direct-mail leaflet. Paid for by Citizens for a Better Essex County, Montclair, NJ.

Curry, Marshall, dir. 2005. *Street fight* [DVD]. United States: Marshall Curry Productions.

Davis, Marilyn, and Alex Willingham. 1993. Andrew Young and the Georgia State elections of 1990. In *Dilemmas of Black politics,* ed. Georgia Persons, 66–84. New York: HarperCollins.

Dawson, Michael. 1994. *Behind the mule.* Princeton, NJ: Princeton University Press.

DeMicco, Steven. 2008. Personal interview. June.

First World. 1977. First World interviews Julian Bond. *First World.* March/April 7.

84   *Andra Gillespie*

Gillespie, Andra. 2005. *Community, coordination and context: A Black politics perspective on voter mobilization.* PhD diss., Yale University.

———. 2006. Race-ing for Newark: Old and new Black politics and the 2002 election. Paper presented at the Annual Meeting of the National Conference of Black Political Scientists. Atlanta, GA, March 25.

Good news for Newark residents! n.d. Direct mail leaflet. Paid for by Committee to Elect Ronald L. Rice—2006, Newark, NJ.

Green, Donald P., and Alan S. Gerber. 2004. Get out the vote! How to increase voter turnout. Washington, DC: The Brookings Institution.

Hajnal, Zoltan. 2007. *Changing White attitudes toward Black political leadership.* New York: Cambridge University Press.

———. 2002. How turnout turned the race. *Newark Star-Ledger*, May 15, 25.

Jacobs, Andrew. 2002. A mayor is his own inspiration; James trumpets his record and Newark's future. *New York Times*, April 25, B1.

James, Oscar Sr. 2006. Personal interview. July 25.

James, Oscar Sidney. 2007. Personal interview. October 8.

Jones, Richard Lezin Jones. 2002. Newark hasn't seen the last of Booker. *New York Times,* May 16.

Kilson, Martin. 2002. Personal letter to Lee Daniels. In How to spot a Trojan horse: A letter From Harvard. *The Black Commentator.* http://www.Blackcommentator.com (accessed April 5 2002).

———. n.d. Maybe if Cory Booker came from Newark, he'd understand…. Direct-mail leaflet. Paid for by Citizens to Elect Sharpe James, Newark, NJ.

Miller, Jonathan, and Richard B. Jones. 2008. Ex-Newark mayor convicted of fraud. *New York Times,* April 2008. http://www.nytimes.com/3008/04/17/nyregion/16end"james.html?_&lscp=1&sig=sharpejames convict&st=cse# (accessed Septemebr 24, 2009)._

Morris, Kevin. 2006. Personal interview. July 28.

Muhammad, Rahman. 2006. Personal interview. June 24.

Orey, Byron D'Andra. 2006. Deracialization or racialization: The making of a Black mayor in Jackson, Mississippi. *Politics and Policy* 34 (4): 814–36.

———. Boris Ricks. 2007. A systematic analysis of the deracialization concept. University of Nebraska Digital Commons. http://digitalcommons.unl.edu/poliscifacpub/24 (accessed September 2008).

Quintana, Luis. 2007. Personal interview. December 17.

Scheme Machine. n.d.. Direct mail leaflet. Paid for by Booker Team For Newark, Newark, NJ.

Sharif, Carl. 2006. Personal interview. July 22.

Webster, Elnardo. 2007. Personal interview. August 22.

Why are they buying your city. n.d. Leaflet. Paid for by Activists Concerned For Newark, Newark, NJ.

Will, George. 2002. Newark's nasty race. *The Washington Post.* March 17, B9.

Wilson, Zaphon. 1993. Gantt versus Helms: Deracialization confronts southern traditionalism. In *Dilemmas of Black politics*, ed. Georgia Persons, 66–84. New York: HarperCollins.

Wright, Sharon. 1996. The deracialization strategy and African American candidates in Memphis mayoral elections. In *Race, governance, and politics in the United States*, ed. Huey L. Perry, 151–64. Gainesville: University of Florida Press.

Part II

Inheritance and Governance

What Black Political Scions Do Once They Get Elected

In popular discussions of Phase III Black leadership, journalists and pundits lavish much of the attention on charismatic Ivy League Upstarts such as Barack Obama and Cory Booker. With all of the attention on young Black politicians with sterling educational credentials, it is easy to forget that many of the young Black politicians who have emerged so far have benefited from a long family tradition of civil rights activism and public service. Harold Ford Jr. has certainly received a great deal of attention, but many of the others have been understudied.

The chapters in this section explore the political styles and careers of two scions of prominent Black political families. In chapter 1, I suggested that family connections were a double-edged sword for the children of Black politicians and activists. On the one hand, scions of political families can leverage their family connections to help them run for political office. In Black communities, certain political and activist families are well respected, and members of these families are less likely to have their racial bona fides challenged, even if they champion addressing racial inequality using nontraditional or even conservative methods.

On the other hand, though, coming from a long Black political lineage may have its drawbacks. If young Black politicians have controversial relatives, they may feel pressure to distance themselves from their families in order to cultivate a crossover appeal. They may also engender conflict at home if they disagree with their families over tactics or campaign style.

The next two chapters focus on two prominent scions of Black political families. In chapter 4, Randy Burnside and Antonio Rodriguez study the legislative career of Jesse Jackson Jr., son of the famed civil rights leader. Is the younger Jackson the legislative mirror of his father's agenda, or has he forged his own path? Is Jackson's legislative agenda different from that of his older Black colleagues in Congress? Does he sponsor substantive or symbolic legislation? Does he sponsor racially specific or race-neutral legislation?

In chapter 5, Athena King, Todd Shaw, and Lester Spence study the career of former Detroit Mayor Kwame Kilpatrick. While many young Black politicians burst onto the political scene pledging to reform their communities, the Kilpatrick example demonstrates that young Black politicians are susceptible to the same human foibles that affect politicians of all parties and all races.

4 Like Father, Like Son?

Jesse Jackson Jr.'s Tenure as a U.S. Congressman

Randolph Burnside and Antonio Rodriguez

If Jesse Jackson Jr. enjoys the benefits of his name, he has also had to endure the challenges of bearing that name. As the son of a famous and controversial American civil rights leader, Jackson parlayed his family's prominence in Chicago to win a special election to Congress in 1995. As one of the first Blacks of the post-Civil Rights generation to win election to a federal office, Jackson Jr. was in a unique position to be able to use his youthful perspective and the values he learned at home to help set a national policy agenda for Blacks and non-Blacks alike. As an emerging leader, he could articulate the concerns of a new generation of Americans with a different perspective. However, as someone who literally grew up in shadow of the Civil Rights Movement, he might also be able to reframe old civil rights issues and articulate them for the modern era, earning the respect of his forebears in both the activist and legislative communities.

How has Jackson used his position to advance such a policy agenda? Has he developed a political persona and a policy agenda similar to his technocratic, politically moderate, heavily credentialed Black peers? Or, is he his father with the power of the legislative vote? In this chapter, Randolph Burnside and Antonio Rodriguez scrutinize Jackson's legislative agenda. They contend that Jackson's bill sponsorship record demonstrates the precarious balance he tries to maintain between aligning with the pragmatism of his generation and the overt racial activism of his father's generation.

Introduction

Jesse Jackson Jr. emerged as a political force after defeating Emil Jones, who had for years been a force to be reckoned with in Illinois politics. Given Jackson's work with the Rainbow Coalition and his obvious attachment to leaders from the Civil Rights era, it is interesting to note his reluctance to accept this frame as his ideological predisposition. Jesse Jackson Jr. provides us with an example of a Black elected official who based on rhetoric may indicate that he is a part of the new generation of Black politicians like Barack Obama, Deval Patrick, and Artur Davis. However, the mere fact that his name is Jesse Jackson Jr. and his father is Jesse Jackson Sr. causes one to wonder what is/was the impact of having one of the leading Black advocates of the Civil Rights generation as a father?

The current literature on the impact of family influence on an individual's political predisposition indicates that individuals are greatly influenced by their parents and are likely to incorporate at least some of their parents' political values into their own adult worldview. One of the best known approaches that supports this conclusion is the transmission model. A study by Beck and Jennings (1991) concluded that "people do tend to carry important political dispositions 'inherited' from their parents into adulthood—in conformity with the parent-to-child transmission model" (760). However, they also posit that this transmission of political attributes is far from being an absolute carryover of political dispositions. For instance, they note that the general political environment of the era in which the child is raised may play an important role in how she orients herself to politics in the future. Hence, the turbulent time period of the 1960s could in effect have a different political socializing affect on the child growing up in that period than her parents and lead her to be different in her orientation to politics. Given the conclusions drawn by Beck and Jennings (1991), the fact that Jackson Jr. grew up after the Civil Rights Movement could support his claims that he is not a carbon copy of his father.

Jackson Jr. suggests—and anecdotal evidence seems to support—that he occupies a nuanced, pragmatic middle position in this emergence of a new style of Black politician. This position incorporates subtle components of both generations' worldviews. Jackson's public statements bear this out. For example he stated: "It's not that I haven't taken positions different from my father's—though we usually agree on the substance of most issues" (Jackson and Watkins 2001, 21). Thus, it appears that Jackson Jr. is very clear on his political philosophy. However, one of the goals of this chapter is to ascertain if we are dealing with Jackson Jr.'s rhetoric or political reality when we examine his legislative record on issues of concern to African Americans. By focusing on this question, we can determine whether Jesse Jackson Jr. is a younger version of his father and his father's movement contemporaries or whether he is a new Black politician in the style of Barack Obama and Artur Davis, who have moved away from seeing politics in Black and White.

This chapter will proceed with an analysis of Jackson Jr.'s election and subsequent reelection to the Illinois 2nd Congressional District seat. We will use Jackson Jr.'s congressional record, public statements, various interviews and information gained from his own writings to gain a better understanding of his position in the hotly debated trichotomy of Black political leadership. In doing this, we will examine and compare his legislative record with those of House members from three distinct phases of Black political leadership as described in chapter 1. By doing this, we can empirically establish whether Jackson Jr.'s style and/or substance places him within one particular group or another. We also analyze public statements made by Jackson Jr. and his father in an attempt to help illuminate the potential differences and similarities between father and son.

"A New Generation": Jesse Jackson Jr. and the 1995 Special Election

Jesse Jackson Jr.'s election to Congress in December 1995[1] was the first time that a member of the highly visible and political Jackson family had ever won an elected office. Running under the slogan "A New Generation," Jackson Jr. successfully converted family political capital into a seat in the U.S. House of Representatives. The Second Congressional District includes the South Side of Chicago and the adjacent suburbs. According to the 2000 Census, the district population is roughly 60 percent African American, 30 percent White, and 10 percent Latino (U.S. Census 2000). Jackson was the third African American to hold the seat (Gus Savage and Mel Reynolds had served the district previously).

In many ways, Jackson Jr. was an electoral neophyte. Though he was from a very influential political family, he was young (30 years old) and had not previously held any elected positions. However, Jackson had been active in civil rights organizations. Prior to his election to the U.S. House of Representatives, Jackson Jr. was the National Field Director of the National Rainbow Coalition. Because of his relative youth and inexperience in electoral politics vis-à-vis his famous name, many people regarded him "as a child of privilege with a famous name who would take predictable stands on the issues and make fiery speeches denouncing the evils of racism in America" (Johnson 1998, 1).

It has to be very hard being the son of the man who is acknowledged as a symbol of the Civil Rights era politics while trying to forge one's own political identity. One of the first things Jackson Jr. did to assure voters that he was not the Jesse Jackson that they were accustomed to seeing was to create his campaign slogan: "A New Generation." Most of the campaign materials carried this slogan with a picture of him on it. The younger Jackson was clearly trying to establish himself as being separate from his father.

Jackson Jr. used a combination of name recognition, technology, and youthful energy to get voters out in a special election where the turnout was 21 percent (Simpson 1996). However, he also took advantage of his famous name and famous father on his way to winning. The elder Jackson introduced him when he announced his congressional candidacy. Father and son publicly campaigned together. The Jackson family name was a huge help to Jesse Jackson Jr. In a *Chicago Tribune* poll released a week before the 1995 special primary election, 97 percent of the people surveyed were familiar with Jesse Jackson Jr. Only 69 percent of respondents were familiar with the next most visible candidate, State Senator Emil Jones (Hardy 1995a). Jones had lived on the South Side of Chicago his entire life and was a force in Chicago politics. He was the Illinois Senate Democratic leader and had served in the legislature for 22 years.[2] When queried about those poll numbers in 1995, Jones responded, "It's a popularity contest. It says nothing about the quality of the candidate. The results are based on the recognition of his father. I always said this race was going to be between me and his daddy, not between me and him" (Hardy 1995a). While Jones was considered the strongest challenger for Jackson Jr., he was not the only politically experienced opponent that Jackson faced that year. He also faced Alice Palmer, a long time educator and member of the Illinois Senate and Monique Davis, a member of the Illinois House of Representatives (Hardy 1995a).

The primary election was in essence the most important election because like most majority-minority districts, the winner of the Democratic primary is the odds-on favorite to win the general election. With this in mind, all of the candidates had strategies in place to win the primary. Jones depended on his relationships with Chicago ward bosses and township committeemen to carry him to a primary victory. Palmer, on the other hand, employed a more deracialized strategy in which she tried to appeal to suburban and White voters. Davis touted the endorsements of former U.S. Congressman Gus Savage and Nation of Islam leader Louis Farrakhan. She also framed herself as an independent who had the best interest of the district at heart (Hardy 1995b).

For his part, Jackson Jr. used a varied approach which combined his obvious name recognition to appeal to older voters, his Rainbow Coalition experience to register new voters, and his youth to appeal to younger voters. Jackson Jr. noted that he was the only one who appealed to younger voters who had been locked out of the political process (Hardy 1995b). However, Jackson's two biggest assets were his name recognition and his use of technology to identify and target those who voted in the two previous elections. This enabled him to enhance his standing among likely voters in the district. This was especially important in the case of a special election, which is notorious for being low in turnout.

Name recognition was important, particularly in a special election. There is little time to cultivate support and meet voters, so any advantage a candidate can muster to spread the word of his candidacy is helpful. Jackson Jr.'s name recognition resonated with voters and provided him access to endorsements and money from outside the district. For instance, Congressman John Conyers of Michigan campaigned on Jackson Jr.'s behalf, noting that age was not an important issue for Jackson Jr. because he was an accomplished young man (Puente and Callahan 1995). Vice-President Al Gore and Mayor Richard Daley were on hand when Jackson celebrated his primary victory (Kokmen and Presecky 1995). There is little doubt that without a famous father, most thirty-year-old political neophytes would not have warranted such attention.

Name recognition can also be a double-edged sword. Jackson Jr.'s opponents criticized him for his relative youth and lack of experience. They also accused him of running on his father's record instead of his own. Emil Jones in particular used these charges to juxtapose what he perceived to be his superior record of experience and know-how (Hardy 1995b).

Despite Jones's best efforts, Jackson was able to post a decisive victory. The results of the primary election are displayed in Table 4.1. Jackson Jr. was able to defeat Jones by nearly 10 percentage points.

The 1995 General Election and Beyond

In the general election, Jackson ran against Republican T. J. Somer, a Chicago policeman, turned lawyer. Somer portrayed himself as someone from the com-

Table 4.1 Democratic Primary Results 1995 Special Election, Illinois
2nd District

Candidate	Vote Total	Vote %
Jackson	30,013	48.2
Jones	24,098	38.7
Palmer	6,343	10.0
Davis	1,519	2.4
Morrow	252	0.7

Source: America Votes. Vol. 22, 7.

munity who could represent the district's distinctive blue collar workers. He campaigned largely on his lifelong connection to the community and his work as a police officer within the district. He tried to paint Jackson Jr. as an outsider whose only reason for moving into the district was so that he could run for the seat vacated by Mel Reynolds. When asked about his chances of beating Jackson Jr. in the general election, Somer noted that "I'm the Rocky Balboa to (Jackson's) Apollo Creed. I'm just a regular guy. I know what people in this district go through" (Miller-Rubin and Presecky 1995). That may well have been the case, but the results of the election were predictable. Jackson Jr. won 76 percent of the vote to Somers's 24 percent. Jackson won 98 percent of the vote inside the part of his district that was in Chicago; he won 51 percent of the vote in the suburban part of the district (Hardy and Presecky 1995).

Since 1995, Jackson Jr. has faced very little electoral competition, and he has managed to consistently garner more than 82 percent of the vote in six general elections. Clearly, name recognition and incumbency advantage have worked to Congressman Jackson's benefit. Moreover, Jackson's strongest 1995 opponents chose not challenge him in subsequent elections. This consistency indicates two things. First, Jackson has been able to avoid a strong challenger to his seat in part because the Democrats have not fielded any strong challengers in the primaries and second because of name recognition. This may have served to dissuade other potentially strong challengers from attempting their own bids. Additionally, it would appear that Jackson Jr. has appealed to at least a portion of the White voters. Jackson continues to perform strongly in the suburban parts of his district as evidenced by his overwhelming reelection victories. Moreover, Jackson has curried favor with suburban voters through his steadfast support for a third Chicago airport to be located in suburban Peotone.

Legislating a Progressive Black Politics

In chapter 1, Andra Gillespie provides us with a three-phase typology that is used to define the current state of Black politics. This typology provides a framework from which we can ascertain Jackson Jr.'s political positioning among members of the U.S. House of Representatives. Using the framework as a guide, we placed forty-four of the Black Members of Congress who have served during part or all of Jackson Jr.'s tenure as a member of the House of Representatives in one of the three phases. We based our categorization of members on several different criteria:

Phase I: Included members who:
- Had direct involvement in the Civil Rights Movement;
- Were elected before 1989;
- Used overt racial appeals in either campaign rhetoric or made overt race based statements while in office; or
- Represented a majority Black district.

Phase II: Included members who:
- Had direct knowledge of the Civil Rights Movement but not necessarily direct involvement;
- Were elected after 1989;
- Ran deracialized campaigns; or
- Represented more heterogeneous districts.

Phase III: Included members who:
- Grew up after the Civil Rights Movement and have no first-hand knowledge of it;
- May have challenged and defeated a Phase I style Black politician for their current seat;
- Ran deracialized campaigns; or
- Have been elected since 1995; or
- Represent more heterogeneous districts.

To gather the necessary information on individual House members' styles, we looked at members' online personal biographies and reviewed journalistic sources on each of these members of Congress. In doing so, we were able to classify each member of Congress as Phase I, II, or III (for a complete listing of the categorical breakdowns, please see appendix 4.1).

Bill sponsorship and enactment are very important parts of each legislator's job. Scholars have long used sponsorship and enactment as measures of a Congress member's productivity and success (Hibbing 1991; Krutz 2005). Furthermore, students of Congress argue that a member's bill cosponsorship activity provides some indication of how members get along with individual members and legislative factions. Furthermore, the number of cosponsors can in effect tell you a lot about how that particular legislator is viewed by their legislative peers (Fowler 2006). This is particularly important when looking at minority legislators because they are least likely of any group to have legislation passed; if a minority legislator can get cosponsors for her proposed legislation or cosponsors more legislation as she acquires greater seniority, then that not only increases the likelihood of passage, but indicates a modicum of respect (Hawkesworth 2003). Thus, the extant literature on the subject would suggest that as time passed he should have received more cosponsors on his legislative proposals.

We analyzed Congressman Jackson's sponsorship and voting behavior by comparing his voting behavior with the average vote of the Black member of Congress who belonged to the different phases of Black political leadership mentioned earlier. We collected the bill cosponsorship data using the Library of Congress online database. We focused on the 108th, 109th, and 110th Congresses. Thus, we could trace any changes in Congressman Jackson's cosponsorship patterns as a result of Democrats taking control of Congress in 2007 (110th Congress).

We also collected roll call data for the 110th Congress and early 2009 (111th Congress). We used Keith T. Poole's NOMINATE data to compare Jackson Jr.'s liberal voting record with the voting records of members of Congress from each of the different phases of Black leadership. Using this data we averaged the NOMINATE scores by the number of U.S. Representatives in the different phases. We use the first dimension NOMINATE scores, which is appropriate for measuring members of Congress along the liberal–conservative continuum. By using the first dimension scores, we are able to capture the ideological location of the legislators' voting patterns (Poole and Rosenthal 1991). In order ascertain the liberal ideology of each member we adjusted the NOMINATE scores by multiplying them by -1; this way, positive scores will indicate liberal ideology, and negative scores will indicate conservative ideology. This enabled us to more easily interpret the location of each phase of leader on the liberal–conservative continuum, since the score is not an individual score but an average of the group's score. Thus, we are comparing each phase's placement on the liberal–conservative continuum and Jackson's placement on the same continuum.

Jackson Jr. has sponsored legislation in each of the congresses in which he has served except for the 104th Congress, which was the first Congress in which he served after his special election. According to Jackson Jr., he spent much of his time in the 104th Congress becoming familiar with how Congress works. Because he entered Congress midterm, he did not have the benefit of going through orientation like other newly elected members (Jackson and Watkins 2001, 20).

If we look at the percentages of new legislation submitted by Jackson Jr. over time, we notice find a marked decline in the amount of new legislation he proposed. For instance, during the 106th Congress, 82 percent of the Bills sponsored by Jackson Jr. were new (i.e., legislation he proposed for the first time). Jackson has not sponsored that much new legislation since. For instance, only 46 percent of Jackson-sponsored legislation in the 107th Congress was new. Thirty percent of Jackson-sponsored legislation in the 108th Congress was new. Only 18 percent of Jackson's sponsored legislation in the 109th Congress was new. In the 110th Congress, Jackson increased his new sponsorship: 50 percent of the legislation he sponsored that session was new. The increase in new bill sponsorship is most likely the result of the fact that Democrats took control of the House of Representatives in the 110th Congress.

Jackson has sponsored less new legislation over time in part because he resubmits legislation that does not pass in one congress in subsequent congresses. For instance, Congressman Jackson has repeatedly proposed eight constitutional amendments, which if ratified would guarantee rights to education, healthcare, and a healthy environment, among other things, since the 107th Congress. Jackson indicates that he proposes these amendments repeatedly because he believes that these amendments are necessary. The substance of these amendments are consistent with the universalist, progressive policy bent that he articulates in his book, *A More Perfect Union: Advancing New American Rights* (2001) (For a full list of legislation that Jackson Jr. has submitted more than once, see appendix 4.2 at the end of this chapter.)

As noted earlier, the number of cosponsors that a member of Congress can recruit does signal a member's standing among his or her colleagues. Individuals perceived as serious legislators should have more cosponsors (Fowler 2006). If we look at the eight constitutional amendments that Jackson has repeatedly submitted, we find that the number of cosponsors has increased over time. This suggests that Jackson Jr. has gained recognition and respect among his legislative counterparts. This is further evidenced by the tremendous increase in his cosponsorship activity on other bills. In Table 4.2 you can see that his cosponsorship activity has increased in every Congress from a low of 258 cosponsors in the 105th Congress (his first full Congress), to 473 in the 110th Congress. So while Jackson solo-sponsored a number of bills, one could argue that his institutional prestige and his willingness to work with others have increased dramatically over time.

Since joining Congress, Jackson has only been able to pass two bills. Both of these bills were symbolic in nature. As Canon (1999) notes, it is oftentimes much easier for members of Congress to get symbolic legislation passed (i.e., naming a post office after someone or some other gesture that does not impose real costs, benefits, regulations on affected parties). He further notes that it is much harder to get cosponsors and pass legislation that has substantive policy implications because it could have serious repercussions for those who sign on as cosponsors. Hence, this explanation could potentially explain why Jackson Jr. has yet to pass any of his substantive legislative proposals. At first glance, Jackson's bill

Table 4.2 Jesse Jackson Jr.'s Bill Sponsorship from the 104th to 110th Congress

Congress	# Bills Where Jackson Was Main Sponsor	# Bills Where Jackson Was Cosponsor	# Jackson Bills Enacted
104th	0	76	0
105th	2	258	0
106th	23	267	0
107th	13	319	0
108th	10	324	0
109th	11	338	1
110th	18	473	1

Source: http//www.Thomas.loc.gov/.

passage rate seems very small, especially for a six-term Congressman. However, it is important to note that minority legislators are less likely than their majority counterparts to have legislation enacted. This point is further evidenced by the results for other African-American congresspersons elected between 1994 and 1998. These nine members passed, on average, 1.77 bills—two members, Danny Davis (D-IL) and Shelia Jackson Lee (D-TX) passed six and five bills respectively. So, Jackson's bill passage rate is slightly above average. It is also important to note that during much of this time the Democrats were the minority party in the House. This would have made it more difficult for a Democrat like Jackson to propose and pass legislation.

Old Generation, New Generation, or "The Bridge"?

One of the ways to get a better insight on Jackson's place among the three phases of Black leadership is to analyze his cosponsorship relationships with Black legislators of all generations. By examining Jackson's cosponsorship relationships, we can determine Jackson's position in the evolving Black political continuum. We track Jackson Jr.'s cosponsorship by simply counting the number of legislative proposals that he cosponsored with other Black members of Congress. We then break this down to reflect the amount of legislation that he cosponsored with members of each distinct phase of Black congress members.

We record Jackson's cosponsorship record with fellow Black legislators in Table 4.3. It is important to note that we start our analysis with the 108th Congress because it is the first to have a critical mass of Phase III Black members of Congress. At a first glance, it would appear that Jackson cosponsors a lot more legislation with more seasoned legislators. Nearly 15% of Jackson's cosponsorship over the three Congresses is with Phase I members of Congress. Nearly 10% of his cosponsorship in the 108th and 109th Congresses was with Phase II members of Congress, and this percentage increases to 13% in the 110th Congress. Jackson's cosponsorship with four legislators in particular seems to be driving this trend: John Conyers (D-MI), John Lewis (D-GA), Barbara Lee (D-CA) and Donald Payne (D-NJ). It would appear that Jackson is clearly connecting himself to experienced and influential members of Congress. This finding supports Fowler's (2006) assertions that cosponsorship networks are an important form of social connectedness. Compared to Phase I, Jackson cosponsored relatively little legislation with Phase III Black members of Congress. Less than 4% of Jackson's cosponsors were Phase III Black members of Congress. Here, we must offer a caveat. There were no more than 5 other Phase III members of Congress serving at one time over this time period (This includes Laura Richardson (D-CA), Yvette Clarke (D-NY), Harold Ford (D-TN), Keith Ellison (D-MN), Artur Davis (D-LA), and Kendrick Meek (D-FL), who neither served together nor necessarily served in all three sessions). Hence, our findings may have more to do with the size of the group than Jackson's unwillingness to cosponsor legislation with certain colleagues. This seems to be at least a plausible explanation when we consider that half of Jackson's cosponsorships with Phase III members are with

Table 4.3 Percentage of Jesse Jackson's Co-Sponsored Legislation with Black Congress Members

Congress	Phase 1	Phase 2	Phase 3
108th	14.2	9.9	.003
109th	13.6	9.5	.009
110th	13.7	13.3	1.6

Source: http//www.Thomas.loc.gov/.

Rep. Keith Ellison (D-MN). That Jackson sponsors so much with Phase I and II legislators is not surprising given that they are the more numerous groups, have more legislative experience and more power. The more important thing to note from Table 4.3 is that Jackson does cosponsor legislation with his younger colleagues and that his cosponsorship with his generational peers increases over the three Congresses that we examine. Hence, it would appear that Jackson is more than willing to cosponsor legislation with all types of Black legislators, which in effect does seem to support the notion that Jackson is a more pragmatic legislator who tries to serve as a bridge between generations and political styles.

However, this conclusion is not supported by the findings in Figure 4.1. In Figure 4.1, we use the same groups and compare them with Jackson Jr.'s ideological positioning on the liberal–conservative continuum. The results indicate that Jackson Jr. is more liberal than any of the combined average scores of Black members of Congress in all three phases. When you take a closer look at the three phases, they actually go in the expected direction: Phase I is the most liberal, with Phases II and III being ideologically similar and more conservative than Phase I.

These findings may seem to be in conflict with each other to a certain degree. However, in many ways, these findings reflect the challenges that a political heir like Jackson faces. Jackson's liberal voting record reflects the enduring connection to his father and his close ties to legislators who sympathize with his father's political views, while his increasing willingness to cosponsor with members of his cohort reflects his simultaneous orientation to his younger colleagues.

Playing Politics with Peotone

The advocacy of a third major airport for the Chicago Metro Area has been the most prominent issue for Jackson during his tenure in the U.S. Congress. Since 1994, Jackson has been the most prominent advocate of building a third major airport for the Chicago metropolitan area. He also helped to organize the Abraham Lincoln National Airport Commission. According to Jackson, the creation of a third airport would bring some equality to what he calls an unequal distribution of economic disparity between the southern part of the Chicago metropolitan area and the rest of the city. In Jackson's estimation, this airport could provide jobs for residents of the southern suburbs of Chicago (Rhodes 2005).

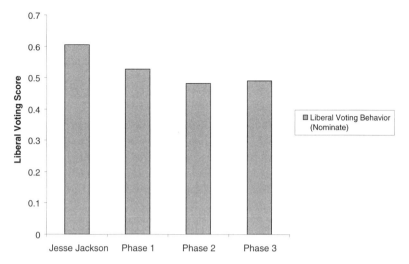

Figure 4.1 Ideological placement of the three phases and Rep. Jackson in the 110th Congress. *Source:* http://voteview.com/dwnl.htm

The following statement, taken from the congressman's Web site, highlights his position on the issue:

> To be built through a public-private partnership, Lincoln National Airport brings together the best of both worlds—private financing and efficiencies, with public governance and accountability. Using only private dollars and posing no cost or risk to taxpayers, Lincoln National Airport is the quickest, cheapest, safest and cleanest way to expand aviation capacity in the State.

> The development partners, LCOR/SNC-Lavalin Joint Venture, have successfully built airports around the world under this model. They, along with the local Abraham Lincoln National Airport Commission, have designed the first airport in the US specifically "priced" to attract low-cost carriers. For the Southland, the Lincoln Airport creates tens of thousands of new jobs, builds a stronger tax base, and provides sound economic development for a generation and beyond" ("Abraham Lincoln National Airport" 2009).

Jackson's support for this airport has put him at odds with longtime Chicago Mayor Richard M. Daley. Daley strongly opposes the development of another major airport because of the potential threat of moving jobs outside the metro area and hampering the expansion of O'Hare International Airport. In Jackson's view, though, Daley opposes the airport because he would be unable to use jobs at the suburban airport as patronage. To Jackson, it is unacceptable to deny southern suburban residents jobs because of petty political considerations (Rhodes 2005).

Mayor Daley's opposition to the airport forced Jackson to develop political relationships outside of the traditional Chicago Democratic machine. He formed unlikely alliances with former Illinois Governors Jim Edgar, George Ryan, and Rod Blagojevich (two Republicans and a Democrat), who supported the idea of a third airport. Because of state support for the airport, the Federal Aviation Administration has begun to review proposals for this new airport (Rhodes 2005).

Jackson's advocacy for a third major airport in Chicago highlights his embrace of universally framed, non-racial issues that appeal to non-Blacks. In this respect, Jackson more closely resembles his more deracialized Phase III Black political peers. However, even in this advocacy, it is clear that Jackson views these issues through a civil rights lens. When asked about the role of race in his pushing for the airport in Peotone, Jackson Jr. stated emphatically:

> The reason people don't identify me as a race leader is no one in Chicago can say that I've interpreted this issue in racial terms…. The airport discussion has been conducted on the plane of economic equality in the south suburbs and the north suburbs. (Mitchell 2006)

Even when Jackson is clearly advocating for all of his constituents, he still pushes a form of progressivism that is commonly associated with Civil Rights generation politics.

Jackson Jr. and the "New" Black Politics

The current state of African-American politics in the United States is not an unexpected development. The differences among the three distinct phases of African-American political leaders can be seen in more areas than just politics. However, the potential impact of what it means politically has been heightened by the recent electoral successes of post-Civil Rights politicians. This is important because this divide can be identified as a philosophical difference between elected officials representing the Civil Rights generation and their younger counterparts who came of age after the Civil Rights struggle. According to a story in the *New York Times* by Matt Bai:

> This newly emerging class of Black politicians, however, men (and a few women) closer in age to Obama and Jackson Jr., seek a broader political belief. Comfortable inside the establishment, bred at universities rather than seminaries, they are just as likely to see themselves as ambassadors to the Black community as they are to see themselves as spokesmen for it, which often means extolling middle-class values in urban neighborhoods….
> Their ambitions range well beyond safely Black seats (sic). (Bai 2008)

While Bai characterizes Jackson and Obama as being symbols of the new Black politicians, Jackson isn't as quick to align himself completely with either of the aforementioned groups. In an interview with NPR, Jackson noted that he and Barack Obama were similar in some ways, being "the first two guys in Chicago who kind of broke the mold" (Cornish 2008). However, he was also clear that there are differences between him and the president. When asked about whether there were two distinct generations of Black leadership, Jackson acknowledged the difference, but asserted that he was the mediator between the old and new generations of Black leadership. He asserted, "I am the bridge, in fact. My biggest concern is that I may be the only bridge between a new generation of young African-American politicians and those who have historically fought to make this possible" (Cornish 2008).

Jackson's statement highlights the ideological and stylistic diversity within the cohort of Phase III Black politicians. As discussed in chapter 1, much of the popular attention on young Black leaders focuses on those leaders with stellar academic credentials who burst onto the national scene in the past decade without prior connections to the Black political establishment. Politicians like Jesse Jackson Jr., who have strong ties to the Black political establishment because of their family connections, are also full-fledged members of this cohort. Their experiences and connections provide them with a different perspective on Black politics and inform their role as the stylistic bridge between the older generations and the new generation.

As a young Congressman, Jackson proposed a more race-conscious, progressive politics. In his book, *A More Perfect Union,* Jackson makes a strong appeal for progressive African-American candidates. It is clear in the book that progressive doesn't necessarily mean a deracialized candidate in the traditional sense. For instance, Jackson was extremely critical of Doug Wilder's deracialized campaign strategy when he explored a presidential bid in 1992. Jackson believed that the strategy essentially rendered Wilder, the candidate of the White establishment, and he asserted that this in part led to the early demise of his campaign. As an alternative, Jackson highlights two examples of progressive Black candidates: his father, who clearly uses race as one of his platforms in addressing larger issues; and Congressman Mel Watt (D-NC). He argues that Watt would have been the best choice for vice president on the Democratic ticket with Al Gore in 2000. Jackson Jr. noted that Watt was "elected in a majority-White congressional district, so I know he could have attracted White southern voters. He is a Constitutional expert who serves on the House Judiciary Committee" (Jackson and Watkins 2001, 460). While Jackson acknowledged that there would have been a White backlash against having an African American on the national ticket in 2000, he believed that this would be countered by the massive registration turnout of new voters. He points to his father's 1988 campaign for president as an example of how it would be possible to have a progressive Black candidate on the Democratic ticket and still win elections (Jackson and Watkins 2001, 456–60).

Clearly, Jackson's ideas about deracialization have evolved since writing *A More Perfect Union.* Jackson strongly supported Barack Obama during his presidential campaign (serving as National Campaign Co-chair); even though Obama ran a deracialized campaign, and Jackson publicly sparred with his father about whether Obama was being authentic in his understanding or approach to "Black issues." Jackson Sr. admonished Obama for not taking an active role in the Jena Six controversy and for talking down to African-American fathers. Most famously, Jackson Sr. was caught on tape (and a live microphone) discussing his desire to castrate Obama for talking down to Black people during a taping break at Fox News ("Jackson Apologizes" 2008). This situation afforded the younger Jackson the opportunity to distinguish himself politically from this father. In response to his father's faux pas, Jackson Jr. said:

> I am deeply outraged and disappointed in Reverend Jackson's reckless statements about Senator Barack Obama. His divisive and demeaning comments about the presumptive Democratic nominee and I believe the next president of the United States contradicts his inspiring and courageous career. ("Jackson Apologizes" 2008)

Conclusion

Jesse Jackson Jr. has had to deal with the reality of being the son of and bearing the name of one of the most polarizing forces in American politics in recent memory. Many people use the adage "it's not what you know but who you know" to describe the current political climate in U.S. politics. It is important to note, as Jackson Jr. has often pointed out, that "I inherited both his friends (in referring to his father) and his detractors, neither of whom I have earned" (Jackson 2001, 21).

While Jackson had a built-in advantage of name recognition in his initial election to Congress, he has since tried to develop a separate image. Jackson Jr. has not just been an extension of his father, and it would appear that he is determined to leave his own mark on politics. This is evident in his seemingly endless pursuit of other offices. For example, in 2006, when it was believed that Mayor Richard Daley was not going to seek reelection, he openly flirted with the idea of running for Mayor of Chicago. When asked about the potential vacancy in the Senate if Barack Obama won the presidency he stated pragmatically that "I wouldn't say no if asked…. There are no African-Americans in the United States Senate should Barack leave it" (Pearson 2008). Furthermore, it would appear that politics have become the full time profession of the family now that Jackson's wife Sandi serves on the Chicago City Council (Zimmerman 2006).

Jackson Jr.'s statement that he "wouldn't say no if asked" left some skeptical about his involvement in the indictment of former Governor Rod Blagojevich on a myriad of charges, one of which was his alleged attempt to sell Barack Obama's Senate seat. Shortly after Blagojevich was arrested, rumors began to surface that Jackson Jr. was one of the people willing to "buy" the Senate seat. In response to these rumors Jackson Jr. issued the following statement. "I reject and denounce pay-to-play politics and have no involvement whatsoever in any wrongdoing. I won't hesitate to cooperate fully and completely with the federal government's investigation" ("Jackson Responds to Rumors" 2008).

The story became more convoluted when the press began to suggest that Jackson Jr. was the infamous Senate candidate number 5 that was referred to in the federal wire tap. In that wire tap, it was suggested that people representing candidate 5 were willing to raise as much as $5 million for an appointment to the Senate seat (Saulny and Drew 2009). Jackson Jr. has steadfastly denied any wrong doing and indicated recently that he was an informant to federal authorities about Blagojevich's attempts to shakedown people attempting to do business in Illinois. Jackson Jr. stated that:

> "I have worked with four governors (including newly installed Gov. Patrick Quinn)," Jackson said. "It wasn't until I came into contact with the Blagojevich administration that they sought to shake down the developers. Their behavior was so unacceptable to me that I took that information to the U.S. Attorney because how can we build our state if every time someone wants to invest and create jobs, they have to go through a political gauntlet of 'gimme, gimme, gimme'?" (McQueary 2009)

While no formal charges were brought against Jackson Jr., many in political circles are suggesting that the implication of wrong doing has done a lot to tarnish his image. Most argue that at the very least he has lost his opportunity to win a statewide election (Saulny and Drew 2009). Given the recent turn of events, it would appear for now that Jackson Jr.'s political ambitions may begin and end with his election to the U.S. House of Representatives.

Jackson's own political philosophy and agenda came to the forefront most recently in his scathing criticism of his father's remarks about Barack Obama during the 2008 presidential election. There are clear philosophical differences between father and son. Jackson Jr. has separated himself from the rhetorical race-based politics of his father and the Civil Rights generation and embraced a more nuanced, pragmatic view of the role of race in politics that approximates his more deracialized generational peers. However, Jackson's more nuanced view of politics is clearly informed by his experiences of having been socialized in Civil Rights Movement circles. This has led to Jackson developing a synchretic political worldview where race is minimized but not completely ignored. Occasionally, this worldview has at times put him at odds with Black politicians in all three phases.

Jackson maintains that he is the link between all the generational and stylistic camps of Black politicians. In examining his legislative record, advocacy on behalf of his constituents and his rhetoric, we would agree with this claim. Jackson clearly is not an extension of his father, nor is he a clone of Barack Obama. He is a pragmatic politician who has been deeply influenced by his father. This influence, coupled with skill and an evolving racial and political landscape, has in some ways made him a uniquely compelling figure even in light of the Blagojevich scandal.

Appendix 4.1 Categorization of CBC Members by Phase, 110th–111th Congress

Phase I		
Corrine Brown	Bill Jefferson	Charles Rangel
Jim Clyburn	Carolyn Cheeks-Kilpatrick	Bobby Rush
John Conyers	Cynthia McKinney	Bennie Thompson
Elijah Cummings	Major Owens	Edolphus Towns
Danny Davis	Donald Payne	Maxine Waters
Alcee Hastings		
Phase II		
Sanford Bishop	Shelia Jackson Lee	Juanita Millender-
G. K. Butterfield	Eddie Bernice Johnson	McDonald
Julia Carson	Hank Johnson	Gwen Moore
William Lacy Clay	Barbara Lee	Bobby Scott
Emanuel Cleaver	John Lewis	David Scott
Al Green	Stephanie Tubbs Jones	Diane Watson
Chaka Fattah	Gregory Meeks	Mel Watt
		Albert Wynn
Phase III		
Yvette Clarke	Keith Ellison	Kendrick Meek
Artur Davis	Harold Ford, Jr.	Laura Richardson

Source: Authors' compilation

Appendix 4.2 Repeat Legislation by Jesse Jackson Jr.

1. H.CON.RES.263 : Expressing the sense of Congress that any Presidential candidate should be permitted to participate in debates among candidates if at least 5 percent of respondents in national public opinion polls of all eligible voters support the candidate's election for President or if a majority of respondents in such polls support the candidate's participation in such debates.
2. H.J.RES.28 : Proposing an amendment to the Constitution of the United States respecting the right to full employment and balanced growth.
3. H.J.RES.29 : Proposing an amendment to the Constitution of the United States regarding the right of citizens of the United States to health care of equal high quality.
4. H.J.RES.30 : Proposing an amendment to the Constitution of the United States respecting the right to decent, safe, sanitary, and affordable housing.
5. H.J.RES.31 : Proposing an amendment to the Constitution of the United States regarding the right of all citizens of the United States to a public education of equal high quality.
6. H.J.RES.32 : Proposing an amendment to the Constitution of the United States relating to equality of rights and reproductive rights.
7. H.J.RES.33 : Proposing an amendment to the Constitution of the United States respecting the right to a clean, safe, and sustainable environment.
8. H.J.RES.34 : Proposing an amendment to the Constitution of the United States relative to taxing the people of the United States progressively.
9. H.J.RES.72 : Proposing an amendment to the Constitution of the United States regarding the right to vote.
10. H.R.321 : To assure protection for the substantive due process rights of the innocent, by providing a temporary moratorium on carrying out of the death penalty to assure that persons able to prove their innocence are not executed.

11. H.R.1038 : To place a moratorium on executions by the Federal Government and urge the States to do the same, while a National Commission on the Death Penalty reviews the fairness of the imposition of the death penalty.
12. H.R.1290 : To amend title VII of the Civil Rights Act of 1964 to make such title fully applicable to the judicial branch of the Federal Government.
13. H.R.5293 : To require States to conduct general elections for Federal office using an instant runoff voting system, to direct the Election Assistance Commission to make grants to States to defray the costs of administering such systems, and for other purposes.
14. H.R.1048 : To amend title VII of the Civil Rights Act of 1964 to make such title fully applicable to the judicial branch of the Federal Government.
15. H.R.1429 : To establish a program under the Secretary of Housing and Urban Development to eliminate redlining in the insurance business. Cosponsors (27)

*The bill number corresponds with the first time the legislation was submitted by Jackson Jr. All bills were submitted at least twice with many of them being submitted four to five times.
Source: Library of Congress. n.d. THOMAS database. http//www.thomas.loc.gov/.

Notes

1. Jackson won his seat in a special election to replace Rep. Mel Reynolds, who was forced out of office after being convicted for having sex with an underage female campaign volunteer (Jackson 2001, 19).
2. Today, he is best known for being the legislative mentor of Barack Obama.

References

Abraham Lincoln National Airport. 2009. Representative Jesse Jackson Jr. website, http://jackson.house.gov/index.php?option=com_content&view=article&id=82&Itemid=78, (accessed August 20, 2009).
America Votes. 1996. Vol. 22. Washington, DC: CQ Press.
Bai, Matt. 2008. Is Obama the end of Black politics? *New York Times,* August 10. http://www.nytimes.com/2008/08/10/magazine/10politics-t.html.
Beck, Paul A., and M. Kent Jennings. 1991. Family traditions, political periods, and the development of partisan orientations. *Journal of Politics* 53 (August): 742–63.
Canon, David T. 1999. *Race, redistricting and representation: The unintended consequences of Black majority districts.* Chicago: University of Chicago Press.
Cornish, Audie. 2008. Jesse Jackson breaking the mold with Obama. NPR, *Morning Edition.* http://www.npr.org/templates/story/story.php?storyId=93970740 (accessed September 15, 2008).
Fowler, James H. 2006. Connecting the Congress: A study of cosponsorship networks. *Political Analysis* 14 (June): 456–87.
Hardy, Thomas. 1995a. Variety is theme in 2nd District—9 diverse hopefuls campaign to replace Reynolds. *Chicago Tribune,* November 26. http://infoweb.newsbank.com.
———. 1995b. Jackson dismisses youth issue—House hopeful says he's got connections. *Chicago Tribune,* November 20. http://infoweb.newsbank.com.
———. William Presecky. 1995. Win for both Jacksons—Son's victory gives dad's national coalition a voice in Congress—Landslide triumph in the 2nd District. *Chicago Tribune,* December 13. http://infoweb.newsbank.com.
Hawkesworth, Mary. 2003. Congressional enactments of race-gender: Toward a theory of race-gendered institutions. *American Political Science Review* 97: 529–55.

Hibbing, John R. 1991. *Congressional careers: Contours of life in the U.S. House of Representatives.* Chapel Hill: University of North Carolina Press.

Jackson apologizes for crude Obama remarks. 2008. http://www.cnn.com/2008/POLI-TICS/07/09/jesse.jackson.comment/ (accessed September 20, 2008).

Jackson, Jesse L. Jr. 2008. Congressman Jackson responds to rumors. http://www.jesse-jacksonjr.org/ (accessed April 17, 2009).

Jackson Responds To Rumors. 2008. http://jackson.house.gov/index.php?option=com_content&task=view&id=318&Itemid=86 (accessed August 20, 2009).

———. Frank Watkins. 2001. *A more perfect Union: Advancing new American rights.* New York: Welcome Rain.

———. 2009. Accomplishments. http://www.house.gov/jackson/AwardedGrants.shtml (accessed September 22, 2008).

Johnson, Dirk. 1998. Jesse Jackson Jr. is his father's son, but he reaches beyond the rainbow. *The New York Times*, March 3. http://www.nytimes.com/1998/03/03/us/jesse-jackson-Jr.-is-his-father-s-son-but-he-reaches-beyond-the-rainbow.html?sec=&spon=&pagewanted=all (accessed August 20, 2009).

Kokmen, Leyla, and William Presecky. 1995. 2nd District race bridges generations. *Chicago Tribune.* December 12. http://infoweb.newsbank.com.

Krutz, Glen S. 2005. Issues and institutions: Winnowing in the U.S. Congress. *American Journal of Political Science,* 49: 313–26.

Library of Congress. n.d. THOMAS database. http//www.thomas.loc.gov/.

McQueary, Kristen. 2009. Jackson Jr.: Blago was all about "gimme, gimme, gimme." *Southtown Star.* February 22. http://infoweb.newsbank.com (accessed April 17, 2009).

Miller-Rubin, Bonnie, and William Presecky. 1995. Time puts superficial focus in 2nd District—Integrity overrides candidates' issues. *Chicago Tribune,* December 11. http://infoweb.newsbank.com.

Mitchell, Mary. 2006. Dreaming big has Jackson Jr. sizing up possible mayoral run. *Chicago Sun-Times,* September 19. http://web.ebscohost.com.

Pearson, Rick. 2008. 5 Questions for Rep. Jesse Jackson Jr. *Chicago Tribune,* August 28. http://infoweb.newsbank.com.

Poole, Keith. n.d. Voteview website. http://voteview.com/dwnl.htm.

———. Howard Rosenthal. 1991. Patterns of congressional voting. *American Journal of Political Science* 35 (February): 228–78.

Puente, Teresa, and Patricia Callahan. 1995. 2nd District foes preach hope. *Chicago Tribune,* November 27. http://infoweb.newsbank.com.

Rhodes, Steve. 2005. What does junior want? *Chicago Magazine,* May. http://www.chicagomag.com/Chicago-Magazine/May-2005/What-Does-Junior-Want/ (accessed May 27, 2008).

Saulny, Susan, and Christopher Drew. 2009. Investigators take closer look at Rep. Jackson in Blagojevich case. http://www.nytimes.com/2009/04/14/us/politics/14jackson.html?ref=global-home (accessed April 18, 2009).

Simpson, Burney. 1996. How Jesse Jackson, Jr. combined new campaign techniques with old-fashioned Chicago-style voter contact. *Campaigns & Elections* June: 34–36.

Zimmerman, Stephanie. 2006. Jesse Jr.'s wife running for alderman. *Chicago Sun-Times,* December 19.

5 Hype, Hip-Hop, and Heartbreak
The Rise and Fall of Kwame Kilpatrick

Athena King, Todd Shaw, and Lester Spence

One of the reasons young Black political candidates have been so attractive in recent years is because of their success in projecting a racially moderate, reformist image. Younger Black politicians are often presented as the antidote to more controversial, racially strident figures of the Civil Rights Movement and to African-American political leaders who fell into ethical trouble. Somehow, these politicians convince voters and journalists that they are above race-baiting and beyond reproach.

Unfortunately, this generation of Black leadership is not immune from scandal. In 2008, Detroit Mayor Kwame Kilpatrick resigned his position after pleading guilty to perjury in an attempt to conceal an affair with his former chief of staff. How did this happen? Kilpatrick had been one of the nation's youngest mayors when he was elected in 2001—after an illustrious career in the Michigan House of Representatives. He had been heralded by the Democratic Leadership Council as one of its "Rising Stars." Kilpatrick, "the Hip Hop Mayor," had been the shining example of melding probusiness political savvy and keen street smarts. What happened?

Athena King, Todd Shaw, and Lester Spence trace the rise and fall of Kwame Kilpatrick. They examine Kilpatrick's attempt to marry a hip-hop sensibility to pragmatic politics. The union could have been politically electrifying, but without accountability, Kilpatrick lost control and eventually lost his career.

Introduction

> I want to tell you, Detroit, that you done set me up for a comeback.
> —Kwame Kilpatrick, September 4, 2008

In the summer of 2003, the Hip-Hop generation witnessed a unique political moment in Detroit, Michigan. Mayor Kwame Kilpatrick, who at age thirty-one was the youngest person ever elected to the office, made a cameo appearance in a video welcoming more than 90,000 Hip-Hop fans to an all-star concert. This event was held at the new Ford football stadium and hosted by the rapper Eminem, star of the Detroit-based movie *Eight Mile* (Watkins 2005). As the birthplace of

the Motown sound that inspired Black activism in the 1960s and 1970s, Detroit
was already known for its legendary ability to blend politics and popular culture
(Smith 1999). So, it is no surprise that it produced the first Black leader to don the
title of "Hip-Hop Mayor." Kilpatrick artfully employed the symbols and language
of Hip-Hop, his generation's culture, to convey ownership over the city's future
and to rebrand the image of Black politics in the post-Civil Rights era.

Among the many events celebrating Kilpatrick's inauguration in 2002 was a
party for Detroit youth at the Charles H. Wright Museum of African American
History (MAAH). Without question, it was a Detroit-style party. The best house
and Hip-Hop music DJs provided the sounds, and a variety of attires—from
"bright purple suits" and matching "gators" (alligator shoes) to throwback t-shirts
and jeans—provided the sights. Arriving fashionably late to his own party, Kilpatrick jumped on stage to accompany the "old school" rap star, Biz Markie, as
they led the crowd in reciting the lyrics to well-known songs. Unfortunately,
politics would ironically imitate art; two of Markie's songs foreshadowed the
mayor's actions and fortunes (Spence 2008). The song "Just a Friend" tells a classic story of romantic infidelity through the refrain: *"But you say he's just a friend."*
True to life, Kilpatrick's criminal conviction as well as political downfall all stem
from a perjury cover up of his extramarital affair with an executive aide. The song
entitled "The Vapors" tells a story of how a capricious fan base does not appreciate the quixotic fame many rap stars experience. Kilpatrick literally "caught the
vapors," for he fundamentally miscalculated how his tacit embrace of a gangsta/
playa persona (of many Hip-Hop locations) would invite public scrutiny not simply of his leadership ethics but his Black urban regime. Because Black politics
often concerns itself with questions of race and redistribution, it frequently touts
progressive social change (Shaw 2009). But true to the genius and contradictions
of Hip-Hop, Black politics is also integrally connected to the market, which
tends to dampen its progressive potential (Iton 2008).

The contentious "postracial" intersection we examine in this chapter is what
we call "Hip-Hop Black Politics"—a political juncture between the politics
of Hip-Hop, most especially the "gangsta/playa" spectacle, and the pragmatic
politics of the newest generation of Black mayors. Both dimensions are well-
represented in the political career of Kwame Kilpatrick, though we do not contend that Kilpatrick consciously embraced this spectacle. A legion of scholars and
commentators have adeptly examined the politics of Hip-Hop culture (Baldwin
2004; Boyd 2004; Bynoe 2004; Forman 2002; Johnson 2008; Lusane 2004;
Rose 1994a) and a smaller group has considered the recent forays Hip-Hop activists and moguls have made into electoral politics—from the National Hip-Hop
Activist Network to the exploits of Sean "Diddy" Combs and Russell Simmons
(Watkins 2005; Forman 2002; Kitwana 2002). However, the rise and fall of
Kilpatrick in Detroit provides us with a unique opportunity to understand how
the outcomes of Hip-Hop Black politics—from its progressive potential to its
retrograde contradictions—depend upon the ideological motives of its handlers
as they claim politically to *represent* the *'hood*—the Black poor and working class
communities (Forman 2002; Spence 2008).

We pursue this task by first examining the extant political and economic landscape in which Black urban politics resides in Detroit and elsewhere; we especially delineate the polarities of Black urban regimes. Next, we define the Hip-Hop generation leader and discuss how and why the competing valences of Hip-Hop Black politics—from grassroots progressivism to neoliberalism—exist as a precarious ideological nexus driven by the gangsta/playa ethic. In the fourth and largest section, we flush out that instability as exhibited by Kilpatrick's political biography and his administration and project him as the political equivalent of the "hip-hop bourgeoisie" such as Jay-Z, Biggie Smalls, and Lil' Kim (Baldwin 2004). All of them are (or were) capable of true genius but their gangsta/playa interpretations of power and "spectacular consumption" embroiled them in the nihilism of the market. In the conclusion, we consider the lessons the Detroit experience offers and how claims of a "postracial" Black politics are far too premature, even though it was not racism, per se, but rather Kilpatrick's gangsta/playa ethics, which complicated his regime designs and led to his undoing.

Black Regime Politics: From Neoliberalism to Progressivism

Before we discuss the unique nexus we call Hip-Hop Black politics, we must first present a conventional theory of when Black mayors and other elected officials are willing and able to serve the needs of the poor and working class. Urbanists have widely used regime theory to explain how city governments amass the political coalitions necessary to promote economic redevelopment and civic reform. Its proponents argue that the economic imperatives of a city often compel informal alliances between politicians, community leaders, and corporate powerbrokers who at their worst ignore or dislocate low-income communities (Elkin 1987; Stone 1989; Horan 1991; Ferman 1996). As opposed to those who argue that cities are simply held hostage to the national and international mobility of capital, these theorists assert that "politics matters" in determining the conditions under which governing coalitions are and are not formed. Until recently, however, the theory fell short in conceptualizing the responses of grassroots activists and the internal dynamics of race as well as African-American politics (Jennings 1992; Horan 2002; Shaw 2009). Although a plethora of regime typologies have emerged since the early 1980s, we simplify matters by discussing the two extreme poles of our continuum—the *neoliberal regime* and the *progressive regime*.

Inspired by the work of Friedrich Hayek and Milton Friedman, two conservative economists, neoliberalism is an alternative form of government that believes the allocational, redistributive, and regulatory functions of government must be conjoined with or shaped by the primacy of the market.[1] Hackworth reasons, "Neoliberalism, simply defined, is an ideological rejection of egalitarian liberalism in general and the Keynesian welfare state in particular...[G]overnment should be used only sparingly in very specific circumstances, rather than interfering within the marketplace" (Hackworth 2007a, 9). At the local level, Dreier, Mollenkopf, and Swanstrom label such governments as "urban conservative regimes" that believe, "Government should be run like a business instead of trying to make social change by targeting spending on minorities or poor neighborhoods. The only real solution to the problem of concentrated poverty is to cut the size and scope of government. This will free up the private sector to invest, so the benefits of private-sector growth will trickle down to the poor" (Dreier, Mollenkopf, and Swanson 2001, 164). In a similar vein, Spence adeptly summarizes the neoliberal regime's imperatives as it pursues this retrenchment,

> Programs to be rolled back are those programs that redistribute resources from those who are highly productive to those who are not. Public resources like housing, utilities, waste management, and education should be privatized. If constituency support for a given public good is too high to privatize that good outright, scale the public aspect of the good back gradually in order to provide the opportunity for a full roll back at a later date. Also rolled back are the various public protections that prevent the flexibility of capital. (Spence 2008, 12–13)

One of the more prominent examples of a neoliberal regime is the administration of former New York Mayor Rudolph Giuliani. He clashed with labor unions, minority constituencies, and various interest groups as he eliminated affirmative action programs, made social spending cuts, enlarged the police force, took on "quality of life" problems such as "homeless people and panhandling," and initially excluded key interests groups from the post 9/11 redevelopment of the World Trade Center site (Dreier et al. 2001, 166). Indeed, the neoliberal project has become such a dominant approach to governmental reform, since its initial inception by the "Reagan Revolution," that many left-of-center politicians from Bill Clinton and the "New Democrats" to Black mayors like Andrew Young in Atlanta or Dennis Archer in Detroit, have embraced its key tenets (Spence 2008; Shaw 2009).

Unlike the neoliberal regime, the *progressive regime* is more willing to balance the demands of monopoly capital with those of grassroots redistribution. Rosdil describes a "populist or progressive regime" as one that emphasizes "balanced economic growth" where: the benefits and costs of this growth are evenly dispersed; citizens are encouraged to substantively participate in the governance of the regime; and the "built environment" fosters "face-to-face interactions" and aesthetically pleasing arrangements of sustainable communities not spatially isolated residences of towering steel, concrete, and glass, or blight and pollution (Rosdil 1991, 78). Progressive regime theorists such as DeLeon, Clavel, and McGovern all assume that despite the overwhelming influence of structural and institutional factors in shaping a city's regime, it is vital to remember that ideational factors—ideologies, political cultures, values—prefigure political conflicts and thus influence how various actors employ structures and institutions in these conflicts. Characteristic of cities like San Francisco, Boston, Berkeley, or Santa Monica is that they are comprised of highly educated, affluent, mobile, and professional classes. Because the political economies of such cities are not held hostage to monopoly capital or at least a single industry, like oil in Houston or automobiles in Detroit, they arguably have the luxury of being liberal by tightly regulating the growth politics of businesses and firms readily competing to locate within their lucrative environs. At least that is the theory (Clavel and Wiewel 1991; DeLeon 1992; McGovern 1998).

Due to the vagaries of race, class, and economy, we students of the "Black Urban Regime" understand it as a governing formation at a complicated juncture that often swings between progressive policy goals and neoliberal outcomes (Bennett 1993; Banks 2000; Shaw and Spence 2004; Thompson 2006). In a very important essay, Reed identifies this dilemma as one in which the "upper-class bias" of Black elected officials often confounds their ability to be accountable to impoverished Black constituents. But he readily concedes, "The problem is not that Black regimes are led by inept, uncaring or mean-spirited elitists; in fact, Black elected officials tend to be somewhat more attentive and liberal than their White counterparts in their attitudes about social welfare issues" (Reed 1988, 161). To the contrary, Reed points out that, "The central contradiction facing the Black regime [is that] it is caught between the expectations of its principally Black electoral constituency, which implies downward redistribution, and those of its [White corporate] governing coalition, which converge around the use of public policy as a mechanism for upward redistribution" (161). Reed notes how the use of effective racial symbolism by a Black politician permits her or him to command Black constituent support while also making this politician "an especially attractive partner in the pro-growth coalition" (Reed 1988, 162). When Black elected leaders like Kilpatrick lead or participate in Black neoliberal regimes, especially during periods of economic decline, racial symbolism becomes their means to deflect attention away from some of the regime's more negative policy outcomes and to quell at least some of the more strident opposition from grassroots advocates. Akin to the troubled and brief career of rap legend Tupac (2Pac) Shakur—who left a profound poetry about racism, love, and ghetto struggles alongside tales of "thug life" misogyny and masculinist brutality (Dyson 2004b; Shakur 1999; Watts 2004)—Hip-Hop Black politics, like the Black urban regime, has the potential to greatly fluctuate between "positive rap" (progressivism) and "negative rap" (neoliberalism) and thus challenge or reinforce the dislocation of the '*hoods* they claim to *represent*. First we discuss the so-called "Hip-Hop generation" and its Black politics before delineating the aforementioned irony found in Kilpatrick's politics.

The Hip-Hop Generation Leader and Post-Civil Rights Era Black Politics

In the book *Deconstructing Tyrone*, Natalie Hopkinson and Natalie Y. Moore identified several characteristics of a Hip-Hop generation leader: mostly male, with a professional degree, middle-class, and members of political or clerical dynasties (usually "inheriting" political office from a parent or utilizing the parent's connections and stature to secure support in future elections) (Hopkinson and Moore 2006, 10). It is a definition with some problems, but we believe it to be largely useful. Along with Kilpatrick, other examples of the Hip-Hop generation leader include U.S. Rep. Jesse Jackson, Jr. (D-IL), Ras Baraka (former Newark City Councilman and son of poet/activist Amiri Baraka), and U.S. Representative Kendrick Meek (D-FL). However, Hip-Hop generation leaders also exist in other fields. With a middle-class upbringing and a father who took part in the Civil Rights Movement as a copastor with Martin Luther King, Sr., the Rev. Otis Moss III of the Trinity United Church of Christ in Chicago is also an exemplar (*Church History—Ebenezer Baptist Church, Atlanta, GA* n.d.).

All of these new leaders, part of a very powerful Black middle and upper class, have emerged and matured in this post-Civil Rights era, largely due to their easily receiving the baton of leadership. Politically, these leaders are relatively able to bridge the gap between race as well as generation. In turn, their success can imbue the younger generation with a newfound sense of purpose and the belief that one of their own will advance their agendas. For instance, the 2001 turnout of Detroit voters between the ages of 18 to 40 was 40 percent higher than the previous election, and this increase was squarely attributed to Kilpatrick's candidacy. Often, the younger generation (rightly) admonishes or castigates the older civil rights establishment for its myopia and failures, including the proliferation of drugs, gang violence, HIV/AIDS, and poverty, which all directly impact the well-being of the urban and rural Black poor (Gamboa 2004).

However, the Hip-Hop generation leader has a difficult and unique set of problems compared to other leaders. Bynoe (2004) highlights what we too see as a key shortcoming. For all of their populist rhetoric and well-meaning intentions, few of them pursue office with a plan for systematic change. In the worst cases, their careers are more helped by their pedigrees of high name value and recognition than their platforms. Thus, Bynoe believes the verdict is still out on this class. She urges newer generations of leadership to possess clear qualifications for political office, build constituencies across generations; to be clear about their relationship with the electorate; and to fully "understand the impact of race, class and age" on the opinions of potential voters (Bynoe 2004, 95). But we reiterate that Hip-Hop Black politics is a pendulum whose kinetics swing between regression and reform.

The Progressive Potential versus Neoliberal Contradictions of Hip-Hop Black Politics

At the heart of the dual potential that confronts Hip-Hop Black politics is the very same configuration of institutions that confound the Black urban regime— the market. The exemplary success of Hip-Hop moguls such as Russell Simmons or Sean "Diddy" Combs reinforces the conventional wisdom that Hip-Hop music and culture, what Kitwana calls a barometer for, "street culture, prison culture, and the new Black youth culture" (Kitwana 2004, 202), is a lucrative if not multibillion dollar industry (Forman 2002). Similar to Phase I Black mayors, however, who insisted upon the incorporation of African Americans into the city's corporate power structure, Lusane observes about Hip-Hop's ability to boldly speak truth to power: "The commodification [sic] of Black resistance is not the same as resistance to a society built upon commodification [sic]. Rap artists, even those who obtained some level of economic power and independence, are still slaves to a market system that requires an economic elite and mass deprivation" (Lusane 2004, 354). In concluding that Hip-Hop's organic Black brilliance has become a form of "Danceable Capitalism," Johnson agrees that the rap world depicted in most contemporary rap videos is a fiction where, "The artist is depicted as having total artistic control and the presence of a largely White corporate management is seldom seen" (D 1997; Johnson 2008, 88). Despite Hip-Hop's eclecticism, this market reality fueled an intense (if not overly simplistic) debate as to whether the "positivity" of rap's Afrocentric, Black nationalism wing—and thus all politically conscious rap—has been supplanted by the "negativity" of the "ghettocentric," realism wing of gangsta rap and its offspring (Baldwin 2004; Dyson 1996, 2004a; Johnson 2008). In fact, these intertwined wings have both exhibited the antiracist genius as well as neoliberal contradictions.

By the early 1990s, this Afrocentric/Black nationalist collectivity of Hip-Hop had appropriated the symbols and rhetoric of the 1960s Black Power and Soul Music era and what emerged was a wide range of groups, such as Public Enemy, Brand Nubian, X-Klan, and A Tribe Called Quest (Henderson 1996). While this wing was not solely responsible for the late 1990s climax of Black youth activism, they and their admirers were closely aligned with a number of campaigns: the Haitian refugee campaign, the defense of Mumia Abu-Jamal, and the various "Million Marches" (Kitwana 2002, 2004). Feminist critics challenged the patriarchy, racial essentialism, and homophobia of this wing, thus celebrating the rise of women rappers such as Queen Latifah and MC Lyte as well as other countervoices (Ransby and Matthews 1995; Rose 1994b). Boyd praised forward-thinking gender dynamics of the rap group Arrested Development. But because their song "Everyday People" demarcated the self-conscious "African" who must protect his "Black Queen" from rude, 40-ounce drinking "niggas," Boyd considers that, "an unconscious co-optation of regressive class politics" (Boyd 2004, 32). Taken to an extreme, such conclusions validate Bill Cosby's neoliberal implication that the ghetto poor are undeserving of social aid because their pathologies besmirch the Civil Rights Movement's bourgeois respectability (Dyson 2005). "But what happens," asks Baldwin, "when the nigga speaks back?" (Baldwin 2004, 165).

Among many other influences, gangsta rap (e.g., Junior MAFIA, The Firm, Roc-A-Fella—Rockerfeller Records, etc.) appropriated the 1970s "Blaxploitation" films and their valorization of the pimp/playa culture as part of the larger American fascination with gangsters. Lurid songs of ghetto life and pimping by Eazy-E, Too Short, the Geto Boys, Snoop Doggy Dogg, and others easily elicited opposition from what Black and White critics saw as virulent displays of brutality, materialism, and an oppressive machismo—take, for example, Dr. Dre's song, "Bitches Ain't Shit But Hoes and Tricks." Watts goes so far as to say gangsta rap, "constitutes some of the ugly and obscene excesses of pop culture constitutive of the mess we've gotten ourselves into…it poses as death-on-a-stick, a low-fat, low-calorie poison that is sure to satisfy anyone's 'appetite for destruction'" (Watts 2004, 602). Mindful of these contradictions, other cultural critics have at least partially defended gangsta rap, because of the trenchant critiques Ice Cube and many other gangsta rappers leveled at racism, poverty, and the prison-industrial complex (hooks 1994; Boyd 2004). Dyson reasoned that, "gangsta rap often reaches higher than its ugliest, lowest common denominator. Misogyny, violence, materialism, and sexual transgression are not its exclusive domain" but are reinforced by the gangsterism of the dominant White culture (Dyson 2004a, 416).

But what are the pitfalls of the gangsta/playa ideology as appropriated by Hip-Hop politicians like Kilpatrick when they sit at the helm of Black urban regimes? Baldwin asserts that Black "moral purists" are concerned with Gangsta rap partly because its adherents—Jay-Z, 'Lil Kim, Foxy Brown, Notorious B.I.G—unabashedly project a "Black good life" ethos that clashes with the respectability anxieties of the Afrocentric middle class or Civil Rights bourgeoisie: "[Gangsta/playas] have all the trappings of the middle and elite classes but wear Versace and Armani in a different way, drive their Bentleys to different places, and play out private inequalities in public arenas" (Baldwin 2004, 161). He points to the endpoint of the "spectacular consumption" they idealize:

> Hip Hop as a musical form could never follow the traditional association of commodification without cooptation, because the revolution of hip hop was fought out within the circuits of the market. These artists have begun to discover that a Black politics can also be organized within the processes of consumption. (Baldwin 2004, 161)

Thus this new generation of hustlers seeks to become new "playas" in the "game," and they, like Hip-Hop Black politicians, label all of detractors as "playa haters" who merely want to "stop Black progress" (Baldwin 2004, 161). However, we find Watts's conclusion telling, for the gangsta/playa is ultimately a neoliberal project; for it hyperidealizes the market, individual acquisition, and private power. Thus, in the most literal way, the "Hustler is ultimately consumed by his own spectacle:" Tupac is criminally convicted and then murdered; The Notorious B.I.G. is gunned down in front of a nightclub; Dr. Dre assaults a female DJ at a New York radio station (Watts 2004, 606). At the figurative level, the Hip-Hop Black politician who seeks progressive change through a neoliberal regime is defeated for, like the rap game, he can only "mediate argumentative tensions," and not transform the bitterly unequal "terms of exchange and interaction" (Watts 2004, 606, 607).

Below, we explain how Kilpatrick was "consumed by his own spectacle" as he attempted to project a new ethic of Hip-Hop leadership. In the end, his nonchalant embrace of the gangsta/playa ethic blinded him to how the race and regime "game" he was playing was untenable.

The Rise of Kilpatrick

Background and Premayoral Career

By the age of ten, Kwame Malik Kilpatrick knew he wanted to be in politics. After meeting Detroit's legendary first Black mayor, Coleman Young, Kilpatrick decided that one day, he would run for the same office. Born on June 8, 1970, in Detroit, Michigan and raised on the city's West Side, Kwame's aspirations were in no small way influenced by his very political family. His mother is Carolyn Cheeks Kilpatrick, the long time U.S. Representative from Michigan's 13th District. His mother's sister, Marsha G. Cheeks, is a Democrat and was a Michigan state representative from 2003 to 2008 ("Michigan Votes—The Honorable Marsha Cheeks" 2009). Kilpatrick's father, Bernard Nathaniel Kilpatrick (who is no longer married to Representative Cheeks Kilpatrick) served as Chief of Staff to former Wayne County Executive Edward H. McNamara. McNamara, a political kingpin in Michigan until his death in 2006, endorsed Kilpatrick's mayoral candidacy and played a central role in his initial campaign (Collins 2001). It has long been rumored in Detroit circles that McNamara cast a very long shadow over Kwame's career.

Kilpatrick was a bright, ambitious, popular, and athletic child. He attended Detroit's Pelham Middle School and later the elite Cass Technical High School (Cohen 2008). After graduating from high school in 1988, Kilpatrick attended Florida A&M University on a football scholarship. While at FAMU, he was named a football All-American in his senior year (1992) and pledged the Alpha Phi Alpha fraternity. In 1992, he graduated with a political science degree and a teaching certificate, although media accounts suggest the teaching certificate was never issued ("Kwame Kilpatrick—Mayor of Detroit," 2008). While taking a political science course at Florida A&M, Kilpatrick met the former Carlita Poles, whom he married in 1995. Their sons Jalil and Jelani were born in 1996, and their third son, Jonas, was born in 2001. After college, Kilpatrick stayed in Tallahassee to teach at Rickards High School. He then returned to Detroit's Marcus Garvey Academy to teach middle school, coach basketball, and serve as a mentor to students. During this time, he enrolled in the Michigan State University College of Law and graduated in 1996. He was admitted to the Michigan Bar in 2000 ("Kwame M. Kilpatrick—P60494" 2008).

When his mother vacated her Michigan House seat in 1996 to run for Congress, Kilpatrick successfully ran for it at the age of twenty-five. In 1998, he won reelection against Republican challenger Kimberly Carter and won by more than 15,000 votes (Michigan Secretary of State 2008). At the age of thirty, he was named Minority Leader of the Michigan House—the youngest individual and the first African American to lead either party in the Michigan State Legislature ("About the Mayor: Kwame M. Kilpatrick—Mayor, City of Detroit" 2008). While a member of the House, Kilpatrick claimed partial or full credit for many pieces of legislation: (1) the creation of a new Detroit area regional transportation authority; (2) the creation of the Tax Reverted Clean Title Act program, to benefit local governments; (3) the appropriation of $1 million to tear down dangerous abandoned buildings in Detroit; (4) and the requirement that the Department of Transportation spend $1.5 million for preliminary "community outreach" and engineering studies of a Lansing to Detroit rail passenger service ("Kwame Kilpatrick (D). Bills Introduced… 2008). However, his legislative career was not without controversy. He steered state grants to two Detroit nonprofit agencies run by friends. In turn, these agencies directed the funds to U.N.I.T.E. Co. Inc., a nonprofit organization created and incorporated by Kilpatrick's wife Carlita in 2000 shortly after the first disbursement was made (Dawson, Schaefer, and Elrick 2008). While this action was legal, it hinted at the opaque dealings that became all too permissible later in Kilpatrick's career.

The First and Second Mayoral Campaigns: Overview of the Spectacle and the Regime

In April 2001, Detroit Mayor Dennis Archer abruptly decided not to run for reelection. Archer had served since the retirement of Coleman Young in 1993 and led the aggressive economic revitalization of downtown, despite occasional grassroots opposition. In the wake of this announcement, Kilpatrick decided to pursue his long-held dream of becoming mayor (Shaw 2009; Bradsher 2001). After declaring he was "on a mission from God," Kilpatrick formally announced his candidacy for mayor in May 2001 from his family's front porch (Collins 2001). While his age was regarded as his biggest impediment, Kilpatrick joined a crowded field of twenty-one other candidates and trailed them all until the September 11, 2001 primary. Until this time, the favored candidate was the popular Detroit City Council President Gil Hill, a former Detroit police officer featured in Eddie Murphy's first *Beverly Hills Cop* movie. The battle between these two men became a confrontation between the older, civil rights generation and Kilpatrick's Hip-Hop generation (Spence 2008; Watkins 2005). By erecting an electoral coalition that included the business community and labor, Kilpatrick won the city's nonpartisan primary with 50.2 percent of the vote to Hill's 34.4 percent ("2001 Newsmaker of the Year" 2002). The two top vote-getters (Kilpatrick and Hill) would move on to face each other in the general election. From the primary until the election, the two candidates were in a statistical dead heat. However, Kilpatrick won the election in November 2001 with 54 percent of the vote ("Detroit Mayor: Kilpatrick the City's Youngest Mayor Ever" 2005).

In 2005, Kilpatrick chose to run again and emphasized his accomplishments over the first term as a justification for his run. There were many governance initiatives for which he claimed credit. He began a $500-million redevelopment of land along the Detroit River (Carr 2002); kept the peace during a three-day, city-wide blackout in 2003 ("Detroit Mayor '05: Kilpatrick Basks…" 2005); initiated the first phase of a Detroit-area industrial park which would bring in at least 275 new jobs (Gallagher 2004); and took an active role in attempting to end state oversight of the city's school district, thus restoring it to the hands of city leaders ("Michigan: Back to the Blackboard" 2003). There were, nonetheless, the myriad problems confronted by the city at the end of his first term that

Table 5.1 Detroit Population and Economic Changes

	1990	*2000*	*2006*
Total Population	1,027,974	951, 270	—
% Black	75.7	81.6	83.1
% White	21.6	12.3	10.0
Median Household Income (inflation-adjusted for 1989)	$18,742	$21,976	$21,111
% Bachelor's Degree	9.6	11.0	11.3
% Individuals below poverty level	31.2	26.1	32.5
% Vacant Housing Units	8.7	10.3	23.0

Source: US Census Bureau (1990, 2000, and 2006 American Community Survey).

speak directly to Kilpatrick's problematic governance ethic as combined with his neoliberal policy solutions.

Table 5.1 reveals that during Kilpatrick's first term, Detroit, an already impoverished city, continued to flounder economically. The city's newest "urban crisis" led to reduced incomes (which were already low), continued exodus from the city, higher poverty, and increased home vacancy, just to name a few indicators. The Archer administration left Kilpatrick with a $69 million deficit; two governors withheld state revenues; and tax collection receipts continued to sag, thus enlarging the budget shortfall to $389 million. As we will shortly discuss, the mayor proposed a series of belt-tightening measures to grapple with shortfall, including slashing the city workforce by 25 percent (more than 4,000 jobs), demanding various rate increases for city services, and proposing aggressive privatization schemes (Spence 2008; Bello 2005).

While demanding these belt-tightening measures, however, Kilpatrick personally assumed a Hip-Hop bourgeoisie lifestyle and charged approximately $210,000 (most of it for travel, meals, alcohol, and entertainment) on a city-issued credit card ("Detroit Mayor Criticized…" 2005). In addition, Kilpatrick signed a two-year lease for a cherry-red Lincoln Navigator for his wife to drive at the cost of $24,995. Any city purchase that exceeded $25,000 had to be approved by council; anything below that amount can be purchased by city officials without council approval. By leasing the Navigator at $24,995, Kilpatrick was able to acquire the vehicle without approaching the council for permission to do so ("Plagued by Scandal…" 2005). In a peremptory move, when he was challenged on such expenditures, he removed the head of internal affairs for "conducting unauthorized investigations," thus prompting an unlawful termination lawsuit (Fowler 2004). Because of these scandals, *Time* magazine dubbed Kilpatrick one of America's worst mayors ("Time Magazine Lists…" 2005).

Consequently, the 2005 mayoral race produced a crowded field. Foremost among the eleven challengers was Freman Hendrix, a fellow Democrat and Dennis Archer's former deputy mayor. Hendrix held a strong fifteen-point advantage over Kilpatrick leading up to the primary ("Poll Shows Challenger Ahead in

Mayoral Race" 2005). In the August primary, Kilpatrick finished second to Hendrix, garnering 34 percent of the total vote to Hendrix's 44 percent ("Primary Results" 2005). This set the stage for a Kilpatrick/Hendrix showdown. Over the next two months, Hendrix emphasized Kilpatrick's scandals and inability to move the city of Detroit forward; Kilpatrick sought absolution for past mistakes from his fellow Detroiters. Surprisingly, Kilpatrick was the city's first incumbent mayor to come in second in a primary in over 50 years ("About the Mayor: Kwame M. Kilpatrick—Mayor, City of Detroit," 2008).

On Election Night, both camps initially claimed victory, even though pre-election polls predicted a Hendrix win ("Poll: Incumbent Kilpatrick Narrows…" 2005). By 3 a.m. the next morning, Kilpatrick was declared the winner with 53 percent of the vote to Hendrix's 47 percent, though a FBI investigation was opened to look "into vote irregularities, including claims of absentee ballots cast by the dead" ("Hendrix Takes Early Lead…" 2005). Kilpatrick's comeback can be partly attributed to his Black populist rhetoric, his apparent contrition for mistakes made in the first term (Slevin 2005), his ability to exacerbate tensions between the inner city and suburbs, and the leadership figure he struck during Rosa Parks' passing and funeral. Many citizens said those factors—most notably Kilpatrick's seemingly heartfelt tribute to Ms. Parks at her funeral—were enough to persuade them to give the young mayor another chance ("Kwame's Passion Pays Off…" 2005). Hendrix petitioned the Wayne County Board of Canvassers for a recount, which was granted (against Kilpatrick's objections). By December 29, 2005, Hendrix conceded the race to Kilpatrick after determining that a recount would not change the outcome ("Challenger Drops Request…" 2005). Kilpatrick was inaugurated for a second term in January 2006.

The Fall of Kilpatrick

Hip-Hop Mayor: The Gangsta/Playa Ethic and the Neoliberal Regime

When initially elected, Kilpatrick proudly assumed the accoutrements of his Hip-Hop bourgeoisie image complete with a large diamond earring, flashy, well-tailored suits and fedoras, frequent club-hopping with his entourage (even on Inauguration Night), and peppering his statements and grandiloquent speeches with rap lyrics and lingo (Gamboa 2004). He caught the eye of Hip-Hop royalty (including Detroit native son Eminem), and was given the "Hip-Hop Mayor" title by none other than Russell Simmons. Kilpatrick's speech, dress, and body language conveyed his connection to the Hip-Hop generation—from his chest bump greetings to his posting a Myspace page ("Kilpatrick, Kwame—Myspace" 2008). But it is also clear that at times Kilpatrick's political intuition and intelligence compelled him to temper this youthful flamboyance and gain the trust of city stakeholders. During each election, he distanced himself from his Hip-Hop moniker. In fact, he routinely removed his trademark earring after polling showed that women between the ages of 40 and 55 were turned off by it. But this was most likely a political calculation, because he resumed wearing it after each election ("Detroit Mayor Sheds Earring" 2005).

True to the "gangsta" image was Kilpatrick's overly large security posse—approximately twenty officers. In fact, Kilpatrick's security detail exceeded that of mayors of cities much larger than Detroit ("Kwame Kilpatrick/Detroit" 2005). It accompanied Kilpatrick everywhere, and its members were accused of threatening and intimidating people whose actions and words went against the "Kilpatrick grain" (i.e., appear to contradict Kilpatrick or otherwise cast him in a negative light) ("Kwame Kilpatrick/Detroit" 2005). For example, an investigative reporter for an ABC television affiliate accused a member of Kilpatrick's team of physical assault when the reporter asked questions in connection to the Navigator lease controversy (Hakim 2005). Furthermore, a May 2008 news story reported that there were at least twenty-nine friends and family members employed in the Kilpatrick administration, some of whom were discovered to have lied on their resumes about college credentials. While it is common for elected officials to distribute patronage among friends, family, and loyalists, Kilpatrick made more personal appointments than all other Detroit mayors combined since 1970; and none of these individuals were subjected to the massive across-the-board layoffs (approximately 4,000 employees) that took place in city government beginning in 2002, which included firefighters and nearly 1,000 police officers (Elrick, Schaefer, and Tanner 2008). In fact, individuals with personal connections to the mayor saw an average 36 percent increase in their salaries between 2002 and 2007, with some receiving as much as an 86 percent increase in salary during this time (Elrick et al. 2008). On the other hand, employees in other departments who received raises got 2 percent in 2003 and another 2 percent in 2004 (Elrick et al. 2008).

Regime Priorities and Fiscal Excesses

The implication of Kilpatrick being a "Hip-Hop Mayor" is that his administration would be in sync with grassroots constituencies and thus more likely to balance the imperatives of economic growth and large scale economic development with the needs of his most economically vulnerable constituencies—the proverbial 'hood. Like his predecessors Archer and to a lesser degree Young, Kilpatrick collaborated with and courted various corporate and financial sectors of Detroit. Thus he claimed several economic development successes, including an additional 500,000 square feet in office space; more than two dozen new downtown restaurants; a successful Super Bowl XL event; a new major league baseball stadium; downtown condominium construction; and three downtown casinos (Spence 2008). But as Spence notes, "This is neoliberal revitalization in a nutshell, representing an attempt to both increase Detroit's status as a unique place for tourism and entertainment, and to use innovative market driven approaches to garner revenue through trickle down effects...or through public–private deals" (Spence 2008, 21). There are many other ways Kilpatrick adopted neoliberal answers to the fiscal shortfalls the city experienced during his administration. But to give a few examples, he: (1) cut more than 5,000 city jobs (including police and firemen) or more than 25 percent of the workforce; (2) reduced the city payroll by

$270 million; privatized the Detroit Zoo and Detroit Historical Museum; (4) added a regressive trash pick-up fee of $300; and (5) increased bus fares while decreasing the number of routes (Spence 2008, 8–9).

To be sure, such decisions exhibit a certain level of fiscal pragmatism in the midst of the city's worsening fiscal state of affairs. But they also contradict any contention that a Hip-Hop mayor like Kilpatrick is what Thompson (2006) labels a "Third Wave," progressive mayor. Such leaders imaginatively defend the interests of the Black poor and other low-income Detroiters—that is, those most in need of such things as increased police protection, city employment, and low-priced bus fares—by ensuring that any necessary fiscal retrenchment does not fall most squarely upon their shoulders (Thompson 2006, 15–19). In a previous budget analysis where Spence compared the budget outlays of the Archer administration to that of the Kilpatrick administration, he found that on average, the Archer administration expended more than did its successor in areas of specific concern to youth—recreation, youth cultural affairs, communication and creative services, and the arts (Spence 2008, 23–27). If Spence's findings are still true, holding constant any fiscal resource differences between each period, then these findings point to the irony of Kilpatrick brandishing the Hip-Hop mayor image while not being fully in sync with the needs of youth—one of the most economically vulnerable groups in Detroit.

Table 5.2 further informs us of what the Kilpatrick regime considered its policy and fiscal priorities between the years of 2006 and 2007 as it tackled Detroit's larger economic problems, specifically housing poverty. This table does not map the intricacies of the policy deliberation process, but it gives us two broad indicators of the regime's policy stances. We see how the mayor and city council each prioritized funding for Community Development Block Grant (CDBG), funding to address problems confronting the poor and working class: that is, housing disrepair, social service needs, small business flight or commercial decline, homelessness, and the construction of affordable housing. In this regard, the city council felt at least $3.1 million more dollars (or 10 percent of the CDBG budget) should be expended in these areas than did the mayor (see all of the expenditure lines above the "Rehabilitation" category). Additionally, Table 5.2 shows that the Kilpatrick regime supported city-led versus community-based development activities. When it came to the expenditure of these funds, Kilpatrick's regime was less willing to funnel many of these dollars to community-based or "grassroots" organizations and their activities than was the city council; he instead wanted to spend more on city-directed activities. Like his predecessors, he may have been less concerned with partnering with grassroots development coalitions to bring about equitable growth than reserving his regime's ability to control and leverage these dollars with those already targeted at downtown and other major development areas (Shaw 2009).

Kilpatrick and his associates' perceived excesses further exacerbated budget disputes with the city council. For example, the mayor had the authority to bypass the Detroit Water Board and City Council on several contracts, including: (1) a $131 million radio system that would be used mostly by the Detroit

Table 5.2 Detroit Community Development Block Grant Budget Analysis, 2006–2007 FY

Community Based Organization Activities	Mayor's Rec	CC Final	Diff.
Minor Home Repair	$2,100,000	$3,431,843	+$1,331,843
Public Service	$4,146,000	$4,900,789	+$754,789
Economic Development Commercial	$440,800	$1,000,000	+$559,200
Matching Incentive Grants	$0	$300,000	+$300,000
Homeless Public Service	$1,233,575	$1,399,628	+$166,053
Rehabilitation	$100,000	$100,000	$0
Technical Assistance	$100,000	$100,000	$0
Public Improvements	$450,000	$150,000	-$300,000
New Housing Construction Public	$1,453,000	$915,003	-$537,997
Facility Rehabilitation (PFR)	$948,929	$180,215	-$768,714
CBO TOTAL	**$10,972,304**	**$12,477,478**	*$1,5,05,174*

City Activities	Mayor's Rec	CC Final	Diff.
Administration/Planning Staff	$8,097,136	$8,325,987	+$228,851
Technical Assistance Staff/Projects	$526,531	$691,531	+$165,000
Demolition-B&SE Staff	$7,243,775	$7,243,775	$0
Minor Home Repair-City	$4,750,000	$4,750,000	$0
Programs Home Repair Staff	$3,780,771	$3,780,771	$0
Acquisition-P&DD Staff	$354,776	$354,776	$0
PFR Technical Assistance Staff	$3,458,059	$3,456,449	-$1,610
Economic Development	$612,771	$568,000	-$44,771
Public Service-P&DD Staff	$430,462	$201,611	-$228,851
Public Improvements-City Projects	$550,000	$200,000	-$350,000
Section 108 Loan Repayments	$2,942,950	$1,669,157	-$1,273,793
CITY TOTAL	**$32,747,231**	**$31,242,057**	**-$1,505,174**

Source: Community Legal Resources. October 2006. Community Development Advocates of Detroit: Community Development Block Grant (CDBG) Briefing Paper. Detroit, MI, p. 14.

Police and Fire Departments; (2) a $21.3 million security upgrade performed by a company tied to the mayor's friend, Bobby Ferguson; and (3) a $38,000 no-bid public relations contract awarded to Bob Berg, the spokesman for Kilpatrick's reelection campaign. In 2006, a U.S. District Court judge ended the mayor's administrative authority when Kilpatrick sought to circumvent "the normal city charter process of approving city contracts and to approve $12 million in additional payments to DWSD contractors, including a $10,000 raise for the DWSD director." They were supposed to be paid to someone close to Kilpatrick (and, at the time, serving time in the county jail for assault). The Michigan State Senate passed a resolution affirming the judge's termination of Kilpatrick's administrative authority (Michigan State Senate 2005–2006).

Gangsta/Playa Excesses

To reiterate, it was not because Kilpatrick embraced the Hip-Hop mayor image, per se, that he had a personal and leadership style that racially rebuffed calls for policy responsiveness and personal accountability. We contend it was his choice to intersect the gangsta/playa dimension of Hip-Hop style with the neoliberal dimension of the Black urban regime that led to his whirlwind of personal and political misconduct. For example, station WXYZ-TV in Detroit discovered in 2007 that Kilpatrick borrowed nearly $9,000 from a civic fund to take his family and babysitter on a week-long vacation to a California resort and spa ("Steve Wilson Investigates…" 2007). Named the Kilpatrick Civic Fund, it was a tax-exempt, public service fund whose purpose was to "educate residents about voting; support crime prevention or economic empowerment and improve social welfare" ("Steve Wilson Investigates…" 2007). Kilpatrick responded to the discovery and subsequent questions by grabbing the microphone out of the hand of a reporter and throwing it against the wall in an on-camera fit of rage ("Steve Wilson Investigates…" 2007). Among the "urban legends" about the mayor's machinations were the rumors of a "wild party" (replete with exotic dancers) at the official residence, Manoogian Mansion. According to members of the mayor's detail, the mayor's wife later interrupted the party and attacked one of the dancers performing for the mayor ("Cox to Investigate…" 2008). While investigating abuses by the mayor's security detail (which included drunk driving, wrecking city-issued automobiles, and falsifying overtime records), members of the police internal affairs units also investigated the rumors surrounding the party ("Old Issues Arise…" 2007). To date, Kilpatrick has categorically denied that a party took place, yet the investigation led to the termination of two officers—Gary A. Brown, former head of Internal Affairs and Harold C. Nelthrope, a former Kilpatrick bodyguard. Shortly after the investigation, the exotic dancer alleged to have performed for the mayor, a 27-year-old by the name of Tamara Greene, was shot and killed in her car on April 30, 2003. Police Lieutenant Alvin Bowman investigated the murder and indicated that Ms. Greene was shot 18 times with .40 caliber bullets. The officer also suggested that the shooter was a member of the Detroit police force (LeDuff 2008).

The Final Straw: The Whistleblower Trial and Text Messaging Scandal

The act that ultimately brought down Kilpatrick's administration was the infamous whistleblower and text messaging scandal that led to his criminal perjury conviction. As mentioned earlier, Officers Brown and Nelthrope filed suit against the city for wrongful termination. In 2007, the two were originally awarded $6.5 million by the jury—$3.6 million to Brown and $2.9 million to Nelthrope, including interest, for four years ("Old Issues Arise…" 2007). However, the Detroit City Council agreed to pay $8.4 million to the two officers and a third officer, effectively increasing the amount of the settlement by nearly $2 million (Carney 2008). During the trial, Kilpatrick and Christine Beatty, the mayor's chief of staff, disavowed contentions that they were involved in an extramarital affair between 2002 and 2003 and likewise had conspired to fire Brown because of his investigation into the alleged Manoogian Mansion incident and murder of Tamara Greene. Prosecutorial discovery conducted during the trial exposed the existence of nearly 14,000 text messages that passed between the mayor and Beatty between September and October of 2002 as well as April and May of 2003. Many of these messages in fact provided evidence that the two were having an affair and planned to fire Brown ("SHOW: Detroit Mayor Kwame Kilpatrick Involved..."). Under the Freedom of Information Act, *The Detroit Free Press*, the *Detroit News*, and the city council sued, requesting the release of all settlement-related documents. It was later discovered that the mayor asked for an increased settlement as part of a confidentiality agreement signed by all parties to cover up the existence of the text messages, which would prove that Kilpatrick and Beatty perjured themselves during the trial (Schaefer and Elrick 2008).

After an investigation by Wayne County Prosecutor Kym Worthy, Kilpatrick and Beatty were charged with obstruction of justice, conspiracy, misconduct in office, and perjury. Kilpatrick and Beatty were arraigned on March 24, 2008 (Ashenfetter, Swickand, and Gorchow 2008). Overall, Kilpatrick was charged with eight felonies and Beatty with seven (Huleh 2008).

Kilpatrick resisted calls to step down from his office, despite the fact that he was the first sitting mayor of Detroit to be indicted ("Detroit Mayor Pleads..." 2008). In the wake of the budget deficit, heavy layoffs, and previous controversies, many citizens felt that a $9 million-plus judgment in the whistleblower trial was the tipping point. In February 2008, the Wayne County Election Commission approved a recall effort against Kilpatrick. Filed by Douglas Johnson, the recall wanted Kilpatrick removed based on the multimillion dollar settlement as well as the scandal involving the Lincoln Navigator and the city credit card abuse. However, the petition was challenged by the Kilpatrick legal team in March 2008 because Mr. Johnson was not an actual resident of Detroit ("Denial of Mayoral Recall..." 2008). Instead, Angelo Brown filed a second recall petition later that month and charged that Kilpatrick was too preoccupied with his legal problems to effectively govern the city. After revisions, the Election Commission approved the second petition ("Panel OKs Recall Language..." 2008).

In addition to the recall petition by private citizens, the council also took action. In March 2008, it passed a 7–1 nonbinding resolution asking Kilpatrick to resign as mayor. The resolution was essentially a vote of no-confidence. In addition, the council conferred with an attorney to determine the steps necessary to remove Kilpatrick from office should he fail to resign of his own volition (Blumer 2008). In May 2008, the council approved a two-pronged measure designed to strengthen its ability to remove Kilpatrick from office. In a 5-4 vote, it approved a request to ask Michigan Governor Jennifer Granholm to remove Kilpatrick from office. By the same margin, the council approved a measure to begin its own proceedings to oust the mayor. Finally, the council voted 7-2 to formally censure Kilpatrick. The removal process gave the council the power to establish a forfeiture hearing for June 2008 (later rescheduled to July 2008). This forfeiture hearing was a trial-like public proceeding where Kilpatrick and his legal counsel had the option to appear and defend him against the council's charges (Gorchow et al. 2008).

Though the two-pronged measure passed, the margin for passage was considerably smaller than the margin for asking Kilpatrick to resign. Three more council members—Monica Conyers, Martha Reeves, and Barbara-Rose Collins—joined together to oppose any dismissal measures against the mayor and emerged as Kilpatrick's most vociferous supporters.[2] In June 2008, the three council members signed a letter drafted and sent to Governor Granholm articulating their solidarity in opposition to the forfeiture hearings. They also requested that Granholm refrain from participating in the removal process and insisted that they were not deceived by Kilpatrick into approving the $8.4 million settlement in the whistleblower case (MacDonald and Josar 2008). The governor decided that the state would remain neutral until the council exhausted all remedies available for it to remove Kilpatrick from office.

In January 2008, Kilpatrick admitted his indiscretions with Christine Beatty in a televised speech and apologized to Detroit's citizens. Still, he vowed to remain in office and do the job to which he was elected. He railed against the attempts to have him removed from office, both in person, with his February 2008 State of the City Address and through his surrogates (i.e., his legal counsel and supporters on the council). With language that clearly identified race and racism as principal fissures within these controversies, he stated: "In the past 30 days I've been called a nigger more than anytime in my entire life. In the past three days I've received more death threats than I have in my entire administration" ("Angry Kilpatrick Attacks Foes, Media" 2008). The controversy was effectively having the city grind to a halt and was bitterly dividing the citizenry (McGraw 2008).

Nonetheless, once Governor Granholm was pressured to proceed with the forfeiture hearing in September of 2008 and the mayor was twice criminally charged—once for exceeding his bail agreement by leaving Detroit for Windsor, Canada and then for assaulting an court officer who delivered a subpoena to a Kilpatrick friend—the weight of public opinion, political pressure, and the possibility of severe jail time forced the mayor to negotiate a plea. Even presidential candidate Barack Obama issued a statement decrying Kilpatrick's actions and insisting that he resign, for it was feared that Kilpatrick would damage Obama's electoral prospects in Michigan. In the end, Kilpatrick agreed: "to pay restitution of $1 million to the city; to surrender his law license, forfeit his state pension to the city and be barred from elective office for five years; and to serve 120 days in the Wayne County jail, followed by five year's probation" (Saulny 2008, A1). After months of intrigue, the mayor admitted that he "lied under oath" (Saulny 2008, A1). Although Black Detroiters expressed differing sentiments about the end of the controversy, it proved to be a disheartening conclusion to the immediate political career of the most prominent of all Hip-Hop Black politicians.

Conclusion: A "Postracial" Black Politics and the Hip-Hop Generation?

At its best, Hip-Hop culture has inspired a brand new generation of grassroots activists and organic intellectuals who through poetry and lyrics have critically analyzed the conditions of the marginalized, such as the ghetto poor, domestically abused women and children, and inmates of the prison-industrial complex (Kitwana 2002). These activists can join others to serve both as accountability agents for Black elected officials and also run for office to lead the progressive changes they and their constituents need. Spence considers this the counter-political potential of Hip-Hop Black politics (Spence 2008).

What we consider problematic about Kilpatrick's embrace of the gangsta/playa ethic is how its particular market-idolatry invited a nihilistic and unaccountable self-aggrandizement. Once Kilpatrick created a narrative of populist justifications for his personal excesses and a fictive accountability to the needs of ordinary Detroiters, he literally spun a tale as to why a defense of him and his actions constituted an anti-racist defense of Blackness. Recall his strong assertions that public debates surrounding his legal troubles were best interpreted through the lens of race and racism. True to the death of Tupac Shakur or Notorious B.I.G, Kilpatrick consciously permitted his political life to imitate art and was "consumed by his own spectacle" (Watts 2004, 606). True to Baldwin's (2004) thesis, he seemed to believe that the Hip-Hop bourgeoisie was *the* political vanguard best able to *represent* post-Civil Rights Movement era aspirations. In actuality, the Kilpatrick case demonstrates that the contradictions of the gangsta/playa pole of Hip-Hop Black politics can reinforce a neoliberal regime that inflicts pain upon the very constituents who it claims to serve.

To the causal observer, Kilpatrick appears to be an outlier from the new generation of Black politicians—Obama, Fenty, Booker, etc.—in that his legal troubles led him to radically depart from the "Third Wave's" brand of deracialized rhetoric and politics (Gillespie 2009). By the very fact that Kilpatrick proudly exhibited Hip-Hop's braggadocio and swagger may lead some to conclude that he touted an ethos more *authentically Black* than the postracial, common ground mantra of his cohort. But, for two key reasons, we warn that the rise and fall of Kwame Kilpatrick is not simply a cautionary tale about the Hip-Hop bourgeoisie's excesses.

First of all, the Kilpatrick case speaks to the potential myopia of the new Black political classes—Hip-Hop and otherwise—who believe they are the unique guarantors of this "postracial" moment and its possibilities. It is not yet clear that for all of this generation's claims of grassroots empowerment and accountability that they can or will use their newly attained political powers in ways that best serve Black grassroots needs. For example, akin to Kilpatrick's fairly even allocations of community and economic development dollars, low-income advocates have praised President Obama's multibillion dollar stimulus package as a pathway to improving the plight of the minority poor. But similar to Kilpatrick targeting funds to preexisting areas of planned development, such advocates also demand that new federal housing subsidies benefit not just middle-class (White) homeowners and that new public infrastructure jobs benefit more than White male construction workers (Inclusion 2009). Second, and more important, we must recognize that, by definition, differing leadership styles are simply different façades if the ultimate policy outcomes are driven by a shared philosophy

(Edelman 1984, 74). For example, Mayor Fenty of Washington, DC has a more deracialized and plainspoken style of Black mayoral leadership than that of the flashy and racially provocative Kilpatrick, but both have been criticized for arguing that market-driven models of school reform are best suited to transforming their beleaguered, inner-city school districts (Mrozowski 2007; Clay 2008). In the final analysis, it is very important not to be distracted by the relative spectacle of this new generation's professed accountability. As Tavis Smiley (2009) insists, we need to verify accountability. Otherwise, the promise of this new Black politics may be, as in the Kilpatrick case, trumped by the "hype" of old racial excuses for political excess.

Note

1. We use the term *neoliberalism* in a way that refers to classic liberal thought or the belief that the protection of individual liberties, the right to own property, and the preservation of a free market are the most important duties of any government by consent (Hackworth, 2007b); and for a discussion of these principles as debated within American thought see Kramnick and Lowi (2009).
2. There is a dearth of information specifying whether Conyers et al. threw support behind Kilpatrick as a nod to U.S. Congresswoman Cheeks-Kilpatrick. Originally, Collins joined the rest of council in a 7-1 vote in favor of a resolution asking Kilpatrick to resign on March 18, 2008 (see MacDonald 2008). Conyers cast the lone dissenting vote; Reeves was not present.

References

2001 newsmaker of the year. *Crain's Detroit Business Online*, January 21, 2002. http://www.crainsdetroit.com/article/20020121/SUB/201210881 (accessed June 9, 2008).

Angry Kilpatrick attacks foes, media. 2008. [Video]. WXYZ.com online, March 12. http://www.wxyz.com/news/story/VIDEO-Angry-Kilpatrick-Attacks-Foes-Media/0fE8VVMfr02Ojw-mjbrkkw.cspx (accessed June 10, 2008).

Ashenfetter, David, Joe Swickand, and Zachary Gorchow. 2008. Kilpatrick and Beatty surrender: Pair are booked after being charged with perjury, conspiracy, misconduct. *The Detroit Free Press Online.* March 24. http://www.freep.com/apps/pbcs.dll/article?AID=/20080324/NEWS01/303250001 (accessed May 30, 2008).

Baldwin, Davarian L. 2004. Black empires, White desires: The spatial politics of identity in the age of hip-hop. In *That's the joint! The hip hop studies reader*, ed. M. Forman and M. A. Neal. New York: Routledge, 159–176.

Banks, Manley Elliott. 2000. A changing electorate in a Black majority city: The emergence of a neo-conservative Black urban regime in contemporary Atlanta. *Journal of Urban Affairs* 22(3): 265–78.

Bello, Marsha. 2005. Detroit's budget crunch worsens. *The Detroit Free Press,* January 15.

Bennett, Larry. 1993. Harold Washington and the Black urban regime. *Urban Affairs Quarterly* 28: 423–40.

Blumer, Tom. AP joins the Kwame Kilpatrick name that party parade. BizzyBlog.com online. March 25. http://www.bizzyblog.com/index.php?s=AP+Joins+the+Kwame+Kilpatrick+Name+That+Party+Parade&search=Search (accessed June 16, 2008).

Boyd, Todd. 2004. Check yo self before you wreck yo self: The death of politics in rap music and popular culture. In *That's the joint! The hip hop studies reader*, ed. M. Forman and M. A. Neal. New York: Routledge, 325–340.

Bradsher, Keith. 2001. Detroit mayor will not seek another term. *The New York Times*, April 18.

Bynoe, Yvonne 2004. *Stand and deliver: Political activism, leadership, and hip hop culture.* New York: Soft Skull Press.

Carney, Mike. 2008. Mayor charged with perjury after denying affair with aide. *The Virginian-Pilot* (Norfolk, VA), March 25.

Carr, Robert. 2002. Group comes up with $500M riverfront project. *GlobeSt.com.* December 13, http://www.globest.com/news/20021213/detroit/65130-1.html (accessed May 30, 2008).

Challenger drops request for recount in Detroit mayor's race. 2005. *The Associated Press State & Local Wire,* December 29.

Church History—Ebenezer Baptist Church, Atlanta, GA. http://www.historicebenezer. org/History.html (accessed June 13, 2008).

Clay, Risen. 2008. The lightning rod. *Atlantic Monthly,* November, 78.

Clavel, Pierre, and Wim Wiewel. 1991. *Harold Washington and the neighborhoods: Progressive city government in Chicago, 1983–1987.* New Brunswick, NJ: Rutgers University Press.

Cohen, George H. 2008. Message from principal George H. Cohen, Jr. Cass Technical High School. http://schools.detroit.k12.mi.us/sites/cass/message.htm (accessed June 8, 2008).

Collins, Lisa. 2001. On the run: Kwame Kilpatrick—Making of a parable. *The Detroit News. Detroit Metro Times Online,* October 10. http://metrotimes.com/editorial/story. asp?id=2552 (accessed June 8, 2008).

———. 2005. Determined Kilpatrick in fight of his life. *The Detroit News,* November 3. http://www.detnews.com/2005/metro/0511/03/B01-370658.htm (accessed June 9, 2008).

Cox to investigate new information in rumored Kilpatrick stripper party. 2008. *Michigan Live Online,* March 13. http://www.mlive.com/news/index.ssf/2008/03/cox_to_ investigate_new_informa.html (accessed June 1, 2008).

Dawson, Bell, Jim Schaefer, and M. L. Elrick. 2008. Kilpatrick helped friends get grants: Money also trickled down to the wife of the mayor. *The Detroit Free Press Online,* May 18. http://www.freep.com/apps/pbcs.dll/article?AID=/20080518/ NEWS01/805180596 (accessed June 8, 2008).

DeLeon, Richard E. 1992. *Left coast city: Progressive politics in San Francisco, 1975 1991.* Lawrence: University Press of Kansas.

Denial of mayoral recall petition appealed. n.d. *Michigan Ballot Initiative News Online.* http://ballotpedia.org/wiki/index.php/Michigan_ballot_initiative_news#cite_ note-4 (accessed June 4, 2008).

Detroit mayor '05: Kilpatrick basks in praise for his handling of blackout. 2003. *The Hotline—The National Journal Group, Inc.,* August 19.

Detroit mayor criticized for charging $210,000 on city credit card. 2005. *The Associated Press State & Local Wire,* May 3.

Detroit mayor: Kilpatrick the city's youngest mayor ever. 2001. *The Hotline—The National Journal Group,* November 7.

Detroit mayor pleads not guilty as prosecutor reveals new text message. 2008. *The Detroit Free Press,* March 25.

Detroit mayor sheds earring. 2005. *USA Today*, October 13.

Dreier, Peter, John H Mollenkopf, and Todd Swanstrom. 2001. What cities can do to address poverty. In *Place matters: Metropolitics for the twenty-first century*. Lawrence: University of Kansas Press.

Dyson, Michael Eric. 1996. *Between god and gangsta rap: Bearing witness to Black culture*. New York: Oxford University Press.

———. 2004a. Gangsta rap and American culture. In *The Michael Eric Dyson reader*. New York: Basic Civitas Books, 411–417.

———. 2004b. "Give me a paper and pen": Tupac's place in hip-hop. In *The Michael Eric Dyson reader*. New York: Basic Civitas Books, 85–99.

———. 2005. *Is Bill Cosby right? Or has the Black middle class lost its mind?* New York: Basic Civitas Books.

Edelman, Murray. 1984.*The symbolic uses of politics*. Urbana and Chicago: University of Illinois Press. (Orig. pub. 1967)

Elkin, Stephen L. 1987. *City and regime in the American republic*. Chicago: University of Chicago Press.

Elrick, M. L., Jim Schaefer, and Kristi Tanner. 2008. Kilpatrick stocks payroll with friends, kin: Mayor's office defends hires; totals excessive, critics say. *The Detroit Free Press online*, May 10. http://www.freep.com/article/20080510/NEWS01/805110582/ (accessed June 4, 2008).

Ferman, Barbara. 1996. *Challenging the growth machine in Chicago and Pittsburgh neighborhood politics*. Lawrence: University Press of Kansas.

Forman, Murray. 2002. *The 'hood comes first: Race, space, and place in rap and hip-hop*. Middletown, CT: Wesleyan University Press.

Fowler, Bree. 2004. Deposition: Top Detroit police official removed after mayor "lost confidence." *The Associated Press State & Local Wire*, June 29.

Gallagher, John. 2004. Detroit-area industrial park begins its first phase. *The Detroit Free Press*, May 15.

Gamboa, Glenn. 2004. Politics gets hip. *The Daily Press Online*, October 10. http://www.dailypress.com/nyc-etpoli1010,0,2550588.story (accessed August 20, 2009).

Gillespie, Andra. 2009. The third wave: Assessing the post-civil rights cohort of black elected leadership. *National Political Science Review* 12: 139–61.

Gorchow, Zachary, Patton Nachii, and Rochelle Riley. 2008. Council takes action to force Kilpatrick out; Narrow votes reflect divided opinion in city on scandal. *Detroit Free Press*, May 14.

Hackworth, Jason. 2007a. *The neoliberal city: Governance, ideology, and development in American urbanism*. Ithaca, NY: Cornell University Press.

———. 2007b. *The neoliberal city: Governance, ideology, and ideology in American urbanism*. Ithaca, NY: Cornell University Press.

Hakim, Danny. 2005. Detroit mayor and TV reporter battle. *The New York Times,* June 2.

Henderson, Errol Anthony. 1996. Black nationalism and rap music. *Journal of Black Studies* 26: 308–39.

Hendrix takes early lead in Detroit mayor's race; FBI investigating absentee ballots. 2005. *The Associated Press*, November 8.

hooks, bell. 1994. Gangsta culture—Sexism, misogyny: Who will take the rap? In *Outlaw culture: Resisting representations*. New York: Routledge, 115–124.

Hopkinson, Natalie, and Natalie Y. Moore. 2006. *Deconstructing Tyrone: A new look at black masculinity in the hip-hop*. San Francisco: Cleis Press.

Horan, Cynthia. 1991. Beyond governing coalitions: Analyzing urban regimes in the 1990s. *Journal of Urban Affairs* 13 (2): 199–35.

———. 2002. Racializing regime politics. *Journal of Urban Affairs* 24 (1): 19–33.

Huleh, Sarah. 2008. Detroit council eyes ouster of Mayor Kilpatrick. *All Things Considered*—National Public Radio (NPR), May 13.

Inclusion, Center for Social. 2009. *Talking points, economic and housing recovery for everyone: Racial equity and prosperity.* New York: Project of the Tides Water Center.

Iton, Richard. 2008. *In search of the black fantastic: Politics and popular culture and in the post-civil rights era.* New York: Oxford University Press.

Jennings, James. 1992. *The politics of black empowerment: The transformation of black activism in urban America.* Detroit, MI: Wayne State University Press.

Johnson, Christopher K. 2008. Danceable capitalism: Hip-hop's link to corporate space. *Journal of Pan African Studies* 2 (4): 80–92.

Kilpatrick, Kwame. *Myspace—Kwame Kilpatrick.* http://www.myspace.com/mayorkwame (accessed May 30, 2008).

———. (D). n.d. *Bills introduced, amendments offered, roll call votes taken from 1/1/2001 to 12/31/2008. Michigan State House of Representatives.* Mackinac Center for Public Policy.

Kitwana, Bakari. 2002. *The hip hop generation: Young blacks and the crisis in African-American culture.* New York: Basic Civitas Books.

———. 2004. The challenge of rap music from cultural movement to political power. In *That's the joint! The hip hop studies reader*, ed. M. Forman and M. A. Neal. New York: Routledge, 341–350.

Kramnick, Issac, and Theodore Lowi. 2009. *American political thought: A Norton anthology.* New York: W.W. Norton.

Kwame Kilpatrick—Mayor of Detroit. 2008. *Citymayors.com. online.* June 4. http://www.citymayors.com/mayors/detroit_mayor.html (accessed June 8, 2008).

Kwame Kilpatrick (D). *Bills introduced, amendments offered, roll call votes taken from 1/1/2001 to 12/31/2008. Michigan State House of Representatives.* Mackinac Center for Public Policy. n.d. http://www.michiganvotes.org/SearchVotes.aspx?EntityID1=133&CategoryID=0&Keywords=&StartMonth=1&StartYear=2001&EndMonth=12&EndYear=2009&Results=10&op=Search (accessed June 8, 2008).

Kwame Kilpatrick/Detroit.*Time Magazine online.* April 17. http://www.time.com/time/magazine/article/0,9171,1050267,00.html. (accessed June 8, 2008).

Kwame M. Kilpatrick—P60494. State Bar Michigan. of n.d. http://www.michbar.org/memberdirectory/detail.cfm?ID=60433506%2D6439%2D86%2DDETAIL (accessed June 8, 2008).

Kwame's passion pays off: Speech at Rosa Parks' funeral influenced voters. 2005. *Windsor Star (Ontario)*, November 10.

LeDuff, Charlie. 2008. Who killed Tamara Greene? *The Detroit News Online.* March 14. http://www.detnews.com/apps/pbcs.dll/article?AID=/20080314/METRO/03140383 (accessed June 10, 2008).

Lusane, Clarence. 2004. Rap, race, and politics. In *That's the joint! The hip hop studies reader*, ed. M. Forman and M. A. Neal. New York: Routledge, 351–362.

MacDonald, Christine. 2008. Mayor Kilpatrick brushes off City Council's call for him to resign. *The Detroit News Online,* March 18. http://www.detnews.com/apps/pbcs.dll/article?AID=/20080318/METRO/803180439 (accessed June 10, 2008).

MacDonald, Christine, and David Josar. 2008. Council trio to gov: Drop mayor action; Letter to Granholm says Kilpatrick didn't deceive them on whistle-blower case. *The Detroit News Online*, June 10. http://www.detnews.com/apps/pbcs.dll/article?AID=/20080610/METRO/806100378 (accessed June 10, 2008).

McGovern, Stephen J. 1998. *The politics of downtown development: Dynamic political cultures in San Francisco and Washington, DC*. Lexington: University Press of Kentucky.

McGraw, Bill. 2008. Kilpatrick's rise and fall. *The Detroit Free Press*, September 5.

Michigan: Back to the blackboard. 2003. *The Bond Buyer*, October 1.

Michigan Secretary of State. *1998 Official Michigan Election Results—9th District State Representative 2 Year Term (1) Position Files in Wayne County*. http://miboecfr.nicusa.com/election/results/98gen/08009000.html (accessed June 8, 2008).

Michigan State Senate. *Senate Resolution No. 109—Resolution to urge the United States District Court, Eastern District of Michigan, to decline a request to circumvent the regular contract approval process with regard to the Detroit Water and Sewerage Department*. State of Michigan Legislature. http://www.legislature.mi.gov/documents/2005-2006/resolutionadopted/Senate/htm/2006-SAR-0109.htm (accessed June 14, 2008).

Michigan votes—The Honorable Marsha Cheeks. n.d. http://www.michiganvotes.org/Legislator.aspx?ID=1469 (accessed April 19, 2009).

Mrozowski, Jennifer. 2007. Kilpatrick school plan opposed: Board fears proposal to open 25 charter schools could pull students, money from public classrooms. *The Detroit News*, May 15.

Old issues arise for mayor in jury verdict against him, city. 2007. *The Associated Press State & Local Wire*, September 11.

Panel OKs recall language on Kilpatrick. 2008. *The Detroit Free Press Online,* April 29. http://www.freep.com/article/20080429/NEWS01/80429038/.

Plagued by scandal, Detroit's mayor faces a tough re-election race. 2005. *The Associated Press State & Local Wire*, July 15.

Poll: Incumbent Kilpatrick narrows gap in Detroit mayor race, though challenger still leads. 2005. *The Associated Press,* November 4.

Poll shows challenger ahead in mayoral race; Freman Hendrix was deputy mayor under Kwame Kilpatrick's predecessor, Dennis Archer. 2005. *Grand Rapid Press (Michigan),* July 18.

Primary Results. 2005. *The Associated Press State & Local Wire*, August 3.

Ransby, Barbara, and Tracye Matthews. 1995. Black popular culture and transcendence of patriarchal illusions. In *Words of fire: An anthology of African-American feminist thought*, ed. B. Guy-Sheftall. New York: New Press, 526–35.

Reed, Adolph Jr. 1988. The black urban regime: Structural origins and constraints. In *Power, community, and the city: Comparative urban and community research*, ed. P. Smith. New Brunswick, NJ: Transaction, 261–81.

Rosdil, Donald L. 1991. The context of radical populism in U.S. cities. *Journal of Urban Affairs* 1: 77–96.

Rose, Tricia. 1994a. *Black noise: Rap music and black culture in contemporary America*. Hanover, NH: Wesleyan University Press.

Saulny, Susan. 2008. Detroit mayor pleads guilty and resigns. *The New York Times*, September 5, A1–3.

Schaefer, Jim, and M. L. Elrick. 2008. Mayor Kilpatrick, chief of staff lied under oath, text messages show. *The Detroit Free Press online*, January 24. http://www.freep.com/apps/pbcs.dll/article?AID=/20080124/NEWS05/801240414/0/NEWS01 (accessed May 30, 2008).

Shakur, Tupac. 1999. *The rose that grew from concrete*. New York: Pocket Books.

Shaw, Todd C. 2009. *Now is the time! Detroit black politics and grassroots activism*. Durham, NC: Duke University Press.

———. Lester K Spence. 2004. Race and representation in Detroit's Community development coalitions. *The Annals of the American Academy of Political and Social Science* 594: 125–42.

SHOW: Detroit Mayor Kwame Kilpatrick involved in sex scandal. NBC News Transcripts, NBC Nightly News, March 21.

Slevin, Peter. 2005. Detroit mayor's race is in home stretch; Democrats face off with plans to reshape city. *The Washington Post*, November 7.

Smiley, Tavis. 2009. *Accountable: Making America as good as its promise*. New York: Atria Books.

Smith, Suzanne E. 1999. *Dancing in the street: Motown and the cultural politics of Detroit*. Cambridge, MA: Harvard University Press.

Spence, Lester K. Stare in the darkness: Rap, hip hop, and black politics. (forthcoming).

Steve Wilson investigates mayor's expenses. 2007. *WXYZ.com online*. May 10. http://www.wxyz.com/content/news/investigators/story.aspx?content_id=bcf27fcb-2679-414c-b84a-4dc27f30e621 (accessed June 1, 2008).

Stone, Clarence N. 1989. *Regime politics: Governing Atlanta, 1946–1988*. Lawrence: University of Kansas.

Thompson, J. Phillip III. 2006. *Double trouble: Black mayors, black communities, and the call for a deep democracy*. New York: Oxford University Press.

Time magazine lists Kilpatrick among worst big city mayors. 2005. *The Associated Press State & Local Wire*, April 17.

Watkins, S. Craig. 2005. *Hip hop matters: Politics, pop culture, and the struggle for the soul of a movement*. Boston: Beacon Press.

Watts, Eric K. 2004. An exploration of spectacular consumption: Gangsta rap as cultural commodity. In *That's the joint! The hip hop studies reader*, ed. M. Forman and M. A. Neal. New York: Routledge, 593–609.

Part III

The Rise of Barack Obama and Its Implications for Black Politics

The election of Barack Obama as the nation's first Black president has completely changed the face of African-American politics. Before Obama, scholars largely assumed that Black presidential candidates could at best hope to use their candidacies to leverage concessions from whichever party enjoyed a preponderance of Blacks' loyalty—most recently, the Democratic Party (Walters 2005, chapter 2). However, with Obama's historic nomination and election, students of Black politics will now be able to see if descriptive representation in the nation's highest executive office actually translates into reduced inequality for Blacks across the country.

While it appears to many that Barack Obama had a charmed path to the presidency, nothing can be farther from the truth. Obama toiled at the local level to win over constituents. In 2000, he suffered a stunning Congressional primary defeat that could have permanently scared him away from pursuing high office. How did Obama emerge from that victory to become the 44th President of the United States?

The next two chapters explore Obama's rise to becoming a transformative political figure in this country. In chapter 6, Lorrie Frasure studies Black constituent attitudes in his 2000 primary defeat and in his 2004 Senate primary victory. Black voters repudiated Obama in 2000, but they roundly supported him in 2004. Frasure argues that Obama's racial moderation was a liability to him at the more racially homogenous local level, but Black voters saw his moderation as an asset when he pursued statewide office.

In chapter 7, Charlton McIlwain shifts the focus to the 2008 Democratic presidential primary. How was Obama able to beat the seemingly invincible Hillary Rodham Clinton? Using content analysis and survey data, McIlwain shows that Obama succeeded, unlike previous Black presidential candidates, at being perceived as a legitimate leader. He was able to best Clinton by espousing a brand of hopeful leadership at an uncertain time in American history when voters were receptive to his kind of inspired leadership.

References

Walters, Ronald. 2005. *Freedom is not enough: Black voters, Black candidates and American presidential politics.* New York: Rowman and Littlefield.

6 The Burden of Jekyll and Hyde
Barack Obama, Racial Identity, and Black Political Behavior[1]

Lorrie Frasure

Today, we popularly know Barack Obama as a man at the top of his game, the man with adoring worldwide audiences who shattered racial barriers on his way to the White House. However, less than a decade before his historic 2008 presidential campaign, Barack Obama was a little known Illinois State Senator who got his hat handed to him by a Black incumbent in a congressional primary.

In 2000, Barack Obama challenged Bobby Rush for the Democratic nomination in the Illinois First Congressional District. This historic district has been represented by a Black member of Congress since 1928, when Oscar DePriest became the first Black elected to Congress in the twentieth century. Obama ran a classic Ivy League Upstart race, charging that his opponent could have done more to help the district and proposing great technocratic ideas to demonstrate his higher legislative acumen. The Black voters in Chicago's South Side were not convinced, though. Satisfied with Rush's leadership in Congress, they delivered him the nomination by a two-to-one margin.

Just four years later, though, the same set of voters would rally around Barack Obama as he sought the Democratic nomination for the U.S. Senate. How could such a thing happen? What factors explain the shift in Black public opinion and subsequent overwhelming turnout favoring Barack Obama? In this chapter, Lorrie Frasure provides a closer examination of the nuanced nature of Black electoral politics. Frasure uses Obama's early political campaigns as a lens through which to examine Black constituent attitudes and political behavior in an era of post-Civil Rights Black political leadership. Her analysis suggests that shifts in Black electoral support for Obama are much more complex than factors related to racial identity alone. Frasure also examines the role of political information and candidate electability on Black political behavior and explores how these factors continued to shape Obama's relationship to the Black electorate during his 2008 presidential election campaign.

Introduction

Securing enough delegates to win the Democratic Party's presidential nomination in June 2008, Senator Barack Obama became the first African American to be nominated by a major political party in the United States. The meteoric rise of Obama to the top of the Democratic presidential ticket is a remarkable moment in U.S. history and politics, but this journey is also a lens through which to examine the intersections of racial identity, political information, and political behavior in an era of post-Civil Rights Black political leadership in the United States. Barack Obama's introduction to the national stage followed a well-executed and widely praised July 2004 Democratic National Convention speech in Boston, followed by his decisive election to the U.S. Senate from Illinois later that year. Obama became the third African-American U.S. Senator elected since Reconstruction, and only the fifth in American history. However, much of the widespread media coverage concerning Obama's "iconic" or "rock-star" ascent into the political spotlight and the American consciousness began with Obama's political campaign against Senator Hillary Rodham Clinton during the 2008 primary election season.

Arguably, it is Obama's early political life in Illinois which uniquely enhances our ability to advance the study of Black political behavior. Numerous questions remain unanswered concerning which factors explain dramatic shifts in Black support for Barack Obama, from a failed attempt to secure a nomination for a seat in the U.S. Congress in a majority Black Chicago district in 2000; to winning overwhelming general election support from the Black electorate during his successful bid for U.S. Senate in 2004; to having to wrestle the Black voting bloc away from Hillary Clinton during the 2008 presidential primaries on his way to becoming the first African-American Democratic presidential nominee and winner in 2008.

During the 2008 presidential primaries, a number of political commentators, Black elites, and academics stirred debate concerning the influence of Obama's racial authenticity, and the extent to which the Black electorate may or may not have supported his political campaigns, in part, because he was "not Black enough" (McIlwain 2007; Walters 2007; Crouch 2006; Dickerson 2006; Giles 2007; Hansen 2007; Valbrun 2007). Though such sentiments were often dismissed as divisive media hype, questions concerning Obama's racial authenticity, in fact, were a common feature throughout each one of his political campaigns dating back to his first Illinois State Senate race in 1996, and they were greatly popularized during the early months of the 2008 presidential primaries against Senator Hillary Clinton. Ron Walters (2007) argues, "it is legitimate that Black Americans raise questions about "Blackness" as an objective issue, because it is the core concept that defines the basic cultural identity of Black people…his [Obama's] identity omitted many of the cultural markers with which Blacks are more familiar to the extent that it has promoted a curiosity of 'cultural fit' that in turn has become an issue of political trust" (12). Walters, further commenting on Obama and the presidential primaries suggests, this perceived lack of credibility in Obama's group or cultural identity affects the confidence of many potential Black voters in his political accountability to their agenda. In this context, whether Obama looks Black, or who his ancestors were, matters, but ultimately less than his commitment to Black interests, and Blacks have historically been cautious about the issue of group representation. (2007, 13)

From his Illinois State Senate run to his bid for the Democratic nomination for president, Obama has arguably led a series of deracialized political campaigns. During a 2007 interview, Obama contended,

In the history of African-American politics in this country there has always been some tension between speaking in universal terms and speaking in very race-specific terms about the plight of the African-American community… by virtue of my background, I am more likely to speak in universal terms. (Crowley and Johnson 2007)

Despite Obama's liberal voting record on matters from civil rights to women's rights, his White crossover appeal and penchant for building broad coalitions across race/ethnicity, class, gender, and party lines has also presented problems for Obama and heightened questions concerning his perceived willingness to position the interests of African Americans into his public policy agenda (see Burnside and Whitehurst 2007 for an examination of Obama's record as an Illinois State Senator).

Largely unexamined is the extent to which Obama's initial lack of widespread Black support stemmed from factors related not only to racial identity and perceived accountability to Black interests, but also factors such as political information and political orientations. In order to better understand the influence of racial and political identity, political information, and sociodemographics on political attitudes and behavior toward Black candidates in the post-Civil Rights era, this study uses a mixed method approach, including preelection and exit poll results, newspaper reports, as well as data from the 2004 Illinois Senate Pre-election Study. I examine the influence of these factors through the lens of three early political campaigns of Barack Obama in Illinois: the 2000 primary election for the U.S. Congress; the 2004 U.S. Senate primary election; and the 2004 U.S. Senate general election. I address the following research questions: (1) Which factors led to Obama's 2000 primary defeat for the U.S. Congress? (2) Which factors influenced a dramatic shift in Black support for Obama during his winning 2004 U.S. Senate primary race? (3) Which factors influenced a vote for Obama in the 2004 U.S. Senate general election, including how the salience of these factors varies by race? I use a mixed method approach to examine these complex questions because there is a lack of systematic empirical data on the early political campaigns of Obama. This makes it difficult to measure the influence of factors related to racial and political identity, political information, and other factors using a single methodology.

This chapter is organized in the following manner. The next section provides a brief review of literature related to racial identity, political information and Black political participation. The third section uses polling data and newspaper reports to provide an overview of Obama's Illinois Congressional and Senate races. In this section, I detail some factors related to Obama's personal background because these characteristics have often served as perceived limitations or strengths in his ability to gain Black and non-Black support during his previous political campaigns. In addition to polling data and newspaper reports used to examine Obama's US Senate primary and general election campaigns, I present some preliminary results from the 2004 Illinois Senate Pre-election Survey, used to construct a multivariate logistic regression analysis of the influence of racial and political identity, political information, along with some standard socio-demographic controls on respondents's intentions to vote for Barack Obama in 2004. The concluding section discusses the persistent influence and development of racial identity on support for Obama during the 2008 Democratic presidential campaign.

Racial Group Identity, Political Information and Political Participation

Barack Obama, like many other twenty-first century Black political leaders who share similar characteristics of having grown up in the post-Civil Rights era, lived in predominantly White or mixed neighborhoods, attended predominately White colleges/universities, and whose political campaigns achieved notable White crossover appeal, has operated in a contested political space between what is deemed "good" or "just" versus what is deemed "bad" or "unjust" in relation to the African-American community. These post-Civil Rights Black political leaders are seemingly plagued by the dilemma of "Jekyll and Hyde politics." Robert Louis Stevenson published the *Strange Case of Dr. Jekyll and Mr. Hyde* in 1886, which recounts the classic, yet tragic tale of the struggle between good and bad.[2] Dawson, Brown, and Allen (1990) assert that:

> to the extent that Black life chances have been historically dominated by the ascriptive factor of race, individual African Americans have been able to use the heuristic of an evaluation of what is "good" or "bad" for the race as a proxy for maximizing individual utility. As long as the perception remains that race is more important than other factors such as social class or gender in influencing life changes, one would expect relatively homogenous group beliefs and behaviors. This perception and the associated heuristic would facilitate the processing of information through the racial-identity belief system. (25)

It is therefore plausible that the personas of good and bad *imposed* upon Barack Obama from those engaging in "Jekyll and Hyde politics" attempt to paint him as a creature of "two faces," where "not Black enough" is the "bad" Obama and

"Black like me" is the "good" Obama, utilizing such markers as cues toward Black political attitudes and behaviors.

In the *Audacity of Hope: Thoughts on Reclaiming the American Dream*, Obama wrote that

> it is not easy for Black politicians to find the right tone—"too angry? not angry enough?"—when discussing the hardships of their constituents.... Even the most fair-minded of Whites...those who would genuinely like to see racial inequality ended and poverty relieved, tend to push back against suggestions of racial victimization—or race-specific claims based on the history of race discrimination in this country. (Obama 2006, 247)

Clearly, then, Jekyll and Hyde politics rubs both ways, as Obama has simultaneously confronted the *inverse* of the African-American racial identity cue among segments of the White electorate, whereas a perception of "too Black" or having a policy agenda too closely aligned with African Americans is the "bad" Obama, while putting forth a universalistic policy agenda which transcends race is the "good" Obama.

Numerous studies have found that voters often cast their vote along racial lines, underscoring the relationship between racial identity cues and political participation (Gurin, Hatchett, and Jackson 1989, Tate 1993, Dawson 1994, Williams 1990). In the study of Black political participation, it is generally assumed that Black voters will vote for Black candidates. As Philpot and Walton (2007) suggest, "regardless of support from White voters, African American candidates typically rely on overwhelming support from Black voters to get elected" (50). Tate's (1993) analysis using data from the 1984–1988 National Black Election Study (NBES), found support for the influence of racial identification on Black political behavior, showing that "Strong race-identifiers were more likely to participate in electoral politics and to support Jesse Jackson's presidential bids than weak race-identifiers" (165). Dawson, Brown, and Allen (1990) argue that,

> political candidates who invoke African American racial identity in their campaigns either explicitly or implicitly, ceteris paribus, can expect increased political mobilization from a Black community that collectively and individually perceived increased group benefits from the results of a successful campaign. Conversely, candidates who base their campaigns in part on what are perceived as attacks on the Black community will also invoke the racial-identity belief system in African Americans, this amplifying Black counter mobilization to a candidate who is perceived to threaten the group interests of African Americans. (25)

Thus, the fact that the Black voting bloc seemed slow to warm to Obama's presidential candidacy created a quandary for the study of Black political behavior.

For over thirty years, much of the existing literature on Black political participation holds that accounting for socioeconomic factors such as income and education, Blacks participate in some political activities at much the same or at even higher rates than Anglo-Whites (Olsen 1972; Verba and Nie 1972; Wolfinger and Rosenstone 1980; Guterbock and London 1983; Bobo and Gilliam 1990; Rosenstone and Hansen 1993; Dawson, Brown, and Allen 1990). These racial differences have often been attributed to theories of racial group identity among African Americans. Shingles (1981) expanded the model of Black political participation based on the group consciousness theory. His explanations of the political overrepresentation of Blacks closely follow the Black consciousness theories of Verba and Nie (1972). Shingles defined Black consciousness as "the awareness among Blacks of their shared status as an unjustly deprived and oppressed group" (Shingles 1981, 77). He also argues that Black consciousness impacts political participation because "it constitutes to the combination of a sense of [high] political efficacy and political mistrust which in turn induces political involvement" (Shingles 1981, 77; see Miller, Gurin, Gurin, and Malanchuk 1981; Gurin et al. 1989). However, Tate (1991) suggests that since findings from early scholars were largely based on data from the 1960s and early 1970s, the effects of these findings may be a function of the political climate or protest atmosphere of the era, calling into question the extent to which racial group consciousness still works to politically mobilize Blacks (1162; also see Tate 1993, 79). [3]

Nevertheless, in some key ways, Tate's (1993) study of Black political participation found support for a "group consciousness" among Blacks surveyed. She writes, "not only does a majority (75 percent) feel that their lives are affected by what happens to Blacks as a group, but many also think about what it means to be Black today. Together, the centrality of racial group membership among Blacks accounts for much of their liberal profiles and political identities as Democrats" (Tate 1993, 165). Dawson (1994) employed a Black utility heuristic, or notion of linked fate, to determine the extent to which African Americans perceive that their own self-interest relates to the racial group interests of Blacks as a whole (see chapter 3). Dawson (1994) finds that Black institutions help to reinforce Blacks' group identity and behavior by emphasizing racial group identity over class group identity among Blacks. This modeling strategy focuses on "group-oriented attitudes that are more relevant to Black participation than the general orientation typically employed in analyses of Anglo participation" (Leighley and Vedlitz 1999, 1095, note).

While these theories have been instrumental in understanding Black political participation, they may not account for evolving dimensions of Black political behavior.

Obama's political campaigns provide an opportunity to better understand the intersections of racial identity, political information, and political behavior. One's information context may include avenues for accessing political information, knowledge of and interests in politics and public affairs, or the extent to which an individual is contacted by a political campaign or even the type of neighborhood in which one lives. Such contexts are important because they are believed to be prerequisites for political efficacy (or the perception that one has the ability to influence the political system). Diana Mutz (1993) writes, "those with high levels of political knowledge, heavy use of mass media, high levels of political interest, and regular involvement in the political process are expected to differ in their decision-making processes from those who are less knowledgeable, less educated, less interested, or less involved" (483–84).

In short, people with high levels of political information, knowledge, and awareness are thought to vote differently from those with low levels; and these individuals are better equipped to form opinions that are consistent with their political predispositions (Converse 1962; Zaller 1991, 1992). Converse (1962) evaluated how some values constrain mass opinion. His work suggests that people rely on contextual information presented to them via political cues from elites to process new ideas.[4] While some individuals are ill-informed, they often take "shortcuts" to make up for their lack of information and knowledge by employing political cues, which come largely from political elites. These cues in turn help them to form positions on issues that are consistent with their political views (Zaller 1991, 1992).

These factors may be particularly important to the study of Black political behavior in the post-Civil Rights era. We still have very little knowledge of the influence of racial and political identity cues as well as political information related to how Black voters will respond to various types of African-American political campaigns, including those involving two or more Black candidates from the same party; two Black candidates from different political parties; or when a Black male candidate opposes a non-Black female candidate for elected office. An analysis of Obama's early political campaigns is uniquely suitable to begin to unpack some of these concerns.

The Early Political Campaigns of Barack Obama

This study uses a mixed method approach that includes preelection and exit poll results, newspaper reports, as well as data from the 2004 Illinois Senate Study, to examine the following research questions: (1) Which factors led to Obama's 2000 primary defeat for the U.S. Congress? (2) Which factors influenced a dramatic shift in Black support for Obama during his 2004 U.S. Senate primary race? (3) Which factors influenced a vote for Obama in the 2004 U.S. Senate general election, including how the salience of these factors varied by race? Using a variety of sources assists in explaining a more nuanced narrative of the events of Obama's political campaigns. The next section analyzes the early political campaigns of Barack Obama, starting with his bid for U.S. Congress, followed by his bid for the U.S. Senate. Then, I summarize and discuss preliminary results from the 2004 Illinois Senate Study used to construct a multivariate logistic regression model of the relationships between racial and political identity, political information, along with some standard demographic controls on Black and White respondent's intention to cast a vote for Obama versus Keyes in 2004.

Obama and the Race for U.S. Congress

In 2000, after having served in the Illinois State Senate since 1997, Obama ran for the U.S. Congress in an attempt to unseat former Black Panther and long-time

Democratic incumbent Representative Bobby L. Rush. Despite the fact that Rush's seat in Congress seemed politically vulnerable following his unsuccessful attempt to defeat Richard M. Daley, the long-time incumbent Mayor of Chicago, Rush defeated Obama in a landslide victory of 60 percent to 31 percent (Federal Elections Commission 2000). Obama won the White vote, which made up 30 percent of the electorate, but lost the Black vote, which was a necessary voting bloc toward winning in this predominantly Black Congressional district (Federal Elections Commission 2000; Scott 2007, 5; also see Obama 2006, 105–107 for a personal account of the 2000 Congressional race).

Obama was successfully painted by Rush as an elitist, opportunistic, outsider, who was too inexperienced and was "out of touch" with Chicagoans in the majority Black, South-side district. Obama's campaign for U.S. Congress was plagued with questions concerning whether he was "Black enough' to be trusted to represent the interests of the district he sought to represent (Scott 2007, 1). To be sure, Obama did not fit the model of traditional Black political leaders in Chicago such as Rush, Jesse Jackson Sr., or Harold Washington, the city's first Black mayor. Born in 1961, Obama was only four years old when Malcolm X was assassinated and six when Martin Luther King was assassinated. He was in his twenties when Harold Washington, who was elected mayor in 1983, died suddenly of a heart attack in 1987. Obama's autobiography, *Dreams of My Father: A Story of Race and Inheritance* (1995, 2006), recounts the story of his biracial heritage and upbringing in Hawaii and Indonesia. His White mother, Stanley Ann Dunham, was from Kansas, and his father was a Kenyan, Barack Obama Sr., who abandoned his family to pursue his studies at Harvard when Obama was a toddler. His mother remarried and later divorced an Indonesian, Lolo Soetero, and Obama was raised in Hawaii by his maternal grandparents Madelyn, whom he called Tutu or Toot and Stanley whom he called Gramps. He attended Occidental College in Los Angeles and graduated from Columbia University in New York with a degree in political science. Prior to attending law school at Harvard University, where he became the first Black editor of the *Harvard Law Review*, Obama served as a community organizer on Chicago's South side. In 1992, he married Michelle Robinson, an African-American native Chicagoan, who was also a Harvard Law graduate and his former mentor, whom he met while he worked as a summer associate at a corporate law firm in Chicago. Obama returned to Chicago after law school, reportedly turning down many prestigious jobs in corporate America to follow his political aspirations.

While this story is fascinating for many, the fact that Barack Obama, an unfamiliar if not "funny" name at the outset, was interracial, graduated from Columbia and Harvard universities, lived in Hyde Park (a racially mixed, largely middle- to upper-middle class neighborhood in Chicago), and taught constitutional law at the University of Chicago, an institution known for less than harmonious ties with the surrounding Black community on Chicago's South Side, made it easier for Rush to tarnish Obama's reputation and bring into question his authenticity as a Black candidate who could best serve the interests of a majority Black district (Obama 1995, 2006; Mendell 2007). Despite Obama's work as a community organizer since 1991, he did not have the upbringing, age, or track record of traditional civil rights activism to mount a successful campaign against a well-liked and well-connected Black incumbent like Bobby Rush. What is more, Obama's inability to connect with and appear relatable to Black Chicagoans beyond the corners of the Hyde Park and wealthy Lake Front neighborhoods reportedly made him less favorable to Blacks on the campaign trail (Scott 2007, 5).

On the other hand, Representative Rush was a long time Chicago politician with strong ties to the Black Civil Rights Movement establishment, and was endorsed by many of its leaders, such as Jesse Jackson Sr. Rush also had a strong relationship with the Clintons and his political campaign benefited from an endorsement from President Bill Clinton in 2000. Following his loss, Obama told the *Chicago Tribune*, "there were elements within the African American community who might have suggested 'Well, he's from Hyde Park' or 'He went to Harvard' or 'He was born in Hawaii, so he might not be Black enough'" (Fletcher 2007, 3). Obama admits that perhaps he miscalculated the favorability of Rush among the district's constituency. He garnered only 11 percent name recognition to Rush's 90 percent six months prior to the primary election and thus, arguably, the Black electorate never got a chance to know him (Obama 2006, 105–107). While the race was about an emerging leader versus an incumbent leader, rife with calls for "change," Obama never posed a viable threat to Rush, who never lost his lead as the frontrunner. Moreover, Obama had no way of knowing that the turn of events that would strengthen Rush's relationship with the district's Black electorate. Rush's 29-year-old son Huey died tragically as a result of random gun violence in October 1999. Rush's favorability was boosted by the so-called sympathy vote. Concomitantly, Obama's failure to return to the Illinois Senate from a Christmas vacation in Hawaii, due to his daughter's illness, caused him to miss an important vote on a crime bill that failed to pass by five votes. It was the combination of these factors that led to Obama's defeat by Congressman Rush in 2000 (Obama 2006, 106).

Obama and the Race for U.S. Senate

Obama learned many lessons from his failed U.S. Congress bid. The next time around, Obama was better prepared and politically connected, benefiting from sound political calculations, and knowledgeable, well-connected allies. He reportedly started campaigning for his Senate seat more than eighteen months prior to the primary election. However, while he worked diligently to build coalitions across race, class, and gender lines, in February, one month prior to the U.S. Senate primary, *Chicago Tribune*/WGN-TV news polls showed Obama with only 15 percent of the likely Democratic vote (Pearson 2004). African-American voters in Illinois were a particularly important voting bloc, accounting for about 23 percent of Democratic likely primary voters. For a short time, it seemed that Obama's primary race may have been plagued with racial identity ghosts, similar to his Congressional bid. In fact, *Chicago Tribune*/WGN-TV news polls showed

Table 6.1 Percent of Democratic Primary Likely Voters for Barack Obama, 2004

Field Dates	All Democrats		African American Democrats	
	Obama	*Undecided*	*Obama*	*Undecided*
January 6-11	14	38	29	36
Feb 11-17	15	34	38	35
March 3-6	33	16	62	17

Source: Market Share Corp. poll conducted among Democratic likely voters prior to the March 17, 2004 primary. Margin of error is +/-4 percentage points.

that one month before the Senate Democratic Primary only 38 percent of likely African-American voters supported him (Pearson 2004).

Table 6.1 provides polling results of several hundred Democratic likely voters as well as a breakdown of African-American voters' support for Obama, revealing a progressive rise in support for Obama over the course of the primary campaign. The *Chicago Tribune*/WGN-TV poll taken in January 2004 found that only 14 percent of all Democratic likely voters surveyed would vote for Obama. In February, this number rose to 15 percent and in March, less than two weeks before the primary election, this number rose to 33 percent. Among African-American Democratic likely voters, Obama's poll numbers grew from 29 percent in January, to 38 percent in February, and 62 percent in March. What factors account for this shift in support?

For weeks, wealthy and well-known businessman Blair Hull led the Senate primary race, averaging about 25 percent of the likely vote in the polls. Then, allegations of domestic abuse surfaced involving his ex-wife, thus derailing his Senate primary campaign. These allegations worked to Obama's political fortune and contributed to his ability to pull ahead a few weeks before the primary. Obama and his campaign advisor David Axelrod scrambled to get Obama on television to increase his visibility among Illinois voters. The campaign ran a series of television ads featuring the late Chicago Mayor Harold Washington and the late U.S. Senator Paul Simon. These ads served to raise Obama's visibility and to introduce him to a larger portion of the Illinois electorate. *Chicago Tribune* pollster Nick Panagakis attributed the doubling of African-American voter support, in part, to the increased name recognition and visibility of Obama during the later stages of the primary campaign. In January and February, Obama was familiar to 51 percent and 52 percent of Illinois Black voters. By March, Obama was familiar to 72 percent of Black voters in Illinois. Obama's campaign was also aided by big endorsements from the *Chicago Tribune and Sun-Times*, Sheila Simon, daughter of Paul Simon, and basketball legend, Michael Jordan. On Primary Election Day, Obama received 54 percent of the overall Democratic vote. Obama's primary campaign won 66 percent of the Chicago vote, including 90 percent of the Black vote in Chicago, 61 percent of suburban Cook County, and 56 to 64 percent in three key counties: DuPage, Kane, and Lake (Panagakis 2004).

The 2004 Senate general election became increasingly peculiar, including another series of events which worked in Obama's political favor. Similar to Obama's chief primary election opponent Blair Hull, the Republican general election front-runner, Jack Ryan, also withdrew from the race in light of allegations concerning a personal scandal involving his ex-wife. In August 2004, Republicans surprisingly selected former Reagan diplomat and conservative radio talk show host Alan Keyes to replace Jack Ryan on the Republican ticket. Keyes moved to Illinois from Maryland in August, a few months prior to the election, to lead the Republican ticket.

With the selection of Alan Keyes, the U.S. Senate race became especially historic because it included two African-American candidates who were backed by the major political parties and running in districts that were *not* majority Black (Harris-Lacewell and Junn 2007, 38; Jackson 2006). In the general election, Obama painted Keyes as an interloping carpetbagger shipped in from Maryland in an attempt to steal the general election. Ironically, Obama used an "outsider" stamp similar to the one which Bobby Rush had placed on him four years earlier. However, Keyes, aware of Obama's perceived racial identity problems, "played the race card" on repeated occasions. He attacked Obama's racial identity and background and touted his "more authentic" roots in the African-American community. During a nationally televised interview with ABC-TV news reporter George Stephanopoulos, Alan Keyes stated,

> Barack Obama claims an African-American heritage...Barack Obama and I have the same race—that is, physical characteristics. We are not from the same heritage.... My ancestors toiled in slavery in this country.... My consciousness, who I am as a person, has been shaped by my struggle, deeply emotional and deeply painful, with the reality of that heritage. (Chase and Ford 2004)

In another televised U.S. Senate debate in Illinois, Keyes suggested that race should be important to the voters suggesting, "Race is involved in this in one way because the heritage that people have has a bearing on who they are and what they consider to be important" (Chase and Ford 2004).

Obama responded to these remarks stating, "I guess Mr. Keyes started off making a point that he's somehow more authentically African-American than I am.... You know, I obviously find that offensive" (Chase and Ford 2004).

Despite Keyes's name recognition and use of racial identity politics against Obama, he lost an uphill battle which was never in his favor. Keyes's political stances on issues from gay marriage to abortion rights aligned with much of the Republican Party ideology. However, the public delivery of his viewpoints and his shock-jock radio persona while on the campaign trail did not fare well with most Illinois voters, Republican or Democrat. Keyes's racial, religious, and moral attacks seemed to be largely ignored by the Obama campaign. One week after his selection as Republican nominee, *Chicago Tribune* polls showed Keyes down by 41 points (Sector 2004). While Keyes was well known by state likely voters at 91 percent, he was not well liked (20 percent favorable vs. 42 percent unfavorable). By mid-October his name recognition grew, but among likely voters his favorability ratings fell (15 percent favorable versus 51 percent unfavorable). Among African-American voters from mid-August to mid-October, Keyes favorability scores went from 3 percent to 7 percent favorable, and 65 percent to 69 percent unfavorable. On the other hand, Obama's name recognitions rose from 96 percent to 99 percent among total likely voters, with a favorability rating of 62 percent to 65 percent favorable, and 14 percent to 15 percent unfavorable. Keyes favorable/unfavorable ratings among Republicans went from 33 percent/35 percent in August to 32 percent/35 percent in October 2004 (Panagakis 2004). In November 2004, Obama defeated Keyes 70 percent to 27 percent—the widest margin in Illinois history (CNN 2004). Obama won the support of nine out of ten Black voters and seven out of ten White voters. Obama received 92 percent of the Black vote and 66 percent of the White vote. Keyes received 8 percent of the Black and 31 percent of the White vote.

Despite such a wide margin of support favoring Obama, this election still posed questions regarding the intersections of race, party identification, religiosity, political information and political behavior, providing a unique opportunity to examine these factors among Black and White Illinois respondents who were presented with the electoral choice of two African-American candidates from different political parties. However, despite Alan Keyes's highly unfavorable ratings among both Whites and Blacks and the persistent divisions within the Illinois Republican Party over his placement on the ticket, it is also interesting to examine why Keyes still managed to garner about one-third of the White vote in Illinois, including 33 percent of all White men. Exit polls show that Keyes received over a third of the Protestant vote. In fact, 77 percent of all White, conservative Protestant voters cast a ballot for Keyes, while Obama received 18 percent of this demographic. In order to gain a better understanding of these election results, the next section uses preelection data from the 2004 Illinois Senate Pre-Election Study to predict which factors influenced an intention to vote for Obama versus Keyes among both Black and White voters during the 2004 U.S. Senate general election.[5]

Predicting Electoral Behavior in the 2004 Senate Race among Black and White Illinois Voters

The 2004 Illinois Senate Study includes a random sample of Illinois residents interviewed in October 2004, prior to the November 2004 U.S. Senate general election. The Illinois sample consists of a random sample of respondents, with an oversample of African Americans. Data collected for the 2004 Illinois Senate Study was part of a larger survey, the 2004 Ethnic Politics Pre-Election Study (Harris-Lacewell and Junn 2004, 49).[6]

Table 6.2 presents the results from three multivariate logistic regression estimates for the dependent variable of the response to the question, "If the election for US Senate in Illinois were held today, who would you vote for?" (Obama = 1/

Table 6.2 Logit Model of Likelihood of Intention to Vote for Barack Obama, 2004

Variables	Model I (Full)		Model II (Whites)		Model III (Blacks)	
	B (SE)	min-max	B (SE)	min-max	B (SE)	min-max
Racial Identity						
Race is Politically Important	-0.597** (0.271)	-0.136	-0.775** (0.303)	-0.185	1.943** (0.974)	0.369
Political Information						
(Low) Interest In Politics	-0.336*** (0.130)	-0.228	-0.221 (0.152)	-0.154	-0.344 (0.427)	-0.141
Contacted	0.440* (0.234)	0.100	0.135 (0.289)	0.031	0.369 (0.716)	0.047
Live in White Community	-0.157 (0.245)	-0.035	-0.215 (0.280)	-0.049	0.034 (0.774)	0.004
Religiosity						
Religious Guidance Important	-0.197 (0.341)	-0.043	-0.343 (0.406)	-0.076	-2.560* (1.373)	-0.151
Other Controls						
Democrat	1.334*** (0.252)	0.282	1.774*** (0.350)	0.354	0.298 (0.726)	0.040
Black	0.830** (0.392)	0.168				
Education	0.450*** (0.132)	0.311	0.508*** (0.156)	0.355	1.173*** (0.365)	0.594
Income	0.017 (0.029)	0.067	0.020 (0.040)	0.081	-0.043 (0.068)	-0.100
Female	0.263 (0.232)	0.059	0.282 (0.276)	0.065	1.179 (0.736)	0.179
Age	-0.001 (0.008)	-0.010	-0.004 (0.008)	-0.056	0.035 (0.031)	0.277
Constant	-0.713 (0.843)		-0.677 (0.974)		-2.568 (3.225)	
Observations	609		418		119	
Log Likelihood	-353.505		-241.400		-49.313	
PseudoR²	0.143		0.152		0.298	

*** p<0.01, ** p<0.05, * p<0.10, Robust standard errors in parentheses.
Source: 2004 Illinois Senate Study.

Keyes = 0). Since the dependent variable measure is dichotomous, I use a logistic rather than ordinary least squares regression analysis. Because logistic regression coefficients are more difficult to interpret than ordinary least squares regression estimates, I also present predicted probabilities (under the columns "min-max") to understand the impact of each independent variable on the dependent measure from its minimum to maximum value. Predicted probabilities are much easier to interpret than logistic regression coefficients; unlike the regression coefficients, one can read the predicted probabilities on a scale of 0 to 1. Thus, for our purposes, if an independent variable has a predicted probability of .5, then a person who changes their score on that variable in question from the minimum to the maximum value, controlling for all other factors, increases their probability of intending to vote for Obama by 50 percent.

Model I presents results from the full sample of Illinois respondents. Model II presents results from White Illinois respondents. Model III presents results from Black Illinois respondents. Disaggregating the full model by race allows for a greater examination of the extent to which racial differences, between Black and White Illinois respondents, exist when declaring an intention to cast a vote for Obama versus Keyes.

The likelihood of voting for Obama versus Keyes was modeled as a function of *racial identity*: the perceived importance of the respondent's racial identity to their ideas about politics (1 = very/somewhat important/0 = not at all); *information context*: the respondent's interest in politics and public affairs (1 = very interested, 2 = interested, 3 = somewhat interested, 4 = not at all interested); the influence of whether the respondent lives in a predominantly White community (1 = yes/0 = no); and whether they were contacted by a political campaign prior to the election (1 = yes/0 = no); as well as *religiosity*: as measured by whether or not religion provides guidance in respondent's daily life (1 = yes/0 = no). The religion control is important for this model because Keyes constantly attacked Obama on religious and moral grounds. Alan Keyes called Barack Obama to task on several occasions concerning not only his racial authenticity but also his moral and religious authenticity, stating on numerous occasions that he did not believe Jesus would support Obama because he supports abortion rights. In a televised Senate debate, Keyes stated, while spreading his arms apart, "Christ is over here, Sen. Obama is over there: the two don't look the same" (Chase and Ford 2004). I also include several standard controls including party identification of the respondent (Democrat = 1/Other = 0) and standard sociodemographic characteristics: race, income, education, age, and gender. Note that only Model I includes a measure of race (Black =0 /Other = 1).[7]

Examining these measures of racial identity, information context, party ID, and religiosity, along with some standard demographic controls in a single model, helps us to untangle which factors influence a respondent's intention to cast a vote for Obama versus Keyes in 2004, and the salience of these factors when the model is disaggregated by race.

First, the racial identity measure posed some interesting results. In the full model, respondents who believed that their race was important to their ideas about politics were 14 percent less likely to declare an intention to vote for Obama than those who did not believe that race was important to their ideas about politics. When the model was disaggregated by race, we find that White respondents who believed that being White is important to their ideas about politics were 19 percent less likely to declare a vote for Obama than White respondents who did not think race is important. On the other hand, Black respondents who believed that being Black is important to their ideas about politics were 37 percent more likely to declare an intention to vote for Obama than Black respondents who do not deem race as important. Interestingly, controlling for all other factors, it appears that racial identity played a role in Blacks' and Whites' intention to vote for Obama.

It also appears that low interest in political and public affairs was also inversely correlated with an intention to vote for Obama in the full sample. Moreover, while being contacted by a candidate or political party to vote was positively correlated with an intention to vote for Obama in the full model. Respondents in the full model with lower levels of interest in politics were 23 percent less likely to declare a vote for Obama, and respondents who were contacted were 10 percent more likely to declare a vote for Obama. However, once the model was disaggregated by race, other factors seemed to "wash away" the influence of these two factors on vote choice.

The findings regarding religiosity were also interesting. The importance of religion has played an important role in the study of political participation, particularly related to electoral mobilization and turnout among Blacks (Harris 1994; Bledsoe, Welch, Sigelman, and Combs 1995; Calhoun-Brown 1996; Dawson, Brown and Allen 1990; Reese and Brown 1997; Secret, Johnson, and Forrest 1990). However, the extant research is largely silent on the relationship between religion and vote choice, particularly when choosing among two Black candidates with starkly different views on issues important to the Black religious community (Harris-Lacewell and Junn 2007 are the exception). Recall that Keyes publicly challenged Obama's moral and religious authenticity throughout the general election season (Chase and Ford 2004).

Both in the full sample and in the samples disaggregated by race, religious guidance posed a negative relationship to an intention to vote for Obama. However, this measure only reached statistical significance for Blacks. Black respondents who stated that religion is important in guiding their daily lives were 15 percent less likely to declare an intention to vote for Obama, controlling for all other factors. Harris-Lacewell and Junn (2007) find somewhat similar results suggesting, "Keyes was unable to reasonably portray himself as the authentically racial candidate. Instead, Keyes was able to gain some ground among religious voters, who used religiosity rather than race as the central decision heuristic" (47).

The finding regarding party identification is somewhat unsurprising. Democrats were 28 percent more likely to declare an intention to vote for Obama than non-Democrats, and the same finding held true among White Democrats, who were 35 percent more likely to vote for Obama than White non-Democrats. However, controlling for all other factors, Black Democrats were no more or less likely to declare an intention to vote for Obama than Black non-Democrats.

Finally, the findings from the demographic measures also support the findings of Harris-Lacewell and Junn (2007), who find that Blacks are more likely to cast a vote for Obama than non-Blacks. This model shows that Blacks are 17 percent more likely to declare an intention to vote for Obama than non-Blacks. The model also shows that respondents with higher levels of educational attainment are also more likely to have declared an intention to vote for Obama than respondents with lower levels of educational attainment. Notably, the influence of education is much more salient for Black than for White respondents; while Black respondents with higher levels of education were 59 percent more likely to declare an intention to vote for Obama, White respondents with higher levels of education were only 36 percent more likely to declare a vote for Obama. Controlling for all other factors, gender, age, and income posed no statistically significant effect on respondents' intention to vote for Obama versus Keyes in 2004.

Results from statistical analysis, while complex, suggest that racial differences, including factors related to one's racial identity, played a role in shaping political behavior for Blacks and Whites in 2004. Religion and educational attainment also served a role in shaping Black political behavior during the 2004 Senate race.

Beyond Illinois: Racial Identity, Electability, and the 2008 Presidential Election

This chapter used Obama's early political campaigns as a lens through which to examine Black constituent attitudes and behavior in an era of post-Civil Rights Black political leadership in the United States. While Black voters rejected Obama's bid during the 2000 Congressional race against an African American male Democrat, Black voters overwhelmingly supported him in his 2004 Senate race against an African-American male Republican. Obama's moderate use of racial identity cues and universalistic policy stances upset his electoral chances to capture a Congressional seat at the more racially homogenous district level. But eventually, Black voters saw his moderation as an asset when he pursued statewide office for the U.S. Senate. In addition, this study suggests that shifts in Black electoral support for Obama are much more complex than factors related to racial identity alone.

Obama's relationship with the Black electorate was also seemingly strengthened by factors related to political information and knowledge as well as candidate electability. Obama entered the Congressional race in 2000 with only six months to attempt to defeat Bobby Rush, a well-liked, well-established political giant on Chicago's Black South Side, leaving him little time to raise money, gain name recognition, connect with Black voters and ultimately get out the vote in his favor. After a devastating loss, Obama ran for the U.S. Senate and subsequently for president having learned valuable rules along the political road. He reportedly started campaigning for U.S. Senate more than 18 months prior to the primary election. Moreover, beyond benefiting from the personal scandals of his opponents, which helped to propel him to frontrunner status, he was successful in increasing his visibility among Illinois voters, including the Black electorate, with television ads featuring well-known political figures in Illinois and in the

Chicago area. This exposure, coupled with numerous celebrity endorsements, helped to position Obama as a viable contender and ultimately a winner of the Democratic nomination and later the U.S. Senate seat from Illinois. While the results from the 2004 Illinois Pre-Election Study revealed that racial identity played a role in shaping Black voters's intentions to vote for Obama for U.S. Senate, notably Obama received a helpful dose of free advertising, benefiting from a national platform during and after a well-received keynote address at 2004 Democratic National convention.

After serving as U.S. Senator from Illinois for less than three years, in February 2007, Obama entered the race for the 2008 Democratic presidential nomination. Yet, it appeared that Obama's burden of Jekyll and Hyde politics was not put to rest back in Illinois. Arguably, the Democratic primaries presented the ultimate challenge, to date, for Obama in confronting the nexus between racial identity and the support of the Black electorate. In a similar fashion to his previous campaigns, African Americans as a voting bloc did not immediately support Obama's candidacy. When Obama found difficulty wrestling the Black voting bloc away from Hillary Clinton in the early months of the Democratic primary, questions concerning his racial identity and the extent to which Obama was "Black enough" or "too Black" garnered national media attention.

Ironically, when Blacks as a voting bloc began to turn their support toward Obama (largely following his historic win in the predominantly White Iowa Caucus and in the wake of Bill Clinton's "fairy tale" remarks during the South Carolina Democratic primary concerning the "seriousness" of Obama as a presidential contender (Fears 2008), it was widely suggested that his newfound support, in part, stemmed from Blacks' racial group consciousness. Media pundits espoused the idea that Blacks moved to the Obama camp because of their shared racial identity (see, for example, "Poll: Blacks Support Obama…" 2008).

Paradoxically, many of the factors that supposedly raised suspicions among the Black electorate (i.e., Obama's White crossover appeal) during his earlier campaigns, now *seemingly* served as the same heuristic cue that facilitated the widespread support among the Black electorate during the 2008 Presidential primaries.

We do not yet know the extent to which a shift in Black support for Obama actually occurred because of racial identity or the role of political information and knowledge of candidate Obama. The perceived electability/viability of Obama as an African-American candidate seemed equally important to Black voters in 2008 as it did in 2004, invoking what some scholars refer to as a bandwagon effect. Herbert Simon (1954) argues that,

> It is supposed that the voting behavior of at least some persons is a function of their expectations of the election outcome; published poll data are assumed to influence these expectations, hence to affect the voting behavior of these persons. If persons are more likely to vote for a candidate when they expect him to win than when they expect him to lose, we have a "bandwagon" effect…. (246)

It seems that a shift in substantial Black support for Obama took hold only after the Black electorate perceived Obama to be a viable presidential candidate. In particular, after Obama won the Iowa Caucus, it was evident that the Obama campaign had reached broad White crossover appeal. Obama won 38 percent of the Iowa caucus vote to John Edwards's 30 percent and Hillary Clinton's 29 percent. This result was a great blow to Hillary Clinton's momentum and arguably, a heuristic cue to the Black electorate concerning the electability of Obama for the Democratic nomination. Tracking a few public opinion polls among Black registered voters further marks the dramatic shift in Black support for Obama post-Iowa. Two combined *Washington Post*-ABC polls, taken among registered Democrats in December 2006 and January 2007 (prior to Obama's announcement that he would run for the Democratic nomination on February 10, 2007), showed that Blacks preferred Hillary Clinton 3 to 1 over Barack Obama—60 percent to 20 percent. Two CNN/Opinion Research polls taken among Black registered Democrats before the Iowa Caucus showed Clinton leading Obama 53 percent to 36 percent and 57 percent to 33 percent (April 10–12, 2007 and October 12–14, 2007, respectively). However, a third CNN/Opinion Research poll taken January 14–17, 2008, following the Iowa Caucus on January 3, showed Obama leading Clinton among Black registered voters 59 percent to 31 percent (CNN/Opinion Research Poll: January 18, 2008).[8] By Super Tuesday on February 5, 2008, exit polls reveal that Obama won about 82 percent of the Black vote (Balz and Cohen 2007).

Going into the general election against Republican presidential nominee Senator John McCain, Obama solidly held the Black voting bloc. In an historic victory, Obama defeated McCain in the general election to become the 44th President of the United States. Obama won 365 Electoral College votes and 53 percent of the popular vote to McCain's 173 electoral votes and 46 percent of the popular vote. Exit poll results showed that Obama was supported by about 95 percent of Black voters, while McCain was supported by 4 percent of Black voters (CNN National Election Day Exit Poll).

Since Obama captured the national imagination in 2004, many scholars and commentators have been preoccupied with the extent to which Blacks would support his political campaigns. While his was a shorter road to the White House than most, it was not an easy road. His political story provides a nuanced view of the often not-so-monolithic Black electorate, at the local, state, and national levels. As the number of post-Civil Rights era African-American candidates increases, the role of racial identity and the extent to which candidates use deracialized campaign strategies, speak in universalistic policy terms, and seek broad support from Whites and other racial/ethnic groups will become increasingly important areas of study. The ways in which such candidates navigate the imposition of Jekyll and Hyde politics on their personal background, character, and policy agendas poses further avenues ripe for study. Such research should examine the influence of racial identity, political information, and perceptions of a candidate's electability beyond a Black/White dichotomy toward an understanding of these factors from a comparative racial/ethnic context.

Notes

1. The author wishes to thank Jane Junn and Melissa Harris-Lacewell for the use of data from the 2004 Illinois Senate Pre-election Study. The author also thanks Nick Panagakis of the Market Shares Corp. for his polling data and useful insight on the 2004 Illinois Senate race.

2. *Dr. Jekyll and Mr. Hyde*, as it is popularly known, introduces us to Jekyll, a wealthy, handsome, and respected scientist. However, Jekyll is of "two-selves" for he is leading a double life. Dr. Jekyll successfully compounds a mixture, that when drunk, transforms his body into Edward Hyde, an unsightly, repulsive being that represents the pure evil dwelling within him. Dr. Jekyll is transformed once again to his original self upon drinking the same potion. For some time Jekyll indulges in his secret life and his ability to practice unspeakable acts without detection or repercussions. However, after Hyde engages in a series of crimes, including murder, Jekyll attempts to rid himself of Mr. Hyde—his evil side. Unfortunately, as the story goes, Dr. Jekyll is unable to shake Edward Hyde as his nature struggles between good and evil. As Edward Hyde struggled to overtake Jekyll's total being, Jekyll found himself transforming into Hyde, without having drank the potion. What is more, the drug intended to transform Hyde back to Jekyll was no longer effective. Jekyll, faced with the fact that he may be forced to live out his days as Edward Hyde, tragically commits suicide.

3. More recent findings by Bledsoe et al. (1995) show that "increasing racial integration of American large cities may well reduce Black solidarity…as the numbers of Asians and Hispanics increase dramatically and increasing income undermines the sense of collective identity and fate…. Blacks living in integrated communities may be less interested in Black interests and Black candidates" (453).

4. Converse (1962), contends that individuals most susceptible to influence in a political campaign, are those of the middling level of political awareness, since they are attentive enough to absorb political information, but their knowledge of politics is not sophisticated enough to resist changing their opinions. On the other hand, the least politically aware individuals pay little attention to political cues or messages and are cut off, for one reason other the other, from most efforts of the media and other elite cues to change their opinions. Moreover, the opinions of the most aware individuals are also stable since they are sophisticated enough to guard their existing views and thus are less susceptible to change.

5. There is surprisingly little available data on the 2004 Illinois Senate race. I was fortunate to receive the unreleased data used in this study from the 2004 Illinois Senate Survey (Harris-Lacewell and Junn 2004).

6. The larger random probability sample includes interviews of equal numbers of Whites, African Americans, Latinos, and Asian Americans in the United States. The survey firm Knowledge Networks of Menlo Park, California conducted self-administered surveys via the Internet. Respondents were selected for the Knowledge Networks panel using standard methods of random-digit dialing. "Respondents were selected for the study on the basis of a series of racial self-classification questions collected by Knowledge Networks in a demographic profile. In addition to the U.S. and Illinois samples, a Florida study was also fielded to capture the dynamics of the U.S. Senate race between Betty Castor and Mel Martinez" (Harris-Lacewell and Junn 2007, 49).

7. See Harris-Lacewell and Junn (2007) for a somewhat similar research design and modeling strategy. However, this study disaggregates by racial/ethnic group and does not use the experimental manipulations used in the Harris-Lacewell and Junn 2007 study.

8. Interestingly, the CNN/Opinion Research poll taken in April 2007 and again after the Iowa Caucus asked if Black and White registered Democrats believed Hillary

Clinton or Barack Obama "understands the problems and concerns of Blacks." In April 2007, 88 percent of Black registered Democrats favored Hillary Clinton on this question, as compared to only 77 percent of Black registered Democrats who favored Obama. However, after the Iowa Caucus, 82 percent of Blacks favored Obama on this question as compared to 74 percent who favored Clinton. The same CNN/Opinion poll showed that 42 percent of Blacks felt that Blacks would be better off, if Obama were elected President in November 2008, as compared to only 35 percent of Blacks who believed that Blacks would be better off, if Clinton were elected president (CNN/Opinion Research Poll: January 18, 2008). The CNN/Opinion Research Poll included 383 Black registered voters. The sampling error was +/- 5 percentage points.

References

Balz, Dan, and Jon Cohen. 2007. Blacks shift to Obama, poll finds. *The Washington Post*, February 28, A1.

———. 2008. Poll: Blacks support Obama over Clinton. United Press International. 11 February 28. http://www.redorbit.com/news/politics/1250859/poll_blacks_support_obama_over_clinton/index (accessed October 2, 2009).

Bledsoe, Timothy. Susan Welch, Lee Sigelman, and Michael Combs. 1995. Residential context and racial solidarity among African Americans. *American Journal of Political Science* 39: 434–58.

Bobo, Lawrence, and Franklin D. Gilliam, Jr. 1990. Race, sociopolitical participation, and black empowerment. *American Political Science Review* 84 (June): 377–93.

Brady, Henry E., Sidney Verba, and Kay Lehman Schlozman. 1995. Beyond SES: A resource model of political participation. *The American Political Science Review* 89: 271–94.

Burnside, Randolph, and Kami Whitehurst. 2007. From the statehouse to the White House? Barack Obama's bid to become the next president. *Journal of Black Studies* 38 (September): 75–89.

Calhoun-Brown, Allison. 1996. African American churches and political mobilization: The psychological impact of organizational resources. *The Journal of Politics* 58: 935–53.

Chase, John, and Liam Ford. 2004. Obama, Keyes exchange fighting words on morals, race and religion. *Chicago Tribune,* October 22.

———. 2004. CNN Illinois Senate election results. http://www.cnn.com/ELECTION/2004/pages/results/states/IL/S/01/index.html.

Converse, Philip. 1962. Information flow and the stability of partisan attitudes. *Public Opinion Quarterly* 26: 578–99.

Crouch, Stanley. 2006. What Obama isn't: Black like me on race. *New York Daily News* November 2. http://www.nydailynews.com/opinions/2006/11/02/2006-11-02_what_obama_isnt_Black_like_me_on_race.html.

Crowley, Candy, and Sasha Johnson. 2007. Is America ready to embrace Obama? CNN Washington Bureau. http://www.cnn.com/2007/POLITICS/02/28/obama.black.vote/index.html?section=cnn_lates,.Dawson, Michael. 1994. *Behind the mule: Race and class in African-American politics.* Princeton, NJ: Princeton University Press.

———, Ronald Brown, and Richard Allen. 1990. Racial belief systems, religious guidance, and African American political participation. *The National Review of Political Science* 2: 22–44.

Dickerson, Debra J. 2006. Colorblind: Barack Obama would be the great Black hope in the next presidential race—If he were actually Black. *Salon*, December 22. http://www.salon.com/opinion/feature/2007/01/22/obama/index_np.html (accessed October 10, 2008).

Fears, Darryl. 2008. Blacks stung by Bill Clinton's remarks. *The Washington Post*, January 25. http://www.cbsnews.com/stories/2008/01/25/politics/washingtonpost/main3751490.shtml.

Federal Elections Commission. 2000. U.S.House of Representatives results—Illinois. http://www.fec.gov/pubrec/fe2000/ilh.htm.

Fletcher, Michael A. 2007. Obama's appeal to blacks remains in question *The Washington Post,* January 25, A1.

Giles, Nancy. 2007. What exactly is "Black enough"? Nancy Giles ponders the question everyone seems to be asking. CBS News. March 4. http://www.cbsnews.com/stories/2007/03/04/sunday/main2534119.shtml,Gurin, Patricia. Shirley J. Hatchett, and James S. Jackson. 1989. *Hope and independence.* New York: Russell Sage Foundation.

Guterbock, Thomas, and Bruce London. 1983. Race, political orientation, and participation: An empirical test of four competing theories. *American Sociological Review* 48 (August): 439–53.

Hansen, M. 2007. "Ridiculous" to doubt Obama's "blackness." *Des Moines Register*, February 22, 1.

Harris, Fredrick. 1994. Something within: Religion as a mobilizer of African American political activism. *The Journal of Politics* 56: 42–68.

Harris-Lacewell, Melissa, and Jane Junn. 2007. Old friends and new alliances: How the 2004 Illinois senate race complicates the study of race and religion. *Journal of Black Studies* 38: 30–50.

Jackson, John S. 2006. *The making of a senator: Barack Obama and the 2004 Illinois senate race.* An Occasional Paper of the Paul Simon Public Policy Institute. Southern Illinois University, Carbondale, Illinois.

Leighley, Jan E., and Arnold Vedlitz. 1999. Race, ethnicity, and political participation: Competing models and contrasting explanations. *The Journal of Politics* 61 (November): 1092–1114.

McIlwain, Charlton D. 2007. Perceptions of leadership and the challenge of Obama's blackness. *Journal of Black Studies* 38: 64–74.

Mendell, David. 2007. *Obama: From promise to power.* New York: Harper Publishers.

Miller, Arthur H., Patricia Gurin, Gerald Gurin, and Oksana Malanchuk. 1981. Group consciousness and political participation. *American Journal of Political Science* 25 (August): 494–511.

Mutz, Diana C. 1993. Direct and indirect routes to politicizing personal experience: Does knowledge make a difference? *Public Opinion Quarterly* 57: 483–502.

Obama, Barack. 1995. *Dreams from my father: A story of race and inheritance.* New York: Times Books.

———. 2006. *The audacity of hope: Thoughts on reclaiming the American dream.* New York: Crown Books.

Olsen, Marvin. 1972. Social participation and voting turnout: A multivariate analysis. *American Sociological Review* 37: 317–33.

Panagakis, Nick. 2004. *Chicago Tribune* poll conducted by Market Share Corp.

Pearson, Rick. 2004. Obama, Ryan out front. *Chicago Tribune*, March 9, 1.

Philpot, Tasha S., and Walton Hanes Jr. 2007. One of our own: Black female candidates and the voters who support them. *American Journal of Political Science* 51 (1): 49–62.

———. 2007. Poll: Presidential races tighten on both sides. CNN.com. http://www.cnn.com/2007/POLITICS/04/16/poll.2008/index.html (accessed April 27, 2007).

Reese, Laura, and Ronald Brown. 1995. The effects of religious messages on racial identity and system blame among African Americans. *The Journal of Politics* 57: 24–43.

Rosenstone Steven J., and John Mark Hansen. 1993. *Mobilization, participation, and democracy in America.* New York: Macmillan.

Scott, Janny. 2007. In 2000, a streetwise veteran schooled a bold young Obama. *The New York Times,* September 9.

Secret, Philip E., James B. Johnson, and Audrey W. Forrest. 1990. The impact of religiosity on political participation and membership in voluntary associations among black and white Americans. *Journal of Black Studies* 21: 87–102.

Sector, Bob. 2004. Obama holds 41-point lead over Keyes. *The Chicago Tribune*, August 22.

Shingles, Richard. 1981. Black consciousness and political participation: The missing link. *American Political Science Review* 75: 76–91.

Simon, Herbert A.. 1954. Bandwagon and underdog effects of election predictions. *Public Opinion Quarterly* 51: 245–53.

Tate, Katherine. 1991. Black political participation in the 1984 and 1988 presidential elections. *American Political Science Review* 85: 1159–76.

———. 1993. *From protest to politics: The new black voters in American elections.* New York and Boston: Russell Sage Foundation/Harvard University Press.

Valbrun, Marjorie. 2007. Black like me? Those asking if Barack Obama is "black enough" are asking the wrong question. *The Washington Post*, February 16.

Verba, Sidney, and Norman H. Nie. 1972. *Participation in America: Political democracy and social equality.* New York: Harper and Row.

Walters, Ron. 2007. Barack Obama and the politics of blackness. *Journal of Black Studies* 38 (September): 7–29.

Williams, Linda F. 1990. White/black perceptions of the electability of black political candidates. *National Political Science Review* 2: 45–64.

Wolfinger, Raymond. E., and Steven J. Rosenstone. 1980. *Who votes?* New Haven, CT: Yale University Press.

Zaller, John. 1991. Information, Values and Opinion. *American Political Science Review* 85: 1215–37.

———. 1992. *The nature and origins of mass opinion.* New York: Cambridge University Press.

7   Leadership, Legitimacy, and Public Perceptions of Barack Obama

Charlton McIlwain

Voter assessments of candidate leadership have long played a role in candidate preferences in American elections. Conventional wisdom holds, for example, that George W. Bush prevailed over John Kerry in part because voters viewed Bush as the stronger leader; the perception of Kerry as a flip flopper undermined assessments of his leadership. When Black candidates run for office, voters assess their leadership skills, too.

In this chapter, Charlton McIlwain asks if voter perceptions of a Black candidate's leadership skills are a proxy for racial resentment and if that could have been used against Barack Obama at any time during the 2008 presidential campaign. Using data from the 1988 primaries, McIlwain correlates White voter perceptions of Jesse Jackson's leadership with vote choice and replicates that model for Barack Obama in the 2008 primary.

McIlwain then turns to a discussion of the role of leadership in the 2008 Democratic primary. While voters were more confident in Obama's leadership skills (compared to Jackson 20 years earlier), he still demonstrated weakness on this dimension, especially when compared to Hillary Clinton. So, if Hillary Clinton was perceived to be the stronger leader, how did Barack Obama end up winning the nomination? The answer, McIlwain argues, is change.

Introduction

Leadership is an individual character trait or skill associated with social movements in general. More specifically, however, the term is inextricably linked to American presidential politics, particularly American public opinion about presidential candidates and office holders. In fact, many argue that it is one, if not the, most important criteria Americans use to assess presidential fitness. In August 2004, Barack Obama's political trajectory transitioned in the direction of his presidential aspirations. His speech on July 27, 2004 at the Democratic National Convention not only galvanized crowds of immediate and mediated spectators, but set the stage for and sparked discussion about the possibility for his run at the nation's highest office.

When Obama gave his first speech on the national political stage, he had not yet even been elected to the U.S. Senate.[1] Up to that point, his political career consisted of organizing community groups on Chicago's South Side and a stint in the Illinois State Legislature where, aside from smoking cigarettes and playing poker with his legislative colleagues, he distinguished himself as an able, but relatively local politician (Mikva 2008, personal communication). He traded his earlier distinction as the first Black to head the prestigious *Harvard Law Review* and the opportunity to pursue a lucrative legal profession for work on the streets and the backroom brawls in the corridors of the capitol building in Springfield, Illinois. Despite all of this, Obama was—as early presidential speculators were quick to point out—woefully inexperienced in terms of government work.

Shortly after Barack Obama decided to run for President, I became interested in this phenomenon of leadership: what it means not only in terms of a candidate's ability to cultivate the skill or the public's assessment of whether one possessed it. I was interested primarily in the relationship between race and individual perceptions of presidential leadership. My first look at this relationship (McIlwain 2007) showed that Whites' reliance on leadership as the litmus test for presidential fitness might have detrimentally affected Obama. In short, I argued that leadership might serve as the vehicle by which Whites would mobilize their racial prejudices, their longstanding opinion that Blacks are, for whatever reason, inferior to Whites in terms of a host of valued presidential character traits such as intelligence, work ethic, and most importantly, leadership (Williams 1990; Terkildsen 1993).

Looking back on the 2008 Democratic Party presidential primary, it is not sufficient to say simply that leadership served as a vehicle mobilizing White prejudice against Obama. What is clearer is that voters—White and Black alike—exercised their opinion and assessment of Obama in large part by choosing between two models of presidential leadership. One of these models conceptualizes and operationalizes leadership in terms of formal qualifications reduced in the single term *experienc*e—a known quantity and measurable trait said to predict future success. The other model conceptualizes leadership as rhetorical skill, the ability to rehabilitate, cultivate, and motivate the masses in support of a cause (even if that cause is one's own presidential candidacy). These two models need not be mutually exclusive in principle, but were mobilized in that way in the 2008 contest by opposing candidates Barack Obama and Hillary Clinton. Bifurcating these models of leadership in the way they were had much to do with race.

I argue that Obama's presidential primary success is predicated on both the foundation of Civil Rights era racial politics, as well as his unique ability to recast his constituency, as perhaps a model for Black, post-Civil Rights era electoral success.

Leadership: Presidential Politics and The Civil Rights Tradition

It may come as no surprise to some that presidential politics and the issue of leadership are inseparable. But this is a relatively recent development, and not an insignificant one at that. When we think of the years, decades, and centuries prior to America's founding, the fall and rise of nations, city-states and dynasties, leadership was the stuff of warrior kings, military men, and brave explorers. National heroes—those that commanded respect, demanded reverence, and cultivated favor among the masses—were not learned men or philosopher kings, but those whose ability to amass legions of followers was proven on the battlefield. General Napoleon Bonaparte ruled France at the end of the French Revolution. We are more likely to think of men like Sir Humphrey Gilbert and his half brother Sir Walter Raleigh when we speak of the expansion of the British Empire into the Americas. And, of course it was the great General George Washington who was the overwhelming favorite to lead America in its first steps toward constituting a united, sovereign nation. This is not to say that such leaders were mere brutes lacking rhetorical sophistication. In fact, in most instances, great leaders possessed both the strength for war as well as the persuasive prowess to lead followers into war.

Of course, great military leaders always ran the risk of becoming tyrants by whipping the masses into an emotional frenzy, as Walter Lippman (1922/1997) would later point out. The founders of our new nation sought above all else to fashion a nation immune from tyranny, based on the rule of law, and by limiting the power and authority of the nation's head. The ability to wage war still reigned supreme. It was the exercise and influence of rhetoric they sought to rein in by limiting the president's role, authority, and visibility among the people. In Jeffery Tullis's (1987) characterization of the rhetorical presidency, it was this separation of powers doctrine that marked the dividing line between what he referred to as the "old way" and the new way of conceptualizing the role and relevance of the president and presidency (Tullis 1987, 25).

This new way, the rhetorical presidency, diminished congressional authority, usurped the power to fashion public policy, and, most importantly, placed the president in direct contact with the American public, a point also taken up by Kernell (2006, 1–5). The most dramatic outcome of the rhetorical presidency is that the American public, as well as elected congressional officials, become subject to the persuasive prerogatives of the president. Tullis argues that this is not merely an interesting development in presidential politics. Rather, he argues that it has fundamentally transformed the relationship between the three branches of government, and the president's role in relation to public policy and public opinion. Further, it forever altered our conception of the role and responsibilities that come with the title and office of President. Chief among this new conception is the reemergence of leadership as an essential and defining aspect of presidential politics and presidential character (Kernell 1986; Tullis 1987; Hart 1989).

Franklin Delano Roosevelt, Harry Truman, Lyndon Johnson, and Ronald Reagan are the presidents who most consistently used the tenets of the rhetorical presidency to shape the modern presidency. They all exemplified the single most important characteristic of the rhetorical president: vision. From Roosevelt's New Deal to Truman's Fair Deal, Johnson's Great Society to Reagan's vision of Peace Through Strength, each campaigned for office reimagining what the nation should look like by the end of their tenure. They entered the Oval Office with a policy agenda to fashion the nation in line with their own vision, and they executed their plan by selling their policy initiatives directly to the public using every personal and mediated means available to them (Gelderman, 1997). This became our modern conception of presidential leadership. Leadership means possessing a grand vision for the country, the foresight to channel that vision into the language of public policy, and the political sophistication and strategic skill to mold public sentiment, will, needs, and desires to match one's own.

But these modern models of the rhetorical presidency also shared something else in common: experience. Roosevelt served in the New York State Senate, was Secretary of the Navy, and served as governor. Truman was a former military officer, senator, and vice president before becoming president. Johnson also served in the Senate as well as in the House of Representatives, and also served as vice president. Reagan was the least experienced among them, and even he was Governor of California before becoming president. Several other presidents, not necessarily known for their rhetorical skill, also possessed similar experience before assuming the office. Somewhere along the way, leadership became synonymous with experience. I refer to this generally as the classical model of leadership, where rhetorical ability and government experience are closely intertwined.

The Civil Rights Era Model of Black Leadership

Prior to and during the height of the Civil Rights Movement, African Americans were either essentially barred from formal participation in elective office or wielded very little influence when they were elected. Certainly, the upper echelons of government—the U.S. Senate and the presidency—were well out of reach to African Americans. At the time that many of the figures above were leading the country, prominent African-American figures were embroiled in trying to secure basic freedoms for themselves and members of the Black community. As opposed to the national model where the president was *the* leader, within the Civil Rights Movement there was a diverse array of "leaders." There was Malcolm X speaking out from his northern, urban, Muslim religious base, and Rev. Martin Luther King Jr. leading Southern boycotts and sit-ins. There was Rev. Ralph Abernathy heading up the Southern Christian Leadership Conference's Poor People's Campaign and Thurgood Marshall's leadership of the NAACP Legal Defense Fund. These are a mere few.

Leadership and leaders in the Civil Rights Movement were identified as having a number of personal qualities and character traits (Smith 1996). Chief among these was rhetorical skill—the persuasive power of speech and the ability to mobilize and motivate individuals to join a cause, often to the peril of those who followed. Interwoven with rhetorical skill was a genuine concern for people and a deep desire to inspire and work for change at the local, state, national, or international level. Smith referred to this prominent aspect of leadership as "charisma," a trait central to Martin Luther King Jr.'s leadership in the Civil Rights Movement (Smith 1996, 34). Smith's observation highlights thinking within the post-Martin Luther King Civil Rights Movement, a general consensus that a new leadership model would tie charismatic, street-level organizers with Black elected officials and the legions of Black grass-roots activists (Smith 1996, 34).

Given this, it is no wonder that many of the civil rights leaders that emerged were preachers, individuals who had the ability, position, and organizational structure to connect these aspects of leadership under one roof, as it were. It is also no wonder that once African Americans began to be increasingly elected following the passage of the Civil and Voting Rights Acts in the 1960s, the African-Americans elected to political office were often either former preachers or had very close ties to the Black church (Lincoln and Mamiya 1990, 216–17). The model of leadership that emerged within the Civil Rights era and beyond has been largely secondary to the experience model, largely because those who exemplified this model had both limited formal government experience, as well as limited political and civic interests. In the words of former Congressman and Congressional Black Caucus pioneer William Clay (D-MO), Black people have "no permanent friends, no permanent enemies, just permanent interests" (Clay 1992, ix, 165).

The civil rights model of Black leadership pursued the interests of African Americans first and foremost. Thus, one might distinguish the classical model of leadership (that emphasizes experience) from the rhetorical model of leadership developed by Tullis (1987), Kernell (1986), and Hart (1989), from the civil rights model that emphasized charisma, collective participation, and racial group interests (Smith 1996; Walters and Smith 1999). During the 2008 Democratic Presidential Primary, Obama exhibited the rhetorical skill of the classical model of leadership, with the charisma and grassroots, collective mobilization characteristics of the civil rights model, while broadening the sphere and object of his rhetorical action to encompass national, rather than narrowly defined racial group interests. Hillary Clinton primarily adhered to the purely classical model of leadership that emphasized individual political experience. I would argue that Barack Obama followed the civil rights model of leadership, though with a significant difference (Obama is still a largely deracialized candidate).

Two Models of Leadership in the 2008 Presidential Campaign

According to Patrick Healy, the *New York Times* reporter assigned to cover Hillary Clinton's presidential campaign in 2008, Obama caught Senator Clinton completely by surprise (Healy 2008, personal communication). Clinton, the New York Senator who had essentially campaigned for president since she took office, began the presidential campaign cycle as the frontrunner. She expected to stay in that position because her chief rivals lacked her level of name recognition, experience, and political machinery. Despite early media speculations pitting her, potentially the first female president, against Obama, potentially the first Black president, Clinton made no room for the possibility of such a competition (Healy 2008).

Then there was Iowa, a state with the first and historically most influential primary contest, a state with a majority White electorate full of Democratic Party loyalists. Clinton fully expected to win. It wasn't until Obama pulled an upset, followed by perhaps his most memorable speech on record, that Clinton and her campaign team began to really take stock of this new kid on the block. Clinton prevailed in New Hampshire, however, and she took it as a sign that Iowa was just a fluke. Confident that running the table on Super Tuesday would demoralize and financially bankrupt her opponents, Clinton planned to be the only candidate left standing. Of course, that didn't happen. In fact, just the opposite took place. Obama raised more money, out-organized the Clinton campaign in the Super Tuesday election states, and ended the day as the overwhelming victor. At the end of the day, it was Clinton who was demoralized and financially bankrupt (Mooney 2008).

Of course the media, pundits, political analysts, and the Clinton campaign team spent the first few days after Super Tuesday taking stock of what had happened. How did Obama win? Everyone seemed to come up with the same basic answer: Obama literally *outperformed* Clinton. At almost every campaign event leading up to and following Super Tuesday, Barack Obama packed venues with unprecedented numbers of supporters, undecided voters, curious onlookers, and a never-ending trail of media. Thousands and tens of thousands routinely packed football stadiums, basketball arenas, and town square lawns just to see him. Cheering and chanting his name and campaign slogan, *Yes We Can*, they came for one reason and one reason only: to hear Barack Obama *speak*. They left inspired, hopeful, motivated. Pundits began making comparisons between Obama and Martin Luther King Jr. They spoke about his ability to connect with crowds through his words. They highlighted his ability to turn a phrase in the style of Black preachers in the pulpit on Sunday morning, enhanced by his ability to reach Whites, Blacks, Latinos, and everyone else in between with his message of hope, change, and national unity (Halicks 2008).

The Clinton campaign also identified this gap in speaking ability and style as a significant cause for Obama's unexpected success. Clinton acknowledged she couldn't compete in this arena, and so, she did the next best thing: she began attacking Obama's strength as a limitation. In what was perhaps her most salient and consistent contrast to Obama, Clinton crafted a campaign message that compared Obama's ability to give a speech with her ability to lead and get things done. Clinton made the contrast in several different ways. Trying out her new message at a mid-February fundraiser, Clinton put it this way:

> It's time we move from good words to good works, from sound bites to sound solutions…. We need to make a choice between speeches and solutions. The best words in the world aren't enough unless you match them with action. (Byun 2008)

In this instance, Clinton separates speech from "action" and finding "solutions," clarifying later in her speech that only someone with the requisite experience can accomplish these ends (Byun 2008). Not too long after, Clinton began making sharper distinctions between speech and action, one that came dangerously close to invoking a longstanding racial stereotype. One of the best examples of this more focused attack is featured in a late February ad Clinton ran in advance of the Texas primary.[2] The ad begins with the image of several White ranch hands throwing bales of hay into the back of a pickup truck. A hot, Texas sun beating down on them in the middle of the day, one can see the fatigue in the men's eyes. "Here in Texas, when there's *work* to be done, *talk* doesn't cut it,"[2] a narrator says in an unmistakable Texas drawl. "You gotta roll up your sleeves, stand your ground and *deliver*,"[2] he continues as the image fades from the ranchers to a silent moving image of Hillary Clinton speaking at a small gathering. The narrator continues talking over the imagery that shifts from a group of children to an image of several senior citizens, to rehabilitating military veterans, to a large group of school children. "That's what Hillary Clinton does. She's fought for and *delivered* coverage for uninsured children, health care and dignity for our veterans, and better schools and better teachers."[2] As the image fades back to the now setting sun back on the wide open Texas plains, the narrator concludes: "In Texas it's better *done* than said, and when it's all *said and done*, Hillary *delivers*."[2] Most of the ad here continues the recent contrast between talk and action, talking about getting things done versus delivering on one's promises. Again, it emphasizes that particular quality of leadership about which she can boast most, doing something, accomplishing something, making a list and completing tasks. It is the beginning of the ad that starts Clinton's tip toe into the zone of racial stereotypes when making speeches is contrasted with "hard work." Obama's ability to speak and Clinton's ability to work hard to get things done insinuates that Obama lacks either or both the ability or willingness to work hard, settling for just shooting off his mouth.

As the competition between Clinton and Obama became more heated, Clinton retreated to and emphasized this speaking versus hard work contrast more often. In her speech following her loss in Wisconsin, Clinton again emphasized, in contrast to Obama, that "we have to have hard work" (McIlwain 2008, A27). As I explained in a February 25 editorial in *Newsday*, Clinton's repeated contrast and insinuations that what distinguishes her from Obama is not simply her experience, but her ability and willingness to work hard conjures the familiar stereotype of the lazy Black. I put it this way at that time:

> The stereotype has a history, especially tied to Black men who deal in the currency of words. The idea is that they dazzle the soft-minded with a persuasive prose, but leave them with nothing more than a feeling, at best. At worst, the charm in their speech leaves unwitting audiences with something quite different from what they were promised. In the blaxploitation films of the 1960s and '70s, the Black slickster was the pimp who charmed women into selling their bodies and remitting the proceeds. He was the drug dealer who seduced the poor and oppressed into a chemical high that left them poorer, physically damaged, in jail or dead. It was he whose inspirational orations were used to set a trap, to lure the innocent into the realm of the criminal. The slick trickster can't be trusted; his words are dishonest, serving only himself. (McIlwain 2008, A27)

With the addition of the "hard work" trope to her litany of distinctions about experience, results and the like, Clinton adds a racial dimension to her appeals.[3] It's not the first time a political candidate has repeatedly used the term *hard work* in the course of describing themselves or distinguishing themselves from an opponent. The fact is, however, that it is most often used by Black and Latino candidates running against White opponents in districts that are heavily or majority White. Explained by McIlwain and Caliendo (2007, 10), minority candidates use this and other tropes in election contests where winning White votes is a necessity to inoculate themselves from commonly held stereotypes Whites have about Blacks being lazy.

A classic example of this comes in a television ad by former Congressman Alan Wheat, when he ran for the U.S. Senate in Missouri in 1994. The ad begins with the quaint visual of a White father playing basketball with his son on their farm in (presumably) rural Missouri. A voice states, "The American Dream. To me it's always meant that if you *worked hard* enough you could find opportunity…. Our kids need to know that if you *work hard* and play by the rules you'll have every opportunity to succeed."[4] Not until the final seconds of the advertisement do we see that the voice is that of Alan Wheat and get the first realization (if one did not know already) that he is Black.

Harold Ford Jr., in his 2006 Senate race in Tennessee, makes a similar admonition, beginning one of his political ads with, "Whenever I talk with kids I tell them three things: *work hard*, play by the rules, and keep God first…. It's about responsibility…."[5] Gary Franks, a Black Connecticut Republican congressional candidate in 1990, added a bit more to the context of these phrases in a biographical ad that emphasized that Franks was "…the great grandson of a slave, the son of a mill worker," before adding, "Gary Franks *worked hard*, graduated from Yale…."[6] In another ad Franks preceded his "worked hard and played by the rules" disclaimer with the statement, "Instead of experiencing privilege, I experienced racism,"[7] emphasizing that he worked his way up from nothing to attain the heights of his success. Despite the racial barriers, Franks' biography attests, anyone can make it if they work hard enough.

These are but a few examples of the degree to which common racial stereotypes have and continue to be tied to Black candidates. That is, they are so much a part of the electoral landscape that Black candidates find it strategically necessary to counter them even before racial attacks have been lodged against them by an opposing candidate. The specific references to hard work, playing by the rules, and responsibility are used to counter the common stereotype that Blacks are lazy and expect to get a free ride—to essentially challenge underlying notions of both welfare policy and affirmative action at the same time (Gilens 1999).

The question in the 2008 campaign became whether voters would link these attributes together—race, leadership, hard work, and experience—and penalize Obama in some way, or would race work to benefit Obama, in conjunction with a model of leadership where rhetoric and collective political action were part of the campaign strategy. To address this question, I look to public opinion data and what it has to say about how American voters interpreted the two divergent models of leadership exhibited by Obama and Clinton and how it may have figured into their candidate preferences.

Methods and Data

My analysis of leadership, and the role it played in American public opinion about the choices voters had in the 2008 Democratic Presidential Primary, follows from two primary sets of data. I begin by analyzing public opinion data longitudinally, across the seventeen months leading into the flood of primary contests beginning in February 2008. The data was drawn from the monthly Gallup/*USA Today* Poll beginning with January 2007 and ending with the May 2008 poll.[8] This polling data was selected both for its longstanding methodological reliability and because it consistently asked a set of the same questions throughout this time period.

I focus on three questions assessing public opinion about the candidates' leadership ability, level of experience, and overall favorability. Barack Obama, Hillary Clinton, and John Edwards, the perceived frontrunners of the election, are included in my analysis. This polling data is treated purely descriptively in my analysis, as a way of providing some overall context to how Americans were thinking about the candidates and their leadership qualities up to the time when actual voting decisions began to be made in the presidential primaries.

Building on this foundation, the remainder of my analysis focuses on the results of the Super Tuesday primary that provide the best initial indication about how voters' perception of the candidates' leadership qualities might be expressed in their actual voting choice. I use the *Newsweek* Post-Super Tuesday Poll for my analysis.[8] I should be clear that this was not an exit poll, but a poll that followed the Super Tuesday elections. The survey is drawn from a national adult sample of 1,394 participants. Thus, my analysis of the poll results—particularly the relationship between various leadership measures and candidate favorability—focuses solely on public opinion and only infers a tenuous connection between those opinions and actual voting choices made by the survey participants in particular, and overall election results more generally.

Results

Trends in Public Opinion about Leadership

Fortunately for my purposes, pollsters were pretty consistent with the questions they asked throughout the more than one year of the Democratic primary season. While these types of questions have been consistently asked during previous elections, pollsters' decision to consistently include the same questions over this long period of time reflects, in part, the stark contrast in the candidates' leadership styles and perceived qualities that made them fit for office. I focus on responses to three primary questions about leadership in general, experience, and overall favorability ratings of the candidates. Looking at how the candidates measured up in the minds of voters over the course of the campaign gives us a general sense not only about the public's opinion of the candidates themselves, and the degree to which these qualities of leadership and experience seem to figure into their decision about who they chose to support.

Table 7.1a shows how the public rated Obama, Clinton, and Edwards on the characteristic of leadership. The exact question participants responded to asks them to think about a particular candidate running for president. It then asks, do you think Barack Obama (or the other candidates) is a "strong and decisive leader?" Most evident in these results is the finding that the public consistently identified Hillary Clinton as a strong leader more than her chief rival, Obama, and John Edwards. Edwards, who was perhaps familiar to more people because of his vice presidential run in 2004, received low leadership ratings almost across the board before dropping out of the race in February. After reaching her peak in July 2007, Clinton's leadership ratings steadily decline, and then moved up and down in small increments. Her ratings never climbed back to their July 2007 height of 75 percent. Obama, whose ratings exhibit a series of sharp, dramatic spikes and sharp declines in the early part of the campaign cycle, levels out in the crucial months of the 2008 primaries. Though he still rates below Clinton on leadership quality, he remains close to her throughout the months that she and Obama traded primary election wins. This general look at leadership ratings, in conjunction with what we know in retrospect about the election outcomes, suggests a relationship between voters' leadership ratings and their voting decisions.

Table 7.1b provides a similar look at how voters rated the candidates in terms of their perceived experience. Again, Clinton leads this category with higher ratings consistently throughout the campaign. A couple of things are interesting here. First, Americans don't seem to inflate John Edwards's experience ratings just because he is White. One might expect that if leadership and experience were purely race-related judgments, people may be tempted to attribute more experience to him. That Obama and Edwards share about the same degree of government experience (though Obama was slightly more experienced) is borne out in people's opinions about them here. Despite a few anomalous spikes, poll respondents consistently rated their experience equally.

Second, no amount of campaigning by Obama seems to affect people's view of his experience. The ratings are consistent throughout the eighteen months covered by the polling data. This also suggests that people don't necessarily seem to underrate his experience given their racial awareness. That is, at specific times throughout the election when Obama's race was more salient to voters (throughout the whole Jeremiah Wright controversy, especially) and a more salient feature of media coverage, people's opinions of Obama did not change by and large. Attacks on Obama's experience by his rival, Hillary Clinton, also do not appear to have made any impact.

The final set of polls I follow throughout the campaign are those that indicate the candidates's overall favorability ratings. Table 7.1 (1c) includes these ratings for Obama, Clinton, and Edwards for the same period of time. After January

Table 7.1 Democratic Presidential Candidate Leadership, Experience, and Favorability Ratings, January 2007–May 2008[1]

	1a.				1b.			1c.	
	Obama Leader	Clinton Leader	Edwards Leader	Obama Experience	Clinton Experience	Edwards Experience	Obama Favorability	Clinton Favorability	Edwards Favorability
Jan07	35%	64%	22%	27%	59%	17%	43%	51%	47%
Feb07	22%	52%	17%	5%	71%	17%	59%	56%	51%
Mar07	-	-	-	-	-	-	49%	46%	42%
Apr07	20%	37%	12%	5%	39%	7%	45%	46%	45%
May07	26%	50%	15%	9%	66%	19%	46%	47%	45%
Jun07	49%	60%	15%	-	-	-	48%	49%	43%
Jul07	62%	75%	15%	38%	70%	55%	50%	48%	45%
Aug07	-	-	-	29%	59%	55%	46%	48%	43%
Sep07	20%	61%	13%	10%	44%	18%	46%	45%	43%
Oct07	24%	64%	12%	-	-	-	49%	49%	44%
Nov07	55%	56%	6%	-	-	-	52%	51%	49%
Dec07	19%	50%	13%	8%	44%	15%	54%	53%	46%
Jan08	40%	55%	12%	25%	68%	10%	59%	52%	48%
Feb08	43%	44%	12%	29%	48%	10%	56%	49%	48%
Mar08	56%	61%	-	-	-	-	62%	53%	-
Apr08	56%	62%	-	-	-	-	60%	53%	-
May08	37%	53%	-	-	-	-	58%	51%	-

1. Missing values indicate months where the specific question was not asked (or asked in the same way) in the poll. Missing values for John Edwards also include the time after he dropped out of the race.

Source: Gallup/USA Today Poll, January 2007–May 2008.

2007, Clinton never again overtakes Obama in voters' overall favorability ratings. This generally matches the way people actually voted over the course of the election and is, of course, consistent with the primary election outcome. While it would be misleading to infer any causal connections based on these data—between overall favorability ratings and specific leadership and experience ratings—the data do seem to suggest that Clinton did not benefit from playing up her experience as a particular facet of presidential leadership.

Obama consistently received relatively high leadership ratings, though his ratings were consistently lower than Clinton's. Voters viewed Clinton overwhelmingly as the most experienced candidate. In fact, voters consistently agreed he had very little experience at all. Yet, Obama won. Taken as a whole, these data seem to bear out my interpretation of the election results, given the particular factor of leadership. Voters did not make a choice between two people they saw as being drastically different in terms of leadership. It seems to be the case that they made a choice between two models or expressions of leadership, rejecting the experience model that Clinton adopted.

Super Tuesday: Public Opinion on Two Models of Leadership

To bear out my informal hypothesis even further, I turn to poll results just following the Super Tuesday election contests. A variety of questions from this poll probe issues of leadership in much more pointed and diverse ways than those I looked at in the previous section. I categorize my analysis of the data by separating the questions depending on which model of leadership they point to: either the "classical (experience) model" or the "civil rights (inspiration) model." Tables 7.2 to 7.4 display responses to questions related to the experience model, asking either how much respondents value experience or how much respondents think the candidates possess certain characteristics. I compare Whites' and non-Whites' responses to each of the questions.

Table 7.2 includes two sets of dichotomous questions, asking respondents which they believed was more important when choosing a president: experience *or* judgment on the one hand; inspiration *or* experience on the other. The chi-square statistic is used to compare White and non-White participants's ratings

Table 7.2 Selected Experience Model Ratings by Race, 2008 Democratic Presidential Primary

	Voter Preferences			
	Experience v. Judgment		*Inspiration v. Experience**	
	Experience	*Judgment*	*Inspiration*	*Experience*
White	27%	66%	47%	47%
Non-White	36%	59%	60%	36%

*p≤ .05, two-tailed chi square test, df=1. N=602.
Source: Newsweek Post-Super Tuesday Poll. Conducted February 6-7 by Princeton Survey Research Associates International. N=602 Democrats and Democratic Leaners. Margin of Error: +/- 5 percentage points.

Table 7.3 Selected Experience Model Ratings, 2008 Democratic Presidential Primary [Trust in Crisis/Best Commander-In-Chief]

	*Who Would Voters Trust in Crisis?**		*Who Would Be Best Commander-In-Chief?**	
	Obama	*Clinton*	*Obama*	*Clinton*
White	29%	49%	33%	49%
Non-White	53%	24%	56%	29%

*p≤ .05, two-tailed chi square test, df=1. N=602.
Source: Newsweek Post-Super Tuesday Poll. Conducted February 6-7 by Princeton Survey Research Associates International. N=602 Democrats and Democratic Leaners. Margin of Error: +/- 5 percentage points.

of which qualities were most desirable in a president and to determine whether the differences between each groups' ratings are statistically different from the other. In both sets of comparisons, experience rated lower than either judgment or inspiration. The racial difference is negligible when it comes to experience versus judgment and participants agree, despite their racial differences, that experience paled in comparison or was at least equal to inspiration as the important presidential ability.

Table 7.3 includes responses to the question of which candidate has the judgment voters would trust most in a crisis. Given the context in which the term *crisis* is used—primarily related to national defense issues—I view this question as part of the "experience" category. The premise is that someone with more experience is best able to handle such crises (Clinton explicitly made the argument during the campaign). Here, we do see a significant difference between respondents's ratings, with Whites saying they would trust Clinton more and non-Whites saying they would trust Obama more. In a similar question, participants were asked which candidate "would make the best commander-in-chief?" Again, we see a significant racial divide in the responses.

Two remaining questions probe voters's perceptions of the leadership traits I categorize under the experience model. Table 7.4 reveals responses to the question "which candidate has the right experience for the job?" and which of the candidates would best "get things done in the White House?" Again, Whites, more than non-Whites, believed that Clinton has the right experience, though 30 percent more non-Whites said Clinton has the right experience than Whites who said Obama does. Results to the question about who can get things done show almost exactly the same results: There is a racial divide along with greater numbers of non-Whites who favored Clinton on this question than the reverse.

When we look at public opinion about the value of the "classical model" leadership traits and the candidates perceived to possess these traits, we see a picture emerging where Whites measured Clinton higher on the experience model and non-Whites evaluated Obama the same way, though to lesser degrees. Another part of the developing picture is that despite these ratings, people—with virtually no racial distinction—say experience was not what they think they most want in the 44th President.

Table 7.4 Selected Experience Model Ratings, 2008 Democratic Presidential Primary [Right Experience/Gets Things Done]

	Which Candidate Has the Right Experience?*		Which Candidate Gets Things Done?*	
	Obama	*Clinton*	*Obama*	*Clinton*
White	17%	67%	27%	53%
Non-White	33%	47%	52%	32%

*p≤ .05, two-tailed chi square test, df=1. N=602.

Source: Newsweek Post-Super Tuesday Poll. Conducted February 6-7 by Princeton Survey Research Associates International. N=602 Democrats and Democratic Leaners. Margin of Error: +/- 5 percentage points.

I begin my analysis of polling questions related to the values and characteristics of the "civil rights model" with what we already know from Table 7.2, that most Americans polled, regardless of race, believed the next President needed to be able to lead by inspiration. Along with this element, there are three remaining questions asked related to this model of leadership. In Table 7.5, participants were asked which candidate "inspires and excites people." Both Whites and non-Whites agreeds that Obama, overwhelmingly, fit this bill. There was a difference, however, when those polled were asked which candidate can best bring change. Whites said Clinton could best do so, while non-Whites picked Obama. In this case, however, more spillover goes in the direction of Obama, rather than Clinton, as was the case when we looked at the experience model. That is, more Whites said Obama could best bring change than non-Whites who said the same about Clinton. The final section of Table 7.5 shows the results of when people were asked which of the candidates could best "bring the country together." Here, there is considerable racial distinction in individuals' responses; that there is more than a 20 percentage point gap between Whites, 47 percent of whom said Obama could best bring the country together, and non-Whites, 71 percent of whom said Obama would be able to accomplish this if elected. However, on average, most agreed that this statement best fits Obama; and again, more Whites say that about Obama than non-Whites do about Clinton.

The picture, now complete, gives us a fairly clear explanation for how voters perceived leadership in this election. The data here demonstrates that while people had very strong, sometimes racially polarizing loyalties to each of the candidates, people, largely regardless of race, agreed on how the candidates measured up to two distinct models of leadership. Thus the primary factor in voters' candidate preferences appears to be the fact that most decided that the country most needed a president, Obama, who could lead by inspiration, despite his lack of formal government experience.

Conclusion

Like other post-Civil Rights Black candidates, Obama was successful, in part, because he ran a deracialized campaign (McCormick and Jones 1993). His

Table 7.5 Selected Inspiration Model Ratings, 2008 Democratic Presidential Primary [Inspires/Change/Bring Country Together]

	Who Inspires?		Who Can Best Bring Change?*		Who Brings Country Together?*	
	Obama	Clinton	Obama	Clinton	Obama	Clinton
White	64%	22%	38%	42%	48%	34%
Non-White	75%	16%	65%	22%	71%	19%

*p≤ .05, two-tailed chi square test, df=1. N=602.
Source: Newsweek Post-Super Tuesday Poll. Conducted February 6-7 by Princeton Survey Research Associates International. N=602 Democrats and Democratic Leaners. Margin of Error: +/- 5 percentage points.

interests were not "Black" interests, and the issues he championed, were not "Black" issues. He carefully appealed to Blacks, convincing us that he indeed was a member of the group. But his real target was White voters. Despite this way of separating himself from the Civil Rights model of political candidates, Obama nevertheless incorporated and based his image on the Civil Rights model of leadership. His reliance on movement politics, rhetorical style, and the kind of inspiration only conjured through a special mix of linguistic flavor, enthusiasm, even some modicum of entertainment kept him anchored in the civil rights tradition. Tailoring his message beyond the interests of the Black community, while simultaneously relying on the elements of style he cultivated from his African-American, urban, church roots, allowed Obama to galvanize what many of us thought would be some of his most ardent critics.[9]

Leadership continues to be a valued commodity for presidential aspirants. The American public still desires and expects that the president can and will lead. It was plausible to think that despite all of the hype, White America might see Obama as just another uppity Negro trying to talk his way into a position he did not deserve and for which he was not qualified (Clinton and some of her supporters made this claim as well and did so quite explicitly).[10] It was plausible to think that they might place him in the mold of Civil Rights era politicians for whom racial interest politics was paramount: Jesse Jackson Sr., Al Sharpton, and others. It was plausible to think the very stereotypes that post-Civil Rights era politicians inoculated themselves against in order to appeal to White voters would be the lens used to evaluate Obama. But it didn't turn out quite this way.

Was leadership employed as a racial construct in the 2008 presidential election? The answer is an unequivocal yes—and no. Did voters say, "Black men are not made of the stuff of leadership," and therefore disregard Obama as a presidential possibility? No. Did voters perceive Obama and Clinton differently based on their own racial backgrounds? Sometimes, yes, but not in any real way that seemed to matter. So where did race come into play in this whole thing? At this particular moment in history, the American people unmistakably wanted inspired change. They wanted their country to change course and they wanted someone who would lead them in a direction diametrically opposed to the course we were set on. Obama was successful because he was selling what the American people wanted—change. But not everyone can sell change. Clinton certainly tried, but failed. Race came into play because Obama's persuasive strategy enlisted a model of leadership from an unmistakable racial tradition, the Black rhetorical tradition, which entailed not only putting to use one's gift of speech, but channeling that speech into a special vision that calls on people to do better, to be a part of something greater than themselves.

I am not saying that other presidents did not share this same skill: John F. Kennedy and Bill Clinton are two examples of inspiring, rhetorically gifted White politicians. However, Obama was different because given the blessing of good luck, good timing, and good strategy, Obama persuaded Americans to deemphasize something that has heretofore been a necessary condition for effective presidential leadership—experience.

Notes

1. Interestingly enough, it was another African American, Republican Alan Keyes, that provided early assurance to Obama and the Democratic Party that Obama would have no trouble winning his 2004 election. This gave Obama the freedom to campaign beyond his election and capture the attention of party leaders who selected him to give his now famous speech. Thus, one Black politician's failures essentially provided the catalyst for Obama's historic presidential run.
2. The text of the ad, titled, "Deliver," is taken from video found on the Stanford Political Communication Lab Web site: http://pcl.stanford.edu/campaigns/2008/hc.html
3. While Clinton may not have intentionally appealed to race, her repeated references to "hard work" as a characteristic that distinguished her from Barack Obama drew on, played into, and referenced one of the longstanding racial stereotypes and resentments about Blacks through a form of character attack. This fact, not necessarily her intention to do so, is what characterizes Clinton's statements as a racial appeal, as defined by Mendelberg (2001, 4–35) and McIlwain and Caliendo (2007, 3, 8–9).
4. Text of the ad taken from video located at the University of Oklahoma's Julian P. Kanter Political Commercial Archive. The ad is titled, "Dream," number 59858 in the archive's online catalog: http://www.ou.edu/pccenter/PCC_Update_09/Online_Catalogue.html
5. Text of the ad is taken from video: http://www.youtube.com/watch?v=ttL_DjHWB6Y
6. Text of the ad taken from video located at the University of Oklahoma's Julian P. Kanter Political Commercial Archive. The ad is titled, "American Dream," number 76041 in the archive's online catalog: http://www.ou.edu/pccenter/PCC_Update_09/Online_Catalogue.html
7. Text of the ad taken from video located at the University of Oklahoma's Julian P. Kanter Political Commercial Archive. The ad is titled, "Bio," number 47060 in the archive's online catalog: http://www.ou.edu/pccenter/PCC_Update_09/Online_Catalogue.html
8. Accessed via the Roper Center for Public Opinion archives. Analysis ends with May 2008, one month short of the official end of the primary. Gallup did not continue asking the same precise questions in its June poll as it had in the previous months included in the analysis.

9. Conducted February 6–7 by Princeton Survey Research Associates International. The survey has a margin of error of +/- 5 for the 602 members of the sample that include registered Democrats and Democratic leaners.
10. Obama employed a brand of deracialization called situational deracialization. For a deeper discussion of this concept, refer to chapter 10 of this volume.
11. Former vice-presidential candidate and Hillary Clinton supporter Geraldine Ferraro most notably made such comments. See, for example: Seelye and Bosman (2008), "Ferraro's Obama Remarks Become Talk of Campaign," *New York Times*, March 12.

References

Byun, Christine. 2008. Clinton says choice between "speeches and solutions." The Radar. http://blogs.abcnews.com/politicalradar/202/clintonsays-ch.html.

Clay, William Lacy. 1993. *Just permanent interests: Black Americans in Congress, 1870–1991.* New York: Amistad Press.

Gelderman, Carol. 1997. *All the president's words: The bully pulpit and the creation of the virtual presidency.* New York: Walker.

Gilens, Martin. 1999. *Why Americans hate welfare.* Chicago: University of Chicago Press.

Halicks, Richard. 2008. Countdown 2008: Obama's youthquake: Is the senator leading a movement, or just an interesting campaign? *The Atlanta Journal Constitution*, February 10, 1C.

Hart, Roderick. 1989. *The sound of leadership: presidential communication in the modern age.* Chicago: University of Chicago Press.

Healy, Patrick. 2008. Personal communication.

Kernell, Samuel. 2006. *Going public: New strategies of presidential leadership.* 4th ed. Washington, DC: CQ Press.

Lincoln, Charles. E., and Lawrence H. Mamiya. 1990. *The Black church in the African-American experience.* Chapel Hill, NC: Duke University Press.

Lippmann, Walter. 1997. *Public opinion.* New York: Free Press. (Orig. pub. 1922)

McCormick, J. P. II, and Charles E. Jones. 1993. The conceptualization of deracialization. In *Dilemmas of Black politics*, ed. Georgia Persons, 66–84. New York: HarperCollins.

McIlwain, Charlton D. 2007. Perceptions of leadership and the challenge of Obama's Blackness. *Journal of Black Studies* 38: 64–74.

———. 2008. *Newsday. Clinton veering close to stereotypes.* February 25, A27

——— and Stephen M. Caliendo. 2009. Black messages, White messages: The differential use of racial appeals by Black and White candidates. *Journal of Black Studies* 39, 5: 732–43.

Mikva, Alona. 2008. Personal communication.

Mooney, Brian C. 2008. Clinton gives her campaign $5m loan. *Boston Globe*, February 7, A16.

Smith, Robert C. 1996. *We have no leaders: African Americans in the post-civil rights era.* Albany, NY: SUNY Press

Terkildsen, Nayda. 1993. When White voters evaluate Black candidates: The processing implications of candidate skin color, prejudice, and self-monitoring. *American Journal of Political Science* 37: 1032–53.

Tullis, Jeffrey K. 1987. *The rhetorical presidency.* Princeton, NJ: Princeton University Press.

Walters, Ronald W., and Robert, C. Smith. 1999. *African American leadership.* Albany, NY: SUNY Press.

Williams, Linda F. 1990. White/Black perceptions of the electability of Black political candidates. *National Political Science Review,* 2: 145–64.

Part IV

New Perspectives on Deracialization

So far in this volume, the concept of deracialization has been an undercurrent in many of the chapters you have read. This campaign strategy has been central to the rise of many young and old Black politicians and has been a source of controversy and consternation for many scholars of Black politics and civil rights activists.

Economist Charles Hamilton, who coauthored *Black Power* with Kwame Turé (Stokely Carmichael), first proposed deracialization as a political strategy for Blacks at the 1973 National Urban League convention. By 1973, the Republican Party had successfully rolled out its infamous Southern Strategy, in which Republican candidates, led by Richard Nixon, adopted coded language such as "antibusing," and "pro-law and order" to appeal to Whites, particularly Southerners, who were uncomfortable with the pace of integration and societal change in the wake of the Civil Rights Movement. Hamilton argued then, and later in a 1977 *First World* magazine article, that Democratic election efforts were hampered by perceptions that the party was under the thumb of civil rights leaders. Hamilton posited that if Democrats could frame their policy positions in generic, universal terms that appealed to all voters, they could appeal to a wider swath of the electorate, remain politically viable, and dispel the idea that the Democratic Party only championed narrow issues that appealed to Blacks and feminists (Orey and Ricks 2007, 326; Hamilton 1977).

In 1989, a number of Black candidates used deracialization strategies to win historic elections. David Dinkins became New York City's first Black mayor; Norman Rice became Seattle's first Black mayor. There were historic first elections for Black mayors in Durham, North Carolina and New Haven, Connecticut. Most notably, L. Douglas Wilder became the nation's first Black governor since Reconstruction when he won Virginia's gubernatorial race. These men used deracialization strategies to win office in majority White jurisdictions and won with sizable percentages of the White vote (McCormick and Jones 1993, 66, 68).

While most people concede the efficacy of this strategy, many question the normative appropriateness of deracialization. Immediately after the historic 1989 election, political scientists specializing in Black politics began a debate about the nature and appropriateness of deracialization. Their efforts resulted in two important edited volumes: Georgia Person's *Dilemmas in Black Politics* (1993) and Huey Perry's *Race, Politics and Governance in the United States* (1996).

The contributors to the Persons volume took a pessimistic view of deracialization. They expressed concern that deracialized candidates, should they be elected, would be hamstrung from vigorously addressing racial inequality. To them, deracialized candidates make a tacit compact with their voters to not ruffle the feathers of their non-Black constituents with civil rights advocacy (see McCormick and Jones 1993; Smith 1993). Moreover, they contended that while those who employ deracialized campaign strategies reap short-term benefits (namely, getting elected to one prominent local office), they may have trouble getting elected to statewide or national offices when their opponents make an issue of their race (Wilson 1993; Davis and Willingham 1993).

The contributors to the Perry volume were a little more sanguine. While they still expressed normative misgivings about deracialization as a strategy for addressing persistent racial inequality, they defended many so-called deracialized politicians as not actually being deracialized. Mary Summers and Phillip Klinkner, for instance, pointed out all of New Haven Mayor John Daniels' racialized campaign strategies (1996). Lenneal Henderson proclaimed that Baltimore Mayor Kurt Schmoke was racially transcendent, not deracialized (Henderson 1996).

In the more than a decade since the publication of these volumes, the anxiety over deracialization has not faded from the Black politics discourse. With the rise of a new generation of deracialized Black politicians who are even further removed from the Civil Rights Movement, these questions are all the more relevant.

The fact that a new generation of Black politicians has embraced deracialization suggests that the strategy will not go away any time soon. However, young Black politicians routinely modify deracialization strategies according to local conditions, ideological commitments, and personal career plans.

The next four chapters present four different perspectives on deracialization using the stories of four young Black politicians. In chapter 8, Angela Lewis presents her analysis of the election of Massachusetts Governor Deval Patrick. On the surface, Patrick's election experience was somewhat similar to the earlier experiences of Harvey Gantt. Like him, he ran a deracialized political campaign in which a White opponent appealed to racial sentiment to try to siphon support away from him. Unlike Gantt, though, Patrick was able to prevail in his election. Lewis finds that unlike Jesse Helms, Patrick's opponent, Kerry Healey, was not an effective race-baiter.

In chapter 9, Rachel Yon turns to an examination of Washington, DC Mayor Adrian Fenty's election. As a Local Boy Made Good with considerable crossover appeal, Fenty could have been susceptible to attacks of racial inauthenticity from his fiercest opponent, City Council President Linda Cropp. However, he was not. Why was that the case? Was the relative tameness of that election idiosyncratic or emblematic of Washington's mature race politics?

Sekou Franklin examines Harold Ford Jr.'s 2006 U.S. Senate campaign in chapter 10. Ford is typically perceived as the quintessential deracialized candidate.

However, Franklin shows that Ford is not perfectly deracialized. By introducing his theory of "situational deracialization," Franklin shows how Ford maintained different personas in the Black and White communities in an attempt to curry favor with both groups.

In chapter 11, Tyson King-Meadows presents a most interesting take on conservative politics. Many typically think of Republicans as being the penultimate deracialized candidates because of common stereotypes of Black Republicans as being racial sellouts. However, using Michael Steele's 2006 Senate bid in Maryland as an example, he shows that Steele actually racialized himself in an attempt to attract Black voters who would otherwise be reluctant to vote for a Republican candidate.

References

Davis, Marilyn, and Alex Willingham. 1993. Andrew Young and the Georgia state elections of 1990. In *Dilemmas of Black politics*, ed. Georgia Persons, 147–75. New York: HarperCollins.

Hamilton, Charles V. 1977. Deracialization: Examination of a political strategy. *First World* 1: 3–5.

Henderson, Lenneal J. Jr. 1996. The governance of Kurt Schmoke as mayor of Baltimore. In *Race, governance, and politics in the United States*, ed. Huey L. Perry, 165–78. Gainesville: University of Florida Press.

McCormick, Joseph II, and Charles E. Jones. 1993. The conceptualization of deracialization: Thinking through the dilemma. In *Dilemmas of Black politics*, ed. Georgia Persons, 66–84. New York: HarperCollins.

Orey, Byron D'Andra, and Boris Ricks. 2007. A systematic analysis of the deracialization concept. *The National Political Science Review* January: 325–34.

Perry, Huey, ed. 1996. *Race, governance, and politics in the United States*. Gainesville: University of Florida Press.

Persons, Georgia, ed. 1993. *Dilemmas of Black politics*. New York: HarperCollins.

Smith, Robert C. 1993. Ideology as the enduring dilemma of Black politics. In *Dilemmas of Black politics*, ed. Georgia Persons, 211–25. New York: HarperCollins.

Summers, Mary, and Phillip Klinkner. 1996. The election and governance of John Daniels as mayor of New Haven. In *Race, governance, and politics in the United States*, ed. Huey L. Perry, 127–50. Gainesville: University of Florida Press.

Wilson, Zaphon. 1993. Gantt versus Helms: Deracialization confronts Southern traditionalism. In *Dilemmas of Black politics*, ed. Georgia Persons, 176–93. New York: HarperCollins.

8   Between Generations
Deval Patrick's Election as Massachusetts' First Black Governor[1]

Angela K. Lewis[2]

Deval Patrick is the oldest politician and only governor featured in this volume. In chapter 1, we learned that he is a "Phase 2.5" politician: too young and contemporary to be the political peer of early deracialized candidates such as Doug Wilder, but too old to be a full-fledged member of the post-Civil Rights cohort of Black leaders. Nevertheless, because of his deracialized style and crossover appeal, he is often mentioned in the same breath as people like Barack Obama and Harold Ford.

Some of Patrick's experiences running for statewide office as a deracialized candidate mirror the experiences of deracialized candidates running in Phase II. Patrick was the victim of subtle racial attacks that were intended to erode support for him in the White community. However, unlike his predecessors, Patrick emerged triumphant. Why? In this chapter, Angela Lewis examines Patrick's campaign against former Lieutenant Governor Kerry Healey. She finds that Patrick ran a deracialized political campaign and that Healey did try to fan the flames of racial resentment. However, voters did not take the bait. It seems as though Healey's unpopularity contributed to those appeals falling flat.

Introduction

On November 6, 2006, the voters of Massachusetts made history for only the second time in the United States, electing a Black governor, Deval Patrick, a political novice virtually unknown before the election, stated he did not campaign as the Black candidate; in fact, he said, "If all I was offering was to be the first Black governor of Massachusetts, I wouldn't have won" (Pierce 2006). Did Patrick's candidacy transcend race? Can scholars classify his campaign as one that represents a new era in Black leadership? In the pages that follow, I show the innovations of the Patrick campaign. For two years, Patrick ran a grassroots campaign, visiting neighborhoods and speaking to voters about restoring hope back and making Massachusetts better. Along the way, he rejected large monetary donations from supporters and survived a brutally negative racial smear campaign from his main rival.

Depoliticizing Race

Scholars have identified several necessary conditions for a Black candidate to win office at the statewide level. Sonenshein (1990) argues that a candidate's campaign strategy, the political leaning of voters in the state, and the viability of the candidate's party in the state all influence his chances of winning. Black candidates must work within the party structure and have as much party support as their opponent. Support from the party legitimizes the Black candidate's campaign and provides him with a myriad of resources including financing, endorsements, and mobilization. Jones and Clemons (1993) create a model of racial crossover voting utilizing five components: political apprenticeship, party apparatus, a media/racial ombudsman role, a deracialized strategy, and the wild-card factor. Jeffries (1998) stresses that the Black candidates must have appropriate political experience. However, certain types of experience can be a liability to a Black candidate. Jones and Clemons (1993) suggest that being a former mayor, representing an area that is majority Black, or losing their last election are all liabilities to Black candidates.[3] In short, their previous experience can racialized them to such an extent that non-Black voters can use that experience as an excuse for White voters to not vote for the Black candidate.

An ideal political situation for Black gubernatorial candidates is a state with a large enough Black population to help the candidate win in the general election so that the party will not publicly oppose their candidacy. Soneshein (1990) and Jeffries (1998) disagree somewhat on this point, though. The latter argues that Blacks should not limit their choices to states with liberal attitudes; doing so would severely limit their choices about where Blacks could run for office.

Additionally, Jones and Clemons (1993) argue that there should be a racial ombudsman, preferably the media, to minimize the use of divisive racial symbols. If a candidate prefers not to play the race card when attacked on racial grounds, having third party advocates to point out explicit and subtle racial discrimination can be helpful (Mendelberg 2001). Having a racial ombudsman will do little to offset a quality challenger or to help a candidate deal with unforeseen events or exogenous shocks to his campaign. However, such advocates do help keep their liabilities to a minimum.

Finally, these authors agree that middle class, highly qualified, and deracialized candidates have the greatest chance of success. The candidate should have a conciliatory style that "attempts to defuse the divisive effects of race by avoiding references to ethnic or racially construed issues, while at the same time emphasizing those issues that appeal to a wide community" (Jeffries 1998, 167). The candidate should transcend race and focus on issues that appeal to all voters regardless of race: issues like education, healthcare, and transportation. However, the Black candidate must delicately balance their deracialized approach while at the same time utilizing race as an asset. In short, they must appeal to Whites without alienating Blacks.

Regardless of the circumstances, scholars conclude that some Whites will not vote for Black candidates. Political scientist Vincent Hutchings asserted in an interview that "There remains a non-trivial faction of White voters who will not vote for a candidate simply because (the candidate is) Black. We are kidding ourselves if we argue these people have disappeared from the landscape" (Hutchings, quoted in Page 2006). If the candidate is a strong advocate for civil rights for Blacks or if the candidate makes this issue prominent during the campaign, this phenomenon is exaggerated. The candidate will likely alienate Whites and prompt them to cast a vote for the other candidate. So despite periodic successes, historically, Black candidates do not win statewide elections because a proportion of Whites will not vote for a Black candidate (Williams 1989; Jeffries 1998; Jeffries and Jones 2006).

Massachusetts Politics

Raphael Sonenshein once said that "Massachusetts is the most liberal and Democratic state in national elections" (Sonenshein 1990, 224). Despite this reputation, Republicans controlled the state's executive office for more than a decade. Michael Dukakis was the last Democrat elected governor (in 1986). In 1990, Republican candidate William Weld beat John Silber for the governor's seat. Weld was able to gain an advantage because of dissatisfaction with Democratic stewardship of the state. Voters were angry over the state's economy, the budget, and one party leadership, and they wanted change. Because of this victory, Republicans held Massachusetts up as an example "that they could win even in the bluest state" (Mehren 2006).

By 2006, though, Massachusetts voters had grown tired of Republican gubernatorial rule. The state had witnessed an increase in the cost of living and a decrease in overall population. Voters were also displeased about how then-Governor Mitt Romney made fun of the state for being too liberal and for being the first to allow same-sex marriage while he traveled the country campaigning for president. In addition, state funding for education had decreased tremendously, causing it to fall behind Alabama and Mississippi in higher education funding (Mehren 2006). In the end, voters were upset and wanted change. Journalists Mooney and Wangsness observed that "Many are considering a vote for Patrick because they are upset by the Big Dig,[4] the high cost of living, and the negative tone of the Healey campaign" (Mooney and Wangsness 2006).

The Candidates

The 2006 Massachusetts gubernatorial election was destined to make history by electing the state's first Black or first female governor.[5] Both major party candidates were self-made millionaires, and both had a mix of experiences that enhanced their candidacies.

Deval Patrick was raised by a single mother, who was briefly on welfare, in his grandparent's South Side Chicago apartment. Although Patrick grew up around crime and gangs, he avoided them, and at age 14, he received a scholarship from the A Better Chance program to attend the prestigious Milton Academy in Massachusetts (Page 2006).

The first in his family to attend college, Patrick graduated from Harvard College with honors. Before returning to Harvard to attend law school, he traveled overseas to Sudan and South Africa on a youth training project funded by a Rockefeller Foundation grant (Pierce 2006).

By the time Patrick was fifty years old, he had gained a variety of work experiences. He clerked for a federal appellate judge and worked at the NAACP Legal Defense and Education Fund. He worked in private practice, becoming partner at the prestigious Hill & Barlow law firm. Patrick also served as a federal prosecutor and as the Assistant Attorney General for Civil Rights under President Bill Clinton. After leaving the Justice Department, Patrick served as Vice-President and General Counsel to both Texaco and Coca-Cola. He also served on numerous corporate and charitable boards (Helman 2006b; Pierce 2006).

Republican Kerry Healey, the incumbent Lieutenant Governor, grew up in Daytona Beach, Florida. Her mother was a public school teacher, and her father served 27 years in the US Army and Army Reserves. Healey earned a bachelor's degree in government at Harvard and a Ph.D. from Trinity College in Dublin, Ireland (Mooney 2005).[6]

Healey twice ran unsuccessfully for state representative. In 2002, she beat Jim Rappaport for the Republican nomination for Lieutenant Governor. Later that year, she and Mitt Romney won Massachusetts top two offices. In addition to her political career, Healey was active in numerous community organizations and had a promising career as a law and public safety consultant at Abt Associates and as an adjunct social policy and criminal justice professor at Endicott College and the University of Massachusetts at Lowell (Mooney 2005).

The Primaries

According to Massachusetts Democratic Party rules, in order for a candidate's name to appear on the primary ballot, he or she must receive 15 percent of the votes at the State Convention. In 2006, three candidates sought to meet this threshold: Deval Patrick, Attorney General Tom Reilly, and millionaire Chris Gabrieli. Even in early March 2006, Patrick was well ahead of his contenders. At the convention that year, Patrick garnered 58 percent of delegate votes, compared to Reilly's 27 percent and Gabrieli's 15 percent. Reilly and Gabrieli performed well enough, however, to guarantee them spaces on the primary ballot (Johnson, 2006). Patrick maintained his edge over Reilly and Gabrieli through the summer of 2006. Polls showed Patrick at 35 percent, Gabrieli at 30 percent and Reilly at 27 percent (O'Sullivan 2006).

Each candidate highlighted different issues to appeal to voters. Patrick criticized school districts charging fees for extracurricular activities and transportation. He argued that the activities are part of a child's education and the parent's ability to pay should not determine a child's participation. He wanted to create a fund to help schools provide these programs for free. Gabrieli focused on making commuting easier for workers. Reilly emphasized that his opponents were millionaires who did not understand the significance of a state income tax rollback.

As a result, Reilly released both his and his wife's tax returns hoping other candidates would do the same. They did not. This move earned Reilly the endorsements of 15 mayors across the state. Both Gabrieli and Patrick attacked Reilly about his lack of supervision of the Big Dig Project and how he handled the gay marriage ballot question. The Big Dig finished late and over budget. Moreover, the finished parts of the project were plagued with defects. Gabrieli and Patrick accused the Romney Administration—including Reilly—of not accepting responsibility for the project's failures, and they charged that Reilly could have done more to hold elected officials and contractors accountable for overspending and the lack of quality control. They also argued that Reilly should have blocked attempts to put the gay marriage question on the ballots because the issue had already been decided by the courts (Monahan 2006c). For his part, Reilly criticized Patrick for his work with Texaco and Coca-Cola, as well as his position as a board member of Ameriquest. In particular, Reilly accused Patrick of exploiting minorities for corporate and personal gain (Mooney 2006).[7]

Patrick eventually won the Democratic primary election by a nearly 30 percentage point margin. Many attribute Patrick's victory in the primary to Reilly's poor performance as Attorney General and Gabrieli's narrow base of support. Most of Gabrieli's campaign was self-funded, and he expected to court the more than 50 percent of Massachusetts voters who had no partisan affiliation. In the end, though, independent voters were more likely to support Patrick (Phillips 2006).

Other candidates in the general election for governor included Independent candidate Christy Mihos and Green Rainbow Party candidate Grace Ross. Mihos was the heir of a convenience store chain who had been unsuccessful at prior bids for elective office (though he had served as Director of the Massachusetts Turnpike Authority). He had the potential to be a spoiler in the race, and some hoped that Mihos would run against Healey in the Republican primary. However, he was more likely to take votes away from Healey, not Patrick in a general election (Phillips and Helman 2006; "About the Candidate: Christy Mihos" n.d.; "Christy Mihos-Portrait…" n.d.).[8]

Patrick's Strategy

As we learned in Chapter 1, in today's political climate, it is often the norm for Black candidates to depoliticize race in order to appeal to White voters. It is very unlikely for White voters to elect a passionate civil rights activist to a statewide office. Depoliticizing race is almost a necessity for Black candidates who must garner White votes to win (Canon, Schousen, Sellers 1996).

Although scholars suggest Whites do not vote for Black candidates, Deval Patrick gained the confidence of White voters in Massachusetts (Williams 1989; Jeffries 1998; Jeffries and Jones 2006). His candidacy met all the requirements for a Black candidate to appeal to Whites. First, Massachusetts is a very liberal state. Second, Patrick had the support of the Democratic Party, which provided him access to its vast resources. Former President Clinton and Senators Ted Kennedy and John Kerry all made public appearances to support Patrick. While he did not have previous experience in elected office, he successfully argued that his work as a United States Assistant Attorney General and the experiences as vice president and general counsel at two of the country's largest corporations gave him just the experience need to run a state government responsibly (Helman 2006b).

Most important, Patrick did not initiate discussions of race or racial issues. When his opponent brought them up, he deflected the issues. In a state that is nearly 90 percent White and approximately 7 percent Black, it was necessary for Patrick to appeal to Whites without alienating large numbers of Blacks, just as Edward Brooke did in his bid for the United States Senate in 1966. Brooke was the nation's first popularly elected Black United States Senator, representing Massachusetts from 1967-1979. Brooke did extensive research before launching his candidacy for the Senate. According to Becker and Heaton (1967), Brooke's campaign conducted public opinion research that was one of the largest research programs carried out for a statewide election. It included seven statewide studies conducted between fall 1965 and Election Day 1966 which detailed his standing relative to his opponents and assessed the racial attitudes of potential voters. This intensive research program proved quite beneficial in helping Brooke win the election.

Forty years later, Patrick's gubernatorial campaign showed strong similarities to Brooke's campaign. Both faced unpopular opponents with electoral vulnerabilities and weak public service records. For example, Brooke's opponent Endicott Peabody was a former incumbent governor who had lost his reelection bid at the party primary stage (losing to Francis X. Bellotti) in 1964. Healey had unsuccessfully run for state representative twice and was part of an unpopular incumbent administration. Brooke's popularity and favorability ratings never slipped in the polls, and neither did Patrick's (Smith 2006a, b).[9] Voters also held both opponents in low esteem. Voters did not believe Peabody accomplished much as governor. In contrast, Brooke had a reputation for honesty. As attorney general, he was part of the investigation that uncovered corruption and indicted many state officials. While Kerry Healey's association with the unpopular Mitt Romney proved to be an albatross, voters knew Patrick as the Assistant Attorney General for Civil Rights at the Justice Department who worked for underrepresented groups. Voters also appreciated the positive tone of his candidacy in the face of Healey's negative campaign. In the end, Healey's strategy helped to diminish her popularity throughout the course of the campaign (Becker and Heaton 1967, 348-351; Smith 2006a, b).

Because of Massachusetts's relatively small Black population, Patrick could more comfortably elide racial issues. Public discourse during the campaign also suggests that Patrick's race was inconsequential to this electorate (Eagon 2006; Page 2006). According to some voters, the subject was passé (Eagon 2006). At a meeting with the local Chamber of Commerce, one business owner even commented, "I don't even see him as Black. It looks like to me that he has a deep tan" (Page 2006). Unfortunately, the fact that some voters looked at Patrick as having a "deep tan" may lend some credibility to Strickland and Whicker's (1992) assertion that in order for Black candidates to win statewide office, they must look White (209).

While voters did not express overtly racist attitudes, there was some evidence that some voters had personal issues with Patrick, even if they did not attribute it to race. When pollsters asked voters why they were supporting Deval Patrick, many suggested that they supported him because they disliked Healey and because of her negative ads. On the other hand, when voters mentioned why they supported Healey, a larger percentage said they disliked Patrick. This dislike for Patrick could be related to his race or to some of Patrick's more controversial positions (Mooney and Wangsness 2006).

The Campaign

A series of *Boston Globe*/CBS 4 Polls, displayed in Table 8.1, bear out the fact that Deval Patrick's favorability rating increased among voters over the course of the election cycle. While fewer than one in four voters knew Patrick in March 2005, by September 2006, more than 60 percent of voters had a favorable impression of him. In contrast, Kerry Healey's unfavorability ratings increased over the course of the election cycle. Just one week before the election, 51 percent of respondents had unfavorable views of Healy, compared to Patrick's 27 percent. Healey's association with outgoing Governor Mitt Romney no doubt contributed to voters' unfavorable perception of her. The week before the election, 54 percent of likely voters reported having an unfavorable review of Romney (Smith 2006). Voters were unhappy with the previous four years of the Romney-Healey administration, and they wanted change. Patrick capitalized on this discontent and presented himself as the candidate with the appropriate corporate experience needed to run a state government and to make it more fiscally responsible (Helman 2006b).

Table 8.1 Favorability Ratings, Kerry Healey and Deval Patrick

	Kerry Healy			Deval Patrick		
	Favorable	*Neutral*	*Unfavorable*	*Favorable*	*Neutral*	*Unfavorable*
March 2005	34%	14%	22%	11%	7%	5%
August 2005	47%	16%	23%	12%	13%	5%
March 2006	41%	17%	28%	26%	13%	11%
September 2006	40%	12%	42%	63%	10%	16%
October 2006	34%	11%	51%	60%	8%	27%

Source: Smith 2006a (Boston Globe / CBS4 Poll, October 26, 2006).

Healey's unfavorable ratings spiked in September 2006 and were likely associated with her negative campaign ads. Healey spent twice as much on campaign advertising than Patrick (Healey had more money; she raised nearly $12 million in donations compared to Patrick's nearly $7.5 million (Mooney 2006)). She used those ads to highlight differences between the two candidates on issues of criminal justice. She attacked Patrick for his work as an attorney involved with rape and death penalty cases. For example, in one televised debate, Healey suggested that Patrick was soft on crime because of his support of Benjamin LaGuer, a Latino convicted of raping a 59-year-old woman. Patrick and other likeminded supporters believed that LaGuer was mistreated by the criminal justice system and was a victim of juror misconduct. During the campaign, the public learned that Patrick had corresponded with LaGuer. DNA evidence later proved LaGuer was guilty of the crime, and Healey hoped to use that development to suggest that Patrick consorted with criminals (Atkins 2006; Page 2006; Wangsness 2006b; Williamson 2006).

Healey ran two notable ads where she suggested that Patrick's defense of LaGuer evinced his softness on crime. On ad, called "Garage," featured an elderly White woman in a garage at night. The script reads:

Announcer: Here's a question. If a teacher at your kid's school, or a friend, or a co-worker –if anyone you knew actually praised a convicted rapist, what would you think?
Deval Patrick: He is eloquent, and he is thoughtful, there's no doubt about that.
Announcer: Here's another question. Have you ever heard a woman compliment a rapist?
Deval Patrick: He should be ashamed, not governor. (*Source*: "Kerry Healey for Governor: 'Garage'" 2006.)

In another ad, "Deval Defends," Healey paints Patrick as the supporter of a rapist. The script of that ad reads:

Announcer 1: First Deval Patrick said it was 15 years since he's helped convicted rapist Ben LaGuer.
Announcer 2: Then he admitted it was recent.
Announcer 1: What kind of person continually defends a brutal rapist?
Deval Patrick: He is eloquent, and he is thoughtful.
Announcer 2: Patrick denied he gave the rapist money.
Deval Patrick: No, in fact I don't…
Announcer 1: Then he admitted he had. But what's worse than Deval Patrick's deceptions?
Announcer 2: "If Deval Patrick had his way, a thug who bound a 59-year old woman and repeatedly raped her over the course of eight hours…" would be free. (*Source:* "Kerry Healey for Governor: 'Deval Defends'" 2006.)

A second set of ads criticized Patrick for his work as an NAACP defense attorney who successfully commuted a death sentence for Carl Ray Songer, a man convicted of killing a state trooper (Wickham, 2006). The ad states, "While lawyers have a right to defend admitted cop killers…do we really want one as our governor?" (Wickham 2006). Although the ads initially narrowed the margin between the candidates, they eventually worked against Healey, and Patrick pulled ahead in the race (Anderson 2006).

Healey supporters also attempted to implicate members of Patrick's family in violent crime. News reports surfaced which referred to Patrick's brother-in-law as a convicted rapist. Healey denied any involvement in the leak, and Patrick was forced to respond by acknowledging that his sister and husband had had problems earlier in their marriage. However, he noted that they recently celebrated their 25th wedding anniversary. In response to the attack on his family, Patrick called for the negative campaigning had to end. He said, "We are going to ask the people to choose whether the politics of fear, division and personal destruction is what they want, or whether we're better than that, and are ready to finally throw out those who dump this trash in the public square" (Monahan 2006a).

The campaign tactics Healey and her supporters used incorporated a strategy called implicit racial priming. Mendelberg (2001), defines an implicit racial appeal "as one that contains a recognizable—if subtle—racial reference, most easily through visual references" (11). Mendelberg contends that in the post-Civil Rights era, it is no longer socially acceptable to make overtly racist appeals. Most voters have been conditioned to reject obvious forms of racism. However, if the racial appeal is more subtle, White voters in particular (that was the sample she studied) are more susceptible to internalize the ad's message and voting accordingly. One can make an implicit attack more obvious (and thus, less effective) by merely pointing out that an attack is racist (Mendelberg 2001; see also Valentino, Hutchings, and White 2002).

Simply put, neither Healey nor her supporters had to mention race; but by showing visuals of minority criminals or implying that Patrick, a Black man, had relatives who were criminals, they could have unobtrusively stoked some voters' subconscious racial fears and reaped their votes. Healey's strategy followed a time honored tradition of trying to undermine political opponents by attacking them as soft on crime. These attacks are more visceral when the candidate and/or the perpetrator is a racial or ethnic minority. There are numerous examples of candidates being successfully linked to minority criminal pathology in elections. For example, when Tom Bradley ran unsuccessfully to be Los Angeles' mayor in 1969, his opponent attacked him as being soft on crime even though Bradley was a former police officer. In 1988, George H.W. Bush solidified his lead over Michael Dukakis after surrogates aired the infamous "Willie Horton" ad, which criticized Dukakis for supporting a prison furlough program in which a Black convict, Willie Horton, crossed state lines and raped a White woman in Maryland. The ad prominently featured a menacing photograph of Horton, who was African American. More recently, Antonio Villaraigosa lost his first bid for

Los Angeles' mayoralty in 2001 when his opponent James Hahn, ran attack ads linking Villaraigosa to a fugitive drug dealer (McClain and Steward 1999, 158; Mendelburg 2001, chapter 5; Purdum 2001).

In many of those early races, attacked candidates tried to take the moral high road and not respond to those kind of attacks. In doing so, Mendelberg (2001) argues that candidates play right into their opponents' hands. Someone has to decry the ad as racist, or voters risk falling prey to the bait. In Patrick's case, he also took the moral high road. However, others were willing to step up and attack Healey for her negative campaigning. In particular, Michael Dukakis, the victim of the "Willie Horton" ad, declared, "This has been the dirtiest campaign in the history of the commonwealth" (Mehren 2006). This seemed to do the job of neutralizing the potentially disastrous impact of those advertisements.

For his part, Patrick refused to engage in negative campaigning. Instead, he focused attention on his grass-roots campaign by holding town hall meetings and drawing attention to the record of the incumbent administration. Patrick argued that the Romney/Healey administration cut police resources to local communities (Atkins 2006). He contended that Healey utilized negative ads to distract voters from her record. Patrick went on to state that Healey's campaign set a toxic tone for Massachusetts politics. The efforts of Patrick and his surrogates seemed to work. Polls immediately following the leak about Patrick's brother-in-law showed Patrick 25 points ahead of Healey. Moreover, polls indicated that 45 percent of voters stated that Healey's negative ads made them less likely to vote for her for (Anderson 2006).

The Issues

Several issues were important to voters in the election. Among them were the candidates' positions on fiscal issues such as taxes, the state's economy, the cost of living, crime, immigration, and social issues such as abortion and gay marriage. Most important to a large percentage of voters was the cost of living. According to voters, one solution was to lower the state income tax, passed in 2000. Healey supported rolling back the state income tax from 5.3 percent to 5 percent while at the same time increasing aid to local communities (Howe 2006). Patrick opposed rolling back the state income tax, arguing that it would be fiscally irresponsible, would shift the burden to local communities, and would result in higher property taxes. Instead, he wanted to reduce property taxes and provide more funding to local communities by proposing a local-options or meal tax to help ease their tax burden (Jonas 2006; Wangsness 2006c).

Patrick and Healey disagreed on issues of crime and public safety. Healey supported the death penalty; Patrick opposed it. They also disagreed about the state's proper role in issuing gun licenses. In 2006, local police chiefs issued gun licenses. Police chiefs supported the status quo because it gave them control over who owned weapons in their towns. Opponents charged that vesting power in local law enforcement gave chiefs of police too much power. Patrick supported the idea of local control of gun licenses. Healey, in contrast, made an about-face during the campaign and issued a proposal that would impose statewide standards for gun licenses. Her proposal provoked the ire of local law enforcement officials who exercised their right to institute more stringent gun policies in their jurisdictions (Croteau 2006).

The candidates also differed on education. Healey proposed raising the dropout age from 16 to 18. Patrick offered no public opinion on this issue. While both candidates supported charter schools, Patrick proposed a cap on local government spending on charter schools. He also supported a bond measure to help fund higher education. The candidates did disagree on whether illegal aliens should receive in-state tuition rates. Patrick supported this proposal, and like many voters, Healey opposed it (Atkins and Wedge, 2006; Mooney and Wangsness, 2006).

Despite Massachusetts' reputation as a bastion of social liberalism, social issues were salient in this campaign. Patrick supported same-sex marriage and agreed with the Massachusetts Supreme Court ruling that legalized such marriages in the state. Healey opposed same-sex marriage, but supported civil unions. She also supported the proposed constitutional amendment banning same-sex marriage (Mooney 2005). Despite their disagreements on marriage, both candidates were pro-choice (McNamara 2006).

There were several other issues important in the campaign. Among them included undocumented immigrants and limiting employers' access to criminal records. Patrick supported giving driver's licenses to illegal immigrants and limiting employers' access to criminal records. Although most voters agreed with Healey on how to handle undocumented immigrants and crime, they still planned to vote for Patrick (Carr 2006).

Endorsements

Overall, Deval Patrick benefitted from key endorsements, even from groups that may have been inclined to support Healey. Not surprisingly, the Democratic establishment, including Bill Clinton, Ted Kennedy and John Kerry, endorsed Patrick. Three notable women's groups, the Massachusetts Chapter of the National Organization for Women, the Planned Parenthood Advocacy Fund, and NARAL Pro-Choice Massachusetts endorsed Patrick over Healey, despite the fact that Healey would have been Massachusetts's first elected female governor. Because of Healey's association with the pro-life Mitt Romney, there was some confusion about Healey's stance on abortion. Her refusal to answer questions about issue only added to the ambiguity, making it easier for women's groups to not endorse her (Williams 2006; Wangsness and Simpson 2006).

Patrick also received support from a myriad of Black political leaders and raised more money from out-of-state contributors than any other candidate in the early days of the campaign. The notable contributors included former National Urban League president Vernon Jordan, former labor secretary Alexis Herman, and then-Illinois Senator, Barack Obama. Reports suggest that 24 percent of

Patrick's funding were from grass-roots, Black individuals who wanted to increase the number of Black governors and senators (Williams 2006).

As common in most political campaigns, major newspapers in Massachusetts also endorsed candidates. Among those, supporting Patrick were the *Boston Globe, Worchester Telegram & Gazette, MetroWest Daily News, Providence Journal, Berkshire Eagle, Boston Phoenix, Newton Tab,* and the *West Roxbury & Rosindale Transcript.* Major newspaper outlets supporting Healey included the *Boston Herald, The Eagle-Tribune, Sentinel & Enterprise, Lowell Sun,* and *Cape Cod Times.* There were two common themes in the newspaper endorsements. The first sets of endorsements were supportive of Patrick's campaign rhetoric, which injected hope into politics with a focus on making Massachusetts a better place to live. They also complimented Patrick on running a campaign that was free of negative advertisements. In the end, Patrick's campaign was one of consensus building and compromise. Those supporting Healey pointed out that the bulk of voters in Massachusetts had the same issue positions as Healey. They also pointed out that Healey agreed to uphold the tax rebate voters supported in 2000.

Other Patrick endorsements included the Massachusetts Teachers Association and the Service Employees International Union (SEIU) Local 119. The teachers's union supported Patrick's education policies and charged that the Romney Administration, including Healey, had failed schoolchildren. SEIU supported Patrick's promise to make healthcare more affordable. The Gun Owners Action League endorsed Healey because of her position on creating a state board to issue gun licenses. However, Chief Gemme of Worcester endorsed Patrick (Croteau 2006).

Methods and Data Analysis

The data for this analysis comes from CNN exit polls. Although the data is descriptive, I do observe patterns in how the voters of Massachusetts made their decisions in the gubernatorial election. I begin with crosstabs of the vote by party identification in Table 8.2. First, neither candidate had much crossover appeal to voters identifying with the opposing party. Exactly the same percentage of

Table 8.2 Massachusetts Vote by Party ID and Ideology, 2006

	Healey	*Patrick*	*Mihos*
Democrat (41%)	9%	85%	5%
Republican (19%)	85%	9%	6%
Independent (39%)	41%	45%	10%
Liberal (26%)	9%	83%	6%
Moderate (51%)	36%	55%	8%
Conservative (23%)	72%	20%	6%

Source: CNN Exit Poll. http://edition.cnn.com/ELECTION/2006/pages/results/states/MA/G/00/epolls.0.html. n=655. Figures in parentheses reflect a category's share of the total electorate.

Table 8.3 Massachusetts Vote by Size of Community and Region, 2006

	Healey	*Patrick*	*Mihos*
Urban (22%)	29%	63%	7%
Suburban (67%)	38%	52%	8%
Rural (11%)	30%	65%	2%
Boston Area (25%)	28%	65%	6%
Other Large Cities (12%)	31%	59%	7%
N.Shore/S.Shore (17%)	44%	46%	8%
Eastern Mass (35%)	40%	50%	8%
Western Mass (11%)	30%	65%	2%

Source: CNN Exit Poll. http://edition.cnn.com/ELECTION/2006/pages/results/states/MA/G/00/epolls.0.html. n=655. Figures in parentheses reflect a category's share of the total electorate.

Republicans voted for Patrick as Democrats voted for Healey. Patrick did have a 4-percentage point lead among Independents, though. It also appears that Patrick also had more crossover appeal to conservatives than Healey had with liberals. Only 9 percent of Liberal leaning voters cast their ballots for Healey, while Patrick was able to garner a fifth of conservative voters.

Table 8.3 breaks down the vote by community size and urbanity. The data on community size indicates that Patrick had more support from voters in urban and rural communities than in the suburbs. He also garnered more votes from large cities and the Boston area. In North and South Shore Massachusetts, there is an even split between Kerry and Patrick voters.

There was no apparent gender gap in this election, as evidenced by the data in Table 8.4. However, when we look at this data by race and gender, two facts emerge. First, White women gave more support to Patrick than White men. While only 45 percent of White men voted for Patrick, 57 percent of White women voted for him. The strong support White women showed for Patrick

Table 8.4 Massachusetts Vote by Gender and Race, 2006

	Healey	*Patrick*	*Mihos*
Male (46%)	38%	51%	9%
Female (54%)	32%	61%	5%
White (83%)	39%	51%	8%
Black (9%)	11%	89%	0%
White Men (37%)	42%	45%	11%
White Women (45%)	35%	57%	7%
Non-White Men (9%)	13%	78%	1%
Non-White Women (9%)	21%	78%	0%

Source: CNN Exit Poll. http://edition.cnn.com/ELECTION/2006/pages/results/states/MA/G/00/epolls.0.html. n=655. Figures in parentheses reflect a category's share of the total electorate.

could be the result of the endorsements from the three major women's groups and Healey's ambiguous position on abortion.

When examining the data by race, it is clear that a large percentage of African Americans, 89 percent, voted for Patrick and 11 percent voted for Healey. These numbers are congruent with nationwide data which indicate that a small percentage of Blacks, usually between 5 percent and10 percent of the population, vote Republican (Bositis 2006). Patrick did outrage some Black ministers and voters because he supported gay marriage, but he made a strong appeal to Blacks to overlook his stance on gay marriage because of policy congruence on issues like unemployment and crime. Still, some Blacks may have withheld their votes from him because of his position on gay marriage (Williams 2006).

More than half of Whites voted for Patrick. However, there was a clear generation gap in this election. This is important because in the 1966 senate election, older voters were the most prejudiced and least likely to vote for Edward Brooke (Becker and Heaton 1967, 354). Table 8.5 breaks down the vote by age. Patrick beat Healey by more than 40 percentage points among voters aged 18–29. However, Patrick also won among voters aged 60 and older by a 12 percentage point margin.

Conclusion

A number of factors contributed to race not undermining Deval Patrick's candidacy. Massachusetts had already elected a Black to a statewide office. Patrick also faced a politically unpopular opponent. Though Healey's supporters tried to

Table 8.5 Massachusetts Vote by Age and Income, 2006

	Healey	*Patrick*	*Mihos*
18-29 (11%)	22%	66%	10%
30-44 (23%)	35%	57%	7%
45-59 (35%)	34%	55%	8%
60 and older (32%)	41%	53%	5%
Under $15,000 (3%)	n/a	n/a	n/a
$15-30,000 (9%)	37%	51%	7%
$30-50,000 (20%)	34%	51%	11%
$50-75,000 (20%)	31%	57%	9%
$75-100,000 (20%)	34%	62%	4%
$100-150,000 (19%)	40%	56%	4%
$150-200,000 (5%)	n/a	n/a	n/a
$200,000 or More (4%)	n/a	n/a	n/a

Source: CNN Exit Poll. http://edition.cnn.com/ELECTION/2006/pages/results/states/MA/G/00/epolls.0.html. n=655. Figures in parentheses reflect a category's share of the total electorate.

subtly inject racial stereotypes to bolster her sagging electoral prospects, Patrick surrogates decried those efforts and neutralized the attack.

Patrick's electoral victory evinces that we may have turned a corner—somewhat—in racial politics. While there are numerous examples of Black candidates falling victim to vicious racial attacks (including an attack against Harold Ford in 2006 that Sekou Franklin discusses in the next chapter), the Patrick example shows that they do not always work. Thus, progress is being made.

Patrick's candidacy does raise interesting research opportunities for those interested in studying race and electoral politics. We know from the Harold Ford example that racial attacks are still occasionally effective in modern political campaigns. How can we predict which attacks will be successful and which will be unsuccessful? The Patrick case suggests that certain factors may be important. The attacker's popularity, partisanship and region may all help to predict whether racial attacks can gain traction among voters. As more Blacks run for high profile offices, we should be able to have enough data points to operationalize these factors and test for statistical relationships.

Notes

1. An earlier version of this chapter appeared as Angela K. Lewis. 2009. "Making History, Again, So Soon? The Massachusetts Gubernatorial Election." *National Political Science Review.* 12(1): 7–22. It is reprinted with permission here. Funding for this project was provided by the UAB Office of Equity and Diversity and the UAB ADVANCE program funded by the National Science Foundation.
2. This chapter is dedicated to my son Aiden-Lewis Wilson you are my inspiration. I also thank Jazmin Nikol Welch and Jessica Victoria Welch who provided him with love and care while I worked on this article. I also send a special thanks to my sister, Regina Warren, Joseph and Cynthia Lewis as well as to my graduate assistant, Luedelia Jackson.
3. Jeffries and Jones (2006) find that several unsuccessful statewide Black candidates were former mayors (Thomas Bradley, Ron Kirk, Harvey Gantt, and Andrew Young). They go on to state that historically the office of mayor has not been a stepping stone to a higher elected office.
4. The Big Dig, an underground tunnel system, was a decade-long transportation project that replaced the Central Artery, an elevated six-lane highway through downtown Boston that could no longer hold the amount of traffic in the city. The project finished late and over-budget (Mehren, 2006)
5. Jane Swift had been elevated to the Governor's office earlier, but she assumed office as a Lieutenant Governor fulfilling the unexpired term of her predecessor.
6. Retrieved May 14, 2007, from http://www.boston.com/news/local/politics/candidates/governor/healey/ and http://www.heleycommitte.com/meet_kerry_healey.html.
7. The Reilly campaign was linked to anti-corporate labor activist Ray Rogers who held protest against Patrick. According to media reports (Vennochi, August 11, 2006), the Reilly campaign provided the activists with media contacts and public relations help to protest against Patrick. Rogers planned to criticize Patrick at campaign events "to hold him accountable" for representing corporate interests over the needs of South Americans who tried to sue Texaco for pollution. Rogers also accused Patrick of representing Coke executives who associated with Columbians who murdered labor leaders (Sullivan, 2006).

8. Retrieved May 7, 2009, from http://www.boston.com/news/local/politics/candidates/governor/mihos and http://christy2010.com/pages/about.cfm.
9. The Opinion Research Corporation directed by John F. Becker conducted the polls for Edward Brooke between 1965 and 1966 as referenced in Becker and Heaton, 1967.

References

About the candidates: Christy Mihos. n.d. Boston.com http://www.boston.com/news/local/politics/candidates/governor/mihos (accessed May 7, 2009).

Anderson, Lisa. 2006. Massachusetts gubernatorial candidates wage brutal campaigns. *Chicago Tribune*, October 27.

Atkins, Kimberly. 2006. Battle for governor; Deval turns up heat on Healey. *The Boston Herald*, October 20, 5.

———. Laurel J. Sweet. 2006. The vote is in 2006; Leaders say 1st Black gov a "bookend" for Mass. race woes. *The Boston Herald,* November 9, 6.

Becker, John F., and Eugene E. Heaton Jr. 1967. The election of Senator Edward W. Brooke. *The Public Opinion Quarterly* 31: 346–58.

Bositis, David. 2006. *Blacks and the 2006 midterm election*. Washington, DC: Joint Center for Political and Economic Studies.

Carr, Howie. 2006. Campaign 2006: Mitt's to blame for muffy's mess. *The Boston Herald*, October 27, 4.

Christy Mihos—Portrait of a true leader. n.d. *Christy Mihos for governor.* http://christy2010.com/pages/about.cfm (accessed May 7, 2009).

CNN exit poll data. 2006. http://edition.cnn.com/ELECTION/2006/pages/results/states/MA/G/00/epolls.0.html (accessed April 1, 2007).

Croteau, Scott J. 2006. Police chiefs blast Healey on gun permits: Gun group endorses proposal. *Telegram & Gazette,* October 19, A1.

Eagan, Margery. 2006. Campaign-trail race baiting? If so, voters aren't biting. *The Boston Herald,* October 29, 9.

Ebbert, Stephanie. 2005. Healey bcks proposed constitutional ban on gay marriage. *The Boston Globe*, November 19, http://www.lexis-nexis.com (acccessed August 20, 2009).

Phillips, Frank. 2006. GOP rallies hehind Healey. *The Boston Globe*, March 3, B1. http://www.lexis-nexis.com (accessed August20, 2009).

Helman, Scott. 2006a. Patrick at pulpit, lists his priorities. *The Boston Globe,* February 27, B1.

———. 2006b. Activism, soaring language, disputes mark Patrick's career. *The Boston Globe,* September 6, A1.

Howe, Peter J. 2006. For job growth, small business is big. *The Boston Globe*, October 8.

Jeffries, Judson. 1998. Blacks and high profile statewide office: 1966–1996. *The Western Journal of Black Studies* 22: 164–73.

———. Charles E. Jones, 2006. Blacks who run for governor and the U.S. Senate: An examination of their candidacies. *The Negro Educational Review*, 57: 243–61.

Johnson, Glen. 2006. Patrick garners most votes: Reilly touts success at convention. *Associated Press State and Local Wire,* June 3.

Jonas, Michael. 2006. Deval Patrick's school choice. *The Boston Globe,* September 10, 8.

Jones, Charles, and Michael Clemons. 1993. A model of racial crossover voting: An assessment of the Wilder victory. In *Dilemmas of Black politics,* ed. Georgia Persons, 128–47. New York: HarperCollins

Kalke, Rushmie. 2006a. Patrick, Mihos trade praise, push local aid: Candidates for governor campaign in central Mass. *Telegram & Gazette,* September 29, A6.

———. 2006b. Kerry Healey for governor: "Deval defends" [Political Advertisement]. *Ad Spotlight.* (NationalJournal.com). http://nationaljournal.com/members/adspotlight/2006/10/1013magov1.htm (accessed November 7, 2007).

McNamara, Eileen. 2006. Women's questions. *The Boston Globe,* September 27, B1. http://www.lexis-nexis.com (accessed August 20, 2009).

Mehren, Elizabeth. 2006. The nation: Blue for Beacon Hill? The man who might be Massachusetts' first democratic governor in 20 years is far from a standard-issue liberal. *Los Angeles Times,* October 31.

Mendelberg, Tali. 2001. *The race card: Campaign, strategy, implicit messages, and the norm of equality.* Princeton, NJ: Princeton University Press.

Monahan, John J. 2006a. Attack ads skew gubernatorial campaign. *Telegram & Gazette.* October 15, A1.

———. 2006b. Democratic gubernatorial debate is tonight. *Telegram & Gazette,* September 7, B1.

Mooney, Brian C. 2005. Healey quietly labors to polish an image; Republican eyes run for governor. *The Boston Globe,* December 11, A1. http://www.lexis-nexis.com (accessed August 20, 2009).

Mooney, Brian C. 2006a. Patrick gets help in ad battle with Healey. *The Boston Globe,* October 18, A1.

———. 2006b. Gabrieli readies run for governor; hires operatives, cites positive polling. *The Boston Globe,* March 22, B1.

———. 2006c. Patrick's path from courtroom to boardroom. *The Boston Globe,* August, A1.

———. 2006d. Healey quietly labors to polish an image: Republican eyes run for governor. *The Boston Globe,* December 11, A1.

———. 2006e. Day of decision in state's costliest campaign ever — spending passes $42.8 million in governor's race. *The Boston Globe.* 7 November 7, A1. http;//www.lexis-nexis.com (accessed August 20, 2009).

———. Wangsness, Lisa. 2006. Voters say change is foremost on minds Mass. Attitude benefits Patrick. *The Boston Globe,* October 29, A1. http://web.lexis-nexis.com.fetch.mhsl.uab.edu (accessed May 25, 2007)

O'Sullivan, Jim. 2006. Patrick critic heading for Mass., intending to dog candidate. *State House News Service,* August 8.

Page, Susan. 2006. Election test how much race matters: African-American candidates for major state offices try to break some "old barriers." *USA Today,* September 13, A1.

Phillips, Frank. 2006. Patrick outpaces two rivals in new poll: Democrat surges to a 21-point lead as vote nears. *The Boston Globe,* September 17, A1.

———. Scott Helman. 2006. In a blow to GOP, Mihos to run as independent. *The Boston Globe,* March 2, A1.

———. Adrienne Samuels. 2006. Healey calls for stripping police chiefs of gun-licensing role. *The Boston Globe,* October 18, B4.

Pierce, Charles. 2006. The optimist "I wasn't campaigning as the Black candidate." And because he didn't, because he ran a hopeful, grass-roots campaign that ended with his election as governor, Deval Patrick is our 2006 Bostonian of the year. *The Boston Globe*, December 31, 28.

Purdum, Todd. 2001. Coalition builder wins Los Angeles mayoral race. *The New York Times*, June 7, A14.

Raju, Phalgun. 2004. Lt. Governor of Massachusetts encourages future public service. *The Harbus.* 20, April. http://media.www.harbus.org/media/storage/paper343/news/2004/04/20/News/Lt.Governor.Of.Massachusetts.Encourages.Future.Public.Service-665730.shtml (accessed August 20, 2009).

Sacchetti, Maria. 2006. Patrick, Healey stand apart on schools. *The Boston Globe*, October 7, A1. http://www.lexis-nexis.com (accessed August 20, 2009).

Smith, Andrew. 2006a. *Boston Globe/CBS4 poll. MA gubernatorial election poll.* October 26. The Survey Center. Durham: University of New Hampshire.

———. 2006b. *Boston Globe/WBZ poll. MA gubernatorial election poll.* September 30. The Survey Center. Durham: University of New Hampshire.

Soneshein, Raphael J. 1990. Can Black candidates win statewide elections? *Public Opinion Quarterly* 105: 219–41.

Strickland, Ruth Ann, and Marcia Lynn Whicker. 1992. Comparing the Wilder and Gantt campaigns: A model for Black statewide success in state wide elections. *Political Science & Politics* 25: 204–12.

Valentino, Nicholas, Vincent L. Hutchings, and Ismail White. 2002. Cues that matter: How political ads prime racial attitudes during campaigns. *The American Political Science Review,* 96 (1): 75–90.

Vennochi, Joan. 2006. For Reilly, things go better with Coke. *The Boston Globe,* August 11, A17.

Wangsness, Lisa. 2006a. At rally, Patrick tries to turn Healey's ads back at her. *The Boston Globe*, October 16, B4.

———. 2006b. Healey will sign antitax pledge: 3 in 4 candidates support rollback. *The Boston Globe,* September 4, B1.

———. A. Simpson. 2006. 3 women's groups to endorse Patrick. *The Boston Globe*, October 12, B4.

Wickham, DeWayne. 2006. In Boston, the smell of a dirty trick. *USA Today*, October 17, A19.

Williams, Joseph. 2006. Black political figures rally around Patrick. *The Boston Globe*, April 18, A1.

Williams, Linda F. 1989. White/Black perceptions of the electability of Black political candidates. *National Political Science Review* 1: 45–64.

Williamson, Dianne. 2006. Patrick caught in cross hairs: Support of LaGuer preceded DNA test. *Telegram & Gazette,* October 5, B1.

9 The Declining Significance of Race

Adrian Fenty and the Smooth Electoral Transition

Rachel Yon

In the District of Columbia, race has always played a major issue in the campaigns and administrations of public officials, particularly mayors. This was clearly seen in the campaigns and/or administrations of Mayors Marion Barry, Sharon Pratt Dixon Kelly, and Anthony Williams, who either appealed to racial solidarity or were accused of racial distancing. However, when Adrian Fenty ran to succeed Anthony Williams in 2006, race was hardly an issue in the all-important primary campaign. How could race apparently not matter in a city steeped in Black Nationalism, and how can it not be used against a candidate such a Fenty, a biracial Black man with a tremendous crossover appeal?

In this chapter, Rachel Yon explores a number of possible contributing factors as to why race never became an issue in his campaign. Preliminary findings suggest that because Fenty grew up in the District, he was able to evade the carpetbagger moniker that people such as Cory Booker faced in other cities. Moreover, Fenty's primary opponent, Linda Cropp, was herself a racially moderate politician who was reluctant to attack Fenty's racial bona fides (though she did attack his youth). In the end, Fenty ran an energetic campaign which knocked on every door in the district, and he won handily.

Introduction

Issues of racial authenticity have loomed large in Washington, DC since residents started popularly electing mayors in the 1970s. Where Mayors Kelly and Williams were "not Black enough," Mayor Barry used "race as a battering ram" (Fisher 2006a, B01). Given this history, it would not have been surprising for racial issues to have dominated the 2006 contest between Adrian Fenty, a young, biracial city councilman, and Linda Cropp, City Council President and a stalwart of the city's Black establishment. However, race did not become an issue in that contest. Why did this occur? How Fenty avoid the charge that he was not "Black enough"?

In the pages that follow, I will try to answer these questions. First, I consider the concept of deracialization, its offshoots, and its importance in African

American political strategies. Second, I look at the demographics and the racial composition of the District. These factors are extremely important for a politician to consider because it contributes to the way a campaign is framed. Next, I examine previous mayoral administrations and determine how their choices and leadership styles affected the District. Considering the different legislative and campaigning styles the major candidates possessed and the context of the environment in which they ran is very important. There will also be a discussion of Fenty's political career before he ran for the mayoralty. I then turn to the 2006 Democratic primary race and election and the 2006 general election to determine how Fenty ultimately became mayor. Finally, I revisit these issues and determine why race was not a factor in this election as it had been in the mayoral elections that came before it.

African American Political Style and Strategy

There have been many authors who have discussed and debated the concept of deracialization. Charles V. Hamilton created the term in the 1970s intending to help the Democratic Party vis á vis Republicans by encouraging the party to focus on issues that would appeal to all voters, rather than any particular racial group (McClain and Tauber 1997, 295).

Kilson (1989) believes that deracialization can be a method of ensuring that greater numbers of African Americans are elected to public office. In order to guarantee such a strategy is successful, increasing numbers of Whites must be willing to vote for African American candidates. His work has broadened the deracialization concept into the realm of transethnicity. He states,

> In the years ahead, what I call a transethnic imperative will increasingly inform Black American life in general and its politics in particular. The goal of such an imperative would be to intertwine the leadership of Black and White sociopolitical institutions…The initial focus of an emergent Black transethnic politics must be to transform Black elected officials into politicians elected by multi-ethnic votes, not simply Black votes. (Kilson 1989, 526)

In order to be successful as crossover candidates, politicians must prove their skill and value to the entire voting public. They must demonstrate that they can provide fair leadership to all citizens without favoring those who share a racial background (Austin and Middleton 2004). To ensure they appeal to races and ethnicities beyond their own, they must emphasize inclusive and egalitarian themes (McClain and Tauber 1997).

According to McCormick and Jones (1993), one must consider the strategy of deracialization realistically in our political times as a process of:

> Conducting a campaign in a stylistic fashion that defuses the polarizing effects of race by avoiding explicit references to race-specific issues, while at

the same time emphasizing those issues that are perceived as racially transcendent, thus mobilizing a broad segment of the electorate for purposes of capturing and maintaining public office. (76)

While it would appear that African American candidates are being asked to make all of the changes in order to appeal to voters outside of their racial and ethnic grouping, by limiting "their natural political-cultural impulses to openly advocate Black causes…rather than White voters having to make some political attitudinal adjustments that would lead them to support Black candidates," in fact, "at the theoretical level, deracialization challenges White voters to be less race-bound in their voting preferences" (Perry 1996, 3).

There is the implication that as long as race is not mentioned during a campaign, White voters will find it palatable to vote for a non-White political candidate—as if not talking about it makes color differences disappear (Summers and Klinkner 1996). Proponents of deracialization claim that when comparing the needs, desires, and political interests of Blacks and Whites, there is little-to-no overlap; and, therefore, when politicians attempt to build multiracial coalitions they inevitably forsake Black interests (Summers and Klinkner 1996, 328). However, this is simply not the case. It is crucial when dealing with a deracialization strategy to remember that the political life of many African Americans in this country is found in those areas that are primarily African American and which elect African Americans to lead them (Perry 1996, 2). Despite the suggestion that candidates may ignore their traditional base in favor of voters of other races, the concept of deracialization does not threaten to destroy this important political foundation which, along with race-specific agendas, has often been the only way for African Americans to break into the political scene (Summers and Klinkner 1996). However, it is also important to realize that simply because an African American candidate has used such methods to obtain entry into politics does not mean that they encapsulate the entirety of his/her political ambitions (Summers and Klinkner 1996, 328). What the deracialization strategy has meant is that candidates need to work towards goals that are important to all racial groups. These politicians must not allow any one group to supersede any other in importance but instead ensure that the most important racially transcendent problems and policies are tackled.

As we become more racially tolerant (for example, an African American was chosen as the 2008 Democratic nominee for president and later won the presidency), it should be clear that the use of different "crossover appeals" will become a possibility in United States politics (Summers and Klinkner 1996, 328). Therefore,

> Rather than assuming that recent African American electoral victories have resulted from centrist, establishment politics and conservative appeals to White voters—as opposed to progressive politics, grassroots organizing, and appeals to Black pride—political scientists should analyze each election in its own particular context. (Summers and Klinkner 1996, 328)

Political style and strategy ranges from nonracial or race-neutral politics (where there is minimal or even no mention of race by the candidates) to hyperracial politics (where candidates engage in race-baiting) (Henderson 1996). Between these two extremes one can find transracialized, racialized (race is made a part of the campaign in different ways depending on the candidate but it is clearly a topic of discussion), and deracialized political strategies which differ with regard to the degree to which race is used as an "operating symbol" within a campaign (Henderson 1996, 172). Those politicians who use transracial political strategies continue to include a discussion of race and ethnicity in their campaigns and their rhetoric. In this strategy, the importance of such issues is not minimized, but, the politician also emphasizes the need to transcend these issues and focus on those agendas that appeal to all groups in our society (Henderson 1996, 172). On the other hand, a politician who uses a deracialized strategy attempts to remove race completely from the political discourse, preferring to focus on issues of importance to all voters.

This continuum is based on theories of deracialization in which Black leaders deemphasize race in order to appeal to a broader audience of voters. They focus on particular styles and symbols which allow them to deliver their message without being labeled as working solely for the benefit of the Black community. However, this can also backfire as candidates can be considered to lack racial authenticity. The continuum looks at both electoral strategies and policy strategies as there may be a difference in how a politician runs for office compared with what that politician does once he/she gets into office (Henderson 1996). The style selected depends on a number of factors: 1) the racial composition of the city; 2) the political environment within the particular jurisdiction that might impact an electoral race (as well as any important external factors that might play a role); 3) the race of the candidates running for election (the continuum distinguishes those races where an African American is running against another African American and those in which an African American is running against an individual of another race); 4) the policies to which these candidates plan to focus their time and attention (the continuum looks at the entire policy-making cycle: agenda setting, policy formulation, policy adoption, policy implementation, and policy evaluation); and 5) their campaigning style (Henderson 1996).

A new breed of African American politician is moving onto the political scene. These individuals have had "little or no direct involvement with civil rights organizations and its youth places it beyond direct contact with the historic advances of the 1950s and 1960s" (Albritton et al. 1996, 181). This has resulted in significant changes in the way voters are recruited, the way political candidates present themselves to the voting public, and the way politicians work within government once elected. These African American politicians appear to have the choice of using either race-neutral politics or race-specific politics. Race-neutral politics lessens the prominence of the Black political agenda in order to ensure that the needs of White supporters are also considered. In race-neutral politics, race is merely a descriptive "cue to mobilize support among African American voters" (Albritton et al. 1996, 180). On the other hand, race-specific politics uses race as the "cue for representation of Black political agendas" (Albritton et al. 1996, 180).

Political strategies based on race neutrality not only deemphasize race, but completely remove it from the voting equation (Albritton et al. 1996, 181). These race neutral strategies allow African American candidates to present themselves as non-threatening to voters of all races and as individuals who will focus attention on the projects and policies that are for the benefit of the entire voting district, not just the African American residents. However, this race neutrality does not have to lead to the abandonment of the issues that are considered important to the African American community or of agendas that work towards fulfilling the "so-called progressive Black agenda;" rather, there is potential for this type of strategy to lead to larger numbers of African Americans in public office (Albritton et al. 1996, 182; Hamilton 1977). Perry (1996b) stated,

> There is the outside chance that the successful application of traditional Black politics and deracialized Black politics will help create a level of consciousness among the American public so that neither style of Black politics in its pure form will be necessary. If that is the case, both traditional Black politics and deracialized Black politics would be positive contributions to the advancement of American politics. (195–196)

Of course, each candidate's campaign will depend on a number of different variables, such as, the balance of conservative and liberal ideology in the area as well as the size of the African American population. Yet, "most deracialized campaigns consist of three elements: promoting "nonthreatening" images, purposely avoiding racially divisive issues, and carrying out aggressive grassroots mobilization efforts" (Austin and Middleton 2004, 284; see also McCormick and Jones 1993). As the African American community remains the primary base of political support, these candidates have to ensure that they have secured a majority of these votes before they can safely move on to obtaining support from other racial groups (Austin and Middleton 2004, 284; see also Hamilton 1978). There is a careful balance that must be maintained among the concepts of racial neutrality, protecting ones base, and being the kind of politician that can lead all races and ethnicities (Orey 2006).

Demographics of the District of Columbia

Washington, DC's demographics demand that Black politicians use a deft hand to balance racial and universal interests and campaign appeals. As Table 9.1 shows, the population distribution of the District in 2006 was 56.5 percent African American, 38.4 percent Caucasian, and 5.1 percent other races (including Hispanics, Native Americans, Alaskans, Hawaiians, Pacific Islanders, Asians, those who classify themselves as two or more races, and those who classify themselves as some other race).

While it is obvious that African Americans compose the largest ethnic group in the District, their percentage of the population has been steadily declining since the 1970s. This has been largely attributed to "Black flight," as many middle-class and professional African Americans left the city for the suburbs

Table 9.1 District of Columbia Population and Racial Composition, 1950–2006

Census year	Total population	White	Percentage White	Black	Percentage Black	Other Race	Percentage Other Race
1950	802,178	517,865	64.6	280,803	35	3,510	0.4
1960	763,956	345,263	45	411,737	53.9	6,956	0.9
1970	756,510	209,272	28	537,712	71.1	9,526	1.2
1980	638,333	171,768	27	448,906	70.3	17,659	2.8
1990	606,900	179,667	30	399,604	65.8	27,629	4.6
2000	572,059	197,168	31	349,390	60	25,501	9
2006*	581,530	223,033	38.4	328,566	56.5	29,931	5.1

*These figures are Census estimates.
Source: U.S. Census Bureau.

surrounding the District. It is also apparent that the percentage of the White population has gradually been increasing since the 1980s. This has been most apparent over the last decade, in part because the process of gentrification, which has revitalized many of the neighborhoods in the District, has also displaced residents of some of the District's traditionally Black communities (Muhammad 2007).

Table 9.2 records 2006 city voter registration by party identification. It is quite clear that the demographics of the District make the likelihood of a Democrat being elected in the mayoral race an extremely safe bet. Nearly three-quarters of registered voters identify as Democrats, with only 7.9 percent identifying as Republicans and the other 18.5 percent dividing themselves among smaller parties and identifying as independents (or those affiliated with no party). Indeed, most non-Democrats and Republicans have no party affiliation.

Washington, DC Mayoral Politics

Despite the influx of newcomers and non-Blacks to the city, Washington, DC remains over 50 percent African American. As a result, race has always played a major role in the campaigns and administrations of public officials, particularly

Table 9.2 Registered Voters by Party, September 12, 2006 Washington DC Mayoral Primary

Party	Democrats	Republican	Statehood Green	No Party	Other	Totals
Registered voters	285,486	30,560	5,044	65,321	1,529	387,940
Percentage	73.60%	7.90%	1.30%	16.80%	0.40%	100.00%

Source: D.C. Board of Elections and Ethics, Monthly Report of Voter Registration Statistics.

the high office of mayor. In fact, all of the District of Columbia's mayors (the city has only elected mayors since 1975) have been of African American heritage.

Marion Barry has long loomed as a prominent political figure in the District. Barry served as the city's second mayor from 1979–1991 and, then after a short prison stint, he served as the city's fourth mayor from 1995–1999. Because of the District's relatively short mayoral history and political traditions, Barry became the government in the eyes of his followers and was seen as the "incarnation of general Black will" (Siegal 1997, 105). Under his leadership, many committed themselves to the achievement of a "Black Zion," i.e., "a city that would be governed on its own terms…independent of White standards" (Siegal 1997, 105). According to Herbert Reid (Howard University professor and legal counsel to Mayor Barry):

> After the Civil War Whites "used the indiscretions and excess of Blacks to successfully disenfranchise Blacks and take them out of office." A Black mayor has to be protected no matter what…because he represents the next phase of the civil rights movement. In other words, breaking with Barry would mean repudiating the civil rights movement and a repeat of the White takeover in the post-Reconstruction era. (Reid quoted in Siegal 1997, 105)

Because Barry's incorporated themes of Black Nationalism into his rhetorical leadership, his tenure was the emblem of Black self-determination. Thus, it was very difficult for some to be critical of his leadership, because criticism could evince racial treason (Siegal 1997, 105).

The nationalist zeitgeist of the day probably shielded Barry from having to address serious critiques of his governance. The District had long had a reputation of being wasteful with resources and severely mismanaging constituent services, grants, and funds. This perception magnified under Barry's stewardship (see Powell 1997). By mid-1997, in its region, the District had the lowest-quality services in the Capital Region, despite the fact that residents were paying a good deal more for them than citizens in other areas (Powell 1997). Funds that were to be used to provide or improve the most basic human services were squandered. Barry was well-known for using the power of patronage to create a base of political support. His decision to provide jobs and contracts to those who would help him, instead of ensuring that these individuals were the best choice for the people of the District, led to a reduction in the quality of services provided as well as the loss of hundreds of millions of dollars each year (Powell 1997, A01). Although Barry promised cost-cutting reforms, he never delivered and the District lost $154 million instead (Powell 1997, A01).

While the District of Colombia's workforce grew tremendously under Barry, the "first-rate, relatively corruption-free police department had its budget repeatedly cut" resulting in lowered police morale (Siegal 1997, 90). This led to an increase in the crime rate, especially homicides and drug activity. Although Barry was warned that the police force no longer had control of the now crime-rampant city, he focused more attention on politics. To some observers, Barry's goal seemed to be to have the "police in his pocket" so that he could be free to engage in illegal behavior without fear of being arrested and charged with criminal behavior (Siegal 1997, 90). This criminal behavior included "openly buying drugs and sex" and eventually led to serious drug and corruption allegations which resulted in his arrest (after being caught on tape smoking crack cocaine) and time in prison (Siegal 1997, 90). In response to the criminal allegations, Barry successfully played the race card, claiming that these allegations were merely part of a "White conspiracy to lynch successful Blacks" (Siegal 1997, 90). Many Blacks sympathized with Barry. When he got out of jail, they voted him back in office (first as city councilman, then as mayor) (LaFraniere 1990; Feldmann 1994; Walters 1994; Barras 1992).

Corruption and mismanagement plagued other parts of city government. For instance, while the public housing budget rapidly grew from $36 million to $130 million, the number of housing units failed to increase. Though the Housing Authority's repair staff was twice as large as maintenance departments in comparably sized cities, many public housing units were in utter disrepair (Siegal 1997, 92).

Marion Barry's criminal problems forced him out of the 1990 mayoral election, thus opening the door for Sharon Pratt Dixon Kelly to become Washington's third mayor. Kelly came from a prominent Black family in Washington (her father was a judge and her first husband was a former city councilman) and had been an executive for the local electric company. She had been active in Democratic Party politics for decades. Kelly united Black and White voters to mount a come-from-behind victory, becoming Washington's first female mayor. She gained particular notoriety in that election when she publicly called for the convicted Marion Barry to resign his office. Even Barry conceded that voters selected her as mayor because she was his polar opposite (Siegal 1997, 100; Jaffe and Sherwood 1994, 298; Sherwood 1989; McCraw 1990; Melton 1990).

Kelly assumed office promising to clean house in City Hall "with a shovel, not a broom" (Nichols and Minzesheimer 1990, 3A). Unfortunately, she was unable to deliver on her pledge. Kelly alienated many experienced city employees who could have been invaluable to her management team. She tried unsuccessfully to close the city's budget gap, which triggered additional federal oversight and drove the city to the brink of bankruptcy. In what was perhaps her biggest symbolic defeat, she failed to nurture a relationship with Washington Redskins owner Jack Kent Cooke, which led him to relocate the football team to the Maryland suburbs. She then further angered some constituents by not trying to lure Cooke back to the District (Henderson 1994). Neil Henderson of the *Washington Post* summed up her tenure in office when he wrote:

> But other analysts, including friends and foes alike, say the mayor was in over her head from the start, lacking the management experience or political skills to take on an extraordinarily difficult job. They characterize her four years as a time when the District government began to crumble visibly, as its finances spun out of control and local courts expanded their control

of troubled municipal programs such as public housing and foster care for children. (Henderson 1994, A1)

Kelly also had a difficult time connecting with city residents, particularly Black residents, on a personal level. Kelly's fair skin and upper-class breeding caused problems with some segments of the city's population (Fisher 2006a, B01). Jaffe and Sherwood note:

> She had the Upper Sixteenth Street upbringing, the father who was a judge, the Howard degrees, the haughty arrogance, and the sanctimonious belief that the capital belongs to native Washingtonians of a certain pedigree. She was a direct political heir to former mayor Walter Washington...she was the revenge of the aristocrats against Marion Barry's civil rights rabble. (Jaffe and Sherwood 1994, 299)

Eventually, as the city's finances continued to deteriorate, Kelly found that she had no real political base. Whites had lost confidence in her leadership ability and were not assuaged when Kelly charged that the loss of confidence was racially motivated. And because she had not cultivated support among Blacks, they were not inclined to support her either. In the end, Marion Barry emerged from prison, reorganized his working-class, Black base, and defeated Kelly for the mayoralty in 1994. He was aided by the candidacy of Councilman John Ray, who had finished second to Kelly in 1990. Ray won the White precincts that had supported Kelly in the previous election (Siegal 1997, 100; Henderson 1994).

Marion Barry recaptured control of City Hall in 1994 by promising to redeem himself in the eyes of District residents (Jones and Lowery 1995). While Barry obtained a good deal of support from the District's voters (except for the predictable loss of White support), he also faced a series of daunting political and financial challenges (Jones and Lowery 1995). Although he stated that he would correct the managerial and financial problems the District faced (some were his fault; others were Kelly's fault), Barry had little opportunity to make good on that promise (Janofsky 1998). By the time he got back into office, the Republican controlled Congress determined that the District was in need of a financial oversight board to help it solve its severe fiscal problems (Janofsky 1998). This board "shifted most of the mayor's responsibilities...leaving Mr. Barry to preside over little more than the Department of Recreation and the Office of Aging" (Janofsky 1998, A14). Although Barry strongly protested what he claimed to be a "raping [of] democracy" in the District, Congress paid little attention (Janofsky 1998, A14). This, in part, led to Barry's decision not to run for a fifth term in office.

Anthony Williams succeeded Barry as Mayor of Washington, DC. The Yale and Harvard trained Williams brought extensive government and managerial experience with him to City Hall. He served on New Haven, Connecticut's Board of Alderman. He worked in municipal government in St. Louis and Boston. He also served as Chief Financial Officer for the U.S. Department of Agriculture (Hansen 1998; Cottman and Woodlee 1998; Powell and Williams

1998). Immediately before running for mayor, Marion Barry appointed him as Chief Financial Officer for the District. In this capacity, Williams "restored fiscal accountability for District agencies, balanced the city's budget, which put the District on a track for the return to self government two years earlier than projected, and delivered a surplus of $185 million in fiscal year 1997" ("The Honorable Anthony A. Williams Mayor, District of Columbia" 1999).

In some ways, Williams represented the antithesis of Marion Barry, much like Sharon Pratt Kelly did when she won the mayoralty in 1990. Williams's municipal management experience, however, set him apart from Kelly. Despite these differences, Williams's personal style did cause some problems for him among some city residents. The shy and bookish Williams had to learn how to politick with residents. Williams' reticence, coupled with his popularity among affluent, White residents, attracted charges that he, too, was racially inauthentic (Cottman 1998; Neibauer 2006). In 2006, Williams explained the disconnect between him and city residents, particularly, the poor, Black residents of the District, this way:

> "I just think it's personality, mannerisms," he said. "The RFK racetrack hurt me in the community. Closing D.C. General [hospital, the only public hospital in the District] hurt me in the African American community. Some of the comments I made when I was CFO about the work force being inept. Baseball was characterized as taking from the poor and giving to the rich, even though it had nothing to do with that. So all those things." (Williams quoted in Neibauer 2006)

Williams also seemed uncomfortable around Black people, as one of his associates said to a reporter:

> Having seen him in action many times in small and large events—and in predominantly White as well as predominately Black gatherings—I suggest that it isn't his manner of dress or speech or his braininess that produces his lower standing among African Americans. The reason is more personal. Williams' fondness for people who don't look like him comes through when he's hobnobbing with them. He's congenial, communicative and relaxed. Not so, when he is "among his own kindred." That Williams…is a poor mixer, even standoffish. His body language conveys a remoteness that says to those around him: "I'm here because I have to be here." (King 2001, A21)

Despite Williams's social awkwardness, the District saw great economic improvement, budget surpluses, and urban renewal under his leadership (Fisher 2006a; Nakamura 2006a). He decided that in order to get the District out of the financial straits it was in, he would work closely with the financial control board that had been created and imposed upon the District by the federal government (King 2001, A21). He also worked hard to promote investment in the District in order to "spruce up a city that had gone to seed" (King 2001, A21).

To be sure, Williams's improvement of the city came at a price. During his tenure in office, Washington, DC saw a great deal of gentrification. Low-income residents of these communities blamed his policies for the loss of their homes (Neibauer 2006). King writes that, "Longtime residents…witnessed, with deep sadness, the conversion of old neighborhoods into enclaves for a growing and politically active new middle class, some of whom have high regard for themselves but low tolerance for the history they are replacing. The beauty parlor and barbershop talk is that under Tony Williams, the District of Columbia has become more worldly, and more wealthy and more White (King 2001, A21).

So, in the quarter-century before Adrian Fenty became Mayor of Washington, DC, residents lived experienced extreme polarity in Black political leadership styles. They had lived under Marion Barry's highly racially conscious regime, and the Black patrician leadership of Sharon Pratt Kelly. In addition, residents had experienced the largely deracialized, technocratic leadership of Anthony Williams. While Williams was clearly the most successful of the three mayors, all three mayors had stylistic flaws. By 2006, voters were looking for someone who could "get down and dirty, someone who [to] fix the basic services that were beyond Barry's ability and beneath Williams' grand vision" (Fisher 2006a, B01). Adrian Fenty thought he was the person who fit that bill.

The Political Career of Adrian Fenty

Adrian Fenty was a lifelong resident of the District of Columbia. Born to an interracial couple (Fenty's mother is White, his father Black) with a thriving sporting goods business, Fenty became well acquainted with running and his hometown (Jaffe 2008; Fisher 2006b). Fenty left Washington to earn a bachelor's degree in economics from Oberlin College. He returned to the District to earn a law degree from Howard University ("Mayor Adrian M. Fenty: Biography" n.d.).

As an adult, Fenty became very interested in "local politics, neighborhood politics, ward politics, politics that would improve the quality of life in the neighborhood and the ward that [he] lived in" (Fenty 2008). He became active within his community in neighborhood and civic associations, and when he felt that his Ward 4 Councilmember, Charlene Drew Jarvis (daughter of the famed physician Charles Drew) was not doing enough to bring change to the ward, he challenged her. In 2000, Fenty decided to run for the Ward 4 council seat (Fenty 2008). Running on a platform of neighborhood responsiveness, he promised to provide better constituent service and improved government services (Fenty 2008). He promised to be a hands-on city council member, and to prove his stamina, relentless energy, and desire to work for the citizens of Ward 4, he mounted an aggressive door-to-door campaign. Fenty's efforts paid off, and he beat Councilwoman Jarvis. According to Fenty, he believes he was elected to the city council because of a "combination of the right philosophy for the position and the right outreach in the campaign" (Fenty 2008).

Once a part of the city council, Fenty became best known for his constituent service. He was focused on improving the quality of life his constituents' lives. He stated in a 2008 interview with Dr. Andra Gillespie:

> As chair of the human services committee we got a lot of legislation and better performance out of the agencies under our review. A lot of focus on the neighborhood economic development and cleaning up corridors that had blighted properties from strip clubs to alcohol establishments to used car lots. (Fenty 2008)

During his two terms as a Councilmember, Fenty took a number of controversial stands. He was one of the few politicians to argue that the owners of the Washington Nationals baseball team—not taxpayers—should be required to shoulder the burden and excessive cost of building a new stadium. He cast the only vote against the emergency crime bill because he felt that it was merely a "feel-good" measure (Nakamura 2006a, A01). Finally, he secured $1 billion in funding for school renovations over the initial objections of his colleagues (Nakamura 2006a, A01).

Some fellow councilmembers took issue with Fenty's style. To some, his "radical, attention grabbing positions" demonstrated his inability to build coalitions and work well with colleagues; however, critics claimed that Fenty's style was "just splash" (Nakamura 2006a, A1).

The 2006 Primary Election

Fenty ran for mayor because he wanted to improve on the work of Anthony Williams. Despite Williams's improvements, Fenty believed that the city could do more to deliver services in a timely, efficient and transparent manner (Fenty 2008). With this in mind, Fenty threw his hat into the 2006 mayoral race.

Fenty chose to run a race that highlighted his youthful energy, not his race (Fisher 2006a, B1). He tried to present himself as physically and mentally strong, seemingly ready to make government responsible to its citizens (Williams 2006, C1). He made clear that while he felt the Williams administration had made solid progress, it was in a state of diminishing returns. Williams had been able to take the city from the brink of financial disaster, but his inability to connect with a large portion of the population (i.e. lower income residents) stymied his effectiveness (Silverman 2006, B4).

According to Fenty, "the District needed someone with a new set of eyes, refreshed and renewed energy to try and quicken up the pace of progress and face the challenges the city had with new focus and new zeal" (Fenty 2008). He thought he was that person. To win office, he ran an unprecedented campaign. Beginning in June 2005, he and his volunteers went door-to-door in an attempt to meet every voter in the District before the election. While Fenty was able to make it to more than half of the houses in the city, his volunteers made it to every single house (Williams 2006, C1).

Fenty's main opposition in the Democratic primary was City Council President Linda Cropp, a longtime councilwoman and ally of Mayor Anthony Williams. Fenty and Cropp served together on the DC City Council. This allowed for voters to witness their two, different political styles. Cropp could best be described as a consensus builder, while Fenty had an "independent, contrarian style" (Nakamura 2006a, A1). According to Nakamura (2006a),

> During their years on the council, six for Fenty and sixteen for Cropp, the two have pursued strikingly different legislative styles. Fenty has focused on constituent services and taken radical, attention-grabbing positions that have irritated colleagues but played well among residents. Cropp, is the quintessential insider, wielding influence quietly, often behind closed doors, and moving legislation forward through negotiation and compromise. (A1)

These styles shed some light on how these individuals would run the mayor's office if elected.

Some claim that these different approaches are the result of differences in experience, in other words, a generational gap. Cropp, having spent over two decades as an elected official, believed that responsible government came from those who were patient and deliberate; responsible government would never be created by those who went forward blindly in the political sphere, not thinking through all of the possible consequences of their actions (Nakamura 2006a, A01). However, Fenty, who began to run for office when he was only in his second term on the city council, "believe[d] that the government [had] not been as ambitious as he [had]" (Nakamura 2006a, A1). Despite a lack of experience, he had an excellent reputation for delivering services to the citizens he represented (Williams 2006, C1).

Fenty had few supporters among his colleagues. His fellow councilmembers believed he was more interested in getting media coverage than putting in the work necessary to create long-lasting and beneficial legislation (Nakamura 2006a; Williams 2006). They did not support his candidacy because they did not think he had the ability to work with others within the governmental structure and therefore would not be an effective mayor (Williams 2006, C1).

Mayor Anthony Williams was among those who thought that Fenty was not ready to be mayor. Williams endorsed Cropp for mayor, publicly proclaiming that Fenty was not prepared for the job. To him, Cropp's longstanding career in politics and experience at the highest levels of DC government made her the best choice for mayor (Stevens 2007; Silverman 2006, B04; Woodlee and Weil 2006). To that end, Williams worked tirelessly to raise money and political support for Cropp during the primary season (Doolittle 2006, *Metropolitan*; Silverman 2006).

For her part, Cropp pledged to continue the good work that Anthony Williams had begun. This won her favor with established politicians as well as the business community. The business leaders in particular had become excited about the economic growth under Williams, and they felt that Cropp she was the best person to continue this development (Nakamura 2006b). They also saw her as a political insider who worked well with the established institutions in the District. While she may have won the support of the city's elders, she had a harder time winning over rank-and-file voters. She had trouble "sell[ing] herself" to the public in the face of an energetic individual who promised to breathe new life into DC politics (Nakamura 2006a, A01; Nakamura 2006b, A1).

Despite the fact that he was greatly favored by the public, Fenty did have his handicaps which came out during the race. According to Williams (2006),

> He is not a great orator, his sentences at times peppered with too many ahs and his thoughts stumbling from his mouth. His platform—good schools, safe streets—is not particularly visionary (although some would argue that his promise of a responsive government is by itself a utopian notion). He has no lyrical catchphrase, a la former presidential and vice presidential candidate John Edwards's "two Americas." (C1)

Still, Fenty's new ideas to fix the District's old problems, such as the educational system, the gulf that was growing between rich and poor citizens, the problems of finding affordable housing in the District, and the issues of crime resonated with voters. Citizens believed that he would hold the government accountable and improve its level of performance (Nakamura 2006b).

By July 2006, polls showed that Fenty had a 10 percentage point lead over Cropp (Barnes and Montgomery 2006, A01). This gap existed in part because "District voters [were] alarmed about crime, more despondent than ever about public schools and increasingly anxious that the city [was] heading in the wrong direction" (Barnes and Montgomery 2006, A1). Plus, at that point in time, 55 percent of voters had come to believe that the path Williams was not leading the District down the right path. These voters were looking for a mayor who would find a new direction for the District (Barnes and Montgomery 2006, A1).

In an attempt to narrow the electoral gap, Cropp initiated a negative campaign against Fenty. Citing an instance where Fenty did not adequately represent the financial interests of an elderly client, Cropp accused Fenty of putting ambition before children and seniors. In an attempt to undercut Fenty's support among poor voters, she accused him of voting to lift rent ceilings on apartments. She also attacked his vote against the emergency crime bill and noted that he had affiliations with a defunct charter school. None of these attacks worked. According to *The Washington Post,* the negative advertising did not reduce Fenty's poll numbers (Silverman and Montgomery 2006, B2; Nakamura and Montgomery 2006).

Ultimately, Fenty prevailed in the primary contest, winning all 142 precincts in the District (a first in the District's political history) (Montgomery 2006, A1). He received 57 percent of the vote to Cropp's 31 percent (see Table 9.3).

Table 9.3 Certified Election Night Results, 2006 Washington, DC Democratic Primary

Candidate	Votes Received	Percentage
Vincent Orange	3,075	2.90%
Adrian Fenty	60,732	57.20%
Michael A. Brown	650	0.61%
Linda Cropp	32,897	30.98%
Artee (RT) Milligan	105	0.10%
Marie Johns	8,501	8.01%
Nestor Djonkam	73	0.07%
Write In Candidates	145	0.14%
Total	106,178	100.00%

Source: District of Columbia Board of Elections and Ethics, Certified Election Night Results, September 26, 2006.

The 2006 General Election

The demographics of the District make it almost a guarantee that the Democratic nominee for the mayoralty will win the general election. In the fall election, Fenty faced David Kranich, who had run unopposed in the Republican primary ("Sample Ballot..." 2006). Kranich faced numerous problems as the candidate of a little supported party (fewer than 8 percent of voters are registered Republicans in the District). He was rarely given any press coverage in the newspapers, television, or radio (Montgomery & Silverman 2006, DZ2; Noah 2006). Even Republican groups who agreed to endorse him could not convince their members to support a candidate they did not see as viable (Stewart 2006, B6).

In November 2006, Fenty received an overwhelming 89 percent of the vote to Kranich's 6 percent. The rest of the vote was split among Chris Otten, the DC Statehood Party candidate and a variety of write-in candidates (see Table 9.4).

If Not Race...Then What?

We have seen in other chapters in this volume how some Phase III Black politicians have had to prove their racial bona fides before Black voters took them

Table 9.4 District of Columbia 2006 Mayoral Election Results

Party	Candidate	Votes	Percentage
Democratic	Adrian Fenty	106,848	88.58%
Statehood Green	Chris Otten	4,914	4.07%
Republican	David Kranich	7,517	6.23%
Write-in		1,341	1.11%
Total		120,620	100%

Source: District of Columbia Board of Elections and Ethics, Certified Official Results Report, November 7, 2006.

seriously. Given the fact that Adrian Fenty is a deracialized politician, one would have expected that his campaign would have faced the same hurdles. He did not face those hurdles in 2006. Why was that the case? There are a number of possible macro and micro explanations for this phenomenon.

First, racial politics in the District are mature and reflect the realities of that multi-cultural community. While politics in the District was synonymous with the heavily racialized Marion Barry for nearly two decades, Fenty assumed office on the heels of a successful, deracialized Black mayor. That mayor came into office with a majority-White city council (Cottman and Woodlee 1998). So, not only were District residents comfortable with the idea of deracialized Black leadership, the changing demographics and heavy incorporation of White residents in the city necessitated a lighter touch when it came to racial issues.

Second, as the candidate of the business establishment, Linda Cropp would have been hard pressed to run a racialized campaign. As the heir apparent to Anthony Williams, whose calm demeanor had won over city business leaders (Cleary 1998), Cropp would have jeopardized her standing among the city elite—both Black and White—if she had resorted to race-baiting to try to win the mayoralty. As such, when she did resort to personal attacks, she tried to attack his youth, the only acceptable characteristic she could attack.

Ironically, Cropp's position as the establishment candidate placed Fenty in the position of being the more populist candidate. So, despite the fact that Fenty ran a deracialized campaign, the fact that he incorporated issues of poverty, class inequality, and greater delivery of services into his campaign platform won him support among poorer residents and largely insulated him from racial attacks.

A Brave New World

Black politics appears to be moving away from a "framework of racial reasoning" towards a new "*prophetic* one of moral reasoning, with its fundamental ideas of a mature Black identity, coalition strategy, and Black cultural democracy" (West 1996, 174). This ensures that there is equality within the community and its supporters and a solidarity and strong coalition structure with other racial groups. Not only do these coalitions enhance the "plight of Black people," but they also "enrich the quality of life in the country" (West 1996, 176). Most importantly, such a strategy moves past a focus on racial authenticity towards a focus on, and respect of, the responses, positions, and qualifications of African Americans. This framework assumes "neither a Black essence that all Black people share nor one Black perspective to which all Black people should adhere. Rather, a prophetic framework encourages *moral* assessment of the variety of perspectives held by Black people and selects those views based on Black dignity and decency that eschew putting any group of people or culture on a pedestal or in the gutter" (West 1996, 175). The prophetic framework of moral reasoning is much broader than a framework based on racial reasoning. The former allows one to move past rating an individual on the color of their skin or their supposed lack of racial authenticity and moves toward a consideration of them based on their qualifications and abilities (West 1996).

The election of Adrian Fenty shows that discussions of racial authenticity need not be at the heart of every political contest between old and young Black politicians. In a city like Washington, with a growing, large, and powerful White middle and upper class, Black candidates need to win White votes. Race-baiting is not the way to do that. Racial politics in Washington have evolved since the days of Marion Barry, and Fenty and Cropp's deracialized campaigns reflect that evolution. At the end of the day, though, Fenty won the election because he was hungrier candidate and he found a way to appeal to voters across the racial line and across the class line.

Notes

1. The scandal primarily involved two employees who worked in the city's tax and revenue office who were "charged with preparing false property tax refunds beginning at least as far back as 2001 and delivering them to relatives and friends" (Nakamura and Stewart 2007, A1). This scandal led to the firing of a number of employees from the tax and revenue office and calls for chief financial officer Natwar M. Gandhi to step down. Fenty, however, stood behind the long-serving Gandhi stating that while this was clearly a "breach of the public's trust…Gandhi should be judged on his decade of work in the city's financial office, including the last seven as CFO" (Nakamura and Stewart 2007, A1). In order to ensure a complete and neutral investigation of the alleged conduct, a special committee was created to look into the activities of the tax and revenue office. This committee discovered that these individuals as well as several accomplices had stolen almost $50 million in public funds (Cauvin 2009). Individuals involved in this scandal are still being prosecuted and sentenced to this day (Cauvin 2009).

References

Adrian Fenty for Mayor. n.d. Fenty 2006 official campaign web site. http://www.fenty06.com.

Albritton, Robert B., George Amedee, Keenan Grenell, and Don-Terry Veal. 1996. Deracialization and the new Black politics. In *Race, politics, and governance in the United States*, ed. Huey L. Perry, 179–192. Gainesville: University Press of Florida.

Austin, Sharon D. Wright, and Richard T. Middleton. 2004. The limitations of the deracialization concept in the 2001 Los Angeles mayoral election. *Political Research Quarterly* 57: 283–93.

Barnes, Robert, and Lori Montgomery. 2006, Fenty emerges from D.C. pack. *The Washington Post,* July 23, final edition, A1.

Cauvin, Henry E. 2009. Niece of principal defendant in tax scam gets 9 years. *The Washington Post,* March 17, final edition, B2.

Certified election night results. 2006. *District of Columbia Board of Elections and Ethics,* September 26.

Doolittle, Amy. 2006. Mayor campaigns for Cropp; Williams says Fenty not ready for top post. *The Washington Times,* September 7, final edition, metropolitan.

Eleveld, Kerry. 2008. Poll: Only 2.9% of Americans are LGB. *The Advocate,* May 1.

http://www.advocate.com/exclusive_detail_ektid53742.asp (accessed February 25, 2009).

Fenty, Adrian. 2006a. Interview by Kojo Nnamdi. WAMU Radio Station/KNS DC. *Politics Hour*, July 14.

———. 2006b. Interview by Brian Lamb. C-SPAN/Q&A. November 12.

———. 2008. Interview by Dr. Andra Gillespie. Tape Recording. Washington, DC, March 7.

Fisher, Marc. 2006a. Mayor Fenty, please sweat the small stuff. *The Washington Post,* December 31, final edition, B1.

———. 2006b. Fenty emerges as an action hero. *The Washington Post,* August 24, final edition, B1.

Hamilton, Charles V. 1977. Deracialization: Examination of a political strategy. *First World* 1: 3–5.

———. 1978. Blacks and electoral politics. *Social Policy* (May/June): 21–27.

Henderson Jr., Lenneal J. 1996. The governance of Kurt Schmoke as mayor of Baltimore. In *Race, politics, and governance in the United States*, ed. Huey L. Perry, 165–78. Gainesville: University Press of Florida.

Jaffe, Harry. 2008. Adrian Fenty: Born to run. *The Washingtonian*, November.

Jaffe, Harry S., and Tom Sherwood. 1994. *Dream city: Race, power, and the decline of Washington, D.C.* New York: Simon & Schuster.

Janofsky, Michael. 1998. Marion Barry isn't running for a fifth term. *The Washington Post,* May 22, final edition, A14.

Jones, Joyce, and Mark Lowery. 1995. Marion Barry: The sequel. *Black Enterprise* 25(6): 26.

Just follow the money. 2006. The Alexander Center. http://thealexandercenter.com/articles/justfollowthemoney.htm.

Kilson, Martin. 1989. Problems of Black politics: Some progress, many difficulties. *Dissent* 36: 526–34.

King, Colbert I. 2001. A success story in his comfort zone. *The Washington Post,* December 30, final edition, A21.

Mayor Adrian Fenty: Biography. *The Washington Post.* http://www.washingtonpost.com/wp-srv/metro/politics/dc/fenty2007.html.

McClain, Paula D., and Steven C. Tauber. 1997. An African American presidential candidate: The failed presidential campaign of Governor L. Douglas Wilder. In *African American power and politics: The political context variable,* ed. Hanes Walton Jr., 294–304. New York: Columbia University Press.

McCormick, Joseph P. and Charles E. Jones. 1993. The conceptualization of deracialization: Thinking through the dilemma. In *Dilemmas of Black politics,* ed. Georgia A. Persons, 66–84. New York: HarperCollins.

Montgomery, Lori. 2006. In sweep, Fenty draws on uniting to conquer. *The Washington Post*, September 14, final edition, A1.

———. Elisa Silverman. 2006. Fenty sweep is one for the record books. *The Washington Post,* September 7, final edition, DZ2.

Muhammad, Nisa Islam. 2007. D.C. "exodus" sparks district renewal efforts for Whites. *The Final Call*, June 21.

Nakamura, David. 2006a. Cropp and Fenty have pursued their legislative agendas by opposite means. *The Washington Post* August 21, final edition, A01.

———. 2006b. Fenty prevails in mayor's race. *The Washington Post,* September 13, final edition, A1.

———. Nikita Stewart. 2007. Gandhi, roiled by tax scandal, still has Fenty's support: City CFO asks for independent probe. *The Washington Post,* November 14, final edition, A1.

———. Jon Cohen. 2008. Fetny's first year gets high marks, but divide persists. *The Washington Post,* January 13, final edition, A1.

Neibauer, Michael. 2006. Mayor Williams contemplates his legacy. Examiner.com, December 20. http://www.examiner.com/a-466542-Mayor_Williams_contemplates_his_legacy.html (accessed September 9, 2008).

Noah, Timothy. 2006. The invisible candidate. Slate November 7. http://www.slate.com/id/2153187/ (accessed August 20, 2009).

O'Bryan, Will. 2006. From the bottom up. *MetroWeekly,* November 2.

Orey, Byron D. 2006. Deracialization or racialization: The making of a Black mayor in Jackson, Mississippi. *Politics & Policy* 34 (4): 814–36.

Perry, Hugh. 1996a. An analysis of major themes in the concept of deracialization. In *Race, politics, and governance in the United States*, ed. Huey L. Perry, 1–14. Gainesville: University Press of Florida.

———. 1996b. The value of deracialization as an analytical construct in American politics. In *Race, politics, and governance in the United States*, ed. Huey L. Perry, 193–196. Gainesville: University Press of Florida.

Powell, Michael. 1997. Poor management, federal rule, undermine services. *The Washington Post*, July 20, final edition, A01.

Romero, Adam P., Amanda Baumle, M. V. Lee Badgett, and Gary J. Gates. 2007. *Census snapshot: Washington, D.C.* Scottsdale, AZ: The Williams Institute.

Sample ballot: Republican primary: District of Columbia. 2006. *District of Columbia Board of Elections and Ethics,* September 12.

Siegal, Fred. 1997. *The future once happened here: New York, L.A., and the fate of America's big cities.* New York: Free Press.

Silverman, Elissa, and Lori Montgomery. 2006. New Cropp fliers attack Fenty. *The Washington Post,* August 22, final edition, B02.

———. 2006. Mayor restates support for Cropp: Williams says he might be a hindrance in some locations. *The Washington Post,* August 24, final edition, B4.

Stevens, Andrew. 2007. Adrian Fenty: Mayor of Washington D.C. *City Mayors*, September 13. http://www.citymayors.com/mayors/washington_mayor.html (accessed June 16, 2008).

Stewart, Nikita. 2006. Dave Kranich fighting the Fenty juggernaut: GOP's man is an optimist unfazed by the odds. *The Washington Post,* October 20, final edition, B6.

Summers, Mary, and Philip A. Klinker. 1996. The election and governance of John Daniels as mayor of New Haven. In *Race, politics, and governance in the United States*, ed. Huey L. Perry, 127–50. Gainesville: University Press of Florida.

West, Cornel. 1996. Race matters. In *Color, class, identity: The new politics of race,* ed. John Arthur and Amy Shapiro, 169–178. Boulder, CO: Westview Press.

Williams, the Honorable Anthony A.: Mayor, District of Columbia. 1999. United States Department of Transportation: Federal Highway Administration. http://www.fhwa.dot.gov/gama/mayorbio.htm.

Williams, Vanessa. 2006. See how he runs: To put his name on the D.C. mayor's door, Adrian Fenty is knocking on as many as he can. *The Washington Post,* August 31, final edition, C1.

Woodlee, Yolanda, and Martin Weil. 2006. Williams endorses Cropp for mayor, D.C. council chairman welcomes support, promise of help on campaign. *The Washington Post,* May 17, final edition, B01.

10 Situational Deracialization, Harold Ford, and the 2006 Senate Race in Tennessee

Sekou Franklin

The 2006 Senate race in Tennessee pitting Harold Ford Jr., the five-term Congressman from Memphis, against Bob Corker, the former mayor of Chattanooga, was one of the most intriguing contests of the 2006 mid-term election cycle. The race garnered a tremendous amount of national media attention and underscored the fact that, if elected, Ford would increase the Democratic Party's chances of winning control of the Senate. A victory by Ford would also make him the South's first Black senator since Reconstruction. Despite Ford's defeat—he lost by only 50,000 votes—he demonstrated a unique ability to connect with voters across racial lines.

This chapter examines Ford's electoral and governance strategies during the Senate campaign and ten years in the U.S. House of Representatives. Collectively, Franklin refers to these strategies as "situational deracialization" because it describes how some Black candidates and elected officials strategically use deracialized frames or methods that are malleable and appeal, quite effectively, to a broad array of voters. It further describes how Black candidates embrace race-neutral positions on purportedly racially divisive or controversial issues to curry favor among White moderates and conservatives, yet still use specially targeted, race-specific cues to appeal to Black voters in insulated, homogenous (Black) districts. Finally, situational deracialization helps to explain why Black candidates may distance themselves from associative preferences or policy positions (i.e., pro-immigration postures, judicious crime measures, privacy rights, economic justice) that are perceived by Whites to have the greatest support or sympathy among Blacks.

Introduction

The Tennessee Senate race featuring Harold Ford Jr., a young African-American politician and five-term congressional representative from Memphis, against Bob Corker, a multimillionaire and the former Mayor of Chattanooga, was among the most closely watched contests of the 2006 midterm congressional elections. Ford's competitiveness throughout the race, his image as a conciliatory and pragmatic African-American politician, and the racial and regional dimensions of the campaign brought him unusually favorable media coverage typically not afforded to African-American candidates in biracial elections in the South (Darman 2006). This attention further underscored the fact that, if elected, Ford would increase the Democratic Party's chances of taking control of the U.S. Senate. A victory would also make him the South's first African-American senator since Reconstruction. Considering that most senators were selected by state legislatures prior to the ratification of the Seventeenth Amendment in 1913, Ford would become the first African-American Southerner elected to the Senate by a popular vote in U.S. history.

By examining the 2006 Senate race in Tennessee, this study gives special attention to assessing the efficacy of Ford's electoral strategy. Ford's electoral strategy—I refer to it as *situational deracialization*—attempted to construct varied, and often contradictory, portraits of himself to African-American and White voters. He did this by deemphasizing race-specific issues and related policy concerns when campaigning in White or conservative jurisdictions; but simultaneously, he relied on the promulgation of race-conscious and class-specific appeals to mobilize African-American voters, as long as these appeals were restricted to racially homogenous (i.e., African-American) districts. Despite the effectiveness of situational deracialization as a campaign strategy as exhibited in the Tennessee Senate race, it does not eliminate racially polarized voting in an election or White racial resentment. This is because racial conservatives and their surrogates (party leaders, activists, and media allies) frequently use racial priming tactics to attack African-American candidates.

Though not exclusive to biracial elections, racial priming is typically employed against African-American candidates by party elites, interest groups, and intellectuals. It occurs when these groups inject negative stereotypes of African Americans into campaigns in order to dissuade a large number of Whites from voting for African-American candidates (Brians and Wattenberg 1996, 172–93; Mendelberg 2001; Valentino, Hutchings, and White 2002, 75–90; Geer 2006; Finkel and Geer 1998, 573–95; Prysby 1996, 30–43). Racial priming tactics are routinely used in the South, where institutional racism and anti-Black discourse are embedded in the region's political culture. I argue that because of the salience of racial priming tactics, Harold Ford, Jr. relied upon a strategy of situational deracialization to reduce reflexive voting patterns among moderate and conservative Whites. Yet because he needed a high African-American voter turnout to win, he also used racially conscious and class-specific cues that were specifically tailored for African-American voters.

The watershed event of the election was the October 20 airing of a controversial political advertisement by the Republican National Committee, which implied that Ford had romantic ties or perhaps a sexual liaison with a White woman at a 2005 Super Bowl Party at the Playboy mansion. Though most Black leaders claimed the advertisement—typically referred to as the "Bimbo" or "Playboy" ad—was racially incendiary, Republicans downplayed its negative allusions to miscegenation and insisted that it was created to chip away at Ford's self-portrait as a politician steeped in traditional mores and Christian faith (Davis 2006a; Sher 2006a, B1). Despite these disagreements, most political observers agreed that the advertisement had the effect of priming White voters about racial stereotypes and interracial taboos.

The first part of the study examines Ford's political lineage, his rise to power, and his ideological predispositions. I then provide a theoretical overview of situational deracialization and its three interrelated variables: the normalizing effect, split messaging, and a favorable political context. Next, I measure Ford's appeal among White and moderate/conservative voters through an analysis of the 2006 National Election Pool exit poll. I also conducted secondary analyses using ecological inference to examine racially (African American and White) polarized voting in the 2006 election. Finally, this study is informed by my own observations of the Ford campaign and correspondence with Democratic Party leaders informs their analysis.

The Ford Dynasty

An assessment of the 2006 Senate race and Ford's campaign strategy would be incomplete without devoting some attention to his political lineage and rise to power. Ford's ascendance is directly tied to the Ford dynasty, Tennessee's most recognizable African-American political family. The family catapulted to prominence as Memphis funeral home directors in the 1890s. The funeral home served as an informal social service organization that assisted South Memphis residents with overdue bills, burial costs, and hospital visits. This allowed the Ford family to cultivate a cadre of allies among both elites and rank-and-file African Americans long before they won elected offices (de la Cruz 2005, A1).

Since the early 1970s, at least seven Fords have been elected to local, state, and federal offices. Harold Ford Jr., elected in 1996 to the U.S. House of Representative while only twenty-six years old, won the congressional seat vacated by his father, Harold Ford Sr. The elder Ford, the state's first ever African-American congressional representative, was elected in 1974 by less than 600 votes. Only twenty-nine years old at the time, he defeated the four-term incumbent and racially conservative Dan Kuykendall in a newly redrawn congressional district that was 45 percent African American. Because of redistricting and White flight, the congressional district soon became majority African American (Wright 2000, 87–90). Ford Sr.'s brother, John Ford, was another well-known political figure in the state. Elected in 1974 at thirty-two years old, he became one of the longest-tenured senators in the Tennessee General Assembly before leaving office in 2005.

Notwithstanding the Fords's emergence as one of the state's influential political families, they were unable to transcend the internal squabbling that plagued African-American politics in Memphis-Shelby County. Indeed, the Fords often exacerbated sectarian politics among African-American political elites, as demonstrated in their two-decade long battle with W.W. Herenton, who became Memphis's first African-American mayor in 1991. Before running for mayor, Herenton's candidacy had to be ratified by the People's Convention and Unity Summit, two nominating conventions that brought together Memphis activists and politicos in order to develop a consensus African-American mayoral candidate. After failing to convince the gatherings to select an alternative candidate, Ford Sr. unsuccessfully tried to subvert Herenton's nomination (Pohlmann and Kirby 1996, 140–48). The quarrel contributed to the rivalry between the Ford and Herenton factions. Some observers believed the rivalry would spill into the 2006 Senate race. Yet due to the microscopic attention given to the election contest, and because prominent Democratic Party leaders such as former President Bill Clinton and Senator Barack Obama traveled to the state to campaign for Ford, the Ford–Herenton factions appeared to have coalesced behind his campaign (Schelzig 2006b; Sher 2006b, B2).

The Ford family's reputation was further harmed by corruption charges levied against the elder Fords. Harold Ford Sr. was indicted and later acquitted of bank and mail fraud in the early 1990s, while John Ford was convicted of bribery charges in 2007. The latter scandal grew out of a 2005 sting operation, officially known as Operation Tennessee Waltz, that resulted in John Ford's arrest in the same week Ford Jr. announced his senatorial candidacy (Dries 2005, A7).

The aforementioned scandals, especially Operation Tennessee Waltz, were a potential liability for the younger Ford. They allowed his opponents to label him an apologist for his father and uncle's unethical activities. The charge was so bothersome to Ford that he made the controversial decision to crash a Corker press conference at a Memphis airport two weeks before the election. The move may have backfired against his campaign because it allowed Republicans to label him as immature and too youthful to be elected senator (Feldman 2006).

The elder Fords were fairly liberal champions of civil rights and New Deal social welfare policies. However, Ford Jr. is more conservative than his elders. Indeed, he was deliberate about presenting himself as a candidate who, despite being African American, was independent of the Democratic Party's progressive-left wing. Throughout his ten-year career in the House of Representatives, his political orientations were clearly distinguishable from the race-conscious politics of the older African-American political vanguard. Though his congressional record was more liberal than most Republicans, he was more conservative than most Congressional Black Caucus (CBC) members, many of whom viewed Ford as overly ambitious and opportunistic. After the 2002 midterm elections, for instance, Ford unsuccessfully challenged Nancy Pelosi for the leadership post of the Democratic Caucus in the House of Representatives, despite being opposed by most CBC members. He was soundly defeated by almost 150 votes (White 2002; Abramson 2004).

Additionally, Ford developed a close relationship with conservative Democrats. He was active with the Blue Dog Coalition and the Democratic Leadership Council, two conservative Democratic Party organizations; and after losing his Senate bid in 2006, he was selected as Chair of the Democratic Leadership Council. He regularly endorsed conservative fiscal and foreign policies that had the strong backing of President George W. Bush and Republican congressional leaders (Kimberley 2004; "Black Point Man…" 2005; "Why We Can't…" 2005; *Memphis Flyer* Staff 2005; Baker 2006). For example, he coauthored (with Republican Senators Trent Lott of Mississippi and Jesse Helms of North Carolina) a letter to Bush in 2001 supporting military action against Saddam Hussein. A year before the 2006 election, he even expressed some sympathy for President Bush's Social Security privatization plan (Baird 2005). However, due to pressures from liberal and progressive organizations, he reversed course and spoke out against the initiative. Ford's centrist-moderate orientation did not win him any key endorsements from Tennessee Republicans. Yet, it earned him the endorsements of two newspapers in the conservative, Eastern part of the state, the *Chattanooga Times* and the *Bristol Herald Courier*, located near the Tennessee–Virginia border (Associated Press 2006, B7). The *Herald Courier's* endorsement was particularly surprising since it also backed Republican Senator George Allen in the Virginia Senate race against his Democratic challenger Jim Webb.

Black progressives have been especially critical of Ford for aligning with conservative Democrats and Republicans on key votes in Congress. Leutisha Stills, a political analyst for the progressive-left *Black Agenda Report*, wrote that Ford "[was] the most anti-Black, pro-Republican member of the CBC" (CBC Monitor 2006, 3). The online magazine conducts a rating system of CBC members evaluating their votes for progressive and antidiscrimination policies. Ford was rated the most conservative CBC member, having received an "F" in the September 2006 report. He never received a score above 60 percent (CBC Monitor 2006).

Ford's centrist and conservative positions notwithstanding, he still worked closely with some liberal Democrats. As Table 10.1 points out, he convinced a number of liberals to cosponsor a significant number of the 166 bills he introduced during his five congressional terms. Twenty-one percent, or thirty-five of the cosponsors were CBC members. Sixty-four, or 39 percent, of the congressional representatives were liberal White, Latino, and Asian legislators who received high ratings (above 75 percent) on the American Federation of State, County and Municipal Employees' (AFSCME) congressional scorecard. The liberal-oriented labor group identified about 15 percent of Ford's cosponsors as very conservative (below 25 percent on its rating scale). The remaining cosponsors are moderates and center-left legislators (between 50 and 75 percent on the rating scale), some conservatives (between 25 and 49 percent on the rating scale), and Tennessee congressional representatives.

There are different ways to evaluate House members' ideological predispositions: roll call votes, sponsorship and cosponsorship of bills, the introduction of nonbinding and concurrent resolutions, amendments to bills, committee and subcommittee votes, and congressional alliances based on narrow state interests. When analyzing the representatives who endorsed Ford's bills, about 60 percent of the cosponsors were African-Americans and non-African-American liberals. While this percentage is less impressive than most CBC members, it does show that Ford's political alliances may be more complicated than his critics would suggest.

Nevertheless, the 2006 Senate race tested the efficacy of Ford's pragmatic centrism and his crossover appeal to White voters. As early as March 2006, he convened a private meeting with some of Nashville's influential African-American

Table 10.1 Harold Ford, Jr.'s Legislative Cosponsors, 1997–2006 (N=166)

The TABLE shows results only for House members who signed on as co-sponsors to 166 bills introduced by Ford.

	Percentage
Congressional Black Caucus	21 %
Progressive Non-Black Congressmembers	39 %
Very Conservative Members of Congress	15 %
Other Members of Congress	25 %

Source: Compiled from http://thomas.loc.gov/. The congressional scorecard rating system was compiled from the American Federation of State, County and Municipal Employees' (AFSCME)
annual congressional scorecards. A progressive score is between 75-100 percent. A "very conservative" rating is 25 percent and below. The remaining co-sponsors are moderates and center-
left legislators (between 50-75 percent on the rating scale), some conservatives (between 25-49
percent on the rating scale), and Tennessee representatives who co-sponsored bills that per-
tained to parochial state interests.

clergy to discuss his electoral strategy and to encourage them to intensify their
voter mobilization efforts in the African-American community. Ford told the
group that his campaign drew inspiration from the successful gubernatorial campaign of Phil Bredesen, a conservative Democrat and Nashville's former mayor.[1]
In 2002, Bredesen pulled together an electoral coalition of African-American
voters, moderate and liberal Whites, and to the surprise of many, White voters from rural counties and the conservative bastion of East Tennessee. Ford
believed he could build a similar electoral coalition, in part, by embracing fiscally
and culturally conservative policies that were attractive to Whites and moderates
who would normally vote for Republicans.

Situational Deracialization as a Campaign Strategy

In the aftermath of the 1989 elections, political scientist Robert Smith insisted
that the wave of deracialized campaigns, which produced winning African-
American candidates in majority-White jurisdictions throughout the country,
represented the degeneration of African-American politics. Smith's conclusion
was colored by the fact that many of these candidates won elections by deemphasizing race and related class-based/economic justice issues. Instead, these
candidates endorsed non-confrontational policies that were attractive to White
moderates and corporate interests, and conflicted with the interests of their core
African-American constituencies. Accordingly, political observers of African-
American politics suggested that deracialized campaigns undermined racial
and economic justice issues (Smith 1990, 160–62; McCormick and Jones 1993,
66–84; Wright 1995, 749–58; Strickland and Whicker 1992, 208–10). Herman
George (2004) offers perhaps the harshest critique of deracialized campaigns in
his assessment of Wellington E. Webb's three-term mayoralty in Denver. Despite
being the city's first African-American mayor, Webb's deracialized electoral and
governance strategies resulted in the implementation of regressive measures such

as pro-growth policies, deregulation, municipal privatization, the weakening of affirmative action, and the reduction of public expenditures for affordable housing and public schools.

These assessments of deracialization are worth considering because almost two decades after Smith's observations, one can hardly point to an election contest in a biracial setting where an African-American candidate does not conduct a deracialized campaign (Perry 1996). To insist on race or class-specificity in a biracial context will most certainly invite opposition from established political leaders in both the African-American and White communities. Moreover, as Jeffries (1999, 583–87) points out, African-American candidates believe deracialized or race-neutral strategies can mitigate the electoral disadvantage often attributed to the racial conservatism of some White voters.

It is further worth noting that candidates in majority African-American districts where there are no competitive White candidates have also used deracialized strategies. In separate studies on municipal elections in New Orleans (Liu 2003) and Memphis (Vanderleeuw, Liu, and Marsh 2004), the authors discovered that African-American candidates used deracialized strategies to appeal to a minority group of White voters who were influential constituents in their governing coalitions. The authors found that deracialized strategies were particularly useful for African-American incumbents seeking reelection, especially when pitted against progressive or racially conscious African-American challengers. The White electorate served as a swing vote and helped these candidates curry the favor of pro-growth interests that were initially hostile to them during their first terms.

Throughout this chapter, I use the term *situational deracialization* to describe a contemporary variation of crossover and race-neutral strategies utilized by African-American politicians. Situational deracialization, similar to the earlier interpretations of crossover strategies, illustrates how African-American candidates will downplay or not talk about racial or social justice policies in jurisdictions that have strong histories of racial resentment. It further explains how these candidates may endorse wedge issues such as laws that ban gay marriage or penalize undocumented immigrants, in part, because they do not want to be labeled as liberal (Sigelman et al. 1995). Accordingly, African-American candidates may distance themselves from associative preferences or policy positions and characteristics (i.e., pro-immigration postures, judicious crime measures, economic justice, etc.) that are perceived by Whites to be viewed with the greatest sympathy by African Americans or liberal Whites.

The major distinction between situational deracialization and earlier types of crossover strategies is its elasticity. African-American candidates will use deracialized approaches to accentuate their moderate or conservative positions on cultural issues as well as economic or class-specific policies. In the same election, these candidates may use race-conscious appeals and will even advance narratives that may be attractive to liberal and progressive African Americans as long as these messages are *contained* in African-American jurisdictions (e.g., neighborhoods, districts, indigenous organizations, and institutions). Yet in predominantly White districts where voters believe progressive economic policies—and their tax dollars—unfairly benefit working-class and poor African Americans, the same candidates may embrace fiscally conservative policies. Hence, situational deracialization is a malleable electoral strategy that is able to energize, quite effectively, a diverse group of voters from different jurisdictions.

Harold Ford's use of situational deracialization was characterized by three interrelated variables. First, he attempted to normalize his image among moderate/conservative Whites and the media, and situate it within the mainstream of the dominant political culture in Tennessee. I refer to this as the *normalizing effect* because it explains how and why African-American candidates will espouse culturally or economically based policy positions that are substantively important to moderate and conservative Whites (Middleton and Franklin 2009). An African-American candidate may normalize her or his image for several reasons: to remove the race variable from a campaign; to convince moderate/conservative Whites that she or he has much in common with them, especially on social welfare issues; and to persuade these Whites that she or he subscribes to their beliefs on an assortment of cultural/wedge issues such as religion, sexual politics, and immigration.

Throughout the senate race, Ford accentuated his conservative credentials on fiscal policy and taxes, national security, gay marriage, religion, and immigration. He accused Corker of hiring undocumented immigrants to work in his contracting business and of raising taxes during his tenure as Chattanooga's mayor (Jubera 2006, 9A). He also proclaimed an avid commitment to evangelical Christian principles. A week before the election he told an audience, "I just believe in the power of a big God…I just know that I serve someone bigger than the Republican Party, somebody bigger than the Democratic Party. I serve the same Lord and savior that all of you serve" (Schelzig 2006a). The next week he visited the Little Rebel Bar and Grill in Jackson, Tennessee. The restaurant rarely, if ever, had a visit from a prominent African-American person and is an outpost for racial conservatives who are sympathetic to the Confederate tradition. Additionally Ford's defense policy positions assuaged the sentiments of the state's military families and national-security voters. As early as 2002, he voted to authorize President George W. Bush to pressure the United Nations to send weapon inspectors to Iraq—legislation that laid the groundwork for the Iraq War (Kiely 2002).

How well African-American candidates use racially targeted or class-specific cues and framing devices, or what is referred to as *split messaging,* is the second factor impacting situational deracialization. Split messaging assumes that African-American candidates (and their campaign staff) will develop contradictory framing strategies for varied racial and socioeconomic-based constituencies (Albritton et al. 1996, 179–92). It assumes that race-neutral, African-American candidates will offer competing portraits of themselves, according to the audiences they are targeting and based on the population density or homogeneity of the specific jurisdiction.

Split messaging is important because African-American candidates who appeal to White constituents but ignore African Americans will have a difficult time winning statewide elections. Despite race-neutrality and crossover appeals, even the most centrist or moderate African-American candidate in the Democratic Party needs a relatively high African-American voter turnout to win in the South (McClain and Tauber 1997, 298–99; Black and Black 2002, 244–50). Indeed, African-American candidates are mistaken if they believe their racial background by itself, instead of the strategic use of racial cues, is enough to convince the African-American electorate about their worth.

The difficulty with split messaging, though, is that race or class-specific cues have to be restricted to African-American districts and cannot spill over into White communities. This containment tactic attempts to ensure that racially segregated communities—White and African American—will be presented with different portraits of an African-American candidate. Each of these portraits is designed to convince disparate communities that the candidate will fight for their conflicting interests.

Throughout the 2006 election, Ford defended his conservative credentials when speaking to White audiences. Yet in African-American communities, he presented himself as a race-conscious candidate and a defender of social welfare policies. He didn't necessarily do this personally, but through aggressive phone-banking and appeals from political surrogates such as African-American clergy, labor activists, students from Black colleges and universities, and Democratic Party functionaries. Through the state Democratic Party, Ford mailed handbills to residents in African-American districts that contrasted him with the Republican Party, and reminded voters about President Bush's neglectful response to New Orleans' residents in the aftermath of Hurricane Katrina (Tennessee Democratic Party n.d. a, b).

Furthermore, split messaging requires an extensive grassroots infrastructure that can mobilize low-income and working-class African Americans who tend to have the fewest resources and who are generally the most neglected group in competitive elections. Impersonal or haphazard phone banking, direct mailing, and the use of African-American surrogates are essential to a campaign, but they do not meet the standard of a serious grassroots infrastructure, especially when non-Black and affluent communities receive more personal forms of mobilization (see Green and Gerber 2004). A grassroots infrastructure requires resources and an ongoing organizing effort designed to educate marginal communities about the vote, and to counteract potential voter disenfranchisement procedures.

The political context during an election year is the third factor influencing situational deracialization. Some political context variables include intra-party cohesion or division, the support that African-American candidates have among party elites, the particular locale or jurisdiction to which candidates are appealing, the impact of the national political environment on a state/local election, and whether candidates will benefit from presidential coattails (Walton 1997).

A significant context variable that favored Ford was that he faced little competition in the Democratic Party. His only primary challenger was Rosalind Kurita, a state senator from the military stronghold of Clarksville, near the Kentucky border. Her candidacy was short-lived; after showing no ability to raise money, she dropped out of the race months before the August primary. Other prominent Tennessee Democrats decided not to enter the race, perhaps because Ford expressed strong interest in the Senate seat as early as 2004 and announced his candidacy long before the primary date (Sullivan and Locker 2005, A1).

Additionally, Tennessee Democrats had become particularly disillusioned in recent years, which may have caused some of the state's prominent Democratic Party leaders to prematurely conclude that Republicans would easily win the Senate race, or that they could only win if a nationally recognized politician such as Ford were to enter the race (Sullivan and Locker 2005, A1; Gang 2004, B1). George W. Bush's victories in Tennessee in 2000 and 2004, as well as Bill Frist and Lamar Alexander's senatorial victories and the Republican Party's capture of the State Senate for the first time since Reconstruction, convinced some political observers that Democrats had lost their competitive advantage in the state (Cilliza 2004). If Democrats were to be competitive in a statewide campaign, political observers believed that candidates waving the party banner needed a substantial amount of campaign or personal funds and had to advance conservative policies. Although Tennesseans elected Democrat Phil Bredesen as governor in 2002 and 2006, he was one of the state's wealthiest individuals and a fiscal conservative (Davis 2006b, A1; Cummins 2005, A1).

Furthermore, the Republican Party primary was intensely competitive. Bob Corker, the eventual winner, defeated Ed Bryant and Van Hilleary in an election which was so malicious that Senator Elizabeth Dole of North Carolina, the head of the National Republican Senatorial Committee, intervened to stop the intra-party bickering. After Corker secured the nomination, his campaign was in disarray. In fact, a month and a half before the November election, he reorganized his campaign staff and hired a new campaign manager (Locker 2006, A1).

The main point is that political contextual factors impact the effectiveness of situational deracialized campaigns. Ford benefited from the lack of competition in his party's primary, electoral disillusionment among high-profile Democratic Party officials which discouraged them from running for the Senate, internal divisions inside the Republican Party, and a poorly run campaign by Bob Corker that was not remedied until a month before the election. This gave Ford time—almost six months more than his Republican challenger—to tailor his image, cultivate alliances in conservative strongholds, and re-direct fundraising efforts toward the general election.

Related to the political context variable is the belief that Ford was the most ideal African-American candidate to run in a statewide contest. As discussed earlier in the study, he came from the most influential African-American political family in the state. In addition, his racial phenotype as a very light-skinned African American made him appear less threatening to Whites. As Strickland and Whicker (1992, 208) point out, African Americans who have a racial phenotype that is proximate to Whiteness tend to do better in deracialized campaigns than dark-skinned African Americans.

However, there were some political context variables that had the potential to harm Ford's campaign. These variables included President Bush's popularity in the state; the growing strength of the Republican Party; his family's corruption scandals; and the fact that most African Americans—almost half of the state's 960,000 African Americans—live in Memphis-Shelby County, which was already part of Ford's base. This meant that there was no real growth market, so to speak, of Black votes for Ford to leverage. As a result, Ford had to make some inroads in homogenous, White districts, including the lily-White and Republican-dominated counties of East Tennessee.

It is equally important to emphasize that situational deracialization did not eliminate the impact of the race variable from the 2006 Senate race, despite Ford's crossover appeal. In addition to partisan divisions, African-American/White polarization was the most distinct feature of the campaign, especially pertaining to perceptions of the Bimbo ad, which African Americans found exceptionally offensive (Middleton and Franklin 2009). Even well-intentioned media reports that celebrate how much a victory by an African-American candidate will improve race relations in the South have the impact of reminding voters about the centrality of race in a campaign (Jeffries 1999; Terkilsden and Damore 1999).

In the remainder of this study, I assess the effect of Ford's situational deracialized strategy. The available data allows for a closer examination of the normalizing effect, the political context variables that impacted the election, and the efficacy of Ford's split messaging approach.

Data and Methods

This study uses a two-tiered analysis to measure the effectiveness of Harold Ford's electoral strategy. The first level of analysis uses logistic regression to measure his crossover appeal among Whites and number of other cohorts. The results of the logistic regression are reported as odds ratios instead of parameter estimates because they are easier to interpret.[2] I rely upon data from the Roper Center's National Election Pool (ABC News/Associated Press/CBS News/CNN/Fox News/NBC News) exit poll conducted on November 7, 2006. The regression analysis controls for sociodemographic characteristics (race, gender, age, social class—measured by education and income), and the jurisdictions (region and locality) of the respondents, as well as partisanship (approval for President Bush and Governor Bredesen) and ideology (liberal, conservative, moderate). Another variable is included for married respondents to determine if they were turned off by Ford's then-single marital status. Two variables examine the respondents's views about negative campaigning and political commercials. A political context variable for corruption is included to account for the Ford family's scandals. The corruption variable should also account for the ethical misconduct of several high-profile, Republican members of Congress in the months before the election. Congressional representatives Mark Foley, Randy "Duke" Cunningham, Bob Ney, and Tom Delay, all prominent Republicans, were involved in scandals that received national press coverage.

I am particularly interested in assessing the success of Ford's normalizing strategy. One would expect that if his normalizing strategy were successful, he would have defused Corker's support among moderate and conservative Whites. Five interaction terms gauged the success of the normalizing effect: White evangelical Christians, Whites who oppose gay marriage, Whites who believed illegal immigration was a major issue, Whites who believed the Iraq War was a major campaign issue, and Whites who were concerned about terrorism. I also look at White and African-American respondents who approved of the Iraq War.[3]

In the second level of analyses, I examine voter turnout estimates and African-American/White voter polarization to measure the efficacy of Ford's split messaging tactic. I hypothesize that a successful split messaging tactic will reduce racially polarized voting among African Americans and Whites. That is, Ford would garner an unusual amount of support among Whites—and will produce an impressively high voter turnout among African Americans. I use ecological inference to test this theory. First, I measure the African-American and White support for Bredesen's reelection as governor. Then, I gauge African-American and White support for Ford. The intent is to determine whether Whites split their vote for Bredesen and Corker, in order to provide further insight into the intersection between partisanship and racially polarized voting.

Gary King's (1997) method is useful for assessing voting patterns because it attempts to correct for the "ecological inference problem," or the challenge of interpreting individual-level results and behavior from aggregate data. Because this approach requires a somewhat sophisticated use of diagnostic testing, it is not without flaws. Critics argue that it is difficult to apply King's ecological inference to elections with a sizable multiracial electorate (Kousser 2001). Further, the method's accuracy can slightly fluctuate depending on the selection of covariates (i.e., African American Democrats, White Republicans, etc.) and the population densities of the election precincts in the study (Liu 2007). Despite these shortcomings, ecological regression is commonly used to measure voter intensity and racially polarized voting (Redding and James 2001; Orey 2006).

For the ecological regressions, I look at African-American and White voting patterns in 1,680 election precincts or voter tabulation districts (VTDs).[4] (Tennessee's voter tabulation districts are officially called "pseudo" districts.) This entails fifty-nine of the state's ninety-five counties, including the four largest metropolitan areas/counties where over 65 percent of the African-American population resides: Memphis-Shelby County, Nashville-Davidson County, Knoxville-Knox County, and Chattanooga-Hamilton County. The remaining VTDs, drawn from midsize and rural counties, represent jurisdictions in the middle, eastern, and western parts of the state.[5] Candidates running statewide campaigns typically develop regional strategies because of the intersection of partisanship and regionalism in Tennessee. West Tennessee is a Democratic Party stronghold with a large African-American population in Memphis-Shelby County and the adjacent rural counties. On the other hand, East Tennessee is politically and culturally conservative and is the epicenter of the Republican Party. With the exception of Chattanooga and Knoxville, which are more conservative than Memphis and Nashville, East Tennessee is small town/rural and racially (White) homogenous. Middle Tennessee is comprised of a mix of urban, suburban, and rural and is viewed as a toss-up region between Democrats and Republicans. With minor adjustments, I use the regional description map produced by the Tennessee Comptroller of the Treasury's Office of Local Government, which disaggregates the counties into their respective regions.[6]

Findings and Discussion

To the surprise of many, including Republican Party strategists and Democratic Party insiders, Ford exhibited tremendous political savvy throughout the campaign, and demonstrated a unique ability to connect with voters across racial and regional lines. However, as Table 10.2 illustrates, Ford's crossover appeal was only partially successful. Race was significant in predicting electoral choice, as Whites were more likely to vote for Corker. When compared to African-American voters, White voters were only 14 percent as likely (or 7 times less likely) to vote for Ford. This is not a surprise considering the racial polarization in Tennessee politics (Wright 2000; Pohlmann and Kirby 1996). On the other hand, self-identified liberals and moderates expressed more enthusiasm for Ford's campaign than conservatives. Liberals were also 1.74 times more likely to vote for Ford compared to moderate voters; while the odds that Ford won the support of self-identified conservatives, at least in comparison to moderates, was about three times less when controlling for the other variables. Corruption as a political context variable neither harmed nor helped Ford. He evaded the corruption charge by linking Corker to the political scandals of Republican congressional representatives in the months leading up to the election.

Surprisingly, Ford neutralized Corker's support in rural areas of the state (Waters 2006, A1). It appears his aggressive campaigning in the rural counties of the western and midregions curried him slightly more favor among the regions' voters, compared to the large cities and those counties in the east. The odds of Ford garnering support among large city (above 500,000 people) voters was about three-fifths less than the odds of him winning the rural vote. Excluding the counties in the middle and western region of the state with populations exceeding 100,000, Ford won eight of the remaining twenty counties in West Tennessee and twenty-one of thirty-four counties in Middle Tennessee. This was unexpected since rural voters are often assumed to be more conservative than urban and suburban voters. Tom Lee, Ford's senior campaign advisor, said: "Rural voters who maybe never had the opportunity to vote for an African-American did" (Jubera 2006, 9A). Ford may have received an additional bounce from a large African-American population—as much as 100,000—in rural West Tennessee counties. This region also has a fairly active political organization called the Rural West Tennessee African American Affairs Council. Furthermore, Ford may have benefited from the recent influx of newcomers to the state from the Midwest and Northeast. According to demographers, 20 percent of the state's 2006 population was born outside the South compared to 13 percent in 1990

Table 10.2 Binomial Logistic Regression Assessing Vote for Harold Ford, Jr.

Independent Variables	Odds Ratio[1]
Whites	.14*
Men	1.06
Married	.92
College Educated	.62*
Income (reference category=under $30k)	
$30,000-49,999	.63
$50,000-74,999	.50*
Above $75k	.38*
Age (reference category=30-59 yrs)	
18-29 yrs	1.0
60 yrs and older	1.82*
Region (reference category=East Tennessee)	
Middle/West Tennessee	1.76*
Southwest Tennessee	1.1
Population of Cities (reference category=Rural/under 50k people)	
50,000-500,000 people	.72
Suburbs	2.1
Cities, 10,000-50,000	.86
Over 500,000	.61**
Voted for Pres. GW Bush	.08*
Voted for Gov. Phil Bredesen	10.1*
Ideology (reference category=Moderate)	
Liberal	1.74**
Conservative	.33*
Attack Ads	26.9*
Both Attacked Unfairly	.06*
Corruption	.92
Normalizing Effect	
Approve of Iraq War	.74*
Whites (Iraq War/Important)	1.66*
Whites (Terrorism/Important)	.82
Whites (Illegal Imm./Important)	.51*
Whites (Ban Gay Marriage)	.28*
Whites (Evangelical Christians)	.96

	B **S.E.**		
Weight	-.97* (.23)	-2 Log Likelihood	709.717
Constant	3.6* (.80)*	Chi-Square	1606.464*
		N	1,698

*p <.05, ** p < .10

1 Readers may be interested comparing the odds ratios with the statistically significant parameter estimates that are not included in Table 10.2: Whites (-2.0*); College Educated (-.48*); Income-$50,000-74,999 (-.69*); Income-Above $75K (-.97*); Age-Above 60 Years (.60*); Region-Middle/West (.56*); Cities-Over 500,000 (-.49**); Pres. GW Bush (-2.5*); Gov. Bredesen (2.3*); Ideology-Liberal (.56**); Ideology-Conservative (-1.1*); Attack Ads (3.3*); Both Attacked Unfairly (-2.8*); Approve of Iraq War (-.30*); Whites-Iraq War/Important (.51*); Whites-Ill. Immigration (-.67*); Whites-Ban Gay Marriage (-1.3*). *p < .05, ** p < .10.

Source: The data are from the National Election Pool (ABC News/Associated Press/CBS News/CNN/Fox News/NBC News) exit poll conducted on November 7, 2006. Weights were included in the exit poll.

(Burch 2006). These newcomers tend to be more liberal and tolerant of African-American candidates than homegrown residents.

Despite performing considerably well in rural counties and the two largest metropolitan areas (Memphis-Shelby and Nashville-Davidson County), Ford's candidacy was hurt by a major contextual constraint that tends to overwhelm Democratic Party candidates in Tennessee. The eastern part of the state is a Republican stronghold and has the lowest number of African Americans out of the three main regions. As exhibited in Table 10.2, the odds of Ford garnering support among Middle/Western Tennesseans was 76 percent higher than the odds of him winning the vote among East Tennesseans. Ford only won two of the thirty-five counties in the eastern region; in contrast, Democrat Phil Bredesen won fourteen eastern counties in his successful 2002 gubernatorial election. Furthermore, Ford's margin of defeat was larger in East Tennessee than in other parts of the state, and the voter turnout rate of registered voters (as opposed to the eligible voting age population) was lower in the western and midregion counties that backed Ford. (Later in this study I look at voting patterns among the African-American and White voting age populations, which includes both those who are registered to vote and those who are not registered.)

Overall, about 45 percent of registered voters turned out in the counties that supported Ford. His support seems to be most robust (as measured by high turnout and strong support for Ford) in small counties. For instance, the eleven Ford leaning counties with 50 percent or higher voter turnout (as measured as a percentage of registered voters) all had populations under 30,000; most of these counties had populations under 21,000. In the two largest Ford leaning counties (Nashville-Davidson County and Memphis-Shelby County), the turnout rate among registered voters was 48 percent and 47 percent respectively. Overall, turnout was roughly 48 to 49 percent in the counties that Corker won; but Corker won eleven counties with populations above 50,000 people whose average turnout was 52 percent (Tennessee Department of State's Division of Elections 2002, 2006a). Accordingly, voters turned out in greater numbers in Corker-leaning counties.

Additionally, Ford was unable to win over President George W. Bush's supporters, many of whom lived in East Tennessee. While President Bush's coattails may have disadvantaged Republican congressional candidates in other parts of the country, they still had traction in Tennessee. The impact of partisanship (measured by approval of Bush) as a contextual variable was as great as (and intertwined with) the race variable; and it was greater than the effect of gender and marital status, both of which had little influence in determining voters' choice for the Senate.

Partisanship is particularly important because Tennessee was once considered a relatively moderate Southern state. Senators Estes Kefauver and Albert Gore, Sr., and Governor Frank Clement earned reputations as racial moderates and center-liberal politicians compared to other Southern officials. During the 1950s and 1960s, they advocated for civil rights measures, backed the expansion of health care and the minimum wage, and in the case of Governor Clement, attempted to abolish the state's death penalty provision (Gardner 1979). Tennessee was actually one of the few Southern states initially exempted from the pre-clearance/Section 5 provision of the Voting Rights Act of 1965 because of the relatively high number of African Americans registered to vote (Graham 1992, 94–97, 140–41).

Yet the end of the Civil Rights era, which coincided with the realignment of Southern voters from the Democratic Party to the Republican Party, altered the political landscape in Tennessee. The 1964 Senate victory of Howard K. Baker was a signature election for the Republican Party. A decade later, Tennessee became the first Southern state to elect two Republican senators since Reconstruction. By the 1990s, Democrats had lost more ground. Despite Bill Clinton's victories in 1992 and 1996, three-term Democratic Party incumbent Jim Sasser lost in a stunning defeat to Bill Frist in the 1994 Senate race (Black and Black 2002, 96). Later in 2000 and 2004, George W. Bush won the state's Electoral College vote, even over favorite son candidate Al Gore Jr. in 2000. Republicans made more inroads in the General Assembly in the 2000s, and in 2004, they captured control of the State Senate for the first time since Reconstruction.

Despite the influence of partisanship, and more specifically, party loyalty, it can be misleading in predicting broad support for Ford. Governor Bredesen, a conservative Democrat, also ran for reelection in the 2006 election year and won 69 percent of the vote. (Tennessee Department of State's Division of Elections 2006b). Table 10.2 shows that Bredesen voters were actually 10.1 times more likely to vote for Ford than non-Bredesen supporters. While this phenomenon translated into votes for Ford, one would have expected the coattails effect to have been even more influential in the Senate race (later in this study I revisit this subject).

The use of negative attack ads was another factor influencing the respondents' attitudes toward both candidates. The Bimbo commercial was the most controversial and racially divisive ad of the midterm elections, and the respondents who believed Ford was unfairly attacked by this and other ads were more enthusiastic about his candidacy. Yet this sentiment was counteracted by Republican Party's efforts to convince voters that both Ford and Corker were involved in negative campaigning. For example, Corker charged Ford with "running the most divisive race in the state's history, politically and religiously" (Schelzig 2006a). Consequently, as the Tennessee Senate race points out, campaigns that employ racially and culturally offensive attacks can minimize criticisms by alleging that their opponents also engaged in negative campaigning. This is intentional and can actually make the electorate more sympathetic to party activists who use racial priming tactics against African-American candidates.

Social class (measured by education and income) provides further insight into how the respondents evaluated the Senate race. College educated voters were more likely to vote for Corker than the least educated, and as projected, middle-class and affluent residents (those with family incomes between $50,000 and $75,000 and respondents who made above $75,000 dollars) were more sympathetic to Corker. On the other hand, senior citizens were more enthusiastic about Ford's candidacy compared to middle-aged respondents between ages 30 to 59 (Middleton and Franklin 2009). Indeed, the odds of Ford winning the support of senior citizens was 82 percent higher than the odds of young adult and middle-age voters (ages 30–59) voting for him. This was probably because of their concerns about health care, prescription drug costs, and Social Security, which are policy issues on which voters consistently rate Democrats as better on than Republicans (Pew Research Center for People and the Press 2006b). Corker, however, defused Ford's support among young adult voters (18–29). This was a surprise because one would have expected that Ford's young age and youthful appearance would have given him an extra advantage among younger adults.

The Normalizing Effect

Equally important for this discussion is that Ford tried to position himself as a non-confrontational, race-neutral candidate by embracing conservative positions on a host of cultural, economic, and national security issues. As Table 10.2 reveals, Ford's normalizing tactics were partially successful. Although more White evangelicals voted for Corker, Ford made enough of an impression upon this group to make this variable statistically insignificant. He also neutralized Corker's support among those who thought the war on terrorism was a major concern. This was unexpected since Bush elevated this as an issue throughout the midterm elections. Yet a closer look at an October 2006 Pew Research Center poll (2006a) reveals that Americans were less interested in "terrorism" as an election issue, and many believed the Iraq War hurt the war on terrorism. A majority of the respondents also believed the Iraq War was going very badly. This perhaps explains why Ford won the vote among Whites who said the Iraq War was a major campaign issue—they were 1.66 times more likely to vote for Ford— despite Corker's strong showing among pro-war, national-security voters.

The exit poll results further show that Ford was unable to convince Whites who opposed gay marriage and those who said illegal immigration was an important concern that he was a more worthy candidate than Corker. The odds of Ford winning Whites who were lukewarm to gay marriage and illegal immigration decreased by factors of .28 and .51 respectively. The fact that he regularly reminded voters about these issues, especially about gay marriage, may have worked to his disadvantage and brought more conservative voters to the polls. In addition to the Senate race, Tennesseans voted on a state constitutional amendment to ban gay marriage in the 2006 election, the language of which said that marriage between a man and a woman is "the only legally recognized marital contract in the state" (Tennessee Department of State's Division of Elections 2006c). The amendment passed by 81 percent and obtained 80 percent of the vote in Shelby County, the state's African-American stronghold. Ford was able to insulate himself from criticisms by African Americans and liberal Whites who were troubled by his stance on gay marriage because African Americans voted overwhelmingly, by over 80 percent, for the gay marriage ban.[7] In fact, due to religiosity, it is common for Southern African Americans to be more receptive to culturally conservative positions than non-Southerners (Smith and Seltzer 1992, 129).

Although the normalizing effect may benefit Southern African-American candidates, it can harm them if the related policy positions are elevated as campaign issues by their challengers. Since issues such as gay marriage and illegal immigration have become intrinsically linked with the official positions of the Southern wing of the Republican Party, Ford's normalizing tactics on these issues may have backfired and benefited Corker. When region and partisanship dovetail with race and conservative policy positions such that Southern Whites are more likely to vote for the Republican Party and adopt conservative positions on gay marriage and illegal immigration, then normalizing tactics by African-American candidates may be less effective. To the contrary, it could actually remind voters about which political party has historically advanced these positions.

Racially Polarized Voting and Split Messaging

Next, I use ecological inference to measure the effectiveness of Ford's split messaging tactic. I conducted analyses of voting patterns in fifty-nine counties: large metropolitan areas (Memphis-Shelby, Nashville-Davidson, Chattanooga-Hamilton, and Knox-Knoxville Counties); small and rural counties in East Tennessee and West Tennessee; and an assortment of midsize and rural counties in Middle Tennessee. As discussed earlier, one would expect that in a competitive election that was shaped by racial priming tactics, a successful split messaging tactic would produce a considerable amount of support among Whites as well as an unusually high turnout among the African-American electorate.

As Table 10.3 points out, the effectiveness of Ford's split messaging approach was not enough to reduce racially polarized voting. Nonetheless, 39 to 45 percent of the White electorate (an average of 42 percent) in the four jurisdictions voted for Ford, an impressive number considering the history of racial conservatism in the state. This support exceeded the expectations of many political observers and corresponds with the finding in the exit poll survey, which also estimated the White vote for Ford at 42 percent.

Ford's support among Whites, however, contrasts sharply with those who voted for Democratic Governor Bredesen. Table 10.4 points out that an overwhelming majority of Whites—between 62 and 67 percent in the four separate analyses—voted for Bredesen. Although this was expected considering that incumbent governors rarely lose elections in Tennessee, the gap in Ford and Bredesen's support among Whites—between 20 and 25 percent—is too wide to ignore. Conservative Whites and Republicans, while bypassing their ideological and partisan allegiances in their vote for Bredesen, refused to do so for Ford. This contradiction was particularly bothersome to rank and file Democratic Party activists, some of whom attributed Ford's defeat to the millstone bugaboo of race. Matt Gross, the Chair of the Washington County Democratic Party in East Tennessee, and Barbara Wagner, who sits on the Democratic Party's State Executive Committee, both said the racialization of the Senate contest adversely

Table 10.3 2006 Senate Turnout Rates among Black and White Tennessee Residents, 18 Years Old and Older

Model I	(Chattanooga-Hamilton County, Knoxville-Knox County, Memphis-Shelby and Nashville-Davidson Counties, 31 Percent Black)	
	Voter Turnout	Vote for Ford
Blacks	34 % (.01)	98 % (.01)
Whites	42 % (.00)	45 % (.01)
Model II	(East Tennessee Counties, 2 Percent Black)	
	Voter Turnout	Vote for Ford
Blacks	13 % (.02)	64 % (.01)
Whites	39 % (.00)	39 % (.00)
Model III	(Middle Tennessee Counties, 6 Percent Black)	
	Voter Turnout	Vote for Ford
Blacks	17 % (.02)	80 % (.01)
Whites	45 % (.00)	44 % (.00)
Model IV	(West Tennessee Counties, 20 Percent Black)	
	Voter Turnout	Vote for Ford
Blacks	31 % (.02)	91 %(.01)
Whites	46 % (.01)	40 %(.00)

Note: Gary King's EiZ package is used for all four models covering 59 counties and 1,680 voter tabulation districts (also called election precincts). Constants were included in the inference analyses. Starndard errors are in parentheses.

affected Whites' perception of Ford (Gross, e-mail correspondence with author 2007; Wagner, e-mail correspondence with author 2007). Fayette County Democratic Party Chairman Steve Butler (e-mail correspondence with author 2007) further stated, "Race, in my opinion was the sole reason Congressman Ford did not get elected." On the other hand Gayle Bruce (e-mail correspondence with author 2007), a Hamblen County election commissioner, believed racial resentment against Ford was more pronounced among Republicans and Independents. Geeta McMillan (e-mail correspondence with author 2007), a member of the Democratic Party's state executive committee, also said that Ford's racial background "had a negative impact on some [but] not all voters." To be certain, these sentiments underscore the persistence of the race variable in biracial elections, but they also suggest that partisanship—and the fact that most White voters in the state are Republican—contributed to Ford's election defeat.

Another important point is that Ford garnered near unanimous support among African Americans in the large cities and in West Tennessee's rural counties. However, in the rural and midsize counties in East and Middle Tennessee which had few African Americans (between 2 and 6 percent), Ford's support dropped among African Americans. Yet because so few African Americans live in these counties, the decrease did not seriously harm his campaign. In fact, based on exit poll data, 97 percent of African Americans voted for Ford. This number was greater than the 90 percent of African Americans in the state who voted for Clinton in 1996; the 92 percent who voted for Al Gore in 2000; and the 89 percent who voted for John Kerry in 2004 (Bositis 2001, 2005).

Ford's consolidation of the African-American vote, however, was overshadowed by a lower than predicted African-American voter turnout. Although turnout rates in mid term elections are lower than presidential elections, the Ford campaign wanted an unusually high African-American turnout. Ford's senior political consultant, Michael Powell, anticipated a *presidential* election year turnout among African Americans or 280,000 to 300,000 (43–46 percent) out of 650,000 voting age African Americans. This would have surpassed the estimated 170,000 African Americans who voted for Governor Bredesen in the 2002 gubernatorial election and equaled the 300,000 African-American votes for John Kerry in 2004 (Sher 2006c, B2). This was overly optimistic, even for a campaign that used split messaging to appeal to both moderate/conservative Whites and African Americans. In all four analyses of the Senate race, the African-American vote does not exceed 34 percent. If this number held true across the state—that

Table 10.4 2006 Gubernatorial Turnout Rates among Black and White Tennessee Residents, 18 Years and Older

Model I	*(Chattanooga-Hamilton County, Knoxville-Knox County, Memphis-Shelby and Nashville-Davidson Counties, 31 Percent Black)*	
	Voter Turnout	*Vote for Bredesen*
Blacks	33 % (.01)	95 % (.00)
Whites	42 % (.00)	67 % (.00)
Model II	*(East Tennessee Counties, 2 Percent Black)*	
	Voter Turnout	*Vote for Bredesen*
Blacks	12 % (.02)	95 % (.01)
Whites	39 % (.00)	62 % (.00)
Model III	*(Middle Tennessee Counties, 6 Percent Black)*	
	Voter Turnout	*Vote for Bredesen*
Blacks	17 % (.01)	89 % (.01)
Whites	45 % (.00)	66 % (.00)
Model IV	*(West Tennessee Counties, 20 Percent Black)*	
	Voter Turnout	*Vote for Bredesen*
Blacks	31 % (.02)	88 % (.02)
Whites	46 % (.01)	67 % (.00)

*SE=.00; **SE=.01; ***SE=.02

Note: Gary King's EiZ package is used for all four models covering 59 counties and 1,680 voter tabulation districts (also called election precincts). Constants were included in the inference analyses. Standard errors are in parentheses.

is, if roughly 35 percent of the African-American electorate turned out to vote—then slightly fewer than 230,000 African Americans voted in the election, which fell short of Powell's expectations.

I argue that Ford's split messaging approach, while earning him strong support in the African-American community, did not go far enough in convincing the requisite number of African Americans to go to the polls. In some respects, when candidates have automatic support from loyal cohorts or from a base group of voters, they may relax their efforts to mobilize these groups or outsource these activities to political surrogates. Ford's campaign relied heavily on the African-American clergy, labor, civil rights and civic groups, and volunteers. Yet in Tennessee, this amounts to an elite driven exercise that lasts for a short time—typically several months leading up to the election—instead of the cultivation of an operational infrastructure that is committed to sustaining a long-term, voter education and mobilization initiative.

Split messaging underestimates how important it is for a candidate—not political surrogates—to vigorously advocate for policy positions that are substantively attractive to their base. Various studies have shown that in competitive elections, the Democratic Party's base is more likely to vote in higher numbers when their preferred candidates strongly advocate for their policies without using split messaging (Hill and Leighley 1993; Hill, Leighley, and Andersson 1995; Hill and Leighley 1996). Ford's campaign took pride in convincing voters that race did not matter, as exhibited by his senior advisor Tom Lee's commentary: "We never talked about race in the campaign because we don't think that's what people [voters in conservative counties] are choosing on anymore…What we found this year is that when people hunger for leadership they begin to drop their old barriers. They'll listen to voices from places they would have never considered before" (Jubera 2006, A9). Unfortunately for Ford's campaign, his deracialized persona may have produced a higher level of support among Whites than expected; but it may have also depressed African-American turnout rates.

To be fair, it was difficult for Ford to give as much attention to African Americans other than through phone banking, direct mailing, and race-conscious or economic justice appeals contained to African-American communities. The fact that many Whites were undecided in their Senate choice—as much as 44 percent a month before the election compared to over 70 percent of African-American voters[8]—may have encouraged Ford to focus a disproportionate amount of attention on enlisting support from moderates, middle-class voters, and rural residents.

In many ways, the story of Harold Ford's 2006 senate campaign reflects the complicated nature of deracialization. By employing situational deracialization as a campaign tactic, Ford demonstrated adroitness in navigating Tennessee's racial minefields. However, the outcome of the election demonstrates that earlier scholars' concerns about the efficacy of deracialization were warranted. Ford's predicament bears a striking resemblance to Andrew Young's 1990 primary bid to be Governor of Georgia. In that election, Young worked very hard to appeal to White voters in middle and southern Georgia, alienating many base voters in metro Atlanta. At the end of the day, turnout was lackluster in metro Atlanta, and Young netted few new voters in the rest of the state (Davis and Willingham 1993).

In assessing the Young defeat, Davis and Willingham noted that Young had tried and failed to successfully balance an emphasis on national economic issues with a hometown charm. To them, such a task would have been difficult for any candidate, but it was more difficult for a Black candidate with a civil rights past and no statewide political connections. They contend that such a circumstance "redirects our attention to the way discrimination in the politics of the past structures the limits of electoral opportunity in the present" (Davis and Willingham 1993, 170). In the final analysis, Ford did a better job balancing his local and national, crossover and racialized personas. However, race still mattered, though perhaps less in 2006 than it did in 1990. While Phase III Black politicians have made strides in refining deracialization as a campaign strategy, they still must be mindful of the fact that some voters may be averse to them because of the color of their skin.

Notes

1. This discussion is based on my conversation with one of the participants immediately after the meeting.
2. Odds ratios can also be interpreted as percentages. For example, in Table 10.2, Whites who believed the Iraq War was a major concern can be interpreted as: (a) they are 1.66 times more likely to cast a vote for Ford compared to Whites who said the war was not a major concern; or (b) the odds of Ford winning the vote among Whites who said the war was a major concern was 66 percent (1.66–1.00 = .66 or 66 percent) higher than the odds of him winning the vote among Whites who said the war is not a major concern.
3. Four sociodemographic variables were coded as dummy variables with the following reference categories: age (30–59 = reference category), region (East Tennessee voters = reference category), locality (rural = reference category), and income (Under $30,000 = reference category). Self-identified ideology also has a reference category (moderates = reference category).
4. The ecological inference analyses only looks at African-American and White support for Harold Ford, Jr. and Bob Corker. Tennessee does not collect VTD data for Latino and other minority voters. Further, the voter turnout findings exclude results for third party candidates. (It is further worth noting that the ecological regression analyses assess only a partial sample (59 out of 95) of Tennessee's counties. I used a partial sample mainly because of the uneven distribution of African Americans in the state; most African Americans reside in West and Middle Tennessee, including Memphis-Shelby County, the rural counties adjacent to Memphis, and Nashville-Davidson County. Despite the partial sample, it includes an equal number of small and large counties as well as counties from the state's three regions (West, Middle, and East). Moreover, African-American and White voters (or majority African-American and majority White election precincts) are adequately represented in the sample. Also, as discussed later in the study, the findings of the ecological regressions mirror the exit poll results, which seem to confirm the validity of the partial sample).
5. Excluding the four largest counties, the East Tennessee counties in this study include: Anderson, Blount, Meigs, Sullivan, Bradley, Campbell, Grainger,

Hamblen, Monroe, Roane, Sevier, Unicoi, Washington, Clairborne, Jefferson, McMinn, Pickett, Rhea, Bledsoe, and Fentress. West Tennessee includes: Crockett, Dyer, Gibson, Hardeman, Haywood, Madison, Hardin, Tipton, Benton, Fayette, and Weakley. Middle Tennessee includes: Bedford, Giles, Maury, Montgomery, Robertson, Rutherford, Williamson, Sequatchie, Franklin, Grundy, Moore, Putnam, Stewart, Sumner, Perry, Wayne, Wilson, Trousdale, Van Buren, Warren, Cannon, Overton, Smith, and Lawrence.

6. Unlike the Tennessee Comptroller's office, I include Hamilton, Bledsoe, Fentress, and Pickett Counties in East Tennessee.
7. This finding was discovered in the exit poll results.
8. This finding was discovered in the preelection poll conducted by Gallup. See the Roper Center, *USA Today/Gallup* Poll #2006/TN, November 1–4, 2006.

References

Abramson, Roger. 2004. Prince Harold: The sky could be the limit for Harold Ford Jr. conventional wisdom be damned. *The Nashville Scene*, March 18. http://www.nashvillescene.com/Stories/News/2004/03/18/Prince_Harold/index.shtml.

Albritton, Robert B., George Amedee, Keenan Grenell, and Don-Terry Veal.1996. Deracialization and the new Black politics. In *Race, politics, and governance in the United States*, ed. Huey Perry, 179–92. Gainesville: University of Florida Press.

Associated Press. 2006. Ford, Corker pick up backing—Newspapers statewide split on senate choice. *The Commercial Appeal,* October 28, B7.

Baird, Woody. 2005. President Bush brings social security pitch to Tennessee. *The Associated Press State and Local Wire*, March 10.

Baker, Jackson. 2006. Is Harold Ford really a new generation of democrat—Or is he just another Ford? (political notes). *The Nashville Scene*, October 21. http://www.nashvillescene.com/Stories/News/Political_Notes/2006/10/12/Family_Matters/index.shtml.

Black, Earl, and Merle Black. 2002. *The rise of Southern republicans.* Cambridge, MA: Belknap Press/Harvard University Press.

Black point man for the right. 2005. *The Black Commentator*, 120. January 6. http://www.Blackcommentator.com/120/120_cover_harold_ford_pf.html.

Bositis, David. 2001. *The Black vote in 2001*. Washington, DC: Joint Center for Political and Economic Studies.

———. 2005. *The Black vote in 2004*. Washington, DC: Joint Center for Political and Economic Studies.

Brians, Craig Leonard, and Martin P. Wattenberg. 2006. Campaign issue knowledge and salience: Comparing reception from TV commercials, TV news and newspapers. *American Journal of Political Science* 40 (1): 172–93.

Burch, Audra D. S. 2006. Change may be afoot in the South: Many political contests in the South, such as the U.S Senate. *The Miami Herald,* November 6.

CBC Monitor. 2006. CBC Monitor report card. September. http://www.Blackagendareport.com/001/CBCReportCard20060829.pdf, 1-6.

Cilliza, Chris. 2004. A tale of two senate seats in Tennessee; Jockeying to succeed Frist has begun. *Roll Call,* November 16.http://www.rollcall.com/issues/50_51/politics/7398-1.html (accessed October 9, 2009).

Cummins, John. 2005. Gov. Bredesen for president? Not now. *Chattanooga Times-Free Press*, February 14, A1.

Darman, Jonathan. 2006. The path to power. *Newsweek*, October 30. http://www.msnbc. msn.com/id/15366095/site/newsweek/.

Davis, Marilyn, and Alex Willingham. 1993. Andrew Young and the Georgia State elections of 1990. In *Dilemmas of Black politics*, ed. Georgia Persons, 147–75. New York: HarperCollins,

Davis, Michael. 2006a. Negative ads make a mark in race. *Chattanooga Times Free Press*, November 5. http://66.18.58.15/news/2006/nov/05/Negative-ads-make-a-mark-in-race/.

———. 2006b. Rep. Ford takes hit from GOP, Democrats. *Chattanooga Times-Free Press,* July 9, A1.

de la Cruz, Bonna. 2005. The Fords of Memphis: Service and scandal define a dynasty. *The Tennessean*, July 31, A1.

Dries, Bill. 2005. Uncle not factor to jr.—Rep. Ford: Voters "know difference." *The Commercial Appeal*, May 27, A7.

Feldman, Linda. 2006. All eyes on the big South race. *The Christian Science Monitor*, October 25. http://www.csmonitor.com/2006/1025/p01s02-uspo.html.

Finkel, Steven E., and John Geer. 1998. A spot check: Doubt on the demobilizing effect of attack advertising. *American Journal of Political Science* 42 (2): 573–95.

Gang, Duane. 2004. Ford points to senate in 2006. *Chattanooga Times-Free Press*, December 15, B1.

Gardner, James Bailey. 1979. Political leadership in a period of transition: Frank G. Clement, Albert Gore, Estes Kefauver, and Tennessee Politics, PhD diss., Vanderbilt University, Nashville, Tennessee.

George, Herman Jr. 2004. Community development and the politics of deracialization: The case of Denver, Colorado, 1991–2003. *The Annals of the American Academy of Political and Social Science* 594 (July): 143–57.

Geer, John. 2006. *In defense of negativity: Attack advertising in presidential campaigns.* Chicago: University of Chicago Press.

Graham, Hugh Davis. 1992. *Civil rights and the presidency: Race and gender in American politics, 1960–1972.* New York: Oxford University Press.

Grann, David. 2003. The price of power. *New York Times Magazine*, May 11, 48–55, 68.

Green, Donald P., and Alan S. Gerber. 2004. *Get out the vote! How to increase voter turnout.* Washington, DC: Brookings Institution Press.

Hill, Kim Quaile, and Jan E. Leighley. 1993. Party ideology, organization, and competitiveness as mobilizing forces in competitive elections. *American Journal of Political Science* 37 (4): 1158–78.

———. 1996. Political parties and class mobilization in contemporary United States elections. *American Journal of Political Science* 40 (3): 787–804.

———. Angela Hinton-Andersson. 1995. Lower-class mobilization and policy linkage in the U.S. states. *American Journal of Political Science* 39 (1): 75–86.

Jeffries, Judson L. 1999. U.S. Senator Edward Brooke and Governor L. Douglas Wilder tell political scientists how Blacks can win high-profile statewide office. *PS: Political Science and Politics* 32 (3): 583–87.

Jubera, Drew. 2006. Political aftershock: Ford campaign opened new doors. *The Miami Herald*, November 6, A9.

Kiely, Kathy. 2002. Iraq war vote looms as a battle of the heart. *USA Today*, October 8, 1A.

Kimberley, Margaret. 2004. Harold Ford, Jr.: Don't know much about history. *The Black Commentator* 79. February 26. http://www.Blackcommentator.com/79/79_fr_ford.html.

King, Gary. 1997. *A solution to the ecological inference problem*. Princeton, NJ: Princeton University Press.

Knuckey, Jonathan. 2006. Explaining recent changes in partisan identifications of SouthernWhites. *Political Science Quarterly* 59 (1): 57–70.

Kousser, J. Morgan. 2001. Ecological inference from Goodman to King. *Historical Methods* 34: 100–26.

Liu, Baodong. 2003. Deracialization and urban racial context. *Urban Affairs Review* 38 (4): 572–91.

———. 2007. EI extended model and the fear of ecological fallacy. *Sociological Methods and Research* 36 (1): 3–25.

Locker, Richard. 2006. Corker hit right focus in victory—Republican downplayed war: Despite loss, Ford made a mark. *The Commercial Appeal,* November 9, A1.

McClain, Paula D., and Steven C. Tauber. 1997. An African American presidential candidate: The failed presidential campaign of governor L. Douglas Wilder. In *African American power and politics: The political context variable*, ed. Hanes Walton, 294–303. New York: Columbia University Press.

McCormick, Joseph, and Charles E. Jones. 1993. Conceptualization of deracialization: Thinking through the dilemma. In *Dilemmas of Black politics: Issues of leadership and strategy*, ed. Georgia Persons, 66–84. New York: HarperCollins.

Memphis Flyer Staff. 2005. Harold Ford, Jr. for Senate? *Memphis Flyer*, August 26. http://www.memphisflyer.com/gyrobase/Content?oid=oid%3A9984.

Mendelberg, Tali. 2001. *The race card: Campaign strategy, implicit messages, and the norms of equality*. Princeton, NJ: Princeton University Press.

Middleton, Richard IV, and Sekou Franklin. 2009. Southern racial etiquette and the 2006 Tennessee senate race. *National Political Science Review* 23, 63–82.

Orey, Byron D'Andra. 2006. Deracialization or racialization: The making of a Black mayor in Jackson, Mississippi. *Politics and Policy* (December): 814–36.

Perry, Huey L. ed. 1996. *Race, politics, and governance*. Gainesville: University of Florida Press.

Pew Research Center for People and the Press Survey. 2006a. Iraq looms large in nationalized election. October. http://people-press.org/reports/pdf/290.pdf.

———. 2006b. Republicans cut democratic lead in campaign's final days. November. http://people-press.org/reports/pdf/295.pdf.

Pohlmann, Marcus, and Michael P. Kirby. 1996. *Racial politics at the crossroads: Memphis elects Dr. W. W. Herenton*. Knoxville: University of Tennessee Press.

Prysby, Charles L. 1996. The 1990 U.S. Senate election in North Carolina. In *Race, Governance, and Politics in the United States,* ed. Huey Perry, 30–43. Gainesville: University of Florida Press.

Redding, Kent, and David R. James. 2001. Estimating levels and modeling determinants of Black and White voter turnout in the South, 1880 to 1912. *Historical Methods* 34 (4): 141–59.

Roper Center. 2006. *USA Today*/Gallup Poll #2006/TN. November 1–4.

Schelzig, Erik. 2006a. Faith continues to be prominent issue in Tennessee senate race. *Political News* (AP Wire). November 4.

———. 2006b. Obama urges Tennessee voters to elect second Black senator. *Political News* (AP Wire), November 6.

Sher, Andy. 2006a. Expert sees racial overtones in TV ad. *Chattanooga Times Free Press*, October 24, B1.

———. 2006b. Clinton: More than race. *Chattanooga Times Free Press*, November 2, B2.

———. 2006c. Ford looks to high Black turnout in U.S. senate race. *Chattanooga Times Free Press,* November 4, B2.

Sigelman, Carol K., Lee *Sigelman*, Barbara J. Walkosz, and Michael Nitz. 1995. Black candidates, White voters: Understanding racial bias in political perceptions. *American Journal of Political Science* 39: 243–65.

Smith, Robert C. 1990. Recent elections and Black politics: The maturation or death of Black politics? *PS: Political Science and Politics* 23 (2): 160–62.

Smith, Robert C., and Richard Seltzer. 1992. *Race, class, and culture: A study of Afro-American mass opinion*. Albany, NY: SUNY Press.

Stills, Leutisha. 2006. CBC monitor report card: The good, bad and ugly of the congressional Black caucus. Fall. http://www.Blackagendareport.com/001/pf/pf_001c_ CBC_Monitor_fall_2006.html, 1-8.

Sullivan, Bartholomew, and Richard Locker. 2005. With Frist leaving, 5 come in—Ford, Jr. is among the early prospects for the open senate seat. *The Commercial Appeal*, February 13, A1.

Strickland, Ruth Ann, and Marcia L. Whicker. 1992. Comparing the Wilder and Gantt campaigns: A model for Black candidate success in statewide elections. *PS: Political Science and Politics* 25 (2): 208–10.

Tennessee Democratic Party. n.d.a. Don't just change the channel. Change America. [Direct Mail Leaflet]. Paid for by the Tennessee Democratic Party, Nashville, Tennessee.

———. n.d.b. Unbelievable. It's time for a change in Washington. [Direct Mail Leaflet]. Paid for by the Tennessee Democratic Party, Nashville, Tennessee.

Tennessee Department of State's Division of Elections. 2002. General election, governor. http://www.state.tn.us/sos/election/results/2002-11/governor.pdf.

———. 2006a., General election, United States Senate. http://www.state.tn.us/sos/election/results/2006-11/en4uss.pdf.

———. 2006b. General Election, Governor. http://state.tn.us/sos/election/results/2006-11/RptNovGov.pdf.

———. 2006c. Constitutional amendment questions, constitutional amendment # 1. http://www.state.tn.us/sos/election/results/2006-11/RptCtyCon1andCon2.pdf.

Terkilsden, Nayda, and David F. Damore. 1999. The dynamics of racialized media coverage in congressional elections. *The Journal of Politics* 61 (3): 680–99.

Valentino, Nicholas A., Vincent L. Hutchings, and Ismail K. White. 2002. Cues that matter: How political ads prime racial attitudes during campaigns. *The American Political Science Review* 96 (1): 75–90.

Vanderleeuw, James, Baodong Liu, and Greg Marsh. 2004. Applying Black threat theory, urban regime theory, and deracialization: The Memphis mayoral elections of 1991, 1995, and 1999. *Journal of Urban Affairs* 26 (4): 505–19.

Walton, Hanes. 1997. *African American power and politics: The political context variable*. New York: Columbia University Press.

Waterhouse, Albert. 2006. Put party affiliation in check; Vote early. *Chattanooga Times Free Press*, November 1, B8.

Waters, David. 2006. Ford country? These rural West Tennessee near always lead to the winner. *The Commercial Appeal*, October 31, A1.

White, Jack E. 2002. Harold Ford, Jr. reaches for the stars. *Time Magazine*, December 10. http://www.time.com/time/nation/article/0,8599,397281,00.html.

Why we can't trust Harold Ford Jr. 2005b. *The Black Commentator*, 130, March 17. http://www.Blackcommentator.com/130/130_cover_ford.

Wright, Sharon. 1995. Electoral and biracial coalition: Possible election strategy for African American candidates in Louisville, Kentucky. *Journal of Black Studies* 25 (6): 749–58.

———. 2000. *Race, power, and political emergence in Memphis*. New York: Garland.

11 The "Steele Problem" and the New Republican Battle for Black Votes

Legacy, Loyalty, and Lexicon in Maryland's 2006 Senate Contest[1]

Tyson D. King-Meadows

Because African Americans are overwhelmingly Democratic, it is easy to overlook the role that Black Republicans play in modern, post-civil rights Black politics. One could easily assume that Black Republicans are the best deracialized candidates because they cannot depend on Black votes to get elected or that they struggle to earn credibility among Black constituents. The reality is more nuanced. Black Republicans do not automatically shed their racial identity when they run under the GOP banner, nor do they always ignore Black, Democratic constituents. In this chapter, Tyson King-Meadows problematizes the notion of the deracialized Black Republican candidate. In his case study of Michael Steele's 2006 Senate campaign, we see that Steele deliberately reached out to Black voters, who may have felt ignored by the Maryland Democratic Party. Moreover, he still received less than average White support in Republican strongholds which should have supported him as a fellow partisan. King-Meadows's case study demonstrates that race, partisanship and candidate preferences are more complex than meets the eye.

Introduction

In the wake of the Civil Rights Movement, the Republican Party has had limited success in fielding and stewarding Black candidates to electoral victory (Fauntroy 2007; Walton 1997). This has been especially true in U.S. Senate contests, where a Black Republican has not served since Massachusetts Senator Edward Brooke stepped down in 1979. Despite this, the Democratic Party was still deeply troubled by the 2006 senatorial campaign of Maryland Republican Lieutenant Governor Michael Steele, even though Maryland is a decisively blue state. And two days after Steele *lost* his bid to capture the open senate seat, then-Democratic National Committee Chairman Howard Dean, asserted "[we need diversity on the ticket so that], we do not have another Michael Steele problem" (Skalka 2006b).

On the surface, the comment seemed out of place: the 2006 Democratic nominee for Governor, Baltimore Mayor Martin O'Malley, had selected Prince George's County Delegate Anthony G. Brown, a rising star of the Legislative

Black Caucus of Maryland, as his running mate; the O'Malley-Brown ticket had won; and Steele had been defeated by ten percentage points. However, Dean's trepidations were not about how Black partisans might remember the immediate past. He was concerned about when and how Republicans might capitalize on Black ambivalence about continued loyalty to the Democrats. Put differently, Dean's concerns were about the elasticity of Black linked fate as it affected the propensity of Blacks to vote for the Democratic ticket (Dawson 1994). If most strong racial identifiers traditionally supported Democratic candidates, could enough of those same identifiers be persuaded by a Black Republican offering partisan defection *as* the embodiment of Black linked fate? Could those embracing linked fate choose race over partisanship?

These were some of the questions raised by the 2006 campaign for Maryland's open U.S. Senate seat. Indeed, the campaign challenged convention, providing an excellent counterfactual to deracialization theory. On one side was conservative one-term Republican Lieutenant Governor Michael Steele, the state's first Black to win statewide elected office. On the Democratic side, ten-term Congressman Ben Cardin fought a competitive contest against former five-term Congressman and NAACP President Kweisi Mfume. There were historical, attitudinal, and pragmatic reasons for Blacks *not* to support Steele. Yet both Mfume and Steele defied expectations. Both ran on race (Mayer 2002), and Steele specifically defied the odds by picking up 25 percent of the Black vote in an election year steeped in anti-Republican sentiment (Jacobson 2007).

This chapter examines the 2006 Senate race in Maryland to outline how Steele defied these expectations. In assessing this contest, I pay particular attention to how Steele spoke about Black empowerment, Black racial consciousness, Republican partisanship, and synergies between the three constructs. In addition, I show how Steele capitalized on Black angst over the substantive and descriptive dividends received from Democratic allegiance—including resentment over Cardin's primary victory—despite the presence of a Black Democratic lieutenant gubernatorial nominee. More important, I situate the 2006 Senate campaign as a counterfactual to the deracialization construct. While the conventional wisdom of deracialization suggests running away from race, here was a case in which both a Black Democrat and a Black Republican seeking statewide office emphasized racial issues over partisanship. Furthermore, while deracialization largely precludes the possibility that either would occur in the same statewide election cycle, the political context (see Walton 1997) of the 2006 Maryland Senate campaign allowed Mfume and Steele to break convention and to run on race. The conclusion addresses what this campaign may portend about both the deracialization construct and the future relationship between Blacks and the Republican Party.

Deracialization Theory

The literature on Black electoral behavior and Black political attitudes continues to betray a love-hate relationship with the deracialization construct (e.g.,

McCormick and Jones 1993; Albritton et al. 1996; Orey and Ricks 2007). The construct refers to a combined rhetorical, electoral, and governance strategy in which Black candidates deemphasize "race-specific issues" (McCormick and Jones 1993, 76). In remarking on the distinctions between the agenda setting and the electoral strategy dimensions of the construct, McCormick and Jones define the latter in the following manner:

> Conducting a campaign in a stylistic fashion that defuses the polarizing effects of race by avoiding explicit reference to race-specific issues, while at the same time emphasizing those issues that are perceived as racially transcendent, thus mobilizing a broad segment of the electorate for purposes of capturing and maintaining public office. (McCormick and Jones 1993, 76)

Moving further into the analysis, McCormick and Jones assert three components that will enable one to certify the existence of a deracialized campaign. First, the Black candidate will employ a political style that projects a "nonthreatening image" to Whites (McCormick and Jones 1993, 76). Second, the Black candidate will avoid "racial appeals in organizing the Black community" (McCormick and Jones 1993, 76). Third, the Black candidate will avoid a specific racial agenda. At its base, the deracialization construct emerged to explain the value of electoral victories in the late 1980s and early 1990s by Black candidates in White jurisdictions, the "second wave" of Black politics, where biracial coalition building replaced direct confrontation as a means of achieving policy goals and elected office (Ardrey and Nelson 1990).

In offering deracialization as an expression of Black politics, McCormick and Jones follow an analytical framework that defines Black politics as actions done for the "expressed purpose of improving the material conditions of African Americans" in a way that is "sensitive to the historical role and continuing impact of White racism in American political life" (McCormick and Jones 1993, 79). As such, Black candidates who attempt to capture public office for this express purpose are working within the analytical parameters of Black politics. "If deracialization as a successful electoral strategy leads its practitioners to ignore the policy-oriented concerns of African-Americans," they warn, "then we should rightly dismiss their political behavior as nonlegitimate expressions of Black politics" (McCormick and Jones 1993, 79).

Such trepidation about deracialization as a strategy in Black electoral politics was also seen in analyses of Republican attempts to recruit and field candidates. For example, Georgia Persons (1993, 194) begins an analysis of the 1990 congressional election of Gary Franks (R-CT) with a pointed question: "Is it or is it not Black politics?" In providing one aspect of an answer, Persons (1993, 206) writes, "Of course the deficiency in Franks' claim to legitimacy as a Black leader is a profound one: the constituency which elected him is overwhelmingly White. His claim to legitimacy thus must be based solely on his racial identity as a Black man." By Persons' logic, one's claim to the mantle of Black leadership rested on the racial character of the followership (as another proxy for the interests represented). Explaining these constituency-leadership connections, Persons (1993, 208) continues, "Thus, [Frank's] political message as such may be significantly viewed as that of a representative of White interests, and/or as the positions of an individual who happens to be an elected official who is Black." In the end, Persons (1993, 208) cautions against Black politics being centered on the "racial identity of the contestant" or being "cut off from any larger philosophical groundings." Nonetheless, Persons' analysis implies a future political utility to "Black linked fate" (Dawson 1994) for strategic voters and strategic office seekers. Strategic voters might evoke linked fate to explain their aspirations for descriptive representation and/or frustrations with the substantive representation provided by one party. And strategic office seekers might evoke linked fate to explain their policy positions and the advantage of partisan defection.

The Making of the 2006 Maryland Senate Race

The 2006 battle for Black votes began in 2002, when Republican Representative Robert Ehrlich chose Michael Steele as a running mate in a campaign against two-term Democratic Lieutenant Governor Kathleen Kennedy Townsend (daughter of the late Senator Robert F. Kennedy) to succeed two-term Governor Parris N. Glendening (D). Townsend had shocked Black activists by choosing U.S. Naval Academy Superintendent Admiral Charles Larson—a White Republican who had recently switched parties, as her running mate. This decision negatively resounded on racial and political dimensions: the Democrats held the majority of elected office positions, and Blacks enjoyed high levels of political incorporation across the state (Montgomery 2002).

A few days later, Ehrlich announced Michael S. Steele as the Lieutenant Governor-nominee. Steele was two years into his leadership of the Maryland Republican Party and was a long-term resident of Prince George's County— a predominately Black jurisdiction wielding increasing political and economic influence across the state. As the first Black elected chair of any state's Republican caucus, the Catholic, pro-life, anti-gun control, and pro-school reform candidate had a natural partisan base. He extended it by securing endorsements from disgruntled Black Democrats and marketing a Black vote for the Ehrlich-Steele ticket as both an historic vote and payback for the Democrats's disrespect of Black interests.[2] Other Blacks criticized Republicans for tokenism, playing the race card, and for suggesting that Democrats were unwilling to advance Black elected office-seeking (Sheckels 2006).

Ehrlich seized some favorable political opportunities to beat Townsend by three percentage points. Governor Glendening suffered from low approval ratings, which did not help Townsend. Townsend also ran a poorly organized campaign. Moreover, Ehrlich benefitted from running in a midterm election year and in a year in which Blacks were demobilized. Finally, the Republican ticket did well in competitive and minority jurisdictions. The Ehrlich-Steele victory rippled through national politics, making Ehrlich the first Republican since Spiro T. Agnew (1967–1969) to lead Maryland and making Steele one of the most prominent elected Black Republican officials in the nation (Hockstader 2006; Sheckels 2006; Sokolove 2006).

The 2006 Democratic Primary: Mfume Versus Cardin

The 2002 Ehrlich-Steele victory spread speculation about Democratic support of future Black statewide office seekers. This speculation would be put to the test in 2005. In March of that year, Senator Paul S. Sarbanes announced his retirement, opening up a Maryland seat in the U.S. Senate for the first time since 1986. Three days later, Kweisi Mfume announced his candidacy. Mfume brought impressive credentials to the table: he was a former Baltimore City Council member (1979–1986); a former five-term incumbent Congressman and Congressional Black Caucus Chair; a former national NAACP president (1996–2004); and an alumnus of historically Black Morgan State University. Yet, his announcement surprised Maryland Democrats, including the state's Black members of Congress, Elijah Cummings (Seventh District) and Albert Wynn (Fourth District) (Wagner and Hsu 2005). It also generated both jubilation and consternation. On the one hand, Mfume had expanded the NAACP's membership, had retired organizational debt, and had remained a spokesperson for race-related causes. However, Mfume's personal and political stories—from gang life, out of wedlock children, and accusations of nepotism and sexual improprieties at the NAACP—produced one tapestry of questions about his judgment (Borger 1993; Mfume 1996).

Even so, Black elites saw Mfume's candidacy as an opportunity to break Maryland's glass ceiling of Black electoral politics. Mfume characterized it this way: "It's time for the Democratic Party to make a bold statement in a blue state where Blacks have always been willing to support White Democrats for office" (Wickham 2005, 13A). Without such a bold statement, Mfume feared a possible "seismic change in terms of voter loyalty (to the Democratic Party) because the Black community will feel betrayed" (Wickham 2005, 13A). When other prominent politicians decided against running for the seat, Black Democrats hoped the party's leadership would clear the field for Mfume.

However, the Democratic Party leadership had other plans. Five weeks later, Representative Ben Cardin of the Third District announced his candidacy. In fact, one journalist remarked that party leaders "scoured the field for a viable alternative to Mfume" until Cardin announced his candidacy (Hockstader 2006). Cardin was a relatively unknown commodity outside of his district (which included parts of Anne Arundel, Baltimore and Howard Counties, and Baltimore City) and outside of local Maryland politics. Cardin, however, secured a host of high profile endorsements from the "neutral" party leadership (including House Minority Whip Steny Hoyer), severely outpaced Mfume's fundraising, made sure that neither Wynn nor Cummings endorsed Mfume until right before the September primary, and paraded out a string of endorsements by Black leaders. For example, Cardin heavily publicized the summer 2005 endorsement by State Senator Delores G. Kelley, member of the powerful Executive Nominations

Committee, leader of Baltimore County's powerful 10th District Democratic Club, and a former contender for Mfume's vacant congressional seat. Cardin also garnered support from Black ministers like Rev. John L. Wright, pastor of the First Baptist Church of Guilford and former Chairman of the Maryland State Conferences of the NAACP; Rev. Bowyer G. Freeman of New St. Mark Baptist Church; Rev. Samuel A. Blow of Pleasant Hope Baptist Church; and Rev. Tyrell Brown of Hebron Baptist Church (Nitkin 2005, 4B). Despite the genteel nature of the Mfume-Cardin debates, Mfume made a point to publicly rail against the Democratic leadership who had seemingly "anointed" Cardin as Sarbanes' successor, and Mfume supporters echoed these points (Mosk 2005).

To be sure, problems besieged the Mfume campaign from the beginning. It lacked support beyond Black circles and experienced fundraising problems. Mfume characterized Cardin as a Washington insider whose votes (e.g., authorizations for military activities in Iraq and the Patriot Act) and campaign contributors (e.g., pharmaceutical companies) placed him out of step with most Marylanders. Cardin countered with his longevity in Maryland politics, widespread backing, and his ability to build coalitions. At one point, Cardin even publicized his "A" ranking by the NAACP for the 109th Congress (Mosk 2006e; "Cardin Earns 'A'…" 2006).

Mfume's conundrum was clear: pitch his candidacy beyond Black circles without alienating Black voters who valued descriptive representation. *The Washington Post*'s Marc Fisher (2006, C01) put it this way: "But despite his efforts to make White audiences comfortable with him, Mfume was not shy about mentioning race as one justification for his candidacy…." As detractors of the deracialization construct understood, Black candidates had to balance both Black voter aspirations and White fear. Fisher then concluded his article with these words, "Race, of course, is the trickiest of weapons in a political campaign. When Mfume uses his prodigious rhetorical skills to neutralize the issue, he is masterful. When he wields race as a threat, he risks losing the advantage he has so carefully gained" (Fisher 2006, C01). Undaunted, Mfume pressed on as Cardin's Black gadfly.

The Cardin team and Democratic operatives took Mfume's candidacy seriously, but not for the reasons one would suspect.[3] Referred to as the "Kweisi Problem," Democrats feared that an Mfume victory in the September Democratic primary portended defeat (and the loss of an important Democratic seat) in the general election (Hockstader 2006, B07). To win, they had to (a) dismiss the Mfume candidacy; (b) heal wounds from the 2002 gubernatorial race; and (c) attack Steele (who had officially announced his candidacy in October 2005). With this in mind, Cardin devoted his energies to attacking Steele. He played up President Bush's support for Steele; highlighted the endorsement of the MD-Washington Minority Contractors Association for his (Cardin's) candidacy; contrasted his vote to override President Bush's veto on stem cell research with what a pro-Bush, "Senator Steele" would have done; and criticized the Bush prescription drug plan. Mfume tried to highlight his role as the underdog and tap into Black discontent, but to no avail. For instance, in mid-2006, Mfume contended, "we've always been considered the underdog. We didn't have the same amount of money or the blessing of the party. We're still trying to reach the ears of the voters," he explained (Mosk and Deane 2006, A1). However, by early 2006, Cardin had become a financial juggernaut and would be hard to beat.[4] Despite the objective facts, Cardin's indirect response to Mfume and Black discord—"I have not been anointed…I have a record"—still seemed dismissive (Nitkin and Green 2005, A1).

For Mfume supporters, Cardin's retort was less than convincing. During the campaign, Mfume consistently and not-so-subtly mentioned the level and visibility of endorsements Cardin had received from mostly White elected officials, some of which came almost immediately after Cardin announced his candidacy.[5] For instance, although Mfume was gracious in public about House Minority Whip Steny Hoyer's immediate endorsement of Cardin, Mfume's response—"We didn't have the same amount of money or the blessing of the party" (Mosk and Deane 2006, A1)—reflected a struggle amongst Black partisans (both elites and regular constituents) over the inconsistency between the Democratic National Committee's official position of 'neutrality' and the overt pro-Cardin support of prominent Democrats ("Hoyer to Back…" 2005, B6). As Minority Whip, Hoyer was Maryland's most prominent House Democrat, and it was widely expected that Representative Hoyer would help Cardin's fundraising efforts (Cardin for Senate 2005a; Hoyer for Congress 2005). Another aspect of the endorsement battle was equally puzzling for Mfume supporters: while White leaders in the Democratic Party threw their weight behind Cardin, the Congressional Black Caucus remained neutral and on the sidelines (Kaplan 2005). It was not until late August, days before the September primary, that Maryland's two Black congressmen (Wynn and Cummings) publicly endorsed Mfume.

All the while, Cardin acted as the presumptive Democratic nominee. It was politically expedient for Cardin to marginalize the campaign of Mfume and to attack Steele. Polls consistently revealed that an Mfume primary victory could create a competitive general election. For example, while an April 2006 survey showed Cardin beating Mfume among likely Democratic primary voters, it also suggested that the outcome of the Senate race could turn on who won the Democratic nomination.[6] In a Cardin-Steele matchup, Cardin was predicted to beat Steele by a double-digit margin. However, if Mfume faced Steele, the Democrats' lead would shrink to five percentage points. In either matchup, significant numbers of voters were undecided (about 16 percent in either matchup), and Steele would pick up between 16 and 21 percent of the African American vote. Later, an August 2006 poll showed Steele picking up 23 percent of the Black vote against Cardin, compared to only 8 percent of the Black vote if Steele faced Mfume. The August poll also showed Cardin with a five percentage point lead over Steele, with 16 percent of voters undecided.[7] In the end, Mfume lost the eighteen way primary election to Cardin, 40.5 percent to 43.7 percent (Maryland Board of Election results).

Even in defeat, Mfume was determined not to be summarily dismissed. Steele exploited this point when the former NAACP President waited three days before conceding defeat. Mfume justified the wait under guise of speculation that absentee and provisional ballots would make the difference. Yet Cardin campaigned as the presumptive victor and challenged Steele to a debate. Steele's campaign responded: "As much as Congressman Cardin and Democratic Party bosses would like to push Kweisi Mfume out of the race, the Maryland Board of Elections still has yet to certify who won Tuesday's primary" (Ward 2006d). Also, "This attempt by Congressman Cardin to anoint himself the nominee is disrespectful to the Lieutenant Governor's friend, Kweisi Mfume and, more importantly, disrespectful to Maryland voters" (Ward 2006d). When they did come, Mfume's concession remarks did not take the air out of Steele's sails; if anything, Mfume's failure to immediately and strongly endorse Cardin tacitly legitimized Steele's campaign ploys. Moreover, Steele's comments about ballot security were clearly aimed at disgruntled Mfume supporters who would have remembered Townsend's running mate choice two years earlier and voting irregularities in Florida and Ohio during the two previous presidential elections.

Mfume's next gaffe, at a pro-unity rally two weeks after the Democratic primary, opened up more space for Steele's appeal to Black racial consciousness. This was the first time that Cardin and Mfume appeared in public together after the primary election. During the rally, which featured then-Senator Barack Obama as the headline speaker, Mfume endorsed Cardin but then added, "We need women in leadership positions in the state. We've got to find a way that African Americans and other minorities are represented statewide in office" (Marimow 2006). That State House Majority Whip Delegate Anthony G. Brown was the 2006 Democratic nominee for Lieutenant Governor seemed unimportant. Steele bounced on Mfume's gaffe by stating: "The challenge of the opportunity is to build a bridge to communities the Democratic Party has taken for granted and has, by its choice of nominee, [decided to tell to wait]…I'm here to say, You don't have to wait any longer" (Marimow 2006). A quote from Mfume in a *Washington Post* article added legitimacy to Steele's comments. Mfume justified his appearance at the event as part "promise keeping" to Senator Mikulski, remarking, "I am here to fulfill my commitment and my obligation" (Marimow 2006). It was clear, then, that Mfume's endorsement of Cardin came with a "caveat" (Brow 2006, 1B).

In short, this jockeying for the Black vote affected all involved. Cardin's electability forced Mfume into the paradoxical position of campaigning to *neutralize* race (so that he would not alienate White Democrats) and campaigning to *exploit* race (so that he could mobilize angry Black Democrats). Steele's prominence, Mfume's discontent, and the possibility of Black defection forced Cardin to present his candidacy as non-threatening to Black interests while simultaneously portraying party as more important than race. Along the way, while both Democrats tried to de-escalate talk of race and to run a genteel campaign, Steele did neither. Steele, like Mfume, portrayed race as more important than party allegiance: The "Kweisi Problem" had become the "Steele Problem." As such, Steele could portray partisan defection as strong racial identification.

Running Against Convention: Steele Versus Cardin

Steele, therefore, did not run a deracialized campaign. He consistently expressed opinions on issues related to race and racism, and he made reference to how Democrats responded to his race and party identification before and after he became the Republican nominee for Lieutenant Governor (Mosk 2005a,b). In short, Steele employed a stylized electoral strategy which was very different from Black conservative predecessors seeking statewide office: racialized partisan politics.[8] This strategy attempted to: (a) capitalize on growing levels of Black dissatisfaction with the Democratic Party, (b) challenge expectations about how racially identified Black candidates should campaign, and (c) exploit Black preferences for descriptive representation and for making history (or legacy). For Steele, a strong sense of Black racial identity provided an attitudinal predisposition towards embracing, rather than rejecting, Republican partisanship.

For example, Steele often recalled the 2001 incident where White Democrat and Maryland Senate President Thomas V. "Mike" Miller called him an "Uncle Tom" because Steele complained about minority vote dilution in the redistricting process. He also referenced a September 2002 "Oreo Cookie" incident, where some crowd member allegedly "pelted" Steele with the racially infamous biscuits at a Morgan State University gubernatorial campaign debate (Sokolove 2006). Although some strongly challenged the veracity of the Oreo incident (Green 2005), Steele and others pressed on with the story. For his part, Steele mentioned the incident during a November 17, 2005, appearance on *Hannity and Colmes* ("Is The Race Card in Play…" 2005).

Using these incidents as a thematic backdrop, Steele presented his official entrée into the Senate contest as an evolution of independent Black politics. "For too long, one party worried more about prices in the stock market than prices in the corner market…And too many in the other party preached reconciliation at the same time they practiced division," he remarked while announcing his candidacy for the Senate seat (Steele 2005). Later, Steele said, "As a young man I realized that the front lines in the New Civil Rights Struggle would be different… instead of the right to sit at the lunch counter… the New Civil Rights Struggle would be a struggle for the right to own the diner and to create legacy wealth for our children." (Steele 2005). During this same speech, Steele criticized both parties and refrained from mentioning his Republican affiliation, proclaiming that he would be "A bridge that not only brings both parties together, but, more importantly, brings all of us closer to one another" (Steele 2005).

Furthermore, Steele tried to conjoin Black racial consciousness with partisanship, and, like Mfume, to present his candidacy as an evolution in Black perseverance against racism. He brought up the federal investigation of two Democratic Senatorial Campaign Committee staffers who illegally obtained Steele's credit report. (One pleaded guilty and avoided jail time; the other resigned.) Steele called this a "low point" in the campaign, remarking that the media did not react to the story as it would have if a Republican Senatorial Campaign Committee employed such a tactic against then-Illinois Senator Barack Obama (Steele 2007).

Steele also reminded Blacks that New Yorker Steve Gilliard, a liberal Black blogger, had depicted him as a minstrel in Black face shortly after Steele announced his candidacy (Mosk 2005a).[9] The picture, titled "I's Simple Sambo and I's Running for the Big House," was decried by Democratic Virginia gubernatorial candidate Timothy M. Kaine and was eventually pulled—to the dismay of liberal bloggers. Reportedly, Gilliard defended the picture by saying "Steele invited the portrayal by failing to criticize Gov. Robert L. Ehrlich Jr.'s (R) decision to hold a fundraiser at an all-White country club" (Miller 2005, B04).

Steele also did not let people forget that a 2002 *Baltimore Sun* editorial, to endorse Kathleen Kennedy Townsend for governor, stated that Steele, as running mate of gubernatorial nominee U.S. Rep. Robert Ehrlich, brought "little to the team but the color of his skin" ("Townsend for Governor" 2002). Nor did Steele let people forget that U.S. House Minority Leader Hoyer had accused him of making "a career of slavishly supporting the Republican Party" (Marinow 2006a, B2; "Democrat Apologizes…" 2006). Reaction to Hoyer's remark underscored the problem Steele faced: Steele called the term racist; Hoyer apologized but stuck to the underlying sentiment; Cardin called Steele's reaction an attempt to "change the subject"; the divided response of Black elites made headlines; and Black Democrats remained on the sidelines (Jacoby 2005).

It was easy for Steele to connect these above incidents to a controversial Democratic National Committee strategy memo leaked to the *Washington Post* in April 2006, long before the Democratic primary. The 37-page internal document, prepared by DNC pollster Cornel Belcher and reportedly done in consultation with the Democratic Senatorial Campaign Committee (DSCC), advised the party to "knock Steele down" by identifying Steele as the "hand-picked candidate" of President Bush (Mosk 2006a, B05). The memo hoped Democrats would capitalize on high anti-Bush sentiment amongst Black voters. The memo also specifically urged the party to "turn Steele into a typical Republican in the eyes of voters, as opposed to an African American candidate" (Mosk 2006a, B05). Why? Because, according to the *Post*, "a sizable segment of likely Black voters—as much as 44 percent—would readily abandon their historic Democratic allegiances 'after hearing Steele's messaging'" (Mosk 2006a).[10] The memo also carried a warning, picked up by another news organization, that Democrats might not press Steele about his relationship with President Bush. According to this other news report, Belcher warned, "Democrats must be aggressive, Steele is a unique challenge" (Miniter 2006). Part of that unique challenge, according to the memo, stemmed from "Steele's messaging to the African American community [which] clearly had a positive effect—with many voters reciting his campaign slogans and his advertising" (Miniter 2006).

Steele's response to the memo was immediate and direct, labeling the strategy instructive of how Democrats valued Black voters: "They're afraid of what I represent. They're afraid of the fact that African American voters have options, and I'm one of them" (Mosk 2006a). Steele surrogates labeled the memo another example of race baiting. Others decried the proposed strategy to discredit and "knock down" Steele's candidacy and objected to depicting Steele as a guaranteed (rather than swing or likely) vote for George W. Bush's policies on Medicare reform and Social Security privatization (Ward 2006a).

While prominent Black Democrats remained silent about these practices, they did respond to Steele's use of Black colloquialisms. In July 2006, Blacks chastised Steele for employing the "homeboy" colloquialism in referencing his relationship to President Bush during a radio interview. It never became clear as to whether Black angst centered on the term, the reference point, or on the belief that Steele was using the term to ingratiate himself with Blacks or with Republicans. Either way, when pressed, Steele explained it this way, "I've been quoted before as calling the president my homeboy, you know, and that's how I feel" (Wagner 2006, B01). Steele also invoked another colloquialism when discussing prior critical comments about the Republican Party and President Bush:

> I'm not trying to dis the president…I'm not trying to distance myself from the president. I'm trying to show those lines where I have a different perspective and a different point of view. If I'm not free to share that as a candidate for the U.S. Senate, how can people expect me to share that and express that as a United States Senator?" (Wagner 2006, B01)

These comments came in response to revelations that Steele was the anonymous Republican whose critiques of the party went public earlier in a July *Washington Post* article, "For One Senate Candidate, the 'R' is a 'Scarlet Letter'." The then-anonymous candidate challenged the president's war policy, the federal response to Katrina, and stated that he would "probably not" want President Bush to campaign for him in the state (Milbank 2006, A02). The title of the article was derived from Steele's comment, "For me to pretend I'm not a Republican would be a lie… [to run as a proud Republican is] going to be tough, it's going to be tough to do…If this race is about Republicans and Democrats, I lose" (Milbank 2006, A01). For Steele and supporters, the campaign had to be about Black political independence (Steele 2007).[11]

Lexicon, Legacy, and Loyalty

Steele's run to race made it difficult for Cardin to directly challenge him on issues about racial inequality. Unwilling to confront Steele on such issues, Cardin hammered Steele as a Bush Republican. A Cardin television commercial even featured President Bush's comments that "Michael Steele is the right man for the United States Senate." Cardin's move was both easy and difficult. It was easy because Republican star power fueled Steele's candidacy. Bush headlined a November 2005 fundraiser and appeared on the same stage with Steele at Baltimore's M&T Bank Stadium. White House insider Karl Rove, President Bush,

Vice-President Cheney, and Arizona Senator John McCain hosted or appeared at fundraisers for Steele in Washington and Maryland. White House Chief of Staff Andrew H. Card Jr. headlined a fundraiser in New York, and Bush "Ranger"[12] Mallory Factor (head of the Free Enterprise Fund in DC) spearheaded a private fundraiser.

Steele's commercials and campaign zingers also made Cardin's job easy. For example, appeared in a television commercial featuring a door saying it was time to "show them [politicians] the door" (OnMessage Inc. 2006a). He also appeared with trash containers, signifying his disgust with mudslinging but also implying that it was time to take "out the trash" ("Ad: Taking Out the Trash" n.d.). In another commercial, Steele appeared with a black and white Boston terrier puppy. He intonated that Democrats would call him anything other than a 'child of God' and say that he "hated puppies" (OnMessage Inc. 2006b). These commercials were edgy and confrontational, but allusive about his stances on the issues. Seizing the opportunity, the Democratic Senatorial Campaign Committee released a satirical counter "puppy ad" which highlighted Steele's support for policies endorsed by President Bush (Democratic "Campaign Committee..." 2006). Also, Cardin surrogates suggested parallels between President Bush and Steele, claiming that both were recalcitrant on Iraq, were confrontational to those with dissimilar views, were short on solutions, and were likely to employ discourse on the edge of acceptable political debate.[13]. Despite this, Cardin surrogates faced a difficult time in rallying Blacks to denounce Steele as a Black Republican or as an individual. Some notable non-Marylanders with racial and partisan cachet failed to publicly campaign for Cardin inside the state. According to Steele, only Illinois Senator Barack Obama and former President Clinton ventured publicly into Maryland to campaign for Cardin, with Al Sharpton, Jesse Jackson, and John Conyers appearing at Cardin events outside of the state (Steele 2007).

The Democratic Party's success in portraying Steele as an unwavering Bush supporter perhaps prompted Steele to employ a variety of rhetorical and aesthetic strategies aimed at persuading Democrats, especially Black Democrats, to reconsider their loyalty. For example, to counter the label as a *Bush* Republican, Steele offered a new twist to the "Reagan Democrat" moniker: "Steele *Democrats.*" Steele believed his personal appeal and public policy vision would win over Black Democrats whose racial consciousness, religious convictions, and belief in economic empowerment would trump partisan affinity. Unlike the Reagan campaign, however, there was never a clear message as to which political orientations differentiated segments of the party. The "Steele Democrat" slogan left constituents wondering about the similarities between a Reagan Democrat (who valued a strong military defense and conservative values) and a Steele Democrat (who valued racial consciousness and conservative values). According to a senior advisor to Lieutenant Governor Steele, the ambiguity was an especially strategic error for a campaign targeting young people born around the presidency of George H.W. Bush (1989–1993) ("White" 2007).

Nonetheless, many Democrats with racial and partisan cachet were nervous about the message and visual presentation of the "Steele Democrat" moniker. Presented in white letters against a light blue background, Democrats believed the "Steele Democrat" moniker to be deceptive—akin to "political identity theft" (Skalka 2006a). This position was exaggerated by news that filmmaker Michael Mfume, son of Kweisi Mfume, proudly sported the moniker ("Black Democrats Pledge…" 2006; Miller and Ward 2006).

Despite outcry against Steele's attempt to carve out a distinctive lexical and historical space for his supporters, the Republican pressed on with its explicit message and its visual display. Regarding the former, in the first debate between Cardin, Steele, and independent Kevin Zeese, on October 3, 2006, Steele chastised Cardin for not learning to "look around the room and shut up and listen" (Mosk and Marimow 2006a). This was, in part, a response to Cardin's attack on Steele for supporting the Bush Administration's policies on health care, Iraq, and Social Security. Steele later remarked, "Stop the noise. Stop the race baiting, stop the fear mongering, and deal with me as a man" (Mosk and Marimow 2006a).

Steele's hyperbolic comments were strategic. The debate was at the headquarters of the Greater Baltimore Urban League headquarters, notable for being both a former church and a stop on the Underground Railroad. Steele, in effect, charged Cardin with racism, myopic partisanship, and indifference to Black voices—charges he hoped would motivate Blacks to think of themselves as Steele Democrats. In an attempt to affirm his loyalty to Black issues, Cardin asserted, "Voters in the African-American community want change, and if they vote for me, they will get change" (Miller 2006b). He went on, "I voted against [President] Bush's budget because Bush's budget is leading America in the wrong direction, and the people in the African-American community know that" (Miller 2006b). Steele responded, "I appreciate your message of change, but it is an outdated message… How can you be a change agent if you vote with your party 95 percent of the time?" (Miller 2006b). For Steele, if Cardin's loyalty to party trumped his loyalty to Maryland, then a citizen's loyalty to his/her economic, social, geographic, or racial interests should then trump (what Steele believed was) atavistic partisan attachment.

During other debates, Steele tried again to depict Democrats, and Cardin, as out of touch with non-elite (or Black) concerns. The second debate, on October 25, 2006, occurred on News Channel 8/WJLA's *News Talk Live.* At one point during the debate (the first to be televised), Steele asked Cardin about the beginning and ending of the proposed Metro Purple Line—a point of contention in Maryland's DC suburbs of Prince George's and Montgomery Counties. For many residents, the state's failure to ameliorate traffic congestion, and the congressional delegation's refusal to direct traffic funds to solve the problem, was unacceptable. Flustered by Steele's aggressiveness and the unexpected question, Cardin stumbled to answer the question and then refused to finish his answer. In response Steele uttered, "This gentleman has no clue about Metro traffic, congestion in this region…I know exactly what the needs are because I live here" (*News*

Talk Live 2006). Steele's words were a not-so-thinly veiled nod to descriptive politics—both racially and geographically; Maryland had yet to elect a Senator from the Washington suburbs, a place of growing minority presence. The debate suggested that Steele was aggressive and that Cardin was a policy-wonk unaware of problems outside the Baltimore City/County corridor.

Steele would make another such nod to descriptive politics during the third debate with Cardin on Tim Russert's *Meet the Press* on October 29, 2006. Steele used the opportunity to characterize himself more as a Reagan or Lincoln Republican than a Bush Republican ("MTP Transcript for Oct. 29" 2006). He also affirmed that Justice Clarence Thomas was his hero, but he couched it this way: "In this sense, that, as an African-American, and the only African-American on the bench. You know, I've disagreed with Clarence Thomas on a number of issues" ("MTP Transcript for Oct. 29" 2006). Steele then went on to explain his support for affirmative action. At a fourth debate, held on November 3, 2006 (the Friday prior to the election), and sponsored by the Collective Banking Group, Inc. (a coalition of Black pastors and churches), all three candidates characterized the contest as an election of "change" and highlighted their activities to advance issues pertinent to minority or underserved communities.[14] Thus, we see that Steele's efforts to balance his need to reach out with Blacks and stay within the Republican mainstream made it difficult for Steele to gain traction among Black voters and easier for Cardin to pick up steam with Black voters (Barnes and Mosk 2006b).

Steele found other ways to appeal to Black voters. He publicized a summer endorsement by hip hop mogul Russell Simmons, who hosted a Baltimore fundraiser in August 2006 (Ward 2006b). Steel and Simmons had previously hosted financial empowerment summits together in the state, and the Senate candidate had addressed Simmons' Hip Hop Summit in Detroit (Steele 2007). By publicizing Simmons's endorsement under the theme of "Change the Game," Steele employed hip-hop phraseology to connect with young voters. After Simmons's endorsement video went viral, political analyst Donna Brazile characterized Simmons's entrée into the Steele camp as "a major endorsement for Lieutenant Governor Steele that will help him attract young people, as well as Black voters" (Ward 2006b). Brazile also noted, "Once again, this should serve as a wakeup call to Democrats not to take their most loyal constituents and voters for granted" (Ward 2006b).

Steele also secured the endorsement of Cathy Hughes, founder and chair of Radio One. The Simmons and Hughes endorsement videos were marketed throughout minority communities. Steele's former brother-in-law and former heavyweight boxing champion Mike Tyson also endorsed Steele,[15] as did Don King, who had endorsed Bush in 2004. While Mfume stated that the Hughes and Simmons endorsements were "lost on him" (Mosk 2006c), others saw potential precursors to an avalanche of weighty endorsements.

While not an avalanche, a flurry of later endorsements did affect how the two party nominees jockeyed for the Black vote. In October 2006, early Mfume supporter and former Prince George's County Executive Wayne K. Curry endorsed

Steele. As the county's first Black executive and a vocal Democrat, Curry's endorsement gained enormous publicity, as did the endorsement by Major F. Riddick Jr., former aide to then-Gov. Parris N. Glendening. Steele coupled the Curry endorsement with the endorsement of five Prince George's county council members.[16] Donna Brazile dismissed the Curry endorsement and put more stock in then-current County Executive Jack Johnson's endorsement of Cardin. Political scientist Ron Walters, however, called the endorsements "audacious," proclaiming "This is going to go through the Black community like a rocket... It's going to be the talk of the county, the state, maybe even the nation" (Wiggins 2006, B1). Despite this, Maryland Democratic Party Chair Terry Lierman dismissed Black angst and defended the party's relationship with Blacks, stating "[those doubting the veracity of the party's commitment] are trying to make an issue out of something that doesn't exist" (Wiggins 2006, B1).

Some did not share Lierman's conviction or his optimism about how Black party resentment could play out. In early October 2006, *The Cook Political Report* had labeled Maryland's open seat a "Toss Up," a decisive turn from its prior ranking in March of "Leaning Democrat" (*Cook Report* 2006, 3). For many, the Steele-Cardin campaign represented a problem of navigating legacy and partisan loyalty. Many onlookers made mention of a September 27, 2006, meeting between a frustrated delegation of Maryland's Black state senators and party leaders. While Baltimore Mayor and 2006 Democratic gubernatorial candidate Martin O'Malley described the meeting between himself, the delegation, Cardin, and Lierman as "cordial," non-elites suspected otherwise (Donovan 2006, 5B). Black elites confirmed these suspicions when Prince George's Senator Nathaniel Exum noted, "They don't take us serious. We're the most loyal constituency, and they don't take us serious. They have never done anything, and they pay us lip service...We'll have to see how it plays out" (Ward 2006e).

Public opinion data shows that voters were ambivalent about their senate choices going into the fall campaign. Figure 11.1 displays the post-primary volatility of public opinion towards Cardin and Steele. Clearly, Steele was gaining momentum in his campaign. Cardin enjoyed his widest margins in late September. After that, the race became more unpredictable. The two candidates were tied by mid-October, and though Cardin regained his lead, the last pre-election polls gave him a mere three percentage point lead.

Hoping to build upon Steele's momentum, the Republicans provided another controversial visual depiction of the "Steele Democrats" moniker. It came in the form of an "election-eve" four-page "Democratic Sample Ballot" mailer sent to Prince George's County residents from the Republican gubernatorial and senatorial campaigns. It immediately garnered public outcry. The mailer was a direct appeal to racial consciousness on multiple levels. First, the cover displayed pictures of Kweisi Mfume, County Executive Jack B. Johnson, and former County Executive Wayne K. Curry. Second, the inside contained a checked box for Ehrlich and Steele. Featured candidates for the other offices listed were Democrats. Third, the text, "These are OUR Choices" and "Official Voter Guide" adorned the cover. Fourth, the mailer's colors were red, Black, and green, the traditional

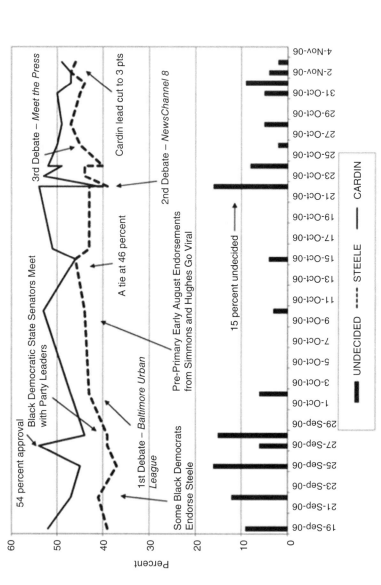

Figure 11.1 Post-primary volatility in approval of Michael Steele and Ben Cardin. *Source*: Compiled by author, from data reported at http://www.reealclearpolitics.com and http://www.pollingreport.com, various dates. Data is for both likely and registered voters.

colors of Black Nationalism. Outraged, the Democrats blasted Republicans for fraudulent electioneering and a veiled attempt at either minority vote dilution or voter deception (Londono 2006). The Steele campaign claimed that the mailers were suggestive, not deceptive. Johnson and Mfume denounced the mailers, with Johnson remarking: "It's untruthful. I'm offended by it, and I'm angry about it" (Mosk 2006d, B02).

Election Results of the 2006 Senate Contest

Ultimately, the 2006 elections proved to be a national referendum on the policies of George W. Bush and the Republican Party (Jacobson 2007). Nearly 58 percent (57.53 percent) of registered voters cast ballots in the 2006 general election in Maryland. This turnout rate was lower than in the 2002 general election (59.69 percent), and understandably, a lower turnout rate than the 2004 presidential election (78.03 percent). Steele carried 18 of the state's 24 counties but lost to Cardin by 10 percentage points (54.2 percent–44.2 percent), or 178,296 votes.

Table 11.1 depicts the breadth and depth of the Steele constituency compared to the constituencies built by other Republican candidates in Maryland. I computed the Republican share of the two-party vote across five elections: the 2006 Senate contest (Steele vs. Cardin); the 2004 Senate contest (Republican E.J. Pipkin vs. Democratic Barbara Mikulski); the 2004 presidential election (George W. Bush vs. John Kerry); the 2002 gubernatorial race (Robert Ehrlich vs. Kathleen Kennedy Townsend); and the 2000 presidential election (George W. Bush vs. Al Gore). Table 11.1 illustrates that in a pairwise comparison between 2006 and 2004, President Bush garnered a larger percentage of the two-party vote for his 2004 reelection than Steele did in his 2006 senatorial bid. In only nine out of the 24 counties did Steele carry a larger percentage of the vote than did Bush in 2004. The percentages in Howard County were identical across the two contests. However, the differences for Baltimore City and Prince George's County are worth noting. In Baltimore City, Steele earned 23.8 percent of the two-party vote while Bush earned 17.2 percent— even while losing to Cardin by over 75,000 votes. In Prince George's County, Steele earned a larger share of the two-party vote (24.2 percent) than did any of his fellow Republicans. Nonetheless, Table 11.1 shows that Steele was largely unable to capitalize whatever cachet, if any, was carried by either the "Steele Democrat" or "Bush Republican" monikers.

Steele's underperformance is especially evident across the 18 counties Bush won in 2004, which vary in size, diversity, and geographical proximity to the state's inner corridor. This is striking for two reasons. First, while Steele and Bush carried Eastern Maryland, these counties tend to be predominately White and rural, and they *vote* Republican. Second, though Steele carried the 18 Bush counties, he was predicted to carry eight jurisdictions where Republicans had a wide registration advantage: Calvert, Carroll, Frederick, Washington,

Table 11.1 GOP Share of Two-Party Vote in Maryland Statewide Elections, by County, 2000–2006

County	2006 Steele (Senate)	2004 Pipkin (Senate)	2004 Bush (President)	2002 Ehrlich (Governor)	2000 Bush (President)
Allegany *	60.6	45.8	64.2	64.8	57.4
Anne Arundel *	55.0	44.3	56.3	65.2	53.8
Baltimore City	23.8	12.1	17.2	24.4	14.6
Baltimore	47.5	36.3	47.6	61.7	45.3
Calvert *	56.8	48.5	59.0	62.2	55.2
Caroline *	67.6	49.5	66.0	75.2	60.9
Carroll *	69.3	58.0	70.6	79.6	67.4
Cecil *	58.4	52.0	60.6	68.9	55.7
Charles	48.5	38.6	49.2	56.5	49.9
Dorchester *	60.2	41.1	59.0	67.7	52.8
Frederick *	58.9	48.8	60.3	66.6	59.6
Garrett *	72.3	61.8	73.4	73.7	72.3
Harford *	63.5	51.4	64.3	74.9	59.7
Howard	45.3	36.1	45.3	55.7	46.0
Kent *	54.9	43.0	53.4	65.5	53.4
Montgomery	32.0	26.7	33.2	38.6	34.9
Prince George's	24.2	13.1	17.6	23.0	18.8
Queen Anne's *	66.4	56.2	67.2	74.7	61.4
Saint Mary's *	58.5	49.1	63.3	63.9	58.6
Somerset *	59.9	40.4	54.8	68.6	48.8
Talbot *	62.4	46.3	60.5	70.3	60.3
Washington *	60.9	52.5	64.4	69.2	60.5
Wicomico *	61.8	45.1	59.2	64.7	53.0
Worcester *	62.1	44.8	61.4	65.4	53.4
Average	44.9	34.2	43.4	52.0	41.5

* Bush County (N=18); Underlined counties reported a 2006 Republican registration advantage
Source: Author calculations of Maryland State Board of Elections data.

Allegany, Garrett, Queen's Anne and Talbot Counties. Unfortunately, Steele underperformed. Take Washington County, for example. In 2004, this jurisdiction gave Bush 64.4 percent of the two-party vote; in 2006, Steele won only 60.9 percent of the vote.

Figure 11.2 shows that Steele seemingly did not fare any better with majority Black voting precincts. As the figure shows, reporting votes for Steele by the percentage of a district's Black voting-age population (BVAP), largely Black dis-

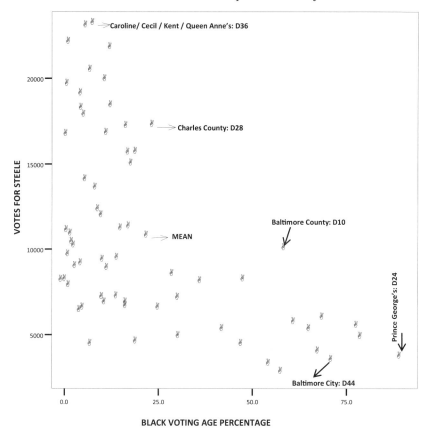

Figure 11.2 Votes for Michael Steele by percentage of Black voting age population, by District. Y=13650.79 – 129.4 BVAP; p<.000. *Source:* Author calculations, Maryland State Board of Elections legislative district data.

tricts rejected the candidate despite endorsements by Black elected officials and celebrities.[17] In Montgomery County, Steele garnered 32 percent of the vote and lost by over 108,000 votes. In Prince George's County, he lost by more than 100,000 votes—a ratio of 3.1:1. Within the county's District 24 (an area with a 90 percent BVAP), Steele received 16 percent of vote. OLS regression shows for every percentage point increase in BVAP, Steele lost 129 votes (F = 26.855; p<.000; adjusted R^2 = .284).[18]

Exit Poll Data

Below, I analyze the 2006 National General Election Poll (also known as the Edison/Mitofsky Exit Poll) weighted national and state sample—with 13,962 and 1,721 respondents. There were 1,334 Blacks in the national sample and there were 394 Blacks in the Maryland sample, respectively. I examined exit

Table 11.2 Black Vote for Michael Steele by Select Demographic Characteristics

Overall	*25%*
GENDER	
Male (44)	30
Female (56)	20
AGE	
18-24 (6)	35
25-29 (10)	14
30-39 (17)	25
40-44 (12)	40
45-49 (15)	27
50-59 (24)	22
60-64 (8)	20
65+ (9)	12
PARTY	
Democrat (77)	17
Republican (8)	84
Independent/Something Else (15)	29
IDEOLOGY	
Liberal (29)	14
Moderate (55)	26
Conservative (16)	38
RELIGION	
Protestant / Other Christian (70)	21
Catholic (14)	37
Something Else (10)	21
None (6)	20

* Parentheses represent proportion of the Maryland Black exit-poll electorate.
Source: Author calculations, Edison/Mitofsky Exit Poll weighted state sample.

poll data for two things: (1) how Steele performed among various socioeconomic demographic groups within the Black electorate; and (2) how Steele performed among Blacks holding negative opinions about the war with Iraq, President Bush, and about the Democratic Party?

Table 11.2 (which shows state, not national data) illustrates that Steele exceeded Democratic expectations by garnering 25 percent of the Black vote. Comparatively, Republican House and Senate candidates nationwide received 10 and 12 percent of the Black vote, respectively. Steele won 35 percent of the vote among Blacks aged 18–24, although this segment was the least mobilized. As expected, Steele did well among married Blacks (28 percent) and among the more affluent. Other Republican congressional candidates did comparatively worse among married Blacks (average: 12.5 percent) and among Blacks making more than $75,000 (average: 22.5 percent). Steele also bested his Republican counterparts among the most educated Blacks. Among Black college graduates, Steele received 33 percent of the vote while his GOP colleagues received an average of 21 percent. Steele failed to capture the majority of Maryland's most affluent and most educated Black voters. Looking further down Table 11.2, a similar pattern emerges highlighting Steele's difficulty in retaining the Republican coalition against heavy pro-Democratic sentiment. While Steele earned 17 percent of the Black Democratic vote, he lost 16 percent of the Black Republican vote. He also lost 62 percent of the Black conservative vote and 74 percent of the Black moderate vote. Given the strong pro-Democratic wave of 2006, these partisan defections are not unexpected. Indeed, what is somewhat remarkable is how well Steele did *against* the Democratic wave. Among liberal Blacks, Steele earned 14 percent of the vote and did better than other Republicans, who only earned 5 percent of this segment. Moreover, despite Steele's pro-life stances, he received a small percentage of the Protestant and Catholic vote and of the vote from frequent church attendees. Among those Blacks attending church once a week (34 percent of the electorate), Steele received only 25 percent of the vote. However, that was a 15-point improvement over other 2006 Republican candidates.

Table 11.3 depicts other dimensions to Black perceptions of the Steele campaign. The Democrats effectively portrayed Steele as a *Bush* Republican, and support from Maryland Blacks reflected nationwide disapproval about the president's agenda. Steele did quite well among Blacks who approved of President Bush and who believed that Iraq was unimportant to their Senate vote. However, nearly two-thirds of Blacks in Maryland and over two-thirds of Blacks nationwide strongly disapproved of Bush's job performance and connected their Senate vote to the Iraq War. Only 5 percent of Blacks expressing disapproval of Bush voted for Steele. Also, 13 percent of Blacks who believed that the Democrats only respected their views voted for Steele, while 37 percent of who believed that both parties respected the views of Blacks voted for him. Cardin garnered 75 percent of those voters who believed neither party respected their views. Thirty-seven percent of those Blacks who voted for Steele indicated that they had reservations.

Conclusion

The 2006 Maryland Senate campaign reveals the need to modify the deracialization construct for examining the nuances of partisan and racial politics in twenty-first century America. The deracialization construct is a rational choice explanation of Black politics practiced against the backdrop of racial antagonism, socioeconomic stratification, and bloc voting. The construct is therefore akin to the Black utility heuristic construct—where individual actions are structured by perceptions of how well Blacks are doing and would do under alternative

Table 11.3 Black Vote for Michael Steele by Select Perceptions

PRESIDENT BUSH'S JOB PERFORMANCE	%
Strongly Approve (6)	59
Somewhat Approve (7)	62
Somewhat Disapprove (22)	28
Strongly Disapprove (64)	14
IMPORTANCE OF IRAQ WAR IN VOTE	
Extremely Important (38)	15
Somewhat Important (27)	24
Somewhat Not Important (23)	33
Not Important at all (12)	37
SENATE VOTE TO EXPRESS:	
Support for President G. W. Bush (2)	86
Opposition to President G. W. Bush (53)	5
President G. W. Bush not a factor (42)	42
RESPECTS THE VIEWS OF BLACKS	
Only the Democratic Party (43)	13
Only the Republican Party (1)	67
Both do (28)	37
Neither does (25)	25
REASONS FOR STEELE VOTE:	
Strongly favor candidate	51
Like candidate but with reservations	37
Dislike the other candidate	7

* Parentheses represent proportion of the Maryland Black exit-poll electorate.
Source: Author calculations, Edison/Mitofsky Exit Poll weighted state sample.

policy regimes (Dawson 1994). The latter explains Black electoral and attitudinal orientations and the former explains Black office seeking practices. Both presume future trajectories of Black politics will remain amenable to Democratic partisanship. Yet, the logic of each construct presents an alternative path: one where Black candidates seeking statewide office reject deracialization in order to raise Black skepticism about the collective dividend produced by Democratic allegiance.

The campaigns of Kweisi Mfume and Michael Steele were decidedly counter to the proscriptions of the deracialization construct. Each sought, albeit in significantly different ways, to (a) threaten White political power, (b) mobilize Black citizens through racial appeals, and (c) to interject issues of race into the contest. Both campaigns reflected consternation over Black office seeking under the Democratic banner. In addition, both campaigns sought to further racialize partisanship by prodding strong Black racial identifiers to deeply consider partisan allegiance as power or powerlessness; that is, to question what scholars call the "structural dependence" upon (Tate 1995) or "electoral capture" (Frymer 1999) of Black voters (and consequently Black interests) within the Democratic Party. Indeed, observers have long pondered about the impact of shifts in Black allegiance and about the willingness and ability for Republicans to capitalize on such shifts (Fauntroy 2007; Philpot 2007; Walton 1997). In fact, going into the 2006 election cycle, journalists had proclaimed it as the "year of the Black Republicans" (Balz and Mosk 2006). Of course, the senatorial and gubernatorial defeats of Steele, Lynn Swann (PA), and Kenneth Blackwell (OH) and the Black proportion of the Republican vote in 2006 suggest otherwise. On the other hand, harbingers are hard to identify at the time of emergence.

Take, for instance, theories explaining voter turnout. The fact that citizens actually turn out to vote successfully paved the way for other critiques of rational choice theory. Morris P. Fiorina (1990, 334) contended that turnout was "the paradox that ate rational choice theory." The theory was inadequate for explaining the expressive value of participation or for why people voted despite the improbability of their vote being decisive. Similarly, both Mfume and Steele continued to reject deracialization despite the improbability of winning—racial bloc voting within a closed primary system prevented the former from winning and a heavy anti-Republican context prevented the latter.

This 2006 Senate contest, however, could foreshadow bigger problems to come for the Democrats. Two things could occur. First, the Republicans could learn how to organize along *racial* lines as they learned to organize along *organizational* lines to win Congress in 1994. Second, the Democrats could (as the national party did in 1988 and as Maryland's state party did in 2002) misread Black willingness to stay home or to defect. If either occurs, Maryland's 2006 contest could become, in retrospect, the campaign that ate deracialization theory as a prism from which to view trajectories of twenty-first century Black politics. The new Republican battle for Black voters could shift slightly away from old adages about similarities in socioeconomic and cultural values. In what could be considered the beginning of a new battle plan, in January 2007 the national Republican leadership appointed Michael Steele to chair GOPAC, the "national organization dedicated exclusively to electing Republicans to state and local offices" ("GOPAC's History" 2009). As the recruitment and political training arm of the Republican Party, Chairman Steele was responsible for diversifying strategies of outreach, for fielding state and local candidates, and for raising awareness about how Republican policies could benefit traditional Democratic constituencies. When I interviewed Chairman Steele, he remarked that he would focus on three key strategies to help Republicans compete for Black votes: education, training, and developing a message (Steele 2007). Steele also remarked that he would employ lessons learned from the 2002 gubernatorial campaign and the 2006 senatorial campaign to teach Republicans "how to communicate, how to reach beyond party label" and how to get beyond the "Scarlet letter" (of R) which plagues party outreach strategies to minority voters (Steele 2007). Steele's words were reminiscent of another Black to chair GOPAC: former Oklahoma U.S. Representative J.C. Watts.

To borrow the words of Prince George's Senator Nathaniel Exum, expressed in the aftermath of a September 2006 meeting between Black state senators and party leaders, only time will tell how it all "plays out," or, more specifically, how the two major parties balance Black voter aspirations and the need to diversify and solidify their partisan bases (Ward 2006e).[19]

Postscript

In late January 2009, GOPAC Chairman Michael Steele bested all competitors in a six-candidate, six-round balloting contest to become the first African American Chairman of the Republican National Committee. Steele's victory was surprising to many. His competitors were then-sitting Chairman Mike Duncan (who eventually withdrew after the third round of balloting), South Carolina Chairman Katon Dawson, former Ohio Secretary of State Ken Blackwell (who is also Black), Michigan Chairman Saul Anuzis, and Tennessee Chairman Chip Saltsman. For many, that Steele's election came on the heels of Barack Obama's inauguration as the first African American President of the United States was uncanny and not quite coincidental.

In reality, the 2008 election ushered in new political realities for the Republican Party. Within two years, they had lost the presidency and both houses of Congress. As Chairman of the Republican National Committee, Steele would be responsible for stemming these losses and for winning new seats. Thus, his personal political fortunes became inextricably tied to the fortunes of the party.

By becoming the face and messenger of the Republican credo, Steele may have unknowingly given fodder to the most reactionary elements of his party while also undermining future party support among Blacks. For example, in February 2009, Steele made an appearance on CNN's *D.L. Hughley Breaks the News.* In this interview, Steele tried to explain to D.L. Hughley, a Black comedian, how he intended to use his party's platform to reach out to Black voters. He noted that Republicans were the first to practice affirmative action, and he affirmed his commitment to use his platform to reach out to Blacks on issues that concerned them ("Transcripts: D.L. Hughley…" 2009).

During this interview, Hughley also asked Steele to respond to the charge that Rush Limbaugh, who had recently professed a desire to see the Obama administration "fail," was the "de facto leader of the Republican party" ("RNC's Michael Steele…" 2009; Associated Press 2009). Steele asserted that he was the leader of the party, and then explained Limbaugh's behavior by saying, "So let's put it into context here. Let's put it into context here. Rush Limbaugh is an entertainer. Rush Limbaugh, his whole thing is entertainment. Yes, it's incendiary. Yes, it's ugly" ("RNC's Michael Steele…" 2009). After this interview, though, Steele felt a backlash and was forced to apologize to Limbaugh (Associate Press 2009).

The D.L. Hughley interview and its aftermath demonstrated the difficulties racialized Black Republicans face, especially when they hold positions of power within their party. Steele tried to simultaneously appeal to Blacks and to appease the part of the conservative base that follows Rush Limbaugh. By all accounts, he failed. His attempt to reach out to Blacks was overshadowed by a turf battle with a radio talk show host. In order to preserve order within his party, Steele chose to emphasize intra-party peace over racial outreach innovation.

It remains to be seen how Steele will fare as Republican National Committee Chairman. He will largely be judged on the outcome of the 2010 midterm elections. If the events of November 2006 and February 2009 are any indication, though, he may have difficulty reconciling the need to maintain the existing Republican base with the need to reach out to Black voters. Whatever the outcome, that Steele actively thinks about recruiting Black voters to the Republican Party demonstrates that Black Republicanism and race consciousness are not necessarily mutually exclusive.

Notes

1. An early version of this chapter was presented at the 2007 National Conference of Black Political Scientists (San Francisco). This chapter also appeared in an earlier form, as Tyson D. King-Meadows. 2009, "Running on Race and Against Conventon: Michael Steele, Kweisi Mfume and Maryland's 2006 Senate Contest." *National Political Science Review* 12(1): 23–44. It is reprinted with permission. The author wishes to thank Brady Walker, an undergraduate political science major at UMBC and activist in Maryland Republican politics, for his research assistance. He also thanks Joe McCormick, Robert Smith, Elka Stevens, and Cheryl Miller for comments on earlier drafts.
2. The parallel is Douglas Wilder's successful 1986 bid for Lt. Governor of Virginia that laid the foundation for Wilder's successful and historic 1989 campaign. Until the 2006 election of Deval Patrick, Massachusetts, Wilder was the first popularly elected African-American governor since Reconstruction.
3. Twenty-eight persons filed for the vacant seat, with eighteen in the Democratic primary (Maryland State Board of Elections 2006).
4. For example, on June 30, 2005, Ben Cardin issued a press release that he had raised over $1 million. An October 12, 2005 press release put Cardin at over $2 million. According to blog news accounts, by late 2005 Cardin had raised "almost $3 million" while Mfume had raised "just over $400,000" and that Cardin had "$2.1 million in cash on hand" compared to "$125,000" raised by Mfume (Holland 2006).
5. Take also comments by Baltimore City resident and Senate Majority Leader Nathaniel J. McFadden, "Kweisi was the first to announce, but the party only came alive when Cardin showed up.… It's caused some chagrin" (Mosk and Craig 2005, B1).
6. Gonzales Research & Marketing Strategies, April 4–13, 2006; N = 819 registered regular voters.
7. Gonzales Research & Marketing Strategies, August 18–25, 2006; N = 843 registered regular voters. The margin of error for the poll was "no more than plus or minus 3.5 percentage points."
8. Of course one could suggest that Steele's tactics were not new. Indeed, some point to the U.S. senatorial campaigns of Alan Keyes—especially the 2004 Illinois

contest against State Senator Barack Obama—and the 2006 Ohio gubernatorial campaign of Secretary of State Ken Blackwell as likely examples. However, I contend that Steele's efforts to appeal to Black voters were different from those of Keyes and Blackwell in two ways. First, Steele's race-based messages were not heavily laden with religious references like those of Keyes and Blackwell; for example, Steele did not publicly suggest that Black women seeking abortions were encouraging or engaging in genocidal murder. Second, Steele frequently referenced Democratic *attacks* on his "authenticity" as a Black man. Unlike Keyes and to some extent Blackwell, Steele did not have to campaign to establish a racial credibility within Black circles. Steele was plagued by a lack of policy credibility, a deficit which enabled him to capitalize on attacks employing racial overtones.

9. A few weeks before Gilliard had depicted Ohio Secretary of State Kenneth Blackwell in Blackface http://stevegilliard.blogspot.com/2005/10/simple-sambo-wants-to-move-to-big.html. For a discussion on the Blackwell incident, see http://www.Blackcommentator.com/157/157_cover_Black_speech_pf.html.

10. Survey based on 489 Black Maryland voters.

11. The supporter interviews were conducted during the ethnographic portion of this project November 7, 2006, at the Comfort Inn in Bowie, Maryland.

12. Rangers were individuals bundling at least $200,000 for the Bush-Cheney 2004 campaign.

13. Field notes of interviews with Cardin supporters in Baltimore City and Baltimore County.

14. In Cardin's opening statement he mentioned his work as Speaker of the Maryland House of Delegates (1979–87) and his success in appointing the first female and first Black chairs of standing committees ("MTP Transcript for Oct. 29" 2006).

15. The Steele campaign did not endorse Tyson's pro-Steele campaign activities (Steele campaign website).

16. The members were David Harrington (D-Cheverly), Samuel H. Dean (D-Mitchellville), Camille Exum (D-Seat Pleasant), Tony Knotts (D-Temple Hills), and Marilynn Bland (D-Clinton).

17. Frequent precinct changes make it impossible to map demographic profile to these small unit lines.

18. A logistic regression running the likelihood of a district giving Steele more than 50 percent of the vote against the percentage of Black voting age population produced an Ex(B) for BVAP of .904. This means that a one-unit change in BVAP decreased the odds of a district voting for Steele by 9.6 percent.

19. See the provocative prescription offered to Democrats in Thomas F. Schaller's *Whistling past Dixie: How Democrats can win without the South* (New York: Simon & Schuster, 2006). Black Democrats are, of course, antagonistic towards the sentiment.

References

Albritton, Robert B., George Amedee, Keenan Grenell, and Don-Terry Veal. 1996. Deracialization and the new Black politics. In *Race, politics, and governance in the United States,* ed. Huey L. Perry, 96–106.Gainesville: University Press of Florida,

Ardrey, Saundra C., and William E. Nelson. 1990. The maturation of Black political power: The case of Cleveland. *PS: Political Science and Politics* 23 (June): 148–51.

Associated Press. 2009. GOP chief apologizes for Limbaugh remarks. MSNBC.com. March 3. http://www.msnbc.msn.com/id/29478402/ (accessed April 20, 2009).

Balz, Dan, and Matthew Mosk. 2006. The year of the Black Republican? GOP targets Democratic constituency in 3 high-profile races. *The Washington Post*, May 10, A1.

Barnes, Robert, and Matthew Mosk. 2006. Steele apologies for Holocaust remarks. *The Washington Post*, February 11, B1.

———. 2006b. Poll puts Maryland Democrats in the lead. *The Washington Post*, October 29, A1.

———. 2006. Black Democrats pledge backing to Steele. *The Washington Times*, September 21.

Brow, Matthew Hay. 2006. Backing Cardin, with a caveat. *The Baltimore Sun,* September 28, B1.

Cardin, Ben. 2006. Cardin earns 'A' rating from NAACP. Press release, February 8. http://www.bencardin.com/news?id=0032 (accessed February 9, 2006).

Cardin for Senate. 2005. Rep. Steny Hoyer endorses Ben Cardin in U.S. Senate race [Press Release]. Catonsville, MD, May 2.

Craig, Tim. 2006. Cheney is featured at Steele fundraiser. *The Washington Post*, April 6, B4.

Dawson, Michael C. 1994. *Behind the mule: Race and class in American politics.* Chicago: University of Chicago Press.

———. 2001. *Black visions: The roots of contemporary African-American political ideologies.* Chicago: University of Chicago Press.

———. 2006. Democrat apologizes for "slavish" remark. CNN.com. October 17. http://www.cnn.com/2006/POLITICS/10/17/democrats.apology/index.html (accessed April 20, 2009).

Democratic Senatorial Campaign Committee: "Dogs." 2006. [Political Advertisement]. http://www.nationaljournal.com/members/adspotlight/2006/09/0927mdsen1.htm (accessed May 20, 2009).

Donovan, Doug. 2006. O'Malley calls talk "cordial." *Baltimore Sun*, October 6, B5.

Face the Nation. 2009. Rahm Emanuel on CBS's "Face the Nation." *CQ Today Online News*, March 1. http://www.cqpolitics.com/wmspage.cfm?docID=news-000003063742 (accessed April 20, 2009).

Fauntroy, Michael. 2007. *Republicans and the Black vote.* Boulder, CO: Lynne Rienner.

Fiorina, Morris P. 1990. Information and rationality in elections. In *Information and democratic processes,* eds. J. A. Ferejohn and J. H. Kuklinski, 329–42. Urbana: University of Illinois Press.

Fisher, Marc. 2006. For Mfume, race cuts both ways. *The Washington Post*, July 2, C1.

Frymer, Paul. 1999. *Uneasy alliances: Race and party competition in America.* Princeton, NJ: Princeton University Press.

———. 2009. GOPAC's history. Gopac.org. http://www.gopac.org/about/default.aspx (accessed May 20, 2009).

GOP chief apologizes for Limbaugh remarks. MSNBC. MSN.com http://www.msnbc.msn.com/id/29478402/ (accessed April 20, 2009).

Green, Andrew. 2005. Ehrlich bristles at Oreo skeptics. *The Baltimore Sun*, November 13 , B1.

Hockstader, Lee. 2006. The "Kweisi Problem." *The Washington Post,* June 11, B7.

Hoyer for Congress. 2005. Key Southern Maryland officials endorse Ben Cardin for Senate, endorsements represent significant widespread support for Cardin throughout southern Maryland [Press Release]. Bowie, Maryland. July 22.

Hutchinson, Earl Ofari n.d. Is the race card in play in the Md. Senate campaign? Foxnews.com. http://www.foxnews.com/story/0,2933,175888,00.html (accessed April 20, 2009).

Jacobson, Gary C. 2007. Referendum: The 2006 midterm congressional elections. *Political Science Quarterly* 122 (Spring): 1–24.

Jacoby, Jeff. 2005. Slurs fly from the left. *The Boston Globe*, December 28, A19.

Kaplan, Jonathan E. 2005. Black lawmakers keep quiet on Cardin V. Mfume primary. *The Hill*, November 22.

Londono, Ernesto. 2006. Sample ballots in Pr. George's misidentify candidates. *The Washington Post*, November 7.

Marimow, Ann E. 2006a. Hoyer remark "racist," GOP's Steele charges. *The Washington Post*, October 18, B2.

———. 2006b. Mfume endorses Cardin, but adds caveat. *The Washington Post*, September 28, A1.

Maryland State Board of Elections. 2006. 2006 gubernatorial general election:-County-wide turnout. http://www.elections.state.md.us/elections/2006/turnout/general/county_wide.html (accessed August 20, 2009).

Mayer, Jeremy. 2002. *Running on race: Racial politics in presidential campaigns, 1960–2000*. New York: Random House.

McCormick, Joseph II, and Charles E. Jones. 1993. The conceptualization of deracialization: Thinking through the dilemma. In *Dilemmas of Black politics: Issues of leadership and strategy*, ed. Georgia A. Persons, 66–84. New York: HarperCollins.

Milbank, Dana. 2006. For one senate candidate, the "R" is a "scarlet letter." *Washington Post,* July 25, A2.

Miller, S. A. 2005. Top Democrats duck on Steele hits. *The Washington Times,* November 3.

———. 2006a. Missed fundraiser wasn't a slap at Bush, Steele says. *The Washington Times*, June 4.

———. 2006b. Steele, Cardin wrangle over race in debate. *The Washington Times*, October 4.

———. Jon Ward. 2006. Mfume son joins Steele to rally Baltimore voters. *The Washington Times*, November 5.

Miniter, Richard. 2006. Democrats plan race-based campaign against Black candidate in Maryland. *The New York Sun*, April 13.

Mosk, Matthew. 2005a. Blog attack on Steele decried, doctored photo criticized by Republicans and Democrats. *Washington Post,* October 28, B4.

———. 2005b. Steele strives for the hearts of Black voters. *The Washington Post*, November 8, B1.

———. 2006a. Cummings and Wynn to back Mfume. *The Washington Post,* August 30, B2.

———. 2006b. Poll finds Steele may be magnet for Black voters. *The Washington Post,* April 6, B5.

———. 2006c. Steele absent from Bush GOP fundraiser. *The Washington Post,* June 1, B5.

———. 2006d. Angling for hip-hop appeal. *The Washington Post*, August 25, B1.

———. 2006d. Democrats denounce flier mailed by GOP. *The Washington Post,* November 7, B2.

———. Dan Balz. 2006. Keep cash coming, Steel tells the GOP. *The Washington Post*, September 29, B6.

———. Tim Craig. 2005. Early support of Cardin stirs talk of a backlash, Mfume backers see opening in senate race *The Washington Post,* December 31, B1.

————. Claudia Deane. 2006. Maryland senate race may hinge on ethnicity. *The Washington Post*, July 2, A1.

————. Ann E. Marimow. 2006a. Steele, Cardin debate draws sharp distinctions. *The Washington Post*, October 4, A1.

————. Ann E. Marimow. 2006b. Cardin, Steele face off in contentious debate. *The Washington Post*, October 25, A1.

MTP transcript. 2006. *Meet the press web site*. October 29. http://www.msnbc.msn.com/id/15473528/ (accessed January 3, 2007).

News talk live 2006. [Television Program]. Washington, DC. WJLA/News Channel 8. October 25.

Nitkin, David. 2005. Cardin finds support among Black clergy. *The Baltimore Sun*, November 16, B4.

————. Andrew A. Green. 2005. Mfume-Cardin contest open: Leading Democrats in dead heat. *The Baltimore Sun*, November 7, A1.

OnMessage, prod. 2006a. Show them the door [Political Advertisement]. Alexandria, VA: On Message. http://www.nationaljournal.com/members/adspotlight/2006/10/1020mdsen1.htm (accessed May 20, 2009).

————, prod. 2006b. Real ideas for change [Political Advertisement]. Alexandria, VA: On Message. http://www.nationaljournal.com/members/adspotlight/2006/09/0919mdsen1.htm (accessed May 20, 2009).

Orey, Byron D'Andra, and Boris E. Ricks. 2007. A systematic analysis of the deracialization concept. *National Political Science Review* 11 (1): 325–34.

Philpot, Tasha S. 2007. *Race, republicans, and the return of the party of Lincoln*. Ann Arbor, MI: University of Michigan Press

RNC's Michael Steele calls Limbaugh's comments "Incendiary and ugly." 2009. [Clip]. *D.L Hughley Breaks the News*. CNN. New York. Posted on http://www.youtube.com/watch?v=W4EWB0Wc4wQ, February 28.

Schaller, Thomas F. 2006. *Whistling past Dixie: How democrats can win without the south*. New York: Simon & Schuster.

Schwartzman, Paul, and Matthew Mosk. 2004. "Racist" label by Ehrlich riles democrats. *The Washington Post,* September 1.

Sheckels, Theodore F. 2006. *Maryland politics and political communication, 1950–2005*. Lanham, MD: Lexington Books.

Skalka, Jennifer. 2006. Mfume won't concede until counting's done. *The Baltimore Sun*, September 15, B5.

————. 2006a. Democrats accuse Steele of "political identity theft." *The Baltimore Sun*. September 22, A1.

————. 2006b. Dean scolds Md. democrats on ticket diversity; Party Chairman wants to avoid replay of "Michael Steele problem." *The Baltimore Sun*, November 10, B5.

Sokolove, Michael. 2006. Why is Michael Steele a *republican* candidate? *New York Times Magazine,* March 26.

Steele, Michael. 2005. Candidate announcement speech. Prince George's Community College, Largo, MD. October 25.

————. 2007. Personal interview. June 22, 2007.

Taking out the trash. n.d. [Political Advertisement]. http://projects.washingtonpost.com/politicalads/132/ (accessed May 20 2009).

Tate, Katherine. 1995. Structural dependence or group loyalty? The Black vote in 1992. In *Democracy's feast: Elections in America*, ed. Herbert F. Weisberg, 111–23. Chatham, NJ: Chatham House.

———. Townsend for governor. *Baltimore Sun*, November 3.

The Cook Political Report, 2006. 20 October 20062006 Senate Race Ratings, October 20, 3. http://www.cookpolitical.com/sites/default/files/2006_sen_ratings_oct27.pdf (accessed August 20, 2009).

Wagner, John. 2006. Steele addresses negative comments on Bush. *The Washington Post,* July 27, B1.

———. Spencer S. Hsu. 2005. Mfume jumps in for Sarbanes's seat. *The Washington Post*, March 15, B5.

Walton, Hanes. 1997. *African American power and politics.* New York: Columbia University Press.

Ward, Jon. 2006a. Plans to knock Steele labeled as "destructive." *The Washington Times*, April 7.

———. 2006b. Steele gaining Blacks' support. *The Washington Times,* August 24.

———. 2006c. Wynn, Cummings back Mfume. *The Washington Times,* August 30.

———. 2006d. Steele, Cardin: Opening shots. *The Washington Times,* September 14.

———. 2006e. Democrats hit for lack of Black candidates. *The Washington Times*, October 6.

———. 2006f. Steele hits Cardin for linking him to Bush, GOP. *The Washington Post*, October 14, A9.

White, John (pseudonym for Steele senior campaign staffer). 2007. Personal interview. June 28.

Wickham, DeWayne. 2005. Blacks deserve something in return from Md. democrats. *USA Today*, March 14, 13A.

Wiggins, Ovetta. 2006. "Black democrats cross party lines to back Steele for U.S. senate. *The Washington Post*, October 31, B1.

You Tube. 2009. RNC's Michael Steele calls Limbaugh's comments "incendiary and ugly." http://www.youtube.com/watch?v=W4EWB0Wc4wQ (accessed April 20, 2009).

Part V

Intersectionality and African-American Politics in the Twenty-First Century

The 2008 presidential election represents one of those fleeting moments of African-American political unity. As during the Civil Rights Movement, Jesse Jackson's 1988 presidential campaign, and during countless historic local campaigns where Blacks were elected for the first time to mayoralties and Congress, there are moments where African Americans close ranks behind a common political purpose.

There is little dispute that Blacks appear to have a remarkable unity of purpose and political preference. For instance, Blacks are the most reliable Democratic voting bloc in the United States and have been so since 1964 (Carmines and Stimson 1989). In groundbreaking work in 1994, political scientist Michael Dawson explains this phenomenon by showing that Black voters put group interests ahead of personal interests when deliberating over candidates and policies (Dawson 1994).

All of this suggests a degree of conformity among Blacks, but it is abundantly clear that Blacks are not a monolithic group. In later work, Dawson demonstrates that African-American political thought includes a range of philosophical influences, including radical egalitarianism, Marxism, feminism, liberalism, and conservatism (Dawson 2003, chapter 1). Furthermore, scholars such as Adolph Reed point out that the apparent unity observed in African-American politics really reflects the domination of one group of Blacks—namely middle- and upper-class Blacks—who dominate the agenda setting process and often ignore the interests of their poorer brothers and sisters (Reed 2000, chapter 1).

The nascent conflict that Reed observed reflects a realization among scholars of race, class, and gender that individuals are not the sum of one identity. People have multiple identities and multiple experiences based upon those identities which inform their perspectives on politics and policy. If a person happens to be a member of more than one disadvantaged minority group, they not only must face being discriminated by mainstream society and by fellow minorities who share one but not all of their identities. In her seminal book *The Boundaries of Blackness* (1999), political scientist Cathy Cohen studied the Black civil rights community's response to the AIDS crisis. Because AIDS was associated with homosexuality and drug abuse and because many Blacks are socially conservative, civil rights leaders chose to ignore the AIDS crisis for its first decade. Instead, they looked for consensus issues which could unify Blacks from all walks of life.

The Black community's response to the AIDS crisis highlights the ways in which some Blacks are doubly marginalized: marginalized by the broader society on account of their race, but also marginalized by both Black and non-Black on account of an additional identity; in this case, sexual orientation or drug addiction (Cohen 1999). The process of being doubly marginalized has ramifications beyond AIDS policy. In the electoral realm, Black candidates who have additional minority identities may have trouble getting elected because of the burden of that additional identity.

In this section, contributors explore these issues in greater depth to determine if candidates' multiple identities have hampered their efforts to win election and if those multiple identities shape their policy agendas once they are elected to office. In chapter 12, Amber Perez and I study the historic election of Keith Ellison as Minnesota's first Black and America's first Muslim congressman. We seek to answer a number of questions. Did his election opponents try to stigmatize him on account of his race, his religion, or both identities? Did the public narrative about Ellison focus on his race or his religion? How do Ellison's identities inform his approach to legislation and policy advocacy?

Chapter 13 shifts the attention to the relationship between race and gender among the cohort of young Black politicians. Because young Black politicians are characterized as post-racial and post-partisan, it would be easy to take for granted that they are progressive on gender issues. This is hard to discern, though, in terms of the cohort's descriptive representation. Young women have only recently emerged onto the national scene as political players in this cohort. Katrina Gamble explores these issues in greater depth to help identify and correct the "pipeline problem."

References

Carmines, Edward, and James Stimson. 1989. *Issue evolution: Race and the transformation of American politics*. Princeton, NJ: Princeton University Press.

Dawson, Michael. 1994. *Behind the mule*. Princeton, NJ: Princeton University Press.

———. 2003. *Black visions*. Chicago: University of Chicago Press.

Cohen, Cathy. 1999. *The boundaries of Blackness: AIDS and the breakdown of Black politics*. Chicago: University of Chicago Press.

Reed, Adolph. 2000. *Class notes*. New York: New Press.

12 Race, Religion, and Post-9/11 America
The Election of Keith Ellison[1]

Andra Gillespie and Amber Perez

In 2006, Minnesota State Representative Keith Ellison made history twice. In the November general election, he became Minnesota's first Black Congressman. He also became the first Muslim member of the U.S. Congress. The latter distinction was particularly notable because it took place five years after September 11 and the beginning of the war on jihadist terror.

The Ellison election presents a perfect case study of the role of intersectionality in elections and governance. Did his campaign face challenges because of his race, his religion, or both? Does Congressman Ellison's race and religion give him a different policy perspective from his non-Black, non-Muslim colleagues?

In this chapter, Andra Gillespie and Amber Perez discuss these issues. Using content analysis of media coverage, they find that most public discussions of Ellison's candidacy and first term of office focused on his religious identity, not his racial identity. There were periods where Ellison's racial identity was salient. It was alternately used to try to marginalize or mainstream him as a candidate and as an American legislator.

Introduction

On Election Day 2006, Keith Ellison won a congressional seat from Minnesota's Fifth Congressional District and made history. Not only did he become Minnesota's first Black congressman, he also became the first Muslim member of Congress in American history. That Ellison shattered two barriers with his historic election evinces the reality that Ellison, like so many people, is a multiple minority, a member of two groups that have been historically marginalized in American society and politics.

For a long time, it would have been acceptable to study Ellison as either a Black politician or a Muslim politician. However, it is essential to understand multiple minorities in the complexity of all of their identities. Moreover, it is important to understand how Ellison's multiple identities helped or hindered his electoral prospects and how constituents and outsiders viewed Ellison as a candidate.

We seek to answer these questions in this chapter. We begin with a discussion of intersectionality, or the study of how people with multiple minority identities negotiate their identities in mainstream society and in their minority communities. Then we use the history of Black Muslims in the United States to illustrate how intersectionality works. The historical overview allows us to place Ellison's candidacy in context. Using content analysis and interview data, we find an interesting irony. At various points before and after the campaign, Ellison's opponents tried to use his religious identity or a combination of his religious and racial identity to either try to keep him out of office or to tarnish his reputation. However, in some ways, his racial identity may have muted the impact of those attacks. Nevertheless, Ellison's public persona is largely defined by his religious identity.

Understanding Intersectionality

> Those of us who stand outside that power often identify one way in which we are different, and we assume that to be the primary cause of all oppression, forgetting other distortions around difference, some of which we ourselves may be practicing. (Audre Lorde 2007, 54)

A generation ago, Black feminists began to push scholars and activists to think actively about the role multiple identities play in shaping some people's life chances and policy preferences. They argued that much of the discourse surrounding second wave feminism focused on issues facing middle-class, White women. As a result, women of color and poor women felt marginalized in the feminist movement, despite the fact that they, too, were victims of gender discrimination. Theorists such as Audre Lorde pushed White feminists to think critically about how racial privilege conferred advantages to White women, even as they experienced gender oppression. Lorde also recognized that Black male civil rights activists used the racial imperative to obscure rampant sexism within the movement. Thus, Black women could find themselves the target of racial discrimination by White feminists on account of their race, and gender discrimination by Black men on account of their sex (Lorde 2007).

The paradox that Lorde described above is commonly known as intersectionality. As Julissa Reynoso writes, "The concept of intersectionality has been defined as the oppression that arises out of the combination of various forms of discrimination, which together produce something unique and distinct from any one form of discrimination standing alone" (Reynoso 2004, 64).

Recognizing that some people have multiple minority identities which affect their experiences and policy preferences represents huge theoretical progress. As Kimberlé Williams Crenshaw, one of the vanguard scholars of this theory, noted, "…the intersection of racism and sexism factors into Black women's lives in ways that cannot be captured wholly by looking separately at the race or gender dimensions of those experiences" (Crenshaw 1995, 358). Crenshaw's statement above evinces that intersectionality is about more than acknowledging that people have many identities and roles in their communities. To simply acknowledge multiple identities implies a certain additive notion of oppression that assumes all people with a certain minority identity are mistreated similarly. If a person has multiple minority identities, then, their oppression doubles, triples, etc., according to the number of minority identities the person embraces or has thrust upon them. Instead, Crenshaw asserts that intersectionality is a more dynamic, synergistic process, where multiple identities collide to create new oppressions and new perspectives on inequality. To use Black women as an example, they may experience gender inequality differently from White women because they are Black; conversely, they experience racism differently from Black men because of their gender (Crenshaw 1995, 359).

Crenshaw, like so many of the pioneers of intersectionality theory, developed the theory to articulate the impact of race, class, and gender on the life chances and political interests of poor women of color. In her seminal article, "Mapping the Margins," Crenshaw uses the issue of domestic violence to show that poor, minority victims often lack the resources and options available to abused wealthy or White women. As such, when policymakers fail to recognize these differences, they minimize the impact of otherwise well-intentioned policies (Crenshaw 1995).

Intersectionality theory also has applications beyond the classic race, class, and gender paradigm. For instance, scholars have acknowledged that sexual orientation can also intersect with racial, class, or gender identity and subject people who are gay and Black or poor, lesbian, and Latina to different forms of discrimination from those experienced by people who are just gay, or female, or poor, or who are just members of a racial or ethnic minority group.

Cathy Cohen perhaps best captured this tension in her book *The Boundaries of Blackness*. Using the AIDS crisis as her case study, Cohen demonstrates how both the mainstream Black civil rights establishment and the White gay community marginalized Black AIDS victims. Civil rights leaders refused to acknowledge AIDS as a pressing issue for the first decade of the crisis, in part because they did not want to appear to condone homosexuality or intravenous drug use. They chose instead to focus on classic civil rights issues upon which all Blacks could agree, such as making Martin Luther King Day a national holiday. Additionally, Black gays and lesbians were marginalized in the White gay rights movement because of race. Before the AIDS crisis hit, White gays had developed their own institutions, such as clinics, and had established contacts with the mainstream epidemiological community. Black gays were excluded from these institutions and contacts. It is through these relationships that doctors and scientists first discovered AIDS; as such, epidemiologists first supposed that AIDS afflicted White, gay men only. In the end, this contributed to Blacks being excluded from the health and information networks that could have provided the early treatment and prevention education that might have reduced the number of AIDS diagnoses and fatalities in the Black community (Cohen 1999).

Intersectionality, Islam, and African Americans

We believe that intersectionality theory applies to religious minorities as well. In the case of African-American Muslims, they have unique social and political experiences which color their worldviews and their political behaviors. As we show in this section, African-American Muslims are marginalized within the larger Muslim community because African-American Islam, with its emphasis on Black Nationalism and racial uplift, has not always been considered doctrinally sound. However, because Black Muslims are largely born in the United States, in contrast to their South Asian and Arab brothers and sisters, they do not experience anti-immigrant bias. Moreover, African-American Muslims' greater familiarity with the American political system allows them to organize politically with greater ease (Elliott 2007). Thus, while African-American Muslims are disadvantaged socially within their religious group, they are advantaged in political terms. It is in this environment that Keith Ellison and other African-American Muslim politicians have found the space to operate politically.

There are an estimated 6 million Muslims who live in the United States. About 25 percent of American Muslims are Black; 34 percent of American Muslims are of South Asian descent; and 26 percent are of Arab descent. While many slaves brought Islam to the United States from Africa during the slave trade, African-American Islam is largely a twentieth century phenomenon, a response born out of racial inequality (Elliott 2007).

Even though many African-American Muslims now subscribe to the tenets of Sunni Islam, most African-American Muslims have had ties to the Nation of Islam at some point in their faith lives (Vohra 1996). The Nation of Islam is a religious movement that had clear ties to the Black Nationalist Movement. It emanated from the Moorish Science Temple, a Chicago-based Black religious movement founded in 1925, which combined Christian and Islamic teachings (Fischer 1985, 392).

Wallace Fard Muhammad founded the Nation of Islam as an offshoot of the Moorish Science Temple in Detroit in 1930. The Nation of Islam combined Islamic teaching with Black uplift and a separatist philosophy. Members rejected integration on the grounds that racial discrimination in the United States prevented Blacks from being able to improve their economic and social standing. Muhammad thought that creating a separate nation within the American nation would be more suitable for African Americans. Wallace Fard Muhammad disappeared in 1934 (followers believe that Muhammad was God and went to Heaven); after his disappearance, Elijah Muhammad took over the movement, leading it until his death in 1975 (Muhammad 1985; Lincoln 1994, 20).

Members of the Nation of Islam sought to make themselves completely independent of Whites, whom they also perceived as the devil.[2] The Nation of Islam employed a doctrine of self-help to aid their efforts (Marsh 1984). Paramount to this self-help philosophy is economic independence and supporting Black owned businesses. Indeed, many members of the Nation of Islam have taken seriously the call to spend money within the Black community, and to not spend money where Blacks cannot work or receive service (Marsh 1984; Lincoln 1994, 20).

Because of the nationalist component of Nation of Islam doctrine, scholars have often classified Blacks Muslims as more of a social movement than a religion. However, changes in the leadership of the movement did help to move Black Muslims toward the more religious aspects of their faith. After Elijah Muhammad died in 1975, his son Wallace Deen Muhammad took over the Nation of Islam and tried to steer followers toward Sunni Islam, renaming the group the World Community of Islam in the West. Minister Louis Farrakhan, leader of the Chicago mosque, challenged Muhammad's efforts and forced a split in the movement. Farrakhan's followers maintained their commitment to the teachings of Elijah Muhammad and resurrected the old name, the Nation of Islam (Marsh 1984; Muhammad 1985, 413; Clegg 2002, 102).

Because most African-American Muslims have been a part of the Nation of Islam at some time in their lives, it is important to understand the relationship between the Nation of Islam and both the African-American community and the larger Muslim community. Many Blacks come to the Nation of Islam as a result of their experiences with racial and class discrimination. They find in the Nation of Islam hope to ameliorate their current economic and social position. The faith has a particular appeal among young, poor Black men. In his landmark study of African-American Muslims, C. Eric Lincoln found that roughly 80 percent of the members of the Nation of Islam were between ages seventeen and thirty-five, predominantly male, and lower class (Elliott 2007; Marsh 1984, 38; Muhammad 1985; Lincoln 1994, 22).

Despite the fact that the Nation of Islam's theology clearly addressed the subordination of Blacks in American society, the Nation of Islam advocated political non-participation until 1983. Elijah Muhammad frowned upon political participation because he believed that voting represented an acquiescence to the devil's system.[3] However, under Louis Farrakhan's leadership, the Nation's policy began to change. When Harold Washington launched his bid to become Chicago's first Black mayor in 1983, and when Jesse Jackson ran for president in 1984, Farrakhan relaxed the prohibition against political participation and encouraged his members to vote. The Nation of Islam formally lifted the ban on political participation in 1993 (Clegg 2002; Walton and Smith 2006, 124).

Part of the reason that Farrakhan changed the policy on political participation was because he wanted to turn the Nation of Islam into a more mainstream religious organization. The Nation of Islam's strict separatist policies marginalized the group in both Black and Muslim circles. The mainstream civil rights community supported integration and found the Nation of Islam's racial exclusivity incompatible with its goals. Louis Farrakhan hoped to make the Nation of Islam more respectable and more relevant by participating in mainstream politics. For example, in 1993, Farrakhan made an agreement with the Congressional Black Caucus to work together on issues of common concern. Farrakhan clearly hoped to bring positive press to his organization, and the connection with a mainstream, civil rights-oriented, legislative organization conferred a certain legitimacy on the Nation of Islam (Muhammad 1985, 413; Clegg 2002).

While the Nation of Islam has made some inroads with the mainstream Black civil rights community, there remains a strain between the Nation of Islam and mainstream Islam. The racial exclusivity of Elijah Muhammad and Louis

Farrakhan's Nation of Islam contradicts traditional Islamic doctrine. Moreover, because African-American Muslims have not had the same religious and language training as their Arab and South Asian counterparts, they have not been viewed as serious Muslims (Elliott 2007).

Class differences also divide African-American Muslims from South Asian-American Muslims and Arab-American Muslims. African-American Muslims tend to come from lower socioeconomic strata. In contrast, South Asian and Arab Muslims are better educated, more likely to be employed in professional occupations, and have higher incomes. Given the class differences between Black and non-Black Muslims, some of the doctrinal differences make sense. The Nation of Islam deliberately recruited Blacks with promises of economic uplift now, and their message appealed to poor people in particular. This message would not resonate as easily with Muslims from more comfortable economic situations (Elliott 2007; Muhammad 1985).

The final difference between Black and non-Black Muslims relates to immigration. South Asian and Arab American Muslims started immigrating en masse to the United States in the 1960s. The Census Bureau and the Office of Immigration and Customs Enforcement are legally barred from tracking immigration according to religion, so demographers infer the size of Muslim immigration according to the rate of immigration from traditionally Muslim countries (Elliott 2006). The fact that bureaucrats use country of origin as a proxy for religion reflects the reality that Americans associate Islam with certain immigrants from certain countries. As such, Muslim immigrants not only have to acclimate to a new political system; they also may have to bear the brunt of anti-Muslim bias in the United States because their ethnicity or national origin, especially since September 11.

In light of the terrorist attacks, many Americans, including African Americans, rationalized prejudice toward Muslims. Communications scholars at Cornell University studied the attitudes of Americans toward Muslims in 2004. Their respondents exhibited a high level of intolerance toward Muslims. For instance, 47 percent of respondents thought that Islam taught its adherents to engage in violent activities. Respondents also assessed Muslims and Muslim countries. Forty-nine percent of respondents believed that Islamic countries and Muslims were violent. Forty-five percent thought that Islamic countries and Muslims were fanatical. Nearly three-quarters of respondents (74 percent) thought that Islamic countries and Muslims oppressed women. Only 21 percent of respondents thought that Islamic countries and Muslims were modern, and 26 percent thought that Islamic countries and Muslims were tolerant of people with different beliefs (Nisbet and Shanahan 2004a, 3, 2004b, 5). Zogby International found that immediately after September 11, Blacks expressed significantly higher levels of support for racially profiling Arabs than Americans generally. This support fell a couple of weeks later, but it still meant that 45 percent of Blacks supported Arab racial profiling in September 2001 (Polakow-Suransky 2001).

Muslim perceptions of this hostility do provide, with some caveats, opportunities for coalescence among Muslims, regardless of race, national origin, or class.

Bareto, Masuoka, and Sanchez examined survey data for Muslim Americans in Seattle, Chicago, Dearborn, Michigan, and Long Beach California. They found that a plurality of their respondents reported feeling a strong sense of commonality with other Muslims. Moreover, two-thirds of respondents professed a sense of linked fate with other Muslims—the belief that what happens to other Muslims affects them (Bareto et al. 2008, 18–19; see also Dawson 1994).

When Bareto et al. look at their data through a multivariate statistical lens, though, they do find interesting correlates of perceptions of Muslim commonality. One would reasonably assume that perceiving religious bias would correlate highly with feelings of pan-Muslim commonality. However, there was no statistically significant relationship between perceiving anti-Muslim bias and feeling commonality with other Muslims. Ironically, perceiving anti-immigrant bias was positively correlated with feelings of commonality with other Muslims (Bareto et al. 2008, 19).

Additionally, the racial and ethnic correlates with Muslim linked fate were mixed. There was no statistically significant difference in Black and Arab-American Muslim perceptions of religious linked fate. However, Asian-American Muslims were more likely to report linked fate, and people who identify racially/ethnically as "other" were less likely to report feelings of linked fate (Bareto et al. 2008, 20).

Collectively, the Bareto, Masuoka, and Sanchez data raise a number of important issues which support the idea that African-American Muslims have a unique religious experience because of their race. While it is clear that Muslims do see commonalities with other co-religionists, they largely perceive themselves in terms of their immigrant status. Approximately two-thirds of Muslim-American adults were born outside of the United States (Bareto et al. 2008, 12). This has the potential to marginalize African-American Muslims, who do not identify as immigrants. Moreover, African-American Muslims' racial background appears to have no relationship to their sense of religious linked fate. Thus, while there is no evidence in this data that Black Muslims identify less with their religious community, they do not report the most linked fate within their faith community.

To be sure, African-American Muslims have not been immune from religious bias. However, because African Americans have been socialized in the American political system, they can more easily navigate the political process to seek redress. In the wake of post-September 11, anti-Muslim bias, Muslims of all racial backgrounds have had a reason to work together. African-American Muslims have been advising immigrant Muslims on how to launch civil rights campaigns. Muslims of all races have started backing the same candidates. As a result of these circumstances, African-American Muslims have seen their status rise in the Muslim community. Both Black and non-Black Muslims have found that they have something to offer one another. Andrea Elliott writes that "African Americans possess a cultural and historical fluency that immigrants lack, as they hold an unassailable place in America from which to defend their faith" (Elliott 2007). As a result, they also have better mobilizing skills that could benefit immigrants. On the other hand, foreign-born Muslims tend to have more money, which could provide needed resources to support these political efforts, and they also "provide a crucial link to the Muslim world and its tradition of scholarship as well as the wisdom that comes with an 'unshattered Islamic heritage'" (Elliott 2007).

In response to anti-Muslim bias in the wake of September 11, there has been an increase in Muslim-American political participation. In 2006, there were 2.2 million Muslim-American voters. During the 2000s, the proportion of registered Muslim voters more than doubled, from 41 percent of eligible Muslim adults in 2000 to 84 percent in 2004. After September 11, Muslim and Arab political action committees stepped up their fundraising and get-out-the-vote efforts. And Muslim Americans became a strong Democratic voting bloc; George W. Bush won 46 percent of the Muslim-American vote in 2000. In 2004, John Kerry won 72 percent of the Muslim-American vote (Marx 2006).

September 11 had a chilling effect on Muslim-American political candidacies, though. According to Braman and Sinno, the number of Muslim-American candidates running at the state, local, and federal level plummeted from 700 in 2000, down to 50 in 2002, and back up to 150 in 2004. They contend that in the wake of the terrorist attacks, Muslim Americans calculated that their chances of winning office had diminished (Braman and Sinno 2006, 5–6; see also Ghazali 2006).

Given the concerns about the viability of Muslim political candidacies, African-American Muslims may be especially advantaged. Historically, native born, African-American Muslims have experienced electoral success. For example, three of the four highest ranking Muslim-American elected officials in the United States in 2004, excluding Keith Ellison, were African Americans (who mostly have Western sounding names): North Carolina State Senator Larry Shaw and Missouri State Assemblymen Yaphett El-Amin and Rodney Hubbard. Since Ellison's election, a second Muslim, André Carson, has been elected to Congress from Indiana. He won a special election to succeed his late grandmother, Congresswoman Julia Carson (Braman and Sinno, 2006, 6; Ellison 2008).

The relative success of African-American Muslim candidates reflects Blacks's integral role in American society. Because African-American Muslims are viewed as intrinsically American, they may have an easier time integrating into American society. Wallace Deen Muhammad perhaps said it best when he said that "Master Fard Muhammad sneaked into America and used a name that made it hard for them to identify him. Because he did not wear a turban, he looked like an American" (Muhammad 1985, 416).

The case of African-American Muslims shows how the intersection of race and religion create synergies, especially in a politically charged environment, serve to both advantage and disadvantage them relative to their non-Black Muslim peers. While African-American Muslims may not have always observed a doctrinally pure form of Islam, their familiarity with the American political system positions them well to be effective advocates for Muslims who feel targeted by anti-Muslim bias in the United States.

Hypotheses and Methods

Keith Ellison's election to Congress in 2006 provides a rich example of how the intersection of race and religion can propel African American Muslims into political office. We hypothesize that Ellison faced an uphill battle as a Muslim-American candidate running for office after September 11. However, because of the intrinsic American-ness afforded Ellison as an African American, he was in a position to be able to combat stereotypes and to convince skeptical voters that he could successfully represent his Muslim and non-Muslim constituents.

To explore these questions in depth, we first explore Keith Ellison's biography and the history of his 2006 election. This analysis helps to shed light on his worldview and on the role that Ellison's Muslim identity played in this election. Political opponents did try to use Islam as a wedge issue, but to little avail, largely because Ellison demonstrated his commitment to core American values. Despite Ellison's ability to rise above anti-Muslim attacks, though, he is still identified largely by his religion.

We use a variety of methods to illumine our points. We use secondary source and interview data in the historical analysis. We also conduct content analysis of national and international newspaper articles. By examining the tenor of media coverage of Ellison's election and its immediate aftermath, we can chronologically chart the salience of racial and religious discourse in this campaign. Additionally, a deep examination of the campaign media frames can show us how voters may have been primed to frame Ellison, whether as a Muslim, a Black or a Black Muslim (see Kinder and Iyengar 1981).

Data

Keith Ellison was born August 4, 1963, in Detroit, Michigan. Ellison's parents, a social worker and a psychiatrist, raised Ellison and his four brothers Catholic. Ellison graduated from Wayne State University and moved to Minnesota to attend law school at the University of Minnesota Law School ("Official Biography" 2008).

It was during college that Ellison decided to convert from Catholicism to Islam. As Ellison explained it, he felt no connection to Catholicism as a young man. And like many African-American Muslims, Ellison was drawn to Islam because of his frustration with systemic racism. When Ellison told us that he was drawn to Islam because he had read Malcolm X, we asked if his conversion had any relation to his identity as a Black person. He responded that it did at the time of his conversion, though he has grown in his faith since then. He said:

> I would say today what sustains me as a Muslim is a spiritual connection with the Divine; it has nothing to do with race, color or even politics, but my introduction to Islam was highly politicized. Because I bought into the ideal that your relationship with the universe, the divine, with God was really important, and so [how] could you be fed and nurtured if what you

are being told [is] that God's White, you're not, you're not? And so I was influenced by those kind of arguments and so, but today I have a much more reflective look on it. (Ellison 2008)

After law school, Ellison practiced in a corporate law firm. He eventually grew tired of that and left to pursue a career in public interest law. As a community organizer, he worked with groups that were advocating on behalf of environmental justice, women's rights, criminal justice, and fair wages (Ellison 2008).

Ellison made his first attempt at public office in 1998, when he ran for Minnesota state representative. He lost that year, but he won a seat in 2002. According to Ellison, his religion was never a factor in his state legislative campaigns, and he made an effort to reach out to all the voters in his district, regardless of their race, ethnicity, or religion (Ellison 2008).

Ellison announced his congressional bid in March 2006. He would be running to fill the seat being vacated by Martin Sabo, a fourteen-term incumbent. Minnesota's Fifth Congressional District is reliably Democratic and extremely diverse for Minnesota: According to the U.S. Census Bureau's 2005–2007 American Community Survey, approximately 28 percent of the district's residents are racial or ethnic minorities: 14 percent of the district is Black; 5 percent is Asian American; 8 percent is Latino; and 14 percent are immigrants, including one of the largest Somali Muslim populations in the United States (U.S. Census Bureau 2005–2007; Smith and Olson 2006; Stachura 2006).

Given the diversity of the district and Ellison's own ideological commitments, Ellison ran on a traditionally liberal platform. His primary issues were peace, working class prosperity, environmental sustainability, and civil and human rights. His strategy seemed to work; Ellison beat out twelve other competitors for the Democratic Farmer Labor Party (DFL)—Minnesota's Democratic Party—nomination (Ellison 2008).

Ellison's primary victory was not easy. He was able to leverage his relationships in the Black and Muslim communities to develop a broad base of support. Muslims of all races in the district rallied around his candidacy. Additionally, Ellison garnered support within the Black community. Though some Black clergy opposed Ellison because of his support for gay rights, he was able to leverage his relationships with other Black clergy because, a decade earlier, Ellison had worked with Black clergy to organize the Minneapolis delegation to the Million Man March; and as a state representative, he had continued to build relationships within the African-American community (Ellison 2008).

However, Ellison's faith did garner him negative attention during the election season. Ironically, the people in the district concerned about Ellison's faith were not concerned about whether he had ties to Middle Eastern terrorists. Instead, the attention focused on Ellison's ties to the Nation of Islam and whether he was an anti-Semite. The Republican congressional nominee, Alan Fine, led the attack against Ellison. Soon after Ellison got the DFL nomination, Fine released information stating that Ellison had been member of the Nation of Islam and was a strong supporter of Louis Farrakhan, whom many condemn as an anti-

Semite (see Anti-Defamation League 2001). Fine noted that Ellison had written several articles in the law school newspaper that supported Farrakhan. Fine also accused Ellison of being anti-Semitic because of his support of former Minneapolis Initiative Against Racism (MIAR) executive director, Joanne Jackson, who had accused Jews of being the most racist White people (Johnson 2006). Based on his line of attack, it would seem that Fine's strategy involved undercutting Ellison's support among liberal Jewish voters.

After those allegations surfaced, Ellison wrote a letter to the director of the Jewish Community Relations Council of Minnesota to set the record straight. In the letter Ellison denounced Farrakhan and the Nation of Islam, and explained that he was briefly involved with the organization in 1995 to help organize delegates to the Million Man March. He explained that he felt that the march promoted good values in the African-American community. In the letter Ellison says: "I did not adequately scrutinize the positions and statements of the Nation of Islam, Louis Farrakhan and Khalid Muhammed" (Ellison quoted in Jewish Telegraphic Agency Staff 2006). Ellison continued, "I saw the Nation of Islam, and specifically the Million Man March, [as] an effort to promote African American self-sufficiency, personal responsibility and community economic development." In a telephone interview, Ellison explained himself by stating, "Young people get into things at certain times in their lives that they think will be helpful to their community" (Ellison, quoted in Jewish Telegraphic Agency Staff 2006).

Soon after penning that letter, Ellison received the endorsement of *American Jewish World*, a Minnesota based newsweekly ("Choices…" 2006).

While Ellison's candidacy raised the specter of anti-Semitism on the local level, national observers did use Ellison's faith to try to imply that he might not be tough on terrorism. Ellison was particularly targeted by anti-Muslim bias after his campaign received money from members of the Council of American-Islamic Relations (CAIR), a Muslim civil rights group, which some conservatives claim has links to the terrorist group Hamas (Johnson 2006). And in an interview just after Ellison's election, then-CNN talk show host Glenn Beck questioned Ellison's loyalty to the United States. Beck pointedly asked Ellison, "Sir, prove to me that you are not working with our enemies" (Beck 2006).

Ellison eventually won the general election with 56 percent of the district's vote in a three-way race (Minnesota Secretary of State 2006). However, even after that victory, more religious controversy erupted. When Ellison announced that he would be sworn in using a copy of the Qur'an previously owned by Thomas Jefferson, it set off a firestorm of criticism. There were two notable critics in this debate. Conservative columnist Dennis Prager suggested that it was treacherous for any politician, much less Ellison, to take the oath of office on anything other than a Bible. In his view, all elected officials, regardless of religion, should take the oath on a Bible to honor America's Judeo-Christian heritage (Prager 2006).[4] Most notably, then-Virginia Congressman Virgil Goode, whose district included Thomas Jefferson's home, Monticello, used Ellison's decision to defend his anti-immigration policy stance. In a letter to constituents that was leaked to the press, he wrote:

The Muslim Representative from Minnesota was elected by the voters of that district and if American citizens don't wake up and adopt the Virgil Goode position on immigration there will likely be many more Muslims elected to office and demanding the use of the Koran…. I fear that in the next century we will have many more Muslims in the United States if we do not adopt the strict immigration policies that I believe are necessary to preserve the values and beliefs traditional to the United States of America. ("Original Text…" n.d.)

The situations described above show that Ellison's religious identity was a constant issue during his general election campaign and shortly thereafter. Ellison's racial identity, on the other hand, seemed to go virtually unnoticed unless critics exposed his ties to the Nation of Islam.

How important were the racial and religious angles to the media coverage of Ellison's campaign. To answer this question, we conducted a content analysis of local, national, and international newspaper articles to see how often journalists mentioned Ellison's religion or his race. We believe that this is important for a number of reasons. When journalists choose to emphasize one or more aspects of a person's background, they are creating a media frame or archetype which influences how readers view the person (Hershey 2001). This frame betrays the reasons why the journalist contends that this subject is newsworthy. If reporters discuss Ellison's race more than they do his religion (or vice versa), then that will either prime voters to think about one aspect of Ellison's identity (Kinder and Iyengar 1981), or reflect in general how the news consuming public already views him.

Using Lexus Nexus Academic Universe, we found 514 unique[5] articles published about Keith Ellison from September 13, 2006 (the day after Ellison's primary win) to January 11, 2007 (the week after he was sworn in as a Member of Congress). One quarter of the articles (129) were published in the local press (i.e., *St. Paul Pioneer Press* or the *Minneapolis Star Tribune*). Most of the articles (335, or about 65 percent) in the database come from national periodicals; and 55 articles (11 percent) appeared in the international press. By collecting articles into mid-January 2007, we could analyze both general election campaign coverage and gather information on the coverage of Ellison's decision to use a Qur'an for his swearing in ceremony. Of particular interest was whether news articles mentioned Ellison's religion or race and which identity was mentioned first. By drawing attention to either Ellison's race or religion first, journalists are priming voters to think about these characteristics (see Kinder and Iyengar 1981).

For this analysis, we coded each article to determine whether or not the text mentioned Ellison's faith, race, whether the article mentioned faith or race first, his association with the Nation of Islam, and the Qur'an controversy. To ensure accurate coding, one author coded the entire database, while an outside coder coded a random sample of 55 articles, or a little more than 10 percent of the articles in the database. Overall, we agreed 86 percent of the time. More than 80 percent of the disagreements related to easily discernible coding disagreements

Table 12.1 Discussion of Keith Ellison's Race and Religion, by News Source

	Local News	*National News*	*International News*	*Total*
Headline Mentions Ellison's Faith	9 (7%)	136 (41%)	20 (36%)	164 (32%)
Headline Mentions Ellison's Race	3 (2%)	6 (2%)	4% (2)	11 (2%)
Article Text Mentions Ellison's Faith	55 (43%)	314 (94%)	54 (98%)	421 (82%)
Article Text Mentions Ellison's Race	25 (19%)	68 (20%)	17 (31%)	110 (21%)
Article Text Mentions Both Ellison's Race and Religion	20 (16%)	66 (20%)	17 (31%)	103 (20%)
Article Text Mentions the Nation of Islam	14 (11%)	37 (11%)	15 (27%)	66 (13%)
Total	129	335	55	514

Source: Authors' compilation. Percentages shown are column percentages. Column percentages are in parentheses.

that were easily resolved. If we do not count those resolvable coding disagreements as errors, our agreement rate jumps to 98 percent.

Table 12.1 presents the basic findings. Not every article mentioning Keith Ellison made reference to his religion, but most of them did. Nearly 82 percent of the articles in our dataset referenced Ellison's Islamic faith somewhere in the text. Thirty-six percent of the articles attempted to prime readers right at the outset by noting Ellison's religion in the headline. The national and international press coverage in particular focused an overwhelming amount of attention on Ellison's faith. All but one of the international articles mentioned that Ellison was a Muslim, as did 94 percent of the national media coverage. In contrast, only 43 percent of the local articles mentioned Ellison's faith.

In contrast, Ellison's racial heritage received paltry coverage. Only 2 percent of the headlines mentioned race, and only one in five articles (21 percent) referenced Ellison's race in the text of the article. Of the 110 articles which mentioned Ellison's race, 103 articles also talked about Ellison's religion. Clearly, journalists focused far more attention on Ellison's faith than they did on his race.

We also coded the articles to see how often media coverage focused on Ellison's prior association with the Nation of Islam. We coded this category separately from whether the article mentioned race or religion; that is, articles could mention the Nation of Islam connection and not note that Ellison was Black or Muslim. Given the Nation's nationalist history, it is very doubtful that there would be White adherents; however, we cannot assume that readers are familiar with the Nation of Islam. Moreover, especially within the context of the Million Man March, which drew Black men of all religions to Washington in 1995, it could be possible for Ellison to support the Nation of Islam without actually being Muslim. For these reasons, we decided to code mentions of the Nation of Islam as a discrete category.

Overall, journalists paid very little attention to Ellison's association with the Nation of Islam. Only 13 percent of the articles mentioned anything about the Nation of Islam, whether they were discussing Alan Fine's accusations that Ellison was still a member of the group and thus guilty of anti-Semitism by association or whether they were discussing Ellison's involvement in the Million Man March. The international press spent more time on this issue than any of the American press. While only 11 percent of the local and national press articles devoted attention to the Nation of Islam, more than a quarter of the international news articles mentioned the Nation of Islam.

It should not be surprising that national and international media outlets took such a keen interest in Ellison's religion. Only a handful of congressional races get national attention in any given election cycle. In order to justify writing such a story, journalists have to convince their editors of the newsworthiness of a story. As such, a local story must have national or global implications or must have a compelling narrative that will be of interest to readers throughout an election season. In the aftermath of September 11, a Muslim candidate with a serious chance of winning easily makes for gripping copy.

Given journalists' interests in creating writing compelling stories, we contend that journalists made deliberate choices in how they presented Keith Ellison. Given the War on Terror and the fear and fascination with Islam, it would not be surprising that newspapers presented Ellison as a Muslim candidate. And although Ellison is African American, we would expect that the media coverage would focus more on Ellison's religion than his race. Despite the fact that Ellison was poised to become Minnesota's first Black Congressman, journalists could determine that his being the first Muslim Congressman in American history was more newsworthy. With this in mind, we delved deeper into the dataset to see if articles mentioning Ellison's race and religion mentioned his race first or his religion first.

The order of mention is important for a number of reasons. One could easily infer from the order which identity the author of an article perceived to be more salient. It makes sense to frontload important information to capture readers' interest in an article. When some fact is presented toward the end of an article, it could evince that it is an afterthought.

We present our basic findings in Table 12.2 below. There were 103 articles that mentioned both Ellison's race and his religion. Of those articles, 63 percent of the articles mentioned Ellison's faith first. Local articles were less likely to do this. The articles that mentioned both Ellison's race and religion were almost evenly split in their tendency to mention race or religion first. However, the national and international coverage clearly privileged Ellison's religious background over his racial heritage. Sixty-five percent of the national coverage mentioned Ellison's religion first, as did 77 percent of the international coverage.

We wanted to see if there might be a relationship between coverage of both Ellison's race and religion and discussions of his association with the Nation of

Table 12.2 Discussion of Keith Ellison's Race and Religion, by News Source (Articles That Mention both Race and Religion Only)

	Local News	*National News*	*International News*	*Total*
Article Text Mentions Ellison's Faith First	9 (45%)	43 (65%)	13 (77%)	65 (63%)
Article Text Mentions Ellison's Race First	11 (55%)	23 (35%)	4 (23%)	38 (37%)
Article Text Mentions the Nation of Islam	5 (25%)	23 (35%)	9 (53%)	37 (36%)
Total	20	66	17	103

Source: Authors' compilation. Percentages shown are column percentages. Column percentages are in parentheses.

Islam. Alan Fine was very deliberate in levying this attack against Ellison. He tried to paint Ellison as an extremist and an anti-Semite, in the hopes of winning usually Democratic, Jewish voters (Fine himself is Jewish, and presumably, he hoped to appeal to religious solidarity) (Olson and Smith 2006). In doing this, Fine points out the relevance of intersectionality. Ellison, as an African American, may not be easily pegged as a jihadist sympathizer; but if he can be linked to the Nation of Islam, he may be able to be perceived as a religious bigot. The strategy, while risky, showed how Ellison's multiple identities could potentially be used against him.

One-quarter (25 percent) of the local articles discussed the Nation of Islam. Approximately one-third (35 percent) of the national articles and more than one-half (53 percent) of the international articles mentioned the Nation of Islam. Overall, thirty-seven of the sixty-six articles mentioning the Nation of Islam noted that Ellison was both Black and Muslim. Of these thirty-seven articles, only ten mentioned race first. Incidentally, all but five articles in the full dataset (61 of 66 articles) that mentioned the Nation of Islam also noted that Ellison was Muslim.

So far, we have seen that the media coverage focused more on Keith Ellison's religious background than they did his race. It is important to consider whether exogenous events had any impact at all on how journalists covered Ellison during this race. It is plausible that in the immediate aftermath of Ellison's election, much of the attention may focus on the novelty of having elected a Muslim congressman. Additionally, the controversy surrounding Ellison's decision to be sworn in on a Qur'an rather than a Bible, particularly Dennis Prager and Virgil Goode's reaction, could also correlate with an increased attention to Ellison's religion rather than his race.

To answer these questions, we divided the dataset into four time periods. We looked at the general election campaign period (September 13–November 8); the immediate postelection period, before Dennis Prager posted his critical editorial (November 9–November 29); the fallout period after the Prager editorial until

Table 12.3 Themes of Keith Ellison Media Coverage over Time

	General Election (9/13/06- 11/8/06)	Post-Election to Prager Blog Post (11/9/06- 11/29/06)	Post-Prager to Swearing-In Ceremony (11/30/06/06- 1/5/07)	Post-Swearing In (1/6/07- 1/11/07)
Article Text Mentions Ellison's Faith	100 (67%)	73 (75%)	205 (94%)	6 (12%)
Article Text Mentions Ellison's Race	43 (29%)	36 (37%)	24 (11%)	7 (14%)
Article Text Mentions Nation of Islam	46 (31%)	10 (10%)	8 (4%)	2 (4%)
Article Text Mentions Oath Controversy	3 (2%)	3 (3%)	190 (87%)	37 (76%)
Total	150	97	218	49

Source: Authors' compilation. Percentages shown are column percentages. Column percentages are in parentheses.

the House swearing-in ceremony (November 30–January 5), and the week after Ellison was sworn in (January 6–January 11).[6]

The bivariate time series relationships are listed above in Table 12.3. Here, we see some interesting findings. First, the discussion of the Nation of Islam largely takes place during the general election season. This is to be expected, as Alan Fine made Ellison's association with the group a campaign issue. After the election, that alleged relationship was no longer as newsworthy. In the immediate postelection period, we see an increasing number of articles mentioning both Ellison's race and religion. Usually, these articles noted the historic nature of Ellison's being the first Muslim and Minnesota's first Black congressman. After the Prager and Goode controversies arose (November 28 and December 5 respectively; Prager 2006; Swarns 2006), we see a significant spike in the number of articles mentioning Ellison's plan to take his oath of office on the Qur'an. While only six articles talk about Ellison's plan to take his oath of office on the Qur'an before November 29, more than 200 articles mention the oath after Dennis Prager went public with his objections. This correlates with increased attention to Ellison's religion (94 percent of the articles published between November 30 and January 5 mention Ellison's religion). However, fewer articles mention Ellison's race after November 29. When they do mention race, it is often to correct the impression that Ellison is an immigrant, in response to Virgil Goode's attempt to tie Ellison's oath-taking to concerns about immigration. For example, when Salt Lake City's *Deseret Morning News* wrote an editorial in support of Ellison, they said, "So we're clear here, Ellison isn't an immigrant. He's an African American who can trace his American ancestors to 1742" ("U.S. Religious Diversity a

Boon" 2006). Thus, the editorial staff used Ellison's race to demonstrate that he was just as American as any other member of Congress.

Analysis/Conclusion

Representative Ellison himself is somewhat dismissive of the idea that his race made him a less threatening Muslim candidate (Ellison 2008). Given the diversity of his district, he has a point; his faith was not an issue to many of his constituents. But Ellison's faith is important to outside observers. Sometimes, race could be a help or a hindrance to that media frame. Over the course and in the immediate aftermath of Ellison's campaign, Ellison's religious identity collided with his racial identity or other exogenous factors to renew interest in him as a newsworthy figure. During his campaign, Ellison's opponent tried to stoke both racial and religious anxiety to leverage opposition to Ellison's candidacy. After the election, when national actors tried to make Ellison's religious identity an issue, defenders used Ellison's racial background to try to blunt the attack. In both instances, we see that Ellison faced different challenges to his candidacy on account of his religion and his race than candidates who were merely black or merely Muslim would face.

In the future, there will be more opportunities to study the intersection of Muslim identity with other relevant political identities. As more White, Arab, and South Asian-American Muslims choose to run for political office, we can expect to have more opportunities to study their campaigns in comparative relief with empirical rigor. Additionally, the rise of prominent Muslim female candidates should provide additional opportunities to study other types of intersectionality, particularly the intersection of religion, gender, and race.

As more and more African-American candidates run for and win political office, we can expect even greater diversity among Black elected officials who win. With this greater diversity comes the recognition that these officials will face different challenges when they run for office. Additionally, these officials may not be identified as primarily African-American leaders. This does not mean that these officials will not be sensitive to the policy concerns of most African Americans. However, we can expect that these politicians will be on the vanguard of expanding the African-American policy agenda to include issues that affect subgroups that heretofore have been ignored in public discourse.

Notes

1. The authors would like to thank Nicole Baerg for her coding assistance.
2. According to Wallace Fard Muhammad, a scientist named Dr. Yakub embarked upon a failed scientific experiment in which he accidentally created a White devil, the ancestor of Caucasian people (Muhammad 1985, 413).
3. Clegg notes that Elijah Muhammad conceded that political participation might be acceptable if Nation members were using the franchise to elect pro-civil rights officials. Louis Farrakhan used this sentiment to justify entering the political arena in the 1980s (Clegg 2002, 104).

4. It is important to note that when members of Congress officially take the oath of office, they take the oath en masse and swear on nothing. Members are free to bring sacred texts with them to a reenactment ceremony in front of cameras and with family (Turley 2007).
5. It was very clear that many articles relied heavily on wire sources for their articles. We deleted identical articles that appeared multiple times in different newspapers. We also eliminated articles that were simply redacted versions of longer wire stories. There are some instances where journalists at one outlet clearly relied on assistance from another source. If the second article included significant new details, then we counted it as a unique article.
6. Time periods end the day after critical events, to accommodate next-day coverage of events like the election.

References

Anti-Defamation League. 2001. 2000 Audit of Ant-Semitic Incidents. Retrieved from http://www.adl/2000audit/2000audit.pdf (accessed October 5, 2009).

Bareto, Matt A., Natalie Matsuoka, and Gabriel R. Sanchez. 2008. Religiosity, discrimination and group identity among Muslim Americans. Paper presented at the annual meeting of the American Political Science Association, Boston.

Beck, Glenn. 2006. *Glen Beck* [Television series transcript]. CNN Headline News Prime. Originally aired 14 November 14. http://transcripts.cnn.com/TRANSCRIPTS/0611/14/gb.01.html (accessed December 18, 2008).

Braman, Eileen, and Abdulkader Sinno. 2006. Can a Muslim represent you? An experimental investigation of causal attributions for the political behavior of Muslim candidates. Paper presented at the annual meeting of the American Political Science Association, Philadelphia.

———. 2006. Choices in the DFL fifth district primary. *American Jewish World,* September 1, 4.

Clegg, Claude III. 2002. You're not ready for Farrakhan: The Nation of Islam and the struggle for Black political leadership. In *Black political organizations in the post-civil rights era*, ed. Ollie Johnson and Karin Stanford, 99–131. New Brunswick, NJ: Rutgers University Press.

Cohen, Cathy. 1999. *The boundaries of Blackness*. Chicago: University of Chicago Press.

Crenshaw, Kimberlé Williams. 1995. Mapping the margins: Intersectionality, identity politics and violence against women of color. In *Critical race theory: The key writings that informed the movement*, ed. Kimberlé Crenshaw, Neil Gotanda, Gary Peller, and Kendall Thomas, 357–83. New York: New Press.

Dawson, Michael. 1994. *Behind the mule*. Princeton, NJ: Princeton University Press.

Elliottt, Andrea. 2006. Muslim immigration has bounced back. *The Seattle Times*. September 10.

———. 2007. Between Black and immigrant Muslims, an uneasy alliance. *The New York Times,* March 11. http://www.nytimes.com/2007/03/11/nyregion/11muslim.html?_r=1&pagewanted=all (accessed December 18, 2008).

Ellison, Keith. 2008. Personal interview. March 7.

Fischer, Miles Mark. 1985. Organized religion and the cults. In *Afro-American religious history: A documentary witness*, ed. Milton C. Sernett, 390–98. Durham, NC: Duke University Press.

Ghazali, Abdus Sattar. 2006. American Muslims in 2006 election. *American Muslim Perspective,* November 10. http://ampolitics.ghazali.net/html/mulslims_in_2006_election.html (accessed December 18, 2008).

Hershey, Marjorie Randon. 2001. The campaign and the media. In *The election of 2000*, ed. Gerald M. Pomper, 46–72. New York: Chatham House.

Jewish Telegraphic Agency Staff. 2006. Confronting the past. Jewish Telegraphic Agency, June 7. http://jta.org/news/article/2006/06/07/14089/muslimcandidatefor (accessed Oct. 5, 2009).

Johnson, Scott W. 2006. Louis Farrakhan's first Congressman. *The Weekly Standard* 12 (4).

Kinder, Donald, and Shanto Iyengar. 1981. *News that matters.* New Haven, CT: Yale University Press.

Lincoln, C. Eric. 1994. *The Black Muslims in America.* 3rd ed. Grand Rapids, MI: Africa World Press.

Lorde, Audre. 2007. Age, race, class and sex: Women redefining difference. In *Race, class and gender: An anthology* (6th ed.), ed. Margaret L. Andersen and Patricia Hill Collins, 52–59. Belmont, CA: Thomson Higher Education.

Marsh, Clifton E. 1984. *From Black Muslims to Muslims: The transition from separatism to Islam, 1930–1980.* Metuchen, NJ: Scarecrow Press.

Marx, Claude R. 2006. Arabs, Muslims emerge in politics. Arab-American Institute Webpage, Press Room: AAI in the News Section, November 6. http://www.aaiusa.org/press-room/2579/aainews110606b (accessed December 18, 2008).

Minnesota Secretary of State. 2006. Official Election Results: November 7, 2006 Election.http://electionresults.sos.state.mn.us/20061107/ElecRslts.asp?M=CG&R=ALL&PN=0000 (accessed December 16 2008).

Muhammad, Wallace D. 1985. Self-government in the new world. In *Afro-American religious history: A documentary witness*, ed. Milton C. Sernett, 413–20. Durham, NC: Duke University Press.

Nisbet, Erik C., and James Shanahan. 2004a. *MSRG special report: U.S. war on terror, U.S. foreign policy, and anti-Americanism.* [Report]. Ithaca, NY: The Media Research and Society Group, Cornell University. December.

———. 2004b. *MSRG special report: Restrictions on civil liberties, views of Islam and Muslim America* [Report]. Ithaca, NY: The Media Research and Society Group, Cornell University. December.

Official biography. 2008. Keith Ellison Congressional Web site. http://ellison.house.gov/index.php?option=com_content&task=view&id=21&Itemid=54 (accessed December 16, 2008).

Olson, Rochelle, and Dane Smith. 2006. Few turned out, now many tuning in. *Star Tribune*, September 14, A1.

Original text of Rep. Goode's letter to constituents. 2008. December 15. http://abcnews.go.com/print?id=2743475.

Polakow-Suransky, Sasha. 2001. Racist profiling goes by Black and White. Arab-American Institute Press Room. October 30. http://www.aaiusa.org/press-room/1782/mustread103001 (accessed October 5, 2009).

Prager, Dennis. 2006. America, not Keith Ellison, decides what book a congressman takes his oath on. Townhall.com. November 28. http://townhall.com/columnists/DennisPrager/2006/11/28/america,_not_keith_ellison,_decides_what_book_a_congressman_takes_his_oath_on (accessed May 18, 2009).

Reynoso, Julissa. 2004. Perspectives on intersections of race, ethnicity, gender and other grounds: Latinas at the margins. *Harvard Latino Law Review* 7 (Spring 2004): 63–73.

Smith, Dane, and Rochelle Olson. 2006. Ellison's kickoff part of crowded fifth scene. *Minneapolis Star Tribune,* March 21, 5B.

Stachura, Sea (Correspondent). 2006. More Somalis in Minnesota turn to Islam. NPR *All Things Considered* [Radio]. July 9.

Swarns, Rachel. Congressman criticizes election of Muslim. *The New York Times,* December 21, A31.

Turley, Jonathan. 2007. The truth about oaths. *USA Today,* January 4, A9.

———. 2006. U.S. religious diversity a boon. *Deseret Morning News,* December 29.

U.S. Census Bureau. 2007. Minnesota Congressional District 5 factsheet. http://fastfacts.census.gov/servlet/ACSCWSFacts?_event=&geo_id=50000US2705&_geoContext=01000US|04000US27|50000US2705&_street=&_county=&_cd=50000US2705&_cityTown=&_state=04000US27&_zip=&_lang=en&_sse=on&ActiveGeoDiv=&_useEV=&pctxt=fph&pgsl=500&_content=&_keyword=&_industry=   (accessed December 16, 2008).

U.S. Religious Diversity a Boon. 2006 *Deseret Morning News,* December, 29. http://www.lexis-nexis.com (accessed December 18, 2008).

Vohra, Smriti. 1996. Al-Islam and African Americans. Part I. *Precinct Reporter,* A6.

Walton, Hanes, and Robert Smith. 2006. *American politics and the African American quest for universal freedom.* New York: Pearson Longman.

13 Young, Gifted, Black, and Female

Why Aren't There More Yvette Clarkes in Congress?

Katrina Gamble

From Harriet Tubman and Sojourner Truth to Ella Baker and Daisy Bates to Shirley Chisholm, African-American women have always played a key role in the Black civil rights struggle, even if their efforts were not acknowledged. While Black women have had to deal with being discriminated against on account of their race and their gender, they have found a way to make their voices heard in both Black and White patriarchal societies.

In her 2003 book *Black Faces in the Mirror*, Katherine Tate noted that while Black women were still underrepresented relative to Black men in the House of Representatives, there were proportionately more Black women in the 106th Congress than White women.

Given the recent track record of Black women in Congress, it would be logical to assume that younger Black women would have seamlessly continued the trend of having higher than average representation among the ranks of prominent Third Wave Black politicians. The reality is more complex, though.

The first Third Wave Black politician to win office at the large city or federal level was Cleo Fields, who won election to Congress from Louisiana in 1992. He was soon followed by Jesse Jackson Jr. in 1995 and Harold Ford Jr. in 1996. A young woman would not join these rarefied ranks until 2006, when Yvette Clarke won her bid to replace Brooklyn Congressman Major Owens in Congress. Why did it take nearly a decade and a half for young, Black women to be elected as a big city mayor, member of Congress, or governor? In this chapter, Katrina Gamble examines the factors that have delayed young women's entry into the elected leadership pipeline.

Individuals have multiple and crosscutting identities, and in many ways these identities shape and inform how one views the world and how one is perceived by society. Some suggest that Black women have a double disadvantage in politics because they must overcome both racialized barriers and gender bias in the political arena (Githens and Prestage 1977; Darcy and Hadley 1988). Black women not only experience racism and sexism simultaneously, but they have unique experiences found at the cross-section of race, gender, and in many cases, class.

Women of color often encounter different obstacles from those encountered by either White women or Black men. "The junction where race, class, and gender meet and intersect is fraught with political challenges. Residential segregation, familial and community responsibility, health issues, criminal justice, and welfare are some issues that take on new meaning from this junction" (Simpson 2007, 152). Whether Black women choose to participate in politics or how they choose to participate politically is influenced, in part, by the intersection of their multiple identities.

In this chapter I use an intersectional framework to examine how factors found to impact racial minorities and women independently might influence the political behavior and campaigns of Black women. Black women of all ages remain underrepresented within American political institutions. Black women make up 2 percent of U.S. congressional members and 3.1 percent of state legislators (CAWP 2009). In 2009, there were only three Black women mayors in the 100 largest U.S. cities and three Black women holding state-wide elected office (CAWP 2009). Many scholars have examined race and gender as potential barriers to elected office, but few have explored how race and gender intersect to affect the political prospects of women of color.

Scholars within this volume have noted the various ways in which a new Black leadership is developing within the American political landscape, but Black women are strangely absent from most discussions about the emerging post-Civil Rights leadership. Why do we not see the same trends among young Black women running for higher office that exist among young Black men? While Black women often confront multiple oppressions and systematic discrimination, they have also always resisted those oppressions (King 1995, 294). Black women have always struggled against subordination and marginalization; and in fact, scholars find that Black women are often more politically engaged than Black men (Cole and Stewart 1996; Tate 1993). For example, Black women accounted for 59 percent of the Black vote and 6.5 percent of the overall vote in the 2004 presidential election (CAWP 2008). Furthermore, at the local level, the number of Black female elected officials is growing at a faster rate than the number of Black male elected officials. Wendy Smooth finds that "since 1990, African-American women have outpaced African-American men in elective office and over the last decade, all of the growth in the number of Black elected officials is attributable to these women" (2006a, 401). When the number of women elected to state legislatures began to plateau in the mid-1990s, the number of Black women elected to state legislatures continued to grow at a steady pace (Sanbonmatsu 2006a; Smooth 2006a). Given Black women's continuous success at the local level and their demonstrated political engagement, what might explain their virtual invisibility in higher political office? I argue, in this chapter, that systemic and structural factors that occur at the intersection of race and gender identity constrain Black female politicians and present particular challenges for Black women's ability to climb the political ladder. I analyze socioeconomic factors, political ambition, and political structures to understand how race and gender influence both candidate emergence and candidate success.

Candidate Emergence

Before analyzing how the intersection of race and gender influences candidate emergence among Black women, it is important to understand what factors affect candidates' decisions generally and what factors are known to mitigate candidate emergence among all women. Candidate emergence is the decision of an individual to run for elective office.

Informal criteria such as education, income, wealth, and occupation are often used to create an "eligibility pool" from which political candidates are recruited and emerge (Darcy, Welch, and Clark 1994, 105). Political candidates tend to have high levels of education and income and are disproportionately from the legal and business fields. Lawyers and businesspeople are not only more likely to have the financial resources to launch a political campaign, but their occupations often provide them with access to valuable political networks (Herrnson 1997).

A quick review of demographic factors reveals that members of the U.S. Congress are a part of the socioeconomic elite. In the 109th Congress, more than 40 percent of members listed their previous occupation as law, 36 percent listed public service or politics, and 36 percent listed business.[1] More than 74 percent of congressional members hold bachelor's degrees and more than 60 percent have graduate degrees. According to opensecrets.org, the average wealth of a House member in 2007 was $684,000; for senators it was $1.7 million. In both education and wealth, congressional representatives are well above the U.S. averages, making it easier for these people to run for elective office (opensecrets.org).

The eligibility pool theory argues that sexual discrimination which limits women's educational and occupational opportunities may also constrain women's political options. Women's historic absence from legal and business fields means they are not part of the groups from which people are typically recruited to serve as elected officials. Furthermore, lawyers and business people also often have the income and wealth to make a political bid without serious financial strain (Darcy, Welch, and Clark 1994). Scholars argue that the expansion of educational and career options for women should translate into more women running for political office, and the increasing similarity between women and men's political background lends credence to the eligibility pool theory. Recent scholarship finds that women elected officials are as educated as their male counterparts. Additionally more women candidates are coming from the legal, political, or business fields. While more women are entering politics from the legal field, they are still more likely than men to be educators before entering Congress (Burrell 1994; Darcy, Welch, and Clark 1994; Gertzog 2002; Fox and Lawless 2004; Ondercin and Welch 2005).

Other factors that influence women's decision to enter politics relate to recruitment and familial obligations. Female congressional candidates and winners are, on average, three years older than their male counterparts (Burrell 1994; Ondercin and Welch 2005). Even with their increased presence in the labor market, women remain responsible for the majority of household work and childcare (Robinson and Goodbey 1999). Women often delay entrance into politics because of familial obligations. It is not unusual for women to wait until their children are older before deciding to seek elective office, especially higher office or national positions that require substantial time away from the home. Younger female candidates are more likely to not have children. Eighty percent of female House members were mothers before entering the institution, but only 50 percent of those under 45 years old had children before entering Congress. The lack of young Black women in Congress may be explained, in part, by familial constraints that affect all women.

Political recruitment and encouragement also play a major role in who runs for higher office. Herrnson (1997) writes, "the drive to hold elective office may be rooted in an individual's personality and tempered by the larger political environment, but potential candidates rarely reach a decision about running for Congress without touching base with a variety of people" (192). Individuals' families and friends often have a significant influence on whether they choose to run, as well as political parties, labor unions, PACs, and other organizations. Political parties and other political organizations offer valuable advice, contacts, and resources to help potential candidates get a campaign off the ground (Herrnson 1997). In fact, scholars find that an individual is much more likely to consider running when she or he receives external encouragement (Fox and Lawless 2004). Prior to 1980, women were rarely recruited to run for elective office, and in some cases, they were discouraged from entering politics (Githens 2003, 34–35). However, recent studies show that women receive as much encouragement as men from political leaders and other organizations at the local level (Welch and Bledose 1988; Burrell 1994; Herrick 1995; Thomas, Herrick, and Braunstein 2002).[2] Given the significance of political ambition and recruitment on candidate emergence, it is important to understand how race and gender may inform political ambition and the political recruitment of young Black women.

Finally, opportunity costs also drive an individual's decision to run for office. Strategic politicians are rational actors who will carefully weigh the costs and benefits of launching a campaign and are likely to only enter a race if there is a strong likelihood of success or if it will enhance a future political bid (Gertzog 2002; Herrnson 1997). Women are just as likely as men to be strategic politicians—weighing both strategic and personal factors to determine whether to run (Gertzog 2002, 104). High reelection rates among congressional incumbents make it particularly difficult to increase women's representation within legislative institutions. Over the past two decades, more than 90 percent of incumbents have been reelected and studies have found that incumbents have a 7 to 10 percent vote share advantage in elections (Levitt and Wolfram 1997, 45; Ansolabehere, Snyder, and Stewart 2000, 17). The resources and time necessary to defeat an incumbent are quite high, and therefore, strategic politicians are more likely to wait for an open seat to run for office. Limited open seats and the power of the incumbency advantage make it difficult for previously marginalized groups such as women and minorities to increase their numbers inside legislative institutions.

Black Women and Candidate Emergence: The Road Less Traveled

The portrait of African-American women members of Congress is quite different from that of the typical politician. The educational and occupational background of Black congresswomen varies widely. For example, neither Cardiss Collins (D-IL) nor Julia Carson (D-IL) had bachelor's degrees before entering Congress, whereas Diane Watson (D-CA) had a doctorate. Approximately two-thirds of African-American women were widowed, divorced, or single when they entered Congress, a much higher percentage than the institution overall. When compared to White female legislators, Black women representatives are also more likely to be single mothers (Tate 2003, 46–47). The twenty-five Black women who have served in Congress, from the nurse to the social worker, demonstrate that there are many routes to elective office. However, some paths to the U.S. House of Representatives may be more difficult than others and may affect one's ability to run for higher office, such as senator or governor.

The most visible young Black male politicians considered a part of the new Black leadership share traits that extend beyond their age and race. President Barack Obama, Artur Davis, Harold Ford, Deval Patrick, and Cory Booker all have Ivy League degrees, graduate degrees, and worked either in law, business, or public service prior to their current position. None are or were single parents. In many ways, their backgrounds correspond with those of more traditional politicians. Some of the younger Black women may have similar profiles. Take Congresswoman Yvette Clarke of New York. She is single, has no children, served three terms on the New York City Council, and comes from a political family. The one factor that distinguishes Clarke from the Black men described above is that she does not have a college degree (*National Journal Magazine* 2006). Given her political background and family ties, her career should take a trajectory similar to male representatives in her age cohort, such as Artur Davis and Harold Ford.

Clearly, the informal criteria for political office such as education, occupation, and income have not made it impossible for Black women to become elected officials, but it does mean that fewer Black women fall into the "eligibility pool." The only way to get more Yvette Clarkes in Congress is to have more young Black women run for political office. While Black women have made significant gains in the business and legal arena, they remain underrepresented in these occupational fields and are underpaid generally compared to their White male and female counterparts. While Black women's earnings have been on a steady increase over the last few decades, contributing to the growth of the Black middle class, they still earn considerably less than White women and face additional barriers to professional development. The median annual earnings for Black women working full time was more than $5,000 less than White women in 2007 (U.S. Census Bureau 2008). Disparities in income and wealth between Black women and White women, White men and Black men may make it even more difficult for qualified Black women to run for elected office. On average, the financial costs to run for office may be much higher for even professional Black women.

Black congresswomen's average net worth was less than half that of the average member of Congress. In 2002, the average net worth for Black women in the House was $305,000 compared to $684,000 for the entire House (opensecrets. org n.d.).

Researchers have also found that Black women are promoted at slower rates than both White women and White men (Higginbotham and Weber 1999). In 2000, 29.7 percent of Black women held professional and managerial positions compared to 38.7 percent of White women. Indeed, the data seem to support the impression of Black female professionals that race and gender are barriers to career success. Women held 15.7 percent of corporate office positions in 2002, but women of color only held 1.7 percent of corporate officer positions (Catalyst 2002). If political parties and organizations focus their recruitment on leaders in the business and legal fields, then the "eligibility pool" is likely to have far fewer Black women than White women. Black women's absence from leadership positions in the private sector may also mean that they have smaller professional networks and less financial security from which to build a political campaign. If the eligibility pool theory is true, these socioeconomic indicators would suggest that Black women will have a more difficult time entering the political arena than White women and this difficulty will likely increase with higher elective offices where more resources and time are required to launch a campaign.

Political ambition can be separated into a two-stage process (Fox and Lawless 2004). Most research on political ambition focuses on strategic decisions made by individuals about political opportunities. Individuals are more likely to run for office when structural factors are in their favor. For example, a strategic politician is more likely to run for office if there is an open seat or the constituent demographics are favorable to a win. However, Fox and Lawless argue that prior to such strategic calculations, one must first understand nascent ambition—an inclination to consider political office (2005, 644). A survey of more than 6,000 individuals from professions that tend to lead to political office (law, business, education, and community activism) shows that race and gender both act as mitigating factors for nascent political ambition. Both Blacks and women are less likely to ever consider running for office. Scholars find that "a White male respondent who self-assesses as 'highly qualified' to run for office and 'very likely' to win a race is approximately one-third more likely than a Black woman with the same self-perception to have considered running for office" (Fox and Lawless 2005, 654). Furthermore, individuals with household incomes over $200,000 are more likely than individuals with lower incomes to express interest in high-level positions (Fox and Lawless 2005). Research on nascent political ambition suggests that the intersection of race, gender, and class may severely depress political ambition among Black women. Low political ambition acts as a significant barrier to increasing Black female leadership. If highly qualified young Black women never even consider running for low-level office, then filling higher positions becomes even more difficult.

Women of color are also less likely to have progressive political ambition, a desire to move from one position to a higher office (see Schlesinger 1966, 10). In a groundbreaking survey of non-White elected officials at various levels of government, scholars found that female elected officials of color are less likely to indicate a desire to run for higher office than their male counterparts (Hardy-Fanta et al. 2006). While 20 percent of the men surveyed indicated a strong likelihood to seek higher office, only 12 percent of the women expressed a strong likelihood to run for a higher position. Black women are nearly absent as statewide candidates. In 2008, Black women were nearly 10 percent of the female candidates running for the U.S. House in the general election, yet no Black women were represented among general election candidates for the U.S. Senate or statewide offices. Local positions often serve as a pipeline to higher political office, and the lack of nascent and progressive political ambition among women of color helps, in part, to explain Black women's underrepresentation in higher offices. The number of Black female elected officials is growing at a steady rate—and in many ways outpaces Black men—but much of that growth is occurring at the local level (Smooth 2006a, 2006b). In order to increase Black women's presence at the federal level, it is important to determine how to increase both nascent and progressive political ambition among Black women.

While it is beyond the scope of this chapter to explain the low levels of political ambition among Black women, there are several factors that should be explored in future research. The same factors that politicize Black women to participate in community activism may also mitigate political ambition for formal office. Scholars have found that women of color (both Black and Latina) often become political activists to better the lives of their children and communities. In many cases motherhood serves as a resource for community organizing (Hardy-Fanta 1993; Pardo 1998; Collins 1990; Naples 1992). Women use their networks and friendships with other mothers to disseminate information and organize. Furthermore, some women of color choose not to run for office because they believe they are more effective as community organizers than as elected officials (Pardo 1998, 222). Women of color are often spurred to action to draw attention to issues ignored by mainstream political institutions, so it is not surprising that some women would rather continue their work outside traditional political institutions. Running for the House or Senate not only requires time and resources, it also requires one to spend a significant amount of time away from home. Given such obligations, qualified Black women may be less likely to seek higher office— choosing local positions closer to home or postponing political efforts until their children are older. Challenges faced by mothers will be even more consequential for single mothers. In 2000, single mothers headed more than 50 percent of Black families, compared to approximately 17 percent of White families (Cantave and Harrison 2001).

Once a Black woman considers running for political office, she still encounters obstacles to becoming an actual candidate for Congress. Women of color are just as likely to be strategic politicians as other groups—they make rational calculations about opportunity structures before launching a political campaign. Incumbency has played a major factor in limiting representation among both women and racial minorities. Favorable opportunities for congressional bids are especially limited for racial minorities. While we have seen increased success among Blacks running in majority White constituencies, most Black congresspersons are elected from districts that are ideologically liberal, highly Democratic, with significant urban populations, and with majority-minority populations. During the 109th Congress, 51 percent of the constituents represented by members of the Congressional Black Caucus racial minorities and 17 percent were in poverty (Covington 2005). Young Blacks—both men and women—seeking congressional office must either wait for a seat to open in a majority-minority district, challenge a Black incumbent, or run in a district that is less likely to elect a Black candidate. Politically ambitious Blacks have fewer favorable opportunities to run for Congress.

Newly drawn majority-minority districts in 1992 led to a dramatic jump in the number of Blacks elected to Congress; the U.S, House of Representatives went from having twenty-six Black members to having forty Black members. However, since 1992 the number of Blacks in the U.S. House has only increased by two (and fell by one in the 111th Congress). New Black faces in the House mostly result from the defeat of Black incumbents or by filling a seat opened by the retirement or death of a Black politician. Yvette Clark lost in 2004 when she challenged Black incumbent Major Owens (D-NY), who had served more than twenty years in Congress. When Owens retired, she eventually obtained the seat after winning a very competitive Democratic primary against two other Black candidates and a White candidate. Donna Edwards (D-MD), another young Black congresswoman, defeated incumbent Albert Wynn in the 2008 Democratic primary. After losing the primary, Wynn resigned from office and Edwards won a special election to replace him in June 2008. Finally, Laura Richardson (D-CA), the only Black congresswoman born after 1960 other than Clarke, was elected in 2007 in a special election to fill a vacant seat after the death of Juanita Millender-McDonald (Kurtz 2006, 2007, 2008; McArdle 2008; Patch and Weinstein 2006). For young Black women running for Congress, the political opportunities are much more limited than for White women. Even if running in an open seat, they are likely to face several Black community leaders vying for an opportunity that does not come around very often.

Some argue that until recently, Democratic leadership was less likely to support Blacks running for statewide office because it was thought they would have a difficult time with White voters. In fact, Barack Obama received only mixed support from Democratic leaders upon his initial decision to run for higher office (Whittington 2004; Neal 2003).[3] One Black congressperson expressed his frustration with the Democratic Party's lack of support for Black candidates running for statewide office:

> Nobody expects anyone to roll over for you in politics. Everybody wants to rise; everybody wants to advance—nobody expects people to roll over for you. But when you see a consistent pattern of Republican politicians being elevated or groomed for state-wide office irrespective of their qualifications. And you see a consistent pattern of Democratic candidates being discour-

aged from running for Governor or Senator on the vague premise that this is not your year or you wouldn't be the strongest candidate. When you see it with highly talented candidates like Obama, Ford, and Patrick it is a source of concern. Make no mistake there are mediocre Black candidates just like there are mediocre White candidates, but the reality is when you have had highly talented candidates like Obama, Ford, and Patrick met at the critical stages in their career with "well wouldn't you want to wait until another time or there is a stronger candidate out there" that's troubling. (personal interview, 2006)

Obama, Patrick, and Ford were able to win the Democratic nomination in their respective contests because they had networks and resources that extended beyond the party. Running for the U.S. Senate or statewide office without such established networks would be extremely difficult. Yvette Clarke (D-NY) and Donna Edwards (D-MD), to some degree, reflect a more traditional path to Congress. Again, Clarke comes from a political family—her mother was the first Jamaican American elected to the New York City Council. Her family background and connections gave her access to extensive political networks and resources. While Edwards's effort to unseat incumbent Albert Wynn was not supported by Democratic Party leaders, she was able to receive support from national organizations such as EMILY's List and the National Organization of Women (NOW). One way to overcome the incumbency advantage or win in competitive seats is to receive an endorsement from a powerful PAC such as EMILY's List, and this worked well for both Clarke and Edwards (Kurtz 2006, 2008; Gonzales 2008).

Several issues must be addressed to increase candidate emergence among Black women. First, decreasing inequities in education, income, wealth, and occupational opportunities would increase the number of Black women that fall into the informal "eligibility pool" of qualified candidates. If more Black women fell into this pool, then they would be more likely to run and be recruited to run for elective office, especially high-level positions. Furthermore, expanding political conceptions about who is qualified to run for office would improve candidate emergence among Black women. Political leaders must look beyond traditional occupations like law and business to find potential candidates. Finally, we must work to understand why nascent and progressive political ambition is suppressed among Black women.

In addition to enhancing nascent and progressive political ambition among Black women, there must be an expansion of political opportunities to increase the presence of young Black women in higher office. In order for this to happen there have to be either some dramatic structural changes in the electoral system or a redefinition of the types of districts that elect Black women. If Black women are able to run successful campaigns in majority-White constituencies, then that obviously expands the universe of options for politically ambitious Black women. A more drastic and unlikely solution would be to shift from single member district to multimember systems, which are much more likely to increase representation among women (Rule 1994). Once Black women make the decision to run, the next question to investigate is what challenges they may encounter on the campaign trail.

On the Campaign Trail and at the Voting Booth

Political underrepresentation among women and racial minorities extends beyond issues with candidate emergence. Scholarship on race and voting behavior finds that racial bias does exist among some White voters (Reeves 1997; Terkildsen 1993; Williams 1989; Sigelman et al. 1995). Studies by Williams (1989) and Sigelman et al. (1995) find that racialized stereotypes drive racial bias in voting. While White voters express a willingness to vote for Black candidates, they are also more likely to describe Black candidates as less qualified (Williams 1989; Sigelman et al. 1995). However, recent elections and studies indicate that racial bias in voting may be fading. More and more, one can find examples of nonincumbent Black candidates winning congressional seats in majority White districts. For example, in 2004 Emanual Cleaver (D-MO) was elected to represent a district with more than a 60 percent White population; and in 2006, Keith Ellison won in a district that was 71 percent White.[4] Furthermore, recent scholarship finds that White voters are just as likely to support Black candidates as White candidates when controlling for party (Highton 2004). Even with increased White support, Black candidates get their strongest support from Black voters, and successful campaigns often combine White support with significant Black support (Philpot and Walton 2007).

When women run they win, and when one controls for party and incumbency, women's share of the vote is equal to men's (Duerst-Lahti 1998; Darcy, Welch, and Clark 1994; Burrell 1994, 1998, 2005; Carroll 1994; Duke 1996). Women candidates seem to be on equal footing with male candidates when it comes to fundraising as well (Burrell 2005). In fact, during the 2004 election cycle, female candidates raised more money than their male counterparts (Burrell 2005, 31). While women candidates run successful campaigns, they still face some obstacles on the campaign trail. Women must manage gender stereotypes. Dolan's research finds that, "the public tends to see female candidates as warm, compassionate, kind and passive. Men are perceived as strong, knowledgeable, tough, direct, and assertive" (Dolan 2005, 41). Female candidates are also thought to be more competent on issues such as health care and education, whereas men are seen as more qualified to represent issues like foreign policy and crime. These gendered stereotypes can either help or harm female candidates dependent on the political context. If voters are most concerned with domestic issues, women candidates may benefit; but if the focus is foreign policy and national security, then a female candidate may have a more difficult time (Dolan 2005).

Race, Gender, and the Political Advantage

How do racial and gender biases impact Black female candidates? Black women candidates, like women candidates in general, are just as likely to win as their male counterparts (Gertzog 2002). In fact, Gertzog (2002, 64) finds that from 1968 to 2000, only two Black women running for Congress in general elections have lost. In some ways the intersection of race and gender works as an advantage for Black female candidates (Philpot and Walton 2007). Black women receive high levels of support from Black female voters, and Black women candidates with political experience get equal support from Black and White voters. In other words, the increased support among Black women voters may actually work to the advantage of Black female candidates with some political experience. Black female voters also turn out at much higher rates than Black men, which means that this voting bloc can really provide Black female candidates with a significant advantage (Philpot and Walton 2007; Smooth 2006a, 405; CAWP 2008).

Some Black female candidates are also able to get financial and organizational support from both Black and women's organizations. Smooth (2006) offers Gwen Moore's (D-WI) successful 2004 congressional campaign as an example of race and gender working to help a Black female candidate. Moore ran a traditionally Democratic campaign, making issues like health care and jobs her central focus. Smooth (2006a, 411) notes:

> Moore embraced the fullness of her identity and employed an intersectional framework in which she drew upon race-based resources and women-based resources. Had she run as a "Black candidate" only or as the "woman candidate" only, she would not have capitalized on crossover appeal needed to secure the vote in her majority White district.

Progressive Black female candidates who adopt liberal positions on women's issues such as health care, education, and childcare, as well as maintain established networks within the Black community can gain a real political advantage in certain political contexts. This advantage may be particularly useful in contests where the Black vote is split among multiple Black candidates. Both Clarke (D-NY) and Edwards (D-MD) gained significant advantage against their Black male competitors when they received support from the powerful PAC EMILY's List (Gonzales 2008; Kurtz 2008). Black women congressional candidates do well once they decide to run, which suggests the biggest barriers to political office for Black women exist at the candidate emergence stage.

Conclusions and Implications

Black women remain significantly underrepresented at all levels of government, but especially at the federal and statewide office level. Black women are highly engaged in the political process. They are leaders in community activism and turn out to vote at significantly high rates. Black women are outpacing Black men in education and in some professional fields, yet they remain almost invisible in national political leadership. The number of young Black female politicians is quite high at the state and local level, but this has not translated into national politics. A survey of local, county, and state officials reveals that 41 percent of female Black elected officials (BEOs) are between 18 and 40 compared to 11 percent of all BEOs (Bositis 2001). The high proportion of young Black representatives disappears at the congressional level. Lower level offices are not serving as a strong pipeline to higher office for young Black women. Black women generally and young Black women in particular are constrained at the candidate emergence stage. When Black women run, they win. The challenge is getting more Black women to run for elected office and getting those holding lower elected office to run for higher office.

In order to increase the number of young Black women in federal and statewide office, there must be an effort to increase nascent and progressive political ambition among Black women. Gains in education, income, and the labor market will place more Black women in the traditional political eligibility pool, which may facilitate more recruitment and encouragement for Black women to run for higher office. While some Black women choose political office as a way to affect change, many focus their efforts on community organizing and grassroots political activism. If party leaders, unions, and other political organizations look outside traditional political contexts to recruit candidates, they are likely to find many highly qualified young Black women. However, factors such as Black mothers' reluctance to run for positions that would require more time away from their children cannot be easily addressed. The reality is that Black women are more likely to be single mothers than are White women, and holding congressional office requires representatives to spend a significant amount of time away from home. Finally, there need to be more political opportunities for ambitious young Black women. Most Black women are strategic politicians and they are more likely to run for office when a positive political context arises. The incumbency advantage and the limited number of majority-minority districts make such political opportunities scarce. However, evidence suggests that politically experienced Black women may be able to expand the universe of political options by capitalizing on both raced-based and gender-based resources. There are certainly more Yvette Clarkes out there, the challenge is getting them to run.

Notes

1. The total adds up to more than a hundred because some members list more than one occupation.
2. Niven (1998) offers evidence to contradict these findings. While not on account of an explicit gender bias, Niven finds that party chairs tend to recruit individuals like them, which often excludes women and other previously marginalized groups (1998).
3. Obama's closest competitor in the Democratic primary for the Illinois senate seat in 2004 was Dan Hynes, who by most accounts was seen as supported by the state Democratic organization (see Whittington 2004 for details). However, Obama made gains with endorsements from several members of the Illinois congressional delegation (see Neal 2003 for details).
4. Ellison was the first Black elected to Congress from Minnesota and is also the first Muslim to serve in the United States Congress.

References

Ansolabehere, Stephen, James M. Snyder, and Charles Stewart III. 2000. Old voters, new voters, and the personal vote: Using redistricting to measure the incumbency advantage. *American Journal of Political Science* 44: 17–34.

Bositis, David A. 2001. *Changing of the guard: Generational differences among Black elected officials*. Washington, DC: Joint Center for Political and Economic Studies.

Burrell, Barbara.1994. *A woman's place is in the house: Campaigning for congress in the feminist era*. Ann Arbor: University of Michigan Press.

———. 1998. Campaign finance: Women's experience in the modern era. In *Women and elective office: Past, present, and future,* ed. Sue Thomas and Clyde Wilcox, 26–37. New York: Oxford University Press.

———. 2005. Campaign financing: Women's experience in the modern era. In *Women and elective office: Past, present, and future*. 2nd ed., ed. Sue Thomas and Clyde Wilcox, 26–40. New York: Oxford University Press.

Cantave, Cassandra, and Roderick Harrison. 2001. Single parent families fact sheet. Prepared for Joint Center for Political and Economic Studies. http://www.jointcenter.org/DB/factsheet/sigpatn.htm (accessed October 31, 2008).

Carroll, Susan. 1994. *Women as candidates in American politics*. Bloomington: Indiana University Press.

Catalyst. 2002. *Census of women corporate offices and top earners*. New York: Catalyst.

Center for American Women and Politics (CAWP). 2009. African American women in elective office fact sheet. http://www.cawp.rutgers.edu/fast_facts/women_of_color/FastFacts_AfricanAmericanWomeninOffice.php (accessed September 10, 2009).

———.2008. Genders differences in voter turnout, fact sheet. http://www.cawp.rutgers.edu/fast_facts/voters/documents/genderdiff.pdf (accessed April 23, 2009).

Cole, Elizabeth R., and Abigail J. Stewart. 1996. Meanings of political participation among Black and White women: Political identity and social responsibility. *Journal of Personality and Social Psychology* 71: 130–40.

Collins, Patricia Hill. 1990. *Black feminist thought: Knowledge, consciousness, and the politics of empowerment*. Boston: Unwin Hyman.

Covington, Kenya. 2005. Congressional Black caucus: Constituents at a glance. Prepared for Congressional Black Caucus Foundation, Center for Policy Analysis and Research. http://www.cbcfinc.org/images/pdf/constituents.pdf (accessed October 31, 2008).

Darcy, R., and Charles D. Hadley. 1988. Black women in politics: The puzzle of success. *Social Science Quarterly* 69: 629–45.

———. Susan Welch, and Janet Clark. 1994. *Women, elections, and representation*. 2nd ed. Lincoln: University of Nebraska Press.

Dolan, Kathaleen. 2005. How the public views women candidates. In *Women and elective office: Past, present, and future*, 2nd ed., ed. Sue Thomas and Clyde Wilcox, 41–59. New York: Oxford University Press.

Duerst-Lahti, Georgia. 1998. The bottleneck: Women becoming candidates. In *Women and elective office: Past, present, and future*, ed. Sue Thomas and Clyde Wilcox, 15–25. New York: Oxford University Press.

Duke, Lois Lovelace, ed. 1996. *Women in politics: Outsiders or insiders?* 2nd ed. Englewood Cliffs, NJ: Prentice-Hall.

Fox, Richard L., and Jennifer L. Lawless. 2004. Entering the arena? Gender and the decision to run for office. *American Journal of Political Science* 48: 264–80.

———. 2005. To run or not to run for office: Explaining nascent political ambition. *American Journal of Political Science* 48: 642–59.

Gertzog, Irwin N. 2002. Women's changing pathways to the U.S. house of representatives: Widows, elites and strategic politicians. In *Women transforming congress*, ed. Cindy Simon Rosenthal, 95–118. Norman: University of Oklahoma Press.

Githens, Marianne. 2003. Accounting for women's political involvement: The perennial problem of recruitment. In *Women and American politics*, ed. Susan J. Carroll, 33–52. New York: Oxford University Press.

Githens, Marianne, and Jewel L. Prestage. 1977. *A portrait of marginality: The political behavior of the American woman.* New York: Longman.

Gonzales, Nathan C. 2008, With risk comes some loss for EMILY's list. *Roll Call,* September 17. http://www.rollcall.com/news/28422-1.html (accessed April 15, 2009).

Hardy-Fanta, Carol. 1993. *Latina politics, Latino politics: Gender, culture, and political participation in Boston.* Philadelphia: Temple University Press.

———. Pei-te Lien, Dianne M. Pinderhughes, and Christine Marie Sierra. 2006. Gender, race, and descriptive representation in the United States: Findings from the gender and multicultural leadership project. *Journal of Women, Politics & Policy* 28: 7–41.

Herrick, Rebekah. 1995. A reappraisal of the quality of women candidates. *Women and Politics* 15: 25–38.

Herrnson, Paul S. 1997. United States. In *Passages to power: Legislative recruitment in advanced democracies*, ed. Pippa Norris, 187–208. Cambridge, UK: Cambridge University Press.

Higginbotham, Elizabeth, and Lynne Weber. 1999. Perceptions of workplace discrimination among Black and White professional/managerial women. In *Latinas and African American women at work*, ed. Irene Browne, 327–53. New York: Russell Sage.

Highton, Benjamin. 2004. White voters and African American candidates for congress. *Political Behavior* 26: 1–25.

King, Deborah K. 1995. Multiple jeopardy, multiple consciousness: The context of black feminist ideology. In *Words of fire*, ed. Beverley Guy-Sheftall, 294–318. New York: New Press.

Kurtz, Josh. 2006. A free-for-all grows in Brooklyn primary. *Roll Call*, September 7. http://www.rollcall.com/issues/52_22/news/14822-1.html (accessed April 23, 2009).

———. 2007. Richardson wins special, will assume Millender-McDonald seat. *Roll Call,* August 22. http://www.rollcall.com/news/19758-1.html (accessed April 15, 2009).

———. 2008. Wynn, Gilchrest lose primaries in Maryland. *Roll Call,* February 13.

Levitt, Steven D., and Catherine D. Wolfram. 1997. Decomposing the sources of incumbency advantage in the U.S. house. *Legislative Studies Quarterly* 22: 45–60.

McArdle, John. 2008. Edwards to be sworn in on Thursday. *Roll Call*, June 18. http://www.rollcall.com/news/26041-1.html (accessed April 23, 2009).

Naples, Nancy A. 1992. Activist mothering: Cross-generational continuity in community work of women from low-income urban neighborhoods. *Gender & Society* 6: 441–63.

National Journal. 2006. Election 2006 biographies—New York. *National Journal Magazine,* November 11. http://www.nationaljournal.com/njmagazine/nj_20061111_48.php (accessed April 23, 2009).

Neal, Steve. 2003, Obama's endorsements stacking up. Chicago Sun-Times, December 31. LexisNexis Academic. http://www.lexisnexis.com:80/us/lnacademic/results/docview/docview.do?docLinkInd=true&risb=21_T7128176733&format=GNBFI&sort=BOOLEAN&startDocNo=1&resultsUrlKey=29_T7128176736&cisb=22_T71

28176735&treeMax=true&treeWidth=0&csi=11064&docNo=2 (accessed April 23, 2009).

Ondercin, Heather L., and Susan Welch. 2005. Women candidates for congress. In *Women and elective office: Past, present, and future.* 2nd ed., ed. Sue Thomas and Clyde Wilcox, 60–80. New York: Oxford University Press.

Opensecrets.org. n.d. Personal finances. http://www.opensecrets.org/pfds/index.php (accessed April 23, 2009).

Pardo, Mary S. 1998. *Mexican American women activists: Identity and resistance in two Los Angeles communities.* Philadelphia: Temple University Press.

Patch, Jeffrey, and Jamie Weinstein. 2006. Three of Tuesday's winners seem headed to Hill. *Roll Call*, September 14. http://www.rollcall.com/issues/52_26/politics/14953-1.html (accessed April 23, 2009).

Patillo-McCoy, Mary. 1999. Middle class, yet Black: A review essay. *African American Research Perspectives* 5: 25–38.

Peter, Katherin, and Laura Horn. 2005. Gender differences in participation and completion of undergraduate education and how they changed over time (NCES 2005-169). U.S. Department of Education, National Center for Education Statistics. Washington, DC: Government Printing Office.

Philpot, Tasha S., and Hanes Walton, Jr. 2007. One of our own: Black female candidates and the voters who support them. *American Journal of Political Science* 51: 49–62.

Reeves, Keith. 1997. *Voting hopes or fears? White voters, Black candidates, & racial politics in America.* New York: Oxford University Press.

Robinson, John P., and Geoffrey Goddbey. 1999. *Time for life: The surprising ways Americans use their time.* 2nd ed. University Park: Penn State Press.

Rule, Wilma. 1994. Women's underrepresentation and electoral systems. *PS: Political Science and Politics* 27: 689–92.

Sanbonmatsu, Kira. 2006a. Gender pools and puzzles: Charting a "women's path" to the legislature. *Politics & Gender* 2: 387–400.

———. 2006b. Do parties know that "women win"? Party leader beliefs about women's electoral chances. *Politics & Gender* 2: 431–50.

Schlesinger, Joseph. 1966. *Ambition and politics: Political careers in the United States.* Chicago: Rand McNally.

Sigelman, Carol K., Lee Sigelman, Barbara J. Walksoz, and Michael Nitz. 1995. Black candidates, White voters: Understanding racial bias in political perceptions. *American Journal of Political Science* 39: 243–65.

Simpson, Andrea Y. 2007. Going it alone: Black women activist and Black organizational quiescence. In *African American perspectives on political science*, ed. Wilbur C. Rich, 151–68. Philadelphia: Temple University Press.

Smooth, Wendy. 2006a. Intersectionality in electoral politics: A mess worth making. *Politics & Gender* 2: 400–14.

———. 2006b. African American women in politics: Journeying from the shadows to the spotlight. In *Gender and elections in America: Shaping the future of American politics,* ed. Susan J. Carroll and Richard Fox, 117–42. New York: Cambridge University Press.

Tate, Katherine. 1993. *From protest to politics: The new Black voters in American elections.* Cambridge, MA: Harvard University Press.

———. 2003. *Black faces in the mirror: African Americans and their representatives in the U.S. Congress.* Princeton, NJ: Princeton University Press.

Terkildsen, Nayda. 1993. When White voters evaluate Black candidates: The processing implications of candidate skin color, prejudice, and self-monitoring. *American Journal of Political Science* 37: 1032–53.

Thomas, Sue. Rebekah Herrick, and Matthew Braunstein. 2002. Legislative careers: The personal and the political. In *Women transforming congress*, ed. Cindy Simon Rosenthal, 397–421. Norman: University of Oklahoma Press.

U.S. Census Bureau. 2008. Current population survey, annual social and economic supplements. http://www.census.gov/hhes/www/income/histinc/p39B.html (accessed October 31, 2008).

Welch, Susan, and Timothy Bledose. 1988. *Urban reform and its consequences*: Chicago: University of Chicago Press.

Whittington, Lauren W. 2004. Man and machine: Will Hynes' institutional support lead to victory? *Roll Call,* March 4. http://www.rollcall.com/issues/49_87/politics/4615-1.html (accessed April 23, 2009).

Williams, Linda. 1989. White/Black perceptions of the electability of Black political candidates. *National Political Science Review* 2: 45–64.

Conclusion
Where Do We Go From Here?

Andra Gillespie

There is little doubt that Election Night 2008 will be a night to remember for many Americans, regardless of their race. Generations from now, people will be able to tell their grandchildren precisely where they were the moment they found out that Barack Obama was elected the country's first Black president.

Obama won in part because Black voters rallied around him in unprecedented numbers. While Democratic candidates generally do well among Black voters—usually winning about nine of every ten Black votes—Obama did even better, winning 96 percent of the Black vote. Moreover, Black voters turned out in unprecedented numbers. Between 2004 and 2008, Black turnout as a share of the overall electorate increased by 2 percentage points. That may not seem like a lot, but that is roughly 3.5 million additional Black voters (Tate 1994; "African Americans, Anger…" 2008; CNN.com 2008).

One of the iconic images of that night was Jesse Jackson weeping in the crowd at Chicago's Grant Park. For a soldier of the Civil Rights Movement like Jackson to witness the election of a Black man was no doubt a cathartic moment for him and for the nation.

To some, the image of Obama winning and Jackson weeping conjures up the notion of a changing of the guard. The Era of Jackson, the man who assumed the mantle of Black activist leadership and made two notable bids for the presidency, was now clearly giving way to the Era of Obama, the man whose cool demeanor and conciliatory tone had swept him past the penultimate racial barrier in American politics.

To others, this historical moment represents the best that Black political unity has to offer. Blacks turned out in record numbers to almost unanimously register their support for an Obama presidency. This level of Black support no doubt contributed to Obama's victories in Virginia, North Carolina, and Indiana ("African Americans, Anger…" 2008). Truly, this election signaled the importance of unity and strength in numbers.

In reality, neither of these interpretations is completely accurate. Without question, the election of Barack Obama brings remarkable change to American and African-American politics, one that will take decades to fully comprehend. However, we should not be lulled by the importance of this moment in our history into thinking that there has been a smooth generational transition in

Black politics or that there is now a unified African-American political agenda. Black politics has always been complex. The election of Barack Obama has not diminished that complexity, nor does it automatically ameliorate the political and social challenges that Blacks face on a daily basis.

As I write this, America is still in the afterglow of the Obama victory. Despite the challenges that face the country (war, a deep recession, growing unemployment), most Americans are hopeful that President Barack Obama will bring order to chaos. Already, the vast majority of Americans have expressed confidence in his early decisions. For instance, 73 percent of Americans approved of Obama's decision making during his transition before taking office (Associated Press 2008). And during the first 100 days of his administration, Obama's job approval ratings hovered between 62 and 66 percent (*New York Times*/CBS News 2009).

As President of the United States and the highest ranking African American in the history of the country, Barack Obama clearly becomes the face of Black politics. However, our analysis of Black politics, even the politics of young, "postracial" Black politicians, does not begin and end with him. Nor does it begin and end with the Ivy League Upstarts who are like him strategically and politically.

In the weeks after the 2008 election, young, moderate Black politicians have gained currency. For instance, during the election season Artur Davis, Harold Ford Jr., Deval Patrick, and Cory Booker were popular commentators and Obama surrogates. Based on the attention that these men receive (Bai 2008; Ifill 2009), it would be easy to assume that the politics that these gentlemen espouse will now become the standard in Black politics.

It is our contention that the politics of postracial Black politicians is one of many standards in Black politics. Adolph Reed recognized this in *Class Notes*, when he asserted that what so many observers mistook for a unified Black body politic was really the politics of middle class Black Americans (Reed 2000). The reality is there is no such thing as monolithic Blackness (Kennedy 1998).[1] If there is no such thing as monolithic Blackness, then there cannot be a monolithic Black political agenda. And if there is no monolithic Black political agenda, then there cannot be one standard Black politician, even if he is president.

Thus, in this volume, we hoped to introduce readers to the diversity and complexity that exists even within the young cohort of Black elected leadership. Not everyone is like Barack Obama, even the ones the media presents as Obama clones. Many did not start their political careers as outsiders to the nation's Black political establishment, and some embrace a political style that is decidedly more racialized than others. Moreover, some people clearly aspire to the highest offices in the land, while others are content to toil in high-profile but lower level positions. The diversity that exists within this cohort of Black politicians has ramifications for the next generation. One should expect continued debate about the nature and direction of Black politics, not coalescence around a common ideal. Moreover, we must be prepared to accept the failures along with the successes of this cohort, just as we did for previous cohorts.

In the final few pages, I would like to make a few predictions about what Black politics will look like in the next generation and what role Black politicians like those featured in this volume will play. Recall from the introductory chapter that this third cohort of new Black politicians is notable because of (1) their embrace of deracialized politics borne out of having benefited from post-Civil Rights integration; (2) the presumption that they are better positioned than their predecessors to deliver with integrity on key policy initiatives of interest to Blacks; and (3) they are expected to hold higher offices more frequently than any previous generation of Black politicians. Based on what we have seen so far among this cohort, a few trends emerge which will be of interest to students, scholars, and general observers.

Rethinking Deracialization

Deracialization has been a controversial topic since Charles Hamilton first raised the idea in the 1970s. Since that time, political scientists have tried to problematize the idea of deracialization. In earlier case studies of Phase II deracialized Black candidates, scholars pointed out that deracialized candidates either did not reflect Black politics (Persons 1993) or were tragically doomed political figures who could never escape the ire of racist constituents who would never vote for them (see Davis and Willingham 1993; Wilson 1993). Later, other scholars responded by charging that many "deracialized" candidates were in fact not deracialized at all; they did talk about race and crafted or supported policies that, stated or unstated, disproportionately benefited Blacks (Summers and Klinkner 1996; Henderson 1996).

This debate evinces the reality that perhaps our definition of deracialization is too narrow. Earlier scholars presented deracialization in stark, Black–White terms (McCormick and Jones 1993). In reality, many politicians are somewhere in the gray range. The chapters in part IV highlight the nuances of deracialization. We believe, as do McCormick and Jones (1993), that deracialization involves deemphasizing racial issues, presenting a nonthreatening demeanor and limiting race-specific appeals to Black constituents. However, we contend that many "deracialized" or "postracial" young Black candidates maintain their crossover appeal and their nonthreatening image without completely abandoning racial issues or appeals. Sekou Franklin showed us how Harold Ford Jr. altered his rhetoric for Black and White audiences. Tyson King-Meadows demonstrated how the penultimate deracialized Black candidate—a Black Republican—used racial solidarity to reach out to disaffected Black Democratic voters. Certain chapters also show us that it is no longer true that deracialized Black candidates are doomed to electoral failure because they can never escape race. In Angela Lewis's chapter on Deval Patrick, we found that not all racial attacks are successful. And in my chapter on Cory Booker, we see that Booker won his second attempt at Newark's mayoralty without fundamentally compromising his commitment to deracialization.

Given Barack Obama's successful, deracialized presidential campaign, it is very likely that deracialization as a political strategy is here to stay. The question now turns to whether deracialized elected officials can be successful in delivering policies that serve to reduce inequality. One of the biggest concerns of scholars such as McCormick and Jones (1993) and Smith (1993) is that deracialized elected officials have made a Faustian bargain with their non-Black constituents to not address civil rights issues. The fear is that if these officials do address racial concerns, White voters in particular will break from the rainbow coalition and prevent the deracialized official from being reelected. It is too early to say whether this will happen. Many Phase III Black politicians have not held office long, especially at the executive level. As such, these officials have not yet had to deal with the type of major crisis[2] that strains racial fault lines. They have not had a Hurricane Katrina or a Jena Six. As such, we, like many other scholars, will be paying close attention when those unfortunate rifts emerge.

Good Government

Recall from the first chapter that many Phase III Black politicians, especially those lacking ties to the Black political establishment, have proffered the idea that they are better suited than their predecessors to hold public office because they are better trained and willing to use innovative methods to address intractable problems. Ultimately, Phase III politicians' ability to deliver on this promise will define the cohort as either successes or failures.

While the country is brimming with hope that Barack Obama and his peers can bring fresh change and innovative reform to their offices, the reality is that many of them—particularly those who hold executive office—have not had their jobs long enough for us to judge their effectiveness. Three Black executives featured in this volume, for instance (Booker, Fenty, and Patrick), were elected to their offices in 2006. After roughly three years in office, they have definitely had their successes (for instance, Booker dramatically reduced Newark's homicide rate; and more people believed that Washington, DC was headed on the right track a year after Adrian Fenty took office than the year before); but they have also had their challenges. Black Washingtonians are far less sanguine about their mayor, with fewer than half giving him high marks. Patrick had to weather a minor scandal about the salary for his wife's chief of staff in his first few months in office. And a group of residents tried to get Booker recalled in his first year in office (Gillespie n.d.; Nakamura and Cohen 2008; Phillips 2007). At this point then, the long term policy impact of the election of these officials remains to be seen. In future editions of this volume, enough time will have elapsed to allow us to conduct an adequate policy analysis.

Inherent with the good government pledges is the idea that Phase III Black politicians somehow have more integrity than other politicians. I would caution readers to disabuse themselves of that idea. Corruption is not the province of one generation of politicians of any race, much less one generation of Black politicians. To suggest otherwise is naïve and maybe slightly racist and classist. Already, one

Phase III Black politician (Kwame Kilpatrick) has fallen in disgrace, and another (Jesse Jackson Jr.), was implicated (unfairly, it now appears) in a major scandal. While we hope that no politician engages in corrupt behavior, we have to prepare ourselves for the possibility that others, too, may fall. Most important, citizens must always be vigilant and hold their elected officials accountable so that no elected official feels that sense of entitlement which breeds corruption.

Progressive Ambitions

The election of Barack Obama now seemingly opens up the possibility that more and more Blacks will run for high political office in the future. While some Blacks are poised to make credible bids for high office in the next few years (Artur Davis will run for Governor of Alabama in 2010, Kendrick Meek will run for U.S. Senate seat from Florida in 2010, and while Harold Ford Jr. has ruled out a 2010 gubernatorial run, he may run for high political office at some point in the future), the change may be slower and harder to detect than we expect (Brown 2009; DeMatteo 2009; Sullivan 2009). Where we are more likely to see change is at the local and state level, which will not be as readily apparent.

One of the biggest potential changes will be the types of communities that Black elected officials will serve. Even Phase III Black politicians by-and-large launched their political careers in majority-Black jurisdictions or in places that have a long history of Black representation. In the future, we may see more Black politicians seeking and winning office in majority-non-Black jurisdictions. *The New York Times* has recently observed Black state legislators winning office in unlikely places such as Iowa and New Hampshire (Swarns 2008).

With all of these changes, we must keep in mind that Blacks are still by and large underrepresented in elective office. If Blacks were proportionately represented in the House of Representatives, there would be fifty-six voting members. Currently, there are forty-one voting Black House members ("Black American Representatives…" n.d.). If Blacks were proportionately represented in the Senate, there would be thirteen Black U.S. Senators. Currently, there is only one Black Senator. If Blacks were proportionately represented among our nation's governors, there would be six Black governors; currently, there are only two Black governors. It will take years to change this reality, but I would expect these numbers to gradually improve.

Other Considerations

A number of additional considerations will be important. Despite the wave of unity that helped usher Barack Obama into office, the African-American community is incredibly and increasingly diverse. As time goes on, racial solidarity may or may not be sufficient to maintain Black political unity. We must prepare ourselves for the reality of multiple Black political communities, not just one Black political community.

Michael Dawson perhaps best articulated the idea of Black political unity when he introduced the Black utility heuristic in *Behind the Mule*. In his landmark book, Dawson argued that perpetual racial discrimination affecting poor and affluent Blacks had inured a sense of linked fate in the African-American community. Linked fate is the idea that what happens to other Blacks affects individual Blacks. Blacks who have a sense of linked fate, then, think about how policies and candidates affect the Black community as a whole, and they choose their policy preferences and candidates accordingly. Dawson finds that Blacks with linked fate, especially middle class Blacks, are more supportive of civil rights and social welfare policies, even though all of those policies do not personally benefit them. Dawson also argues that linked fate helps to explain the overwhelming Democratic identification among Blacks of all classes. Because Democrats are perceived to be more likely to champion policies that benefit Blacks (Tate 1995; Carmines and Stimson 1989), Blacks support Democratic candidates (Dawson 1994).

At the end of his book, Dawson acknowledges that the Black utility heuristic may not be a permanent fixture of Black politics. He contends that if class stratification within the Black community changes or if levels of racism drastically change, a new paradigm could emerge. If both class stratification and racism increase, then Dawson argues that Black politics could bifurcate into two movements: one for poor Blacks and one for affluent Blacks. If class stratification increases but racism decreases, then it may be more appropriate for people of all races to organize around class differences, not racial differences. If both class stratification and racism decrease, Dawson contends that America will have reached a utopian ideal. If class stratification decreases, but racism increases (or stays the same), then the Black utility heuristic will still function (Dawson 1994, 210).

It is very likely that residual racism and increased class stratification will lead to greater balkanization in the Black community (i.e., Dawson's "Two Black Americas" scenario; Dawson 1994, 210). Already there is public opinion data suggesting that Blacks recognize differences between middle and lower class Blacks. In a 2007 Pew Center survey on race relations, 61 percent of Blacks saw increasing divergence between the values of poor and middle class Blacks. Moreover, 53 percent of Blacks were apt to blame Blacks for their own condition, compared to 30 percent of Blacks who blamed discrimination (Pew Research Center 2007, 1, 5). Given the fact that so many questions of racial inequality are inextricably linked to questions of poverty, it is very likely that there will be greater intraracial contestation about the origins of Black inequality and how to address it. Some Black politicians will share the values of those who will minimize the role of systemic factors; and others will share the values of those who see structural racism as the culprit.

Part of the implicit concern with deracialized politics is the fear that deracialized politicians are likely to ignore the role that structural racism plays in perpetuating inequality. If deracialized candidates deemphasize race in order to get elected, then the fear is that they will deemphasize addressing structural issues once in office (McCormick and Jones 1993; Smith 1993). Additionally, there is the possibility that deracialized candidates will pander to the worst stereotypes about Blacks in order to curry favor with non-Black voters. There is evidence supporting and confounding such fears. For instance, there were many who took issue with Barack Obama's 2008 Father's Day address, in which he admonished Black men to be better fathers. To critics, the speech smacked of paternalism, reified stereotypes, and seemed to blame all of the problems in the Black community on bad parenting (see "Obama's Father's Day Speech..." 2008).

There will likely be significant numbers of acolytes to both the individualistic and systemic perspectives on inequality for the foreseeable future. The question will be whether those who speak the language of individual responsibility will have disproportionate access to the tools needed to run successfully for office (i.e., fundraising, political consultants, media attention). If this happens, and deracialized, individualist Black politicians have an advantage getting elected to office, then that guarantees even greater contestation.

It is also very likely that future work will focus greater attention on skin tone. Many of the current crop of Phase III Black politicians are light-skinned, and some will no doubt wonder if having a light skin tone helps or hinders one's chances of being elected to high political office. Jennifer Hochschild and Vesla Weaver note that lighter complexioned Blacks have historically been overrepresented among Black members of Congress; moreover, recent election cycles have also featured disproportionate numbers of fair-skinned Black congressional candidates. While they acknowledge that Blacks of every hue find it difficult to get elected, experimental evidence suggests that White voters may be more inclined to support lighter-skinned candidates in head-to-head matchups between light and dark skinned Black candidates (Hochschild and Weaver 2007, 650–52).

These questions are important because they also raise the issue of whether skin tone correlates with a candidate's decision to use deracialized campaign strategies or if people of different hues perceive linked fate and discrimination differently. Right now, the evidence suggests that these types of correlations do not exist. Hochschild and Weaver note that skin tone has no relationship with perceptions of discrimination or feelings of linked fate (Hochschild and Weaver 2007, 653–54). Considering the historic political postures of light- and dark-skinned Black politicians also seems to bear out this conclusion. For nearly a century, there have been light-skinned politicians who were racialized (i.e., Adam Clayton Powell Jr.), just as there have been dark skinned politicians who were deracialized (i.e., Harvey Gantt). When we look at this current cohort of Black politicians, we see that despite the fact that many high-profile, deracialized politicians are light skinned, there are examples of light-skinned, racialized politicians (i.e., Keith Ellison) and dark-skinned, deracialized politicians (i.e., Mark Mallory).

For now, this cohort of Black politicians is too small to make any conclusions about skin tone. As more young Blacks get elected to high-profile offices, we may be able to pinpoint and answer meaningful research questions related to this issue.

Finally, it is important to remember that many Blacks are more than just Black. They have other identities that may expose them to discrimination; these other identities may or may not have voice in our current political discourse. As time goes on, Blacks with other identities will likely make the case for their perspectives to receive full recognition. Currently, the third phase of new Black politics is very patriarchic, middle to upper class, nominally Christian and implicitly heterosexual. Increasingly, we should expect Blacks with additional identities to make credible attempts to run for public office. These candidates will do more than just provide descriptive representation. They will bring insight about other forms of inequality that will further add to the dynamic debate about how to combat inequity in American society.

Thus, the future is likely to hold increased debate, not greater unity. On some levels, this may seem frightening. There is always this implicit fear among some Blacks that the mainstream elite is always trying to divide and conquer Blacks. These individuals might cite the Willie Lynch letter, which called for controlling slaves by making distinctions between slaves of different genders and skin tones, for instance (see Finalcall.com 2005). On the other hand, though, there can be strength in diversity. When everyone in a group thinks alike and has the same perspective, bad ideas and policies emanating from that group go unchallenged. When bad ideas and policies go unchallenged, they wreak havoc on Black communities and perpetuate suffering. Disagreement and resolution can help combatants identify the weaknesses in their proposals and spur everyone toward creating better policies. Moreover, the recognition of a diverse Black community will likely increase greater mainstream attention toward the Black constituents. As it currently stands, Blacks largely feel shunned by the Republican Party and ignored within the Democratic Party, in part because Black political preferences are supposed to be so predictable (Walton and Smith 2006, 143–47). As more and more observers garner the sophistication to realize that Blacks really do not suffer from groupthink, then this could lead to greater attention from both sides of the aisle.

In order for this diversity to be successful, everyone must agree to certain ground rules. All sides need to agree to respect the perspectives of their opponents. Everyone needs to be willing acknowledge when opponents make good points and have good ideas. And everyone needs to be humble enough to accept when they are wrong or to accept defeat. So far, the transition from old style to new style Black politics has been a little less than civil. With a little more respect from both sides, there is a way to represent all sides, even if everyone cannot agree all the time.

Notes

1. I am also indebted to Gertrude Fraser for her insights on this matter.
2. One could make the argument that the 2007 Mount Vernon School shootings in Newark were a racial crisis. In August 2007, a group of Latino teenagers and young adults murdered three Black college students and critically injured another Black college student in an unprovoked attack. Cory Booker was lauded for his handling of the situation, largely because his office deftly coordinated the efforts to catch the suspects. Within a week, all the suspects were in custody. Given the fact that

the crime involved victims and perpetrators of different races, this could have been a racial crisis. However, race and ethnicity did not become salient in this crisis because all of the public officials involved focused their energies on catching the criminals (Gillespie n.d.).

References

African Americans, anger, fear and youth propel turnout to highest levels since 1960. 2008. [Press Release]. Washington, DC: American University. December 17.

Associated Press. 2008. Obama transition going well, most in AP poll say. *International Herald Tribune*, December 11.

Brown, Robbie. 2009. Black congressman eyes Alabama governor's seat. June 4. http://www.nytimes.com/2009/06/05/us/05davis.html?_r=1 (accessed October 12, 2009).

Bai, Matt. 2008. Is Barack Obama the end of Black politics? *The New York Times Magazine*, August 6.

Black American representatives and senators by congress, 1870–Present. n.d. http://baic.house.gov/historical-data/representatives-senators-by-congress.html?congress=110 (accessed December 23, 2008).

Carmines, Edward, and James Stimson. 1989. *Issue evolution: Race and the transformation of American politics*. Princeton, NJ: Princeton University Press.

CNN. 2008. Election center 2008: National exit polls. http://www.cnn.com/ELECTION/2008/results/polls/#USP00p1 (accessed December 23, 2008).

Davis, Marilyn, and Alex Willingham. 1993. Andrew Young and the Georgia state elections of 1990. In *Dilemmas of Black politics*, ed. Georgia Persons, 147–75. New York: HarperCollins.

Dawson, Michael C. 1994. *Behind the mule*. Princeton, NJ: Princeton University Press.

DeMatteo, Anthony. 2009. Meek pursues senate seat. *The St. Augustine Record*, October 5. http://www.staugustine.com/stories/100509/news_2044597.shtml (accessed October 12, 2009).

Finalcall.com News. 2005. Willie Lynch letter: The making of a slave. Finalcall.com http://www.finalcall.com/artman/publish/article_2167.shtml (accessed May 19, 2009).

Gillespie, Andra. n.d. *Newark and the clash of two Black Americas: Race, class and the breakdown of linked fate, 2002–2008*. Unpublished manuscript.

Henderson, Lenneal J. Jr. 1996. The governance of Kurt Schmoke as mayor of Baltimore. In *Race, governance, and politics in the United States*, ed. Huey L. Perry, 165–78. Gainesville: University of Florida Press.

Hochschild, Jennifer, and Vesla Weaver. 2007. The skin color paradox and the American racial order. *Social Forces* 86(2): 643–70.

Ifill, Gwen. 2009. *The breakthrough: Politics in the age of Obama*. New York: Doubleday.

Kennedy, Lisa. 1998. The body in question. In *Black popular culture*, ed. Gina Dent, 106–11. New York: New Press.

McCormick, Joseph II, and Charles E. Jones. 1993. The conceptualization of deracialization: Thinking through the dilemma. In *Dilemmas of Black politics,* ed. Georgia Persons, 66–84. New York: HarperCollins.

Nakamura, David, and Jon Cohen. 2008. Fenty's first year gets high marks, but divide persists. *Washington Post*, January 13.

The New York Times/CBS News. 2009. *The New York Times*/CBS News Poll, April 1–5. http://graphics8.nytimes.com/packages/images/nytint/docs/new-york-times-cbsnews-poll-on-the-approval-ratings-of-president-barack-obama/original.pdf (accessed May 19 2009).

Obama's father's day speech stirs reaction. *Tell Me More* [Nationally Syndicated Radio Broadcast]. National Public Radio. June 20.

Persons, Georgia. 1993. The election of Gary Franks and the ascendancy of the new Black conservatives. In *Dilemmas of Black politics,* ed. Georgia Persons, 194–208. New York: Harper Collins.

Pew Research Center. 2007. *Optimism about Black progress declines.* Monograph. Washington, DC: Pew Research Center.

Phillips, Frank. 2007. Poll shows concerns on Patrick but popularity high despite his missteps. *The Boston Globe*, April 8.

Reed, Adolph. 2000. *Class notes.* New York: New Press.

Smith, Robert C. 1993. Ideology as the enduring dilemma of Black politics. In *Dilemmas of Black politics*, ed. Georgia Persons, 211–25. New York: HarperCollins.

Sullivan, Bartholemew. 2009. Harold Ford Jr. won't seek Tennessee governor's office. *Memphis Commercial Appeal.* http://www.commercialappeal.com/news/2009/apr/13/harold-ford-jr-wont-seek-tennessee-governors-offic/ (accessed October 12, 2009).

Summers, Mary, and Phillip Klinkner. 1996. The election and governance of John Daniels as mayor of New Haven. In *Race, governance, and politics in the United States*, ed. Huey L. Perry, 127–50. Gainesville: University of Florida Press.

Swarns, Rachel L. 2008. Quiet political shifts as more Blacks are elected. *The New York Times.* October 14. http://www.nytimes.com/2008/10/14/us/politics/14race.html (accessed August 20, 2009).

Tate, Katherine. 1995. *From protest to politics: The new Black voters in American elections.* New York and Cambridge: Russell Sage Foundation/Harvard University Press.

Walton, Hanes, and Robert Smith. 2006. *American politics and the African American quest for universal freedom.* New York: Pearson Longman.

Wilson, Zaphon. 1993. Gantt versus Helms: Deracialization confronts Southern traditionalism. In *Dilemmas of Black politics*, ed. Georgia Persons, 176–93. New York: HarperCollins.

Contributors

Randolph Burnside is an Assistant Professor of Political Science at Southern Illinois University, Carbondale.

Sekou Franklin is an Associate Professor of Political Science at Middle Tennessee State University.

Lorrie Frasure is an Assistant Professor of Political Science at UCLA.

Katrina Gamble is an Assistant Professor of Political Science at Brown University.

Andra Gillespie is an Assistant Professor of Political Science at Emory University.

Athena King is a PhD Candidate in Political Science at the University of South Carolina.

Tyson D. King-Meadows is an Assistant Professor of Political Science at the University of Maryland, Baltimore County.

Angela K. Lewis is an Associate Professor of Government at the University of Alabama at Birmingham.

Charlton McIlwain is an Associate Professor of Communications at New York University.

Amber Perez graduated from Emory University in 2008.

Antonio Rodriguez is a PhD Candidate in Political Science at Southern Illinois University.

Todd Shaw is an Associate Professor in Political Science and African American Studies at the University of South Carolina.

Lester Spence is an Assistant Professor of Political Science at Johns Hopkins University.

Emma Tolbert graduated from Emory University in 2008. She is currently pursuing a master degree in political science and public administration at Jacksonville State University

Rachel Yon is a PhD Candidate in Political Science at the University of Florida.

Index